JB JOSSEY-BASS

THE JOSSEY-BASS
READER ON THE BRAIN
AND LEARNING

Introduction by Kurt Fischer and
Mary Helen Immordino-Yang

John Wiley & Sons, Inc.

Published by Jossey-Bass
A Wiley Imprint
989 Market Street, San Francisco, CA 94103-1741 www.josseybass.com

Wiley Bicentennial logo: Richard J. Pacifico

Jossey-Bass books and products are available through most bookstores. To contact Jossey-Bass directly call our Customer Care Department within the U.S. at 800-956-7739, outside the U.S. at 317-572-3986, or fax 317-572-4002.

Jossey-Bass also publishes its books in a variety of electronic formats. Some content that appears in print may not be available in electronic books.

Page 455 constitutes a continuation of the Copyright page.

Library of Congress Cataloging-in-Publication Data
The Jossey-Bass reader on the brain and learning / foreword by Kurt Fischer and Mary Helen Immordino-Yang. — 1st ed.
      p. ; cm.
Includes bibliographical references.
     ISBN-13: 978-0-7879-6241-8 (pbk.)
     1. Learning—Physiological aspects.   2. Cognition in children—Physiological aspects.   3. Brain—Physiology.   4. Learning, Psychology of.
   I. Jossey-Bass Inc.   II. Title: Reader on the brain and learning.
   [DNLM: 1. Brain—physiology.   2. Cognition—physiology.   3. Learning—physiology.
   WL 300   J84   2008]
   QP408.J67   2008
   612.8'2—dc22

                                                              2007028788

Printed in the United States of America
FIRST EDITION
PB Printing   10 9 8 7 6 5 4 3 2 1

CONTENTS

PART FOUR
The Feeling Brain: Emotional and Social Foundations

PART FIVE
The Learning Brain: Language, Reading, and Math

PART SIX
The Learning Brain: The Arts

PART SEVEN
The Exceptional Brain: When It Works Differently

Welcome to *The Jossey-Bass Reader on the Brain and Learning*. With the Jossey-Bass education readers we hope to provide a clear, concise overview of important topics in education and give our audience a useful knowledge of the theory and practice of key educational issues. Each volume in this series is designed to be informative, comprehensive, and portable.

SOURCES

CHAPTER ONE

Richard Restak. *The Naked Brain: How the Emerging Neurosociety Is Changing How We Live, Work, and Love.* New York: Harmony Books, 2006.

CHAPTER TWO

Scientific American, November 2006, 295(5).

CHAPTER THREE

Robert Sylwester. *How to Explain a Brain: An Educator's Handout of Brain Terms and Cognitive Processes.* Thousand Oaks: Corwin, 2005.

CHAPTER FOUR

British Journal of Educational Psychology, 2004, 74.

CHAPTER FIVE

Phi Delta Kappan, May 1999, 80(9).

CHAPTER SIX

Marian Diamond and Janet Hopson. *Magic Trees of the Mind: How to Nurture Your Child's Intelligence, Creativity, and Healthy Emotions from Birth Through Adolescence.* New York: Plume, 1998.

CHAPTER SEVEN

National Research Council (US) Committee on Learning Research and Educational Practice, National Research Council, John Bransford, and Ann L. Brown. *How People Learn: Brain, Mind, Experience, and School.* Washington, D.C.: National Academies Press, 2000.

CHAPTER EIGHT

Sarah-Jayne Blakemore and Uta Frith. *The Learning Brain: Lessons for Education.* Oxford: Blackwell, 2005.

CHAPTER NINE

Howard Gardner. *Intelligence Reframed: Multiple Intelligences for the 21st Century.* Cambridge, Mass.: Basic Books, 1999.

CHAPTER TEN

Robert J. Sternberg. *Wisdom, Intelligence, and Creativity Synthesized.* Cambridge: Cambridge University Press, 2003.

CHAPTER ELEVEN

Joseph LeDoux. *The Emotional Brain.* London: Phoenix (an Imprint of The Orion Publishing Group Ltd), 1998.

CHAPTER TWELVE

Mind, Brain & Education, March 2007, 1(1).

CHAPTER THIRTEEN

Robert M. Sapolsky. *Why Zebras Don't Get Ulcers,* 3rd ed. New York: Owl Books, 2004.

CHAPTER FOURTEEN

Ronald Kotulak. *Inside the Brain: Revolutionary Discoveries of How the Mind Works.* Riverside: Andrews McMeel Publishing, 1996.

CHAPTER FIFTEEN

Sarah-Jayne Blakemore and Uta Frith. *The Learning Brain: Lessons for Education.* Oxford: Blackwell, 2005.

CHAPTER SIXTEEN

Sally Shaywitz. *Overcoming Dyslexia: A New and Complete Science-Based Program for Reading Problems at Any Level.* New York: Vintage Books, 2003.

CHAPTER SEVENTEEN

Patricia Wolfe and Pamela Nevills. *Building the Reading Brain, PreK-3.* Thousand Oaks: Corwin, 2004.

CHAPTER EIGHTEEN

Stanislas Dehaene. *The Number Sense: How the Mind Creates Mathematics.* New York: Oxford University Press, 1997.

CHAPTER NINETEEN

James P. Byrnes. *Minds, Brains, and Learning.* New York: Guilford, 2001.

CHAPTER TWENTY

David A. Sousa. *How the Brain Learns.* Thousand Oaks: Corwin, 2006.

CHAPTER TWENTY-ONE

Elliot W. Eisner. *The Arts and the Creation of Mind.* New Haven: Yale University Press, 2004.

CHAPTER TWENTY-TWO

Daniel J. Levitin. *This Is Your Brain on Music: The Science of a Human Obsession.* New York: Dutton, 2006.

CHAPTER TWENTY-THREE

Eric Jensen. *Enriching the Brain: How to Maximize Every Learner's Potential.* San Francisco: Jossey-Bass, 2006.

CHAPTER TWENTY-FOUR

Michael Gurian and Kathy Stevens. *The Minds of Boys: Saving Our Sons from Falling Behind in School and Life.* San Francisco: Jossey-Bass, 2005.

CHAPTER TWENTY-FIVE

Temple Grandin. *Thinking in Pictures: My Life with Autism.* New York: Vintage Books, 1995, 2006.

CHAPTER TWENTY-SIX

Scientific American, November 2006, 295(5).

ABOUT THE AUTHORS

SARAH-JAYNE BLAKEMORE is a Royal Society Dorothy Hodgkin Research Fellow at the Institute of Cognitive Neuroscience at University College London. She is engaged in research on the development of the brain during adolescence and social cognition in autism.

JOHN D. BRANSFORD is professor of education and psychology at the University of Washington in Seattle. He has also served as cochair of several National Academy of Science committees. Author of seven books and hundreds of articles and presentations, Bransford is an internationally renowned scholar in cognition and technology.

ANN L. BROWN was an educational psychologist and pioneer in the field of metacognition. She was a professor at University of California, Berkeley's Graduate School of Education before her death in 1999. She served as president of the National Academy of Education as well as the American Educational Research Association, and she won three major career awards from national associations in psychology and education.

JOHN T. BRUER is president of the James S. McDonnell Foundation and an adjunct professor of philosophy at Washington University. He works to facilitate collaboration between the national educational research community and educators who desire to apply cognitive research in their classrooms.

JAMES P. BYRNES is associate dean of psychological studies in education at Temple University. He has published research in the areas of mathematics learning, decision making, language, deductive reasoning, and gender differences in cognition.

RODNEY R. COCKING is a senior program officer at the National Research Council and director of the Board on Behavioral, Cognitive, and Sensory Sciences.

ANTONIO DAMASIO is professor of neuroscience at the University of Southern California, where he is also director of the Brain and Creativity

Institute. His widely translated books include *Descartes' Error: Emotion, Reason and the Human Brain, The Feeling of What Happens: Body and Emotion in the Making of Consciousness*, and *Looking for Spinoza: Joy, Sorrow, and the Feeling Brain*.

STANISLAS DEHAENE is a professor at the Collège de France and a researcher at the Institut National de la Santé. He has worked on a number of topics, including cognitive neuropsychology of language and number processing in the human brain.

MARIAN C. DIAMOND is professor of anatomy at the University of California, Berkeley, and is one of the world's foremost neuroanatomists. She is author of more than one hundred scientific articles and three books.

ELLIOT W. EISNER is professor of education and art at Stanford University where he is known for his scholarship in three fields: arts education, curriculum studies, and educational evaluation. He was awarded the Brock International Prize in Education in 2004.

KURT FISCHER, the Charles Bigelow Professor of Education and Human Development at Harvard University, studies cognition, emotion, and learning and their relation to brain development and educational assessment. He is the author or editor of over a dozen books, as well as more than two hundred scientific articles. Leading an international movement to connect biology and cognitive science to education, he is founding president of the International Mind, Brain, and Education Society and founding editor of the new journal *Mind, Brain, and Education*.

LEONARDO FOGASSI is associate professor of human physiology at the University of Parma in Italy. In 2007 he and his colleagues, Vittorio Gallese and Giacomo Rizzolatti, were awarded the Grawemeyer Psychology Award for their discovery of mirror neurons.

UTA FRITH is professor of cognitive development and deputy director of the Institute of Cognitive Neuroscience at University College London. She is a leading authority on autism and dyslexia and is the author of several books on autism and Asperger syndrome.

VITTORIO GALLESE is professor of human physiology at the University of Parma in Italy. In 2007 he and his colleagues, Leonardo Fogassi and Giacomo Rizzolatti, were awarded the Grawemeyer Psychology Award for their discovery of mirror neurons.

HOWARD GARDNER is the John H. and Elisabeth A. Hobbs Professor of Cognition and Education at the Harvard Graduate School of Education. Among numerous honors, Gardner received a MacArthur Prize Fellowship in 1981. The author of over twenty books translated into twenty-four languages and several hundred articles, Gardner is best known in educational circles for his theory of multiple intelligences.

USHA GOSWAMI is professor of education at the University of Cambridge and a fellow of St John's College, Cambridge. She is also editor of *Applied Psycholinguistics,* and is on the editorial boards of *Journal of Experimental Child Psychology, Reading and Writing, Reading Research Quarterly, Dyslexia, Journal of Child Psychology and Psychiatry, Cognitive Development,* and *Developmental Science.*

TEMPLE GRANDIN is a gifted animal scientist, as well as a prominent author and speaker on the subject of autism. She is arguably the most accomplished and well-known adult with autism in the world. Her books include *Animals in Translation, Thinking in Pictures and Other Reports from My Life with Autism,* and *Unwritten Rules of Social Relationships.*

MICHAEL GURIAN is a social philosopher, family therapist, corporate consultant, and author of twenty-one books published in twenty languages. He is cofounder of The Gurian Institute.

JANET HOPSON is coauthor with Marian Diamond of *Magic Trees of the Mind: How to Nurture Your Child's Intelligence, Creativity,* and *Healthy Emotions from Birth Through Adolescence.*

MARY HELEN IMMORDINO-YANG studies the neuroscience of emotion and its relation to cognitive, linguistic, and social development at the Brain and Creativity Institute/Rossier School of Education, University of Southern California. She lectures nationally and abroad on the implications of brain and cognitive science research for curriculum and pedagogy, and is the North American editor for the journal *Mind, Brain, and Education.*

ERIC JENSEN is an internationally recognized educator known for his translation of neuroscience into classroom applications. He is the author of over twenty books, including *Teaching with the Brain in Mind.*

RONALD KOTULAK was awarded the Pulitzer Prize in Journalism in 1994. He writes on science topics for the *Chicago Tribune.*

JOSEPH LEDOUX is professor of neural science and psychology at New York University. His research is aimed at understanding the biological mechanisms of emotional memory.

DANIEL J. LEVITIN runs the Laboratory for Musical Perception, Cognition, and Expertise at McGill University, where he holds the Bell Chair in the Psychology of Electronic Communication.

PAMELA NEVILLS is a teacher who works with multiage learners from primary grades through postgraduate students. She is also a speaker and consultant on the topic of the brain and education.

LINDSAY M. OBERMAN is the primary investigator on several studies investigating human cognitive and behavioral neuroscience in the Brain and Perception Laboratory in the department of psychology at the University of California, San Diego.

VILAYANUR S. RAMACHANDRAN is director of the Center for Brain and Cognition and professor with the Psychology Department and the Neurosciences Program at the University of California, San Diego, and adjunct professor of biology at the Salk Institute. Ramachandran has published over 120 papers in scientific journals and is author of the critically acclaimed book *Phantoms in the Brain*.

RICHARD RESTAK is a neurologist, neuropsychiatrist, and clinical professor of neurology at George Washington University's Medical Center. He has written over eighteen books about the human brain.

GIACOMO RIZZOLATTI is director of the neurosciences department at the University of Parma in Italy. In 2007 he and his colleagues, Vittorio Gallese and Leonardo Fogassi, were awarded the Grawemeyer Psychology Award for their discovery of mirror neurons.

ROBERT M. SAPOLSKY is professor of biological sciences and of neurology and neurological sciences at Stanford University. He has received numerous honors and awards for his work, including the prestigious MacArthur Fellowship, an Alfred P. Sloan Fellowship, and the Klingenstein Fellowship in Neuroscience.

SALLY SHAYWITZ is professor of pediatrics and child study at the Yale University School of Medicine, where she codirects the Yale Center for the Study of Learning and Attention. Her research interests include both the development of skilled reading and the study of disorders of reading and math in children, adolescents, and young adults.

DAVID A. SOUSA is an international educational consultant and author of several books, including *How the Brain Learns: A Classroom Teacher's Guide* and *Learning Manual for How the Brain Learns*. He has conducted workshops in hundreds of school districts on brain research, instructional skills, supervision, and science education at the elementary, secondary, and university levels.

ROBERT J. STERNBERG is professor of psychology at Yale University. He served as president of the American Psychological Association in 2003 and is the author of roughly 950 books, book chapters, and articles in the field of psychology.

KATHY STEVENS is the training director of the Gurian Institute and has worked in education, child development, and the nonprofit world for more than thirty years in programs as diverse as juvenile and adult corrections, teen pregnancy prevention, cultural competency training, domestic violence prevention, and women's issues.

ROBERT SYLWESTER is an emeritus professor of education at the University of Oregon, where he studies the educational implications of new developments in science and technology. He is the author of several books and many journal articles, and also writes for the acclaimed internet journal, *Brain Connection* (www.brainconnection.com).

PATRICIA WOLFE is an independent consultant who speaks to educators in schools across the United States and abroad. Her focus is on the educational implications and applications of neuroscience, cognitive science, and educational research for teaching and learning.

ACKNOWLEDGMENTS

The Jossey-Bass Education Team would like to thank the following people for their insightful feedback on this Reader: Michael Atherton, David Sousa, James Kaufman, Allison Kaufman, Barbara Given, Renate Caine, and Robert Sylwester.

We are also indebted to Kurt Fischer and Mary Helen Immordino-Yang for a thoughtful Introduction that sets the stage for the Reader and harmoniously brings the pieces together. A special thanks to Mary Helen, who generously shared her knowledge on all things brain-related and whose input greatly influenced the book's content.

In addition, we'd like to thank Leslie Tilley for her development work, Sheri Gilbert, a magnificent permissions editor, and Bev Miller, an extraordinary copyeditor. Last, we are grateful for the amazing production efforts and patient nature of Susan Geraghty.

INTRODUCTION: THE FUNDAMENTAL IMPORTANCE OF THE BRAIN AND LEARNING FOR EDUCATION

People learn. Learning is fundamental to human beings. It is the specialization that we use to become fully human. A major part of that specialization is our exceptionally large brain, the primary organ for learning. We spend the many years of childhood learning the extensive knowledge of our cultures and families. In complex modern cultures, we have created schools as the main institution for promoting learning beyond the family. Modern culture requires that we spend years going to school to learn the special tools and skills of literacy, mathematics, history, science, art, music, and much more. That means that schools and the brain belong together, joined by the common purpose of learning (Battro, Fischer, & Léna, 2007).

The Biological Revolution and Education

There is a revolution afoot that is bringing brain and cognitive science into education and creating new tools to vastly improve how students learn. Or is there? Expectations for educational neuroscience are extremely high, but at this point, it could turn out to be not a revolution but just another fad, a popular enthusiasm that fades with time as the unreality of exaggerated expectations becomes clear (Bruer, Chapter Five, this volume). What is needed is not a quick fix from neuroscience, which will not work for education, but the creation of a new field that integrates neuroscience and other areas of biology and cognitive science with education (Immordino-Yang, 2007; Szücs & Goswami, 2007). Creating this field, which some of us call *mind, brain, and education* (Fischer, Daniel, Immordino-Yang, Stern, Battro, & Koizumi, 2007), can transform schools and education in the long term by creating a scientific basis for educational practice.

This is a new era in science and education—a time when biology is the leader of the sciences, and new discoveries about the brain, genes, and the processes of life make headlines every day. In the popular media, we see amazing pictures of what happens in the brain and how it changes in positive and negative ways, such as in learning to read or becoming addicted to a drug. These advances in tools for imaging the brain promise to improve education by showing, for example, how learning occurs; how a math class can change the ways that neurons connect to form networks for processing information in the brain; how different languages can shape perception and memory in the brain; and how fundamentally emotions shape thinking, learning, and beliefs.

In the midst of all this new science, the deep need for extending and improving education is clear, for North America and for the rest of the world. Education has proven to be one of the best ways of improving people's lives, leading them not only to better jobs but to better health for themselves and their children and to greater prosperity for their community and nation (Graham, 2005). Schooling is the best single way not only to promote learning to read but also to stimulate economic growth, improve the health of infants and their mothers, and reduce the birth rate and prevent overpopulation. With such great needs and hopes, the expectations for schools and other forms of education have surged to extremes, often extending beyond what is possible. These high expectations are coming together with the advances in brain science and related disciplines, leading to hope that science will bring about fast advances in educational practice.

The potentials of brain science for education are indeed enormous. But realizing them requires building a new interdisciplinary science that explicitly links brain science and education in a collaboration, with both playing strong roles. For this interdisciplinary approach to prosper in a way that moves beyond a fad, educators need to know about brain science, and scientists need to know about education. Using scientific research to answer questions about education requires that educators and scientists work together to ask useful questions and ultimately build usable knowledge that will inform educational practice, illuminating how learning occurs in schools and other settings.

To many people, educational implications seem like a natural extension of neuroscientific research. After all, when we educate children, we are shaping the ways that their brains and minds develop and learn. Unfortunately, most of what is called "brain-based education" today has no grounding at all in brain or cognitive science. The only way that brains are involved in most brain-based education is that the students have brains. In typical claims for brain-based education, beliefs about learning and schooling are restated in the language of brain science, but there is no brain research on which those restatements are based. Brain science is a young field, not a mature science, and educational neuroscience is even younger, with only a small number of researchers examining brain processes for learning in educational settings. Even if claims for brain-based education ultimately prove to be true, there is currently no scientific basis for most of them because the research has not yet been done.

The good news is that the first glimmers of educational neuroscientific research are highly promising. For example, research on reading difficulties such as dyslexia uses brain imaging to test how students learn to read and what methods can improve their learning (Szücs & Goswami, 2007; see the chapters in Part Five of this book). Research on brain and cognitive processes in development and learning suggests new tools for assessing learning—tools that promise powerful ways of tracking how individual students learn effectively as they move along specific learning pathways, which often differ across people and topics (Bransford & Donovan, 2005; Fischer & Bidell, 2006). Research on how children learn with distinctly different brains (different ways of processing information and acting based on brain organization) suggests a remarkable flexibility in the ways that people adapt their abilities to learn important skills such as emotional communication in language (Immordino-Yang, 2007; Parts Four and Seven in this book). These and many other research questions can eventually produce major improvements in education. Many young educators and scientists are entering this emerging field to make these improvements possible, and a few training programs have recently been established, such as the Mind, Brain, and Education program that we began at Harvard University in 2000 (http://gseweb.harvard.edu/-mbe) and the new program in Neuroscience and Psychology in Education at the University of Cambridge in England (http://www.educ.cam.ac.uk/randd/npe.html).

Yet there will be no quick fix from educational neuroscience. Building a new field takes time—to bring together educators and brain scientists to figure out how learning occurs effectively in educational settings, formulate questions that will be useful for improving educational practice, and study how students learn, both effectively and ineffectively. If neuroscience can help inform the educational process, then it is important that teachers and others in educational roles know something about the brain and learning. This book makes small steps toward this goal as it helps educators begin to build a foundation of knowledge about brain and cognitive science as it relates to education.

Using This Book

This book can play an important role in creating the new field by helping educators learn about brain and cognitive science so that they can shape effective questions and build a research base to improve education. The book can be an excellent teaching tool for educators and teachers in training. It includes readings from many of the foremost thinkers in the field of cognitive neuroscience, as well as interpretive and summarizing readings by master educators. The main strength of this book is that it offers readings by diverse scientific researchers that have the potential to inform learning and education. To our knowledge, this book is the first to bring such writings together in one place.

There are sections introducing the brain and neuroscience, the debate about brain-based learning and the nature of intelligence, and work about traditional academic skills such as reading and mathematics. Then the book goes beyond those obvious topics to connect neuroscience to other essential components of an education: the arts, emotion, social functioning, and exceptional and atypical thinkers. Too often discussions of neuroscience and learning follow the unfortunate lead of much of education, heavily emphasizing traditional skills and omitting or neglecting other important areas involved in being a person. Learning about emotions, the arts, social interaction, and exceptional learners provides the perspective of the whole person, including the ways that neuropsychological strengths and weaknesses interact in brain and behavior (Fischer, Bernstein, & Immordino-Yang, 2007). The design of effective learning environments requires breaking down the artificial disciplinary boundaries of traditional educational approaches and considering both the whole person and relations between the specific skills that are so important for education, such as literacy and mathematics.

One of the lessons of educational neuroscience, even at this early point in its development, is that children learn along specific pathways, building skills and concepts for particular content—a pathway for understanding American history, a pathway for doing arithmetic, a pathway for playing guitar. At the same time they do not act or think in rigidly separated compartments but can relate different contents (Fischer & Bidell, 2006). As they develop their learning along specific pathways defined by content, they are also forming connections among those pathways. Indeed, reading is a perfect example. It requires the integration of the separate domains of visual analysis (written words), sound analysis (spoken words), and meaning, and it also connects children's interests with their literacy skills, because it is such a powerful tool for learning about topics of interest. Many children learn to read because of a personal passionate interest: they are driven to read to find out more about animals or how a lawn mower works or the Civil War (Fischer & Fusaro, in press). To become educated persons and effective citizens, students ultimately need to learn a wide range of skills, built on an educational foundation that their teachers and parents carefully construct to foster learning, motivation, personal responsibility, and creativity.

The brain is the central organ for learning, and scientific research on learning and the brain promises many important new insights and tools that will improve education around the world. But educational neuroscience is young and just emerging as a field in its own right. It does not offer quick and easy solutions to the tough problems of education. Its contributions to education will come in the long term, as educators and scientists work together to create the new science of learning and the brain.

October 2007   KURT W. FISCHER
Harvard University Graduate School of Education

MARY HELEN IMMORDINO-YANG
University of Southern California

REFERENCES

Battro, A. M., Fischer, K. W., & Léna, P. (Eds.). (2007). *The educated brain: Essays in neuroeducation*. Cambridge: Cambridge University Press.

Bransford, J., & Donovan, S. (Eds.). (2005). *How students learn: History, science, and mathematics in the classroom*. Washington, DC: National Academy Press.

Fischer, K. W., Bernstein, J. H., & Immordino-Yang, M. H. (Eds.). (2007). *Mind, brain, and education in reading disorders*. Cambridge: Cambridge University Press.

Fischer, K. W., & Bidell, T. R. (2006). Dynamic development of action and thought. In W. Damon & R. M. Lerner (Eds.), *Theoretical models of human development: Handbook of child psychology* (6th ed., Vol. 1, pp. 313–399). Hoboken, NJ: Wiley.

Fischer, K. W., Daniel, D., Immordino-Yang, M. H., Stern, E., Battro, A., & Koizumi, H. (2007). Why mind, brain, and education? Why now? *Mind, Brain, and Education, 1*(1), 1–2.

Fischer, K. W., & Fusaro, M. (in press). Using student interests to motivate learning. In R. P. Fink & J. Samuels (Eds.), *Inspiring success: Reading interest and motivation in an age of high-stakes testing*. Newark DE: International Reading Association.

Graham, P. A. (2005). *Schooling America: How the public schools meet the nation's changing needs*. New York: Oxford University Press.

Immordino-Yang, M. H. (2007). A tale of two cases: Lessons for education from the study of two boys living with half their brains. *Mind, Brain, and Education, 1*(2), 66–83.

Szücs, D., & Goswami, U. (2007). Educational neuroscience: Defining a new discipline for the study of mental representations. *Mind, Brain, and Education, 1*(3).

In the interest of readability, the editors have slightly adapted the following selections for this volume. For the complete text, please refer to the original source.

PART ONE

AN OVERVIEW OF THE BRAIN

HOW OUR BRAIN CONSTRUCTS OUR MENTAL WORLD

Richard Restak

Von Hemholtz's Darkroom Experiment

Look up from this book and focus your attention for a few seconds on the first thing that meets your eye. Then return to the book. When you looked up, you didn't have any problem understanding what I meant by attention, did you? One moment you were engaged in reading a sentence, and the next moment you had shifted your attention and you were looking at . . . whatever. It was as if you had directed the beam of a flashlight from one portion of a darkened room to another. Yet attentional shifts don't necessarily involve eye movements. You could just as easily have shifted your attention by simply thinking of something you had to do later today. But what is it exactly that you would be shifting at such a time? This question tantalized the eminent nineteenth-century German scientist Hermann von Helmholtz, who carried out an experiment on attention.

Helmholtz was intrigued with the question of how much information a person could process in a brief period of time. To find out, he used a flashbulb to briefly illuminate an otherwise dark scene consisting of letters painted onto a sheet suspended at one end of his lab. When Helmholtz triggered the flash of light in the dark it provided a short-lived illumination of the letters. He immediately discovered that he couldn't take in all of the letters during the brief illumination; he could see only some of them. But if he decided ahead of time which portion of the screen he would attend to during the illumination, he could easily discern those letters despite his continued inability to perceive letters elsewhere on the screen.

Helmholtz was paying what psychologists now refer to as *covert visual attention* to a chosen region of the sheet of letters: "By a voluntary kind of intention, even without eye movements, . . . one can concentrate attention on the sensation from a particular part and at the same time exclude attention from all other parts."

Today neuroscientists can illustrate what's going on in the brain during Helmholtz's ingenious experiment. When you focus your visual attention on something in your immediate surroundings, the blood flow immediately increases in the visual areas of your brain. But this increase in activity isn't just a generalized increase; it occurs in a highly specific pattern. If you attend to something off to your left, your brain's right visual area is activated; if you attend to something off to your right, it's the left visual area that comes alive. (Remember that the visual hemispheres on the two sides of the brain scan the opposite visual fields.)

Think for a moment what such findings imply. As you direct your visual attention to something in your surroundings, your brain has already begun—thanks to your intention to look at one thing rather than another—to selectively focus on that one aspect of the world in front of you. Thus, in the words of George R. Mangun of the Center for Mind and Brain, University of California, Davis, "Changes in visual brain processing significantly affect how we perceive and respond to the world around us."

Magicians have known about this intention-attention link for centuries and take advantage of it via the technique of misdirection. If a trick "works," it's often because the magician has successfully fooled his audience into purposely (intentionally) focusing their attention on an unimportant aspect of the trick, thus preventing them from seeing what he's actually doing.

Thinking Is for Doing

Not only intention and attention but all other states of mind and body are related to and oftentimes determined by our brain. As an example of my point, say the word *zeal* out loud. Now without changing the position of your lips and mouth in any way, simply imagine saying it. Hold that imagined feeling. Now open your mouth as wide as you can and imagine once again saying *zeal*. Feels quite different, doesn't it?

This simple exercise underscores an important point: Our mental processes are sufficiently tethered to our bodily senses that we have difficulty with situations when the brain and other parts of the body aren't in sync. You'll experience difficulty in any mental activity when your body executes movements that thwart it: it's hard to think critically while slumped in an armchair, hard to meditate on compassion while punching a bag.

Here's another example. Clench your fists, hard, and grit your teeth. At the same time imagine yourself pushing a heavy piece of furniture across the living room. Then quickly change the thought to lying on a beach in the Caribbean listening to gentle waves. Notice how much harder it is to maintain that thought with those clenched fists and that tightened jaw? Now unclench your fists and loosen your jaw and return to the image of pushing that furniture. That doesn't feel quite right either: We don't push furniture with hands and jaw relaxed.

Next, sit for a few moments with your forearm flexed as if you're about to pull something toward you. Now imagine me showing you a series of items or speaking a series of words and then asking you how you feel about them. I then ask you to repeat the exercise with your arm held straight out in a fully extended position. Would it surprise you—as it did me—to learn that you'll tend to like the various items you encountered while holding your arm in the flexed position, and dislike the items heard while your arm is extended? That's what was found in a test measuring the association of arm posture and attitude.

Flexing the arm, of course, is a motion we all carry out when we're pulling something toward us, "embracing" it; straightening the arm, or "strong-arming," in contrast, is what we do when we want to push something away. For those requiring more convincing evidence of the connection between our personal evaluations and our bodily positions, the experimenters repeated the experiment, but this time with a twist: half of the participants in the experiment were asked to push a lever away from them if they reacted positively to a particular word but pull it toward them if the word gave rise to negative associations, while the other half of the participants were told to do the opposite, pulling forward with positive words and pushing away with negative words. Overall, people were faster to respond to positive words when they were pulling instead of pushing the lever, and faster to respond to negative words when they were pushing rather than pulling the lever.

The experimenters tried the experiment again, only this time they didn't say anything about likes or dislikes. Half the volunteers simply responded by pushing the lever as quickly as possible whenever a word appeared; the other half of the participants in this reaction time experiment pulled the lever at the instant they became aware of the word. Again, those pushing the lever reacted more quickly to negative words, while the lever pullers responded faster to positive words.

"Immediately and unintentionally a perceived object or event is classified as either good or bad, and this results, in a matter of milliseconds, in a behavioral predisposition toward that object or event," according to Yale University psychologist John Bargh, who carried out the research just described.

Think for a moment about the usefulness of such an arrangement. Thanks to these automatic responses, it's not necessary to consciously evaluate everything that's happening from moment to moment. Rather, our bodily movements automatically bring us closer to positive events and experiences but increase the distance between negative ones and us. This is especially helpful when our conscious mind is otherwise engaged in thinking about other matters, such as our presentation at tomorrow's weekly staff meeting.

This intimate association between body and thought intrigued the nineteenth-century psychologist William James, who emphasized the intimate association that exists between thinking and action. In 1890 James wrote, "It is a general principle of psychology that consciousness deserts all processes where it can no longer be of use. . . . We grow unconscious of every feeling which is useless as a sign to lead us to our ends." Unlike his brother, the novelist Henry James, William James favored tightly compressed aphorisms over lengthy and baroque paragraphs: "Thinking is for doing," he wrote. These four words simplify without oversimplifying the notion that merely thinking about doing something increases the likelihood that one will actually do it. While this seems a fairly commonsense notion—most of us can readily bring personal examples to mind—James developed it a good bit further. Indeed, he took the notion quite literally and argued for the then-maverick view that thinking about doing something activates the same brain regions that come into play when one actually does it.

A hundred years later PET [positron emission tomography] scan studies confirm James's proposal. Starting in the early 1990s, neuroscientists provided PET scan evidence that thinking about a word or about carrying out a movement activates the same area in the anterior cingulate that is activated when actually saying the word or carrying out the movement.

"These studies support the notion that thinking about something and doing it are neurologically similar. And the two activities activate the same regions of the brain, suggesting they share representational systems," says Duke University psychologist Tanya L. Chartrand, an expert on the link between thinking and doing.

Chartrand's comment is important because it's in line with the advice of psychotherapists and motivational experts who suggest imaginational exercises as the first step toward self-improvement. They advise envisioning yourself as the person you want to become, or changing a situation that's troubling you by imagining that change as a prelude to making it happen.

Mirror Neurons

Although we like to think of ourselves as independent and self-actualizing, our thoughts and behavior are powerfully influenced by other people's actions. This holds true even at the level of simple observation. When we watch another person move, our observation of the movement activates those areas in our brain that we would use if we moved the same way. This was first discovered in macaque monkeys, where "mirror neurons" in the prefrontal cortex respond both when the monkey grasps a peanut and when it watches another monkey grasp it. Even hearing sounds suggestive of a monkey grasping and then breaking a peanut activates the mirror neurons. This suggests that the mirror neurons for vision and hearing aren't just coding movements and sounds but rather goals and meanings: What is the monkey doing? Further, mirror neurons can be trained. If a monkey is taught to rip paper or perform some other action that doesn't come naturally to the animal, specific mirror neurons will start to fire at the mere sound of ripping paper.

A similar perception-action matching system exists in the human brain. Imagine yourself watching me reach out and grasp the cup of tea that now sits on the small table next to my word processor. As you observe my hand reaching for the cup, the motor cortex in your brain will also become slightly active in the same areas you would use if you reached out to pick up that teacup. Further, if you watch my lips as I savor the tea, the area of your brain corresponding to lip movements will activate as well.

No, that doesn't mean you can taste my tea. But it does mean that I'm directly affecting your brain as you watch me go through the motions of drinking my tea. In such a situation the neat division between you and me breaks down and we form a unit in which each of us is influencing the other's actions at the most basic level imaginable: I am altering your brain as a result of your observations of me, and vice versa.

Notice that it isn't necessary for you to consciously think about the movement in order to get your brain working. Merely observing me move my hand toward the teacup will activate those portions of your brain that would come into play if you actually moved your hand. But if I move my hand toward the teacup for a purpose other than sipping tea, the mirror neurons fail to fire. We know this because of a clever experiment carried out by a team led by Marco Iacoboni of the University of California, Los Angeles.

In this test of mirror neuron responses, volunteers watched video clips taken before and after a tea party. The "before" clip showed a steaming teapot and cup placed alongside a neatly arranged plate of cookies. The "after" clip depicted an empty teapot, scattered cookie crumbs, and a used napkin. At the conclusion of both video clips a hand reached in from off-camera and grasped the teacup. Since the hand motion was identical in each clip, only the context suggested two different intentions: drinking the tea in the "before" clip versus tidying up in the "after" clip.

As fMRI [functional magnetic resonance imaging] scans of the volunteers' brains showed, brain activity in these two situations differed markedly. The greatest activity in the right frontal cortex (known from previous research to process mirrorlike responses to hand movements) occurred while the volunteer watched the grasping movement associated with drinking the tea. Thus mirror neurons are affected not just by motion but also by the motivation behind it, according to Iacoboni.

Think for a moment of the implications of this. You can activate my brain if you can attract my attention enough to get me to watch what you're doing, and vice versa. Thanks to the mirror neurons in each of our brains, a functional link exists between my brain and yours.

Nor does any actual movement have to take place in order for this mutual influence of one brain on another to take place. For instance, imagine someone reading to you the following list of words: *plain, rip, geography, stomp, Ireland, wistful, lift.* If you are listening to the words while in a PET scan, the action verbs *rip, stomp,* and *lift* will activate areas of the brain normally engaged if you were actually ripping, stomping, or lifting. Called into play would be the dorsolateral prefrontal cortex, the anterior cingulate, and the premotor and parietal cortices. The same thing would happen if you were watching someone else rip, stomp, and lift, if you spoke the words aloud, or if you dredged up those words from memory.

Valeria Gazzola of the BCN Neuroimaging Center in Gröningen, the Netherlands, has spun the mirror neuron concept in a more intimate direction. In her experiments on auditory empathy she discovered that when a person listens to a sound associated with an action such as kissing, the act of listening activates the same area in the premotor cortex that would come online if that person actually kissed someone: the kissing sounds activated areas of the premotor cortex controlling the mouth movements associated with kissing. Certainly Gazzola's findings are in sync with our everyday experience. As Gazzola puts it: "If in a hotel room, we hear the neighbor's bed squeaking rhythmically, we can't help hearing more than just a sound."

Part of that intuition comes from the capacity of mirror neurons to distinguish between biological and nonbiological actions. Beds don't move on their own and, with one notable exception, usually don't squeak rhythmically. Monkeys make a similar distinction when another monkey is involved in an action compared to a machine carrying out that action. It will grasp something when it sees another monkey do it, but remains unmoved when pliers or a mechanical tool performs the same action. Human infants show a pattern much like this. At eighteen months an infant will imitate and even complete an action made by a human but will fail to imitate a robot making the same movement. This also holds true for sounds. Infants older than nine months can learn new speech sounds to which they have never been exposed, but only if the new sounds come from a real person. Learning the new sound doesn't occur at this age if the infant hears the same word on a tape recorder or video.

In adults, speaking action words activates the same brain structures as actually carrying out the actions (the verb-behavior link, as neuropsychologists refer to it). That linkage is one of the reasons we become annoyed when someone asks us a question while we're trying to concentrate. The question automatically activates those parts of our brain involved in formulating the answer to that question. We're annoyed because of the conscious effort we must exert not to become distracted— that is, direct our attention away from our current thoughts in order to formulate a response to the question. In such situations we learn firsthand that although our brain can carry out many processes simultaneously, the focus of our conscious attention is limited to a few things at a time.

Mental imagery is actually an offshoot of our capacity for activating those mirror neurons. Think for a moment about a pleasant experience you had, say, during your last vacation. I'm thinking at the moment of the view of the beach from the patio of my hotel room at Maui in Hawaii. Although I can "see" the scene very clearly in my imagination, the experience obviously isn't the same as actually being there. From the point of view of physical location, thousands of miles separate the two experiences. But what about the representation of these two experiences in my brain? How does my creation of a mental image within my brain differ from the original experience? Actually, not nearly as much as you might expect.

Over the last decade neuroscientists have discovered that the visual imagery employed in an imaginative re-creation of an earlier experience shares important features with the original visual perception. As I think about the beach many of the same areas will be activated in my brain that were active when I was physically there. And the time that it took me to scan the view of the beach from my patio is equal to the time it takes me now to mentally imagine the same scene. Moreover, if you ask me a question about the beach, my brain will direct my eyes to look downward, just as it would if I were once again looking down from the patio. A question about how the beach appeared from the right of the patio will provoke an unconscious shift of my eyes to the right (or to the left if you asked about how the beach appeared from that direction).

Thanks to mirror neurons, we can mentally rehearse physical activities without actually doing them. If you've learned a physical exercise and then later mentally rehearse it, you will induce an increase in muscle strength comparable to what would happen if you actually did the exercise. What's more, your heart rate and breathing frequency will increase linearly with the increase in the imagined effort: the greater the exertion you imagine yourself making, the more your heart and breathing rates will increase. If you are put into an fMRI scan, many of the same areas will activate as when you actually did the exercise (the primary motor cortex, the premotor cortex, the SMA [supplementary motor area], the basal ganglia, and the cerebellum).

Not everyone shows the same degree of mirroring. When observing someone playing the piano, skilled pianists show stronger motor activation than the musically naive. But if they watch random finger movements instead, the brain responses of the pianists are indistinguishable from people with no special musical expertise or interest. A similar situation exists among dancers. In an ingenious study Bentriz Calvo-Merino of the Institute of Movement Neuroscience, University College London, compared the brain activation patterns of ballet dancers and capoeira dancers (capoeira is an Afro-Brazilian martial dance first developed by slaves in Brazil more than four hundred years ago as a means of fighting back against the slave owners). She found greater brain activation when the dancers viewed movements they had been trained to perform compared to movements they had not. That is, the ballet dancers showed stronger brain activation while observing ballet movements than when observing capoeira movements, and among capoeira dancers, the greater activation occurred while watching capoeira.

In response to this demonstration of the power of imagery for elaborate movement sequences, coaches and trainers have incorporated various imaging exercises into athletic and physical fitness training programs. Obviously, this reliance on imaging can only go so far. That's why the world is still waiting (and will continue to wait, I expect) for the first winner at Wimbledon whose training has consisted only of mental exercises. While thinking and doing activate the same brain areas, the winning of a tennis game, as any regular player knows quite well, requires physical and not just mental effort.

So think about those mirror neurons the next time someone talks to you about the power of human imagination. Imagination involves the activation of sensory and action centers in the brain. Not only can we now locate it within specific areas of the brain, but we can also quantify it. And for the most part imagination is a power that we control: We consciously invoke the images in our imagination or, on those occasions when an image spontaneously springs to mind, we can consciously suppress it. Further, we can "build up" our imaginative powers just as we do our muscular strength.

MIRRORS IN THE MIND

Giacomo Rizzolatti
Leonardo Fogassi
Vittorio Gallese

JOHN WATCHES MARY, who is grasping a flower. John knows what Mary is doing—she is picking up the flower—and he also knows why she is doing it. Mary is smiling at John, and he guesses that she will give him the flower as a present. The simple scene lasts just moments, and John's grasp of what is happening is nearly instantaneous. But how exactly does he understand Mary's action, as well as her intention, so effortlessly?

A decade ago most neuroscientists and psychologists would have attributed an individual's understanding of someone else's actions and, especially, intentions to a rapid reasoning process not unlike that used to solve a logical problem: some sophisticated cognitive apparatus in John's brain elaborated on the information his senses took in and compared it with similar previously stored experiences, allowing John to arrive at a conclusion about what Mary was up to and why. Although such complex deductive operations probably do occur in some situations, particularly when someone's behavior is difficult to decipher, the ease and speed with which we typically understand simple actions suggest a much more straightforward explanation. In the early 1990s our research group at the University of Parma in Italy, which at the time included Luciano Fadiga, found that answer somewhat accidentally in a surprising class of neurons in the monkey brain that fire when an individual performs simple goal-directed motor actions, such as grasping a piece of fruit. The surprising part was that these same neurons also fire when the individual sees someone else perform the same act. Because this newly discovered subset of cells seemed to directly reflect acts performed by another in the observer's brain, we named them mirror neurons. Much as circuits of neurons are believed to store specific memories within the brain, sets of mirror neurons appear to encode templates for specific actions. This property may allow an individual not only to perform basic motor procedures without thinking about them but also to comprehend those acts when they are observed, without any need for explicit reasoning about them. John grasps Mary's action because even as it is happening before his eyes, it is also happening, in effect, inside his head. It is interesting to note that philosophers in the phenomenological tradition long ago posited that one had to experience something within oneself to truly comprehend it. But for neuroscientists, this finding of a physical basis for that idea in the mirror neuron system represents a dramatic change in the way we understand the way we understand.

Instant Recognition

Our research group was not seeking to support or refute one philosophical position or another when we first noticed mirror neurons. We were studying the brain's motor cortex, particularly an area called F5 associated with hand and mouth movements, to learn how commands to perform certain actions are encoded by the firing patterns of neurons. For this purpose, we were recording the activity of individual neurons in the brains of macaques. Our laboratory contained a rich repertoire of stimuli for the monkeys, and as they performed various actions, such as grasping for a toy or a piece of food, we could see that distinct sets of neurons discharged during the execution of specific motor acts. Then we began to notice something strange: when one of us grasped a piece of food, the monkeys' neurons would fire in the same way as when the monkeys themselves grasped the food. At first we wondered whether this phenomenon could be the result of some trivial factor, such as the monkey performing an unnoticed movement while observing our actions. Once we managed to rule out this possibility and others, including food expectation by the monkeys, we realized that the pattern of neuron activity associated with the observed action was a true representation in the brain of the act itself, regardless of who was performing it. Often in biological research, the most direct way to establish the function of a gene, protein, or group of cells is simply to eliminate it and then look for deficits in the organism's health or behavior afterward. We could not use this technique to determine the role of mirror neurons, however, because we found them spread across important regions on both sides of the brain, including the premotor and parietal cortices. Destroying the entire mirror neuron system would have produced such broad general cognitive deficits in the monkeys that teasing out specific effects of the missing cells would have been impossible. So we adopted a different strategy. To test whether mirror neurons play a role in understanding an action rather than just visually registering it, we assessed the neurons' responses when the monkeys could comprehend the meaning of an action without actually seeing it. If mirror neurons truly mediate understanding, we reasoned, their activity should reflect the meaning of the action rather than its visual features. We therefore carried out two series of experiments. First we tested whether the F5 mirror neurons could "recognize" actions merely from their sounds. We recorded the mirror neurons while a monkey was observing a hand motor act, such as ripping a sheet of paper or breaking a peanut shell, that is accompanied by a distinctive sound. Then we presented the monkey with the sound alone. We found that many F5 mirror neurons that had responded to the visual observation of acts accompanied by sounds also responded to the sounds alone, and we dubbed these cell subsets audiovisual mirror neurons.

Next we theorized that if mirror neurons are truly involved in understanding an action, they should also discharge when the monkey does not actually see the action but has sufficient clues to create a mental representation of it. Thus, we first showed a monkey an experimenter reaching for and grasping a piece of food. Next, a screen was positioned in front of the monkey so that it could not see the experimenter's hand grasping the food but could only guess the action's conclusion. Nevertheless, more than half the F5 mirror neurons also discharged when the monkey could just imagine what was happening behind the screen. These experiments confirmed, therefore, that the activity of mirror neurons underpins understanding of motor acts: when comprehension of an action is possible on a nonvisual basis, such as sound or mental representation, mirror neurons do still discharge to signal the act's meaning. Following these discoveries in the monkey brain, we naturally wondered whether a mirror neuron system also exists in humans. We first obtained strong evidence that it does through a series of experiments that employed various techniques for detecting changes in motor cortex activity. As volunteers observed an experimenter grasping objects or performing meaningless arm gestures, for example, increased neural activation in their hand and arm muscles that would be involved in the same movements suggested a mirror neuron response in the motor areas of their brains. Further investigations using different external measures of cortical activity, such as electroencephalography, also supported the existence of a mirror neuron system in humans.

But none of the technologies we had used up to this point allowed us to identify the exact brain areas activated when the volunteers observed motor acts, so we set out to explore this question with direct brain-imaging techniques. In those experiments, carried out at San Raffaele Hospital in Milan, we used positron-emission tomography (PET) to observe neuronal activity in the brains of human volunteers as they watched grasping actions performed with different hand grips and then, as a control, looked at stationary objects. In these situations, seeing actions performed by others activated three main areas of the brain's cortex. One of these, the superior temporal sulcus (STS), is known to contain neurons that respond to observations of moving body parts. The other two—the inferior parietal lobule (IPL) and the inferior frontal gyrus (IFG)—correspond, respectively, to the monkey IPL and the monkey ventral pre-motor cortex, including F5, the areas where we had previously recorded mirror neurons. These encouraging results suggested a mirror mechanism at work in the human brain as well but still did not fully reveal its scope. If mirror neurons permit an observed act to be directly understood by experiencing it, for example, we wondered to what extent the ultimate goal of the action is also a component of that "understanding."

On Purpose

Returning to our example of John and Mary, we said John knows both that Mary is picking up the flower and that she plans to hand it to him. Her smile gave him a contextual clue to her intention, and in this situation, John's knowledge of Mary's goal is fundamental to his understanding of her action, because giving him the flower is the completion of the movements that make up her act. When we perform such a gesture ourselves, in reality we are performing a series of linked motor acts whose sequence is determined by our intent: one series of movements picks the flower and brings it to one's own nose to smell, but a partly different set of movements grasps the flower and hands it to someone else. Therefore, our research group set out to explore whether mirror neurons provide an understanding of intention by distinguishing between similar actions with different goals. For this purpose, we returned to our monkeys to record their parietal neurons under varying conditions. In one set of experiments, a monkey's task was to grasp a piece of food and bring it to its mouth. Next we had the monkey grasp the same item and place it into a container. Interestingly, we found that most of the neurons we recorded discharged differently during the grasping part of the monkey's action, depending on its final goal. This evidence illustrated that the motor system is organized in neuronal chains, each of which encodes the specific intention of the act. We then asked whether this mechanism explains how we understand the intentions of others.

We tested the same grasping neurons for their mirror properties by having a monkey observe an experimenter performing the tasks the monkey itself had done earlier. In each instance, most of the mirror neurons were activated differently, depending on whether the experimenter brought the food to his mouth or put it in the container. The patterns of firing in the monkey's brain exactly matched those we observed when the monkey itself performed the acts—mirror neurons that discharged most strongly during grasping-to-eat rather than grasping-to-place did the same when the monkey watched the experimenter perform the corresponding action. A strict link thus appears to exist between the motor organization of intentional actions and the capacity to understand the intentions of others. When the monkeys observed an action in a particular context, seeing just the first grasping component of the complete movement activated mirror neurons forming a motor chain that also encoded a specific intention. Which chain was activated during their observation of the beginning of an action depended on a variety of factors, such as the nature of the object acted on, the context and the memory of what the observed agent did before. To see whether a similar mechanism for reading intentions exists in humans, we teamed with Marco Iacoboni and his colleagues at the University of California, Los Angeles, for a functional magnetic resonance imaging (fMRI) experiment on volunteers. Participants in these tests were presented with three kinds of stimuli, all contained within video clips. The first set of images showed a hand grasping a cup against an empty background using two different grips. The second consisted of two scenes containing objects such as plates and cutlery, arranged in one instance as though they were ready for someone to have afternoon tea and in the other as though they were left over from a previously eaten snack and were ready to be cleaned up. The third stimulus set showed a hand grasping a cup in either of those two contexts.

We wanted to establish whether human mirror neurons would distinguish between grasping a cup to drink, as suggested by the ready-for-tea context, and grabbing the cup to take it away, as suggested by the cleanup setting. Our results demonstrated not only that they do but also that the mirror neuron system responded strongly to the intention component of an act. Test subjects observing the hand motor acts in the "drinking" or "cleaning" contexts showed differing activation of their mirror neuron systems, and mirror neuron activity was stronger in both those situations than when subjects observed the hand grasping a cup without any context or when looking only at the place settings.

Given that humans and monkeys are social species, it is not difficult to see the potential survival advantage of a mechanism, based on mirror neurons, that locks basic motor acts onto a larger motor semantic network, permitting the direct and immediate comprehension of others' behavior without complex cognitive machinery. In social life, however, understanding others' emotions is equally important. Indeed, emotion is often a key contextual element that signals the intent of an action. That is why we and other research groups have also been exploring whether the mirror system allows us to understand what others feel in addition to what they do.

Connect and Learn

As with actions, humans undoubtedly understand emotions in more than one way. Observing another person experiencing emotion can trigger a cognitive elaboration of that sensory information, which ultimately results in a logical conclusion about what the other is feeling. It may also, however, result in direct mapping of that sensory information onto the motor structures that would produce the experience of that emotion in the observer. These two means of recognizing emotions are profoundly different: with the first, the observer deduces the emotion but does not feel it; via the second, recognition is firsthand because the mirror mechanism elicits the same emotional state in the observer. Thus, when people use the expression "I feel your pain" to indicate both comprehension and empathy, they may not realize just how literally true their statement could be. A paradigmatic example is the emotion of disgust, a basic reaction whose expression has important survival value for fellow members of a species. In its most primitive form, disgust indicates that something the individual tastes or smells is bad and, most likely, dangerous. Once again using fMRI studies, we collaborated with French neuroscientists to show that experiencing disgust as a result of inhaling foul odorants and witnessing disgust on the face of someone else activate the same neural structure—the anterior insula—at some of the very same locations within that structure. These results indicate that populations of mirror neurons in the insula become active both when the test participants experience the emotion and when they see it expressed by others. In other words, the observer and the observed share a neural mechanism that enables a form of direct experiential understanding. Tania Singer and her colleagues at University College London found similar matches between experienced and observed emotions in the context of pain. In that experiment, the participants felt pain produced by electrodes placed on their hands and then watched electrodes placed on a test partner's hand followed by a cue for painful stimulation. Both situations activated the same regions of the anterior insula and the anterior cingulated cortex in the subjects. Taken together, such data strongly suggest that humans may comprehend emotions, or at least powerful negative emotions, through a direct mapping mechanism involving parts of the brain that generate visceral motor responses. Such a mirror mechanism for understanding emotions cannot, of course, fully explain all social cognition, but it does provide for the first time a functional neural basis for some of the interpersonal relations on which more complex social behaviors are built. It may be a substrate that allows us to empathize with others, for example. Dysfunction in this mirroring system may also be implicated in empathy deficits, such as those seen in children with autism [see Chapter Twenty-Six, "Broken Mirrors: A Theory of Autism," by Vilayanur S. Ramachandran and Lindsay M. Oberman]. Many laboratories, including our own, are continuing to explore these questions, both for their inherent interest and their potential therapeutic applications. If the mirror neuron template of a motor action is partly inscribed in the brain by experience, for instance, then it should theoretically be possible to alleviate motor impairments, such as those suffered following a stroke, by potentiating undamaged action templates. Recent evidence indicates, in fact, that the mirror mechanism also plays a role in the way we initially learn new skills. Although the word *ape* is often used to denote mimicry, imitation is not an especially well developed ability among nonhuman primates. It is rare in monkeys and limited in the great apes, including chimpanzees and gorillas. For humans, in contrast, imitation is a very important means by which we learn and transmit skills, language, and culture.

Did this advance over our primate relatives evolve on the neural substrate of the mirror neuron system? Iacoboni and his group provided the first evidence that this might be the case when they used fMRI to observe human subjects who were watching and imitating finger movements. Both activities triggered the IFG, part of the mirror neuron system, in particular when the movement had a specific goal. In all these experiments, however, the movements to be imitated were simple and highly practiced. What role might mirror neurons play when we have to learn completely new and complex motor acts by imitation? To answer this question, Giovanni Buccino at our university and collaborators in Germany recently used fMRI to study participants imitating guitar chords after seeing them played by an expert guitarist. While test subjects observed the expert, their parietofrontal mirror neuron systems became active. And the same area was even more strongly activated during the subjects' imitation of the chord movements. Interestingly, in the interval following observation, while the participants were programming their own imitation of the guitar chords, an additional brain region became active. Known as prefrontal area 46, this part of the brain is traditionally associated with motor planning and working memory and may therefore play a central role in properly assembling the elementary motor acts that constitute the action the subject is about to imitate. Many aspects of imitation have long perplexed neuroscientists, including the basic question of how an individual's brain takes in visual information and translates it to be reproduced in motor terms. If the mirror neuron system serves as a bridge in this process, then in addition to providing an understanding of other people's actions, intentions, and emotions, it may have evolved to become an important component in the human capacity for observation-based learning of sophisticated cognitive skills. Scientists do not yet know if the mirror neuron system is unique to primates or if other animals possess it as well.

Our own research group is currently testing rats to see if that species also demonstrates mirror neuron responses. Such internal mirroring may be an ability that developed late in evolution, which would explain why it is more extensive in humans than in monkeys. Because even newborn human and monkey babies can imitate simple gestures such as sticking out the tongue, however, the ability to create mirror templates for observed actions could be innate. And because lack of emotional mirroring ability appears to be a hallmark of autism, we are also working with young autistic children to learn whether they have detectable motor deficits that could signal a general dysfunction of the mirror neuron system. Only a decade has passed since we published our first discoveries about mirror neurons, and many questions remain to be answered, including the mirror system's possible role in language—one of humanity's most sophisticated cognitive skills. The human mirror neuron system does include Broca's area, a fundamental language-related cortical center. And if, as some linguists believe, human communication first began with facial and hand gestures, then mirror neurons would have played an important role in language evolution. In fact, the mirror mechanism solves two fundamental communication problems: parity and direct comprehension. Parity requires that meaning within the message is the same for the sender as for the recipient. Direct comprehension means that no previous agreement between individuals—on arbitrary symbols, for instance—is needed for them to understand each other. The accord is inherent in the neural organization of both people. Internal mirrors may thus be what allow John and Mary to connect wordlessly and permit human beings in general to communicate on multiple levels.

3

ALPHABETIZED ENTRIES FROM
HOW TO EXPLAIN A BRAIN

Robert Sylwester

Note: The following definitions are from a nontechnical encyclopedic handbook designed for educators. The entries cover various brain concepts and terms and "typically comprise two parts: (1) an initial short functional definition of the concept or term and (2) an expanded commentary that will provide useful background and supplementary information." Please refer to original source for complete text and related entries.

Brain imaging technology. Recently developed computerized machines that measure and display the variations in chemical composition, blood-flow patterns, and electromagnetic fields that occur in normal and abnormal brains.

. . . Recent advances in computerized imaging technology have made it possible to technologically pass through the skull and brain tissue and to observe, amplify, record, rapidly analyze, and graphically display the brain substances and signals that reflect activity in very specific brain regions. This technology has revolutionized brain and mind research, and the diagnosis and treatment of many brain-related diseases and malfunctions.

The first imaging technologies, the X-ray and EEG (electroencephalogram), were primitive by today's standards, but both have been considerably improved—and provided the conceptual base of other amazing imaging technologies that have recently emerged.

Computerized brain imaging technologies now measure and display the variations in chemical composition, blood-flow patterns, and electromagnetic fields that occur in normal and abnormal brains. Each of the several current forms of brain imaging technology has strengths and weaknesses, and new developments are continually making the technology faster, more powerful, less invasive, and less expensive. Imaging technology was initially used primarily in medical diagnosis, but it is increasingly being used in pure neuroscience and psychological research.

Educational researchers are just beginning to use imaging technologies, but this use will dramatically increase in the coming years. It will revolutionize educational research and many elements of educational policy and practice.

The various computerized imaging technologies differ, but the following analogy demonstrates how someone can examine internal differences in something (a brain) that has a protective cover (a skull). Imagine that you're looking for similarities, differences, and imperfections in successive slices of a thinly sliced apple or potato. A brain imaging machine is basically a camera that can rapidly and successively change its focus as it photographs and digitally stores thin slices of a brain to create a comprehensive three-dimensional image of selected properties of the entire brain.

The graphic displays in imaging technology use the color spectrum gradations to represent the activity levels of the various brain areas in a scan (the red end of the spectrum representing a high level of activity in a brain area, the purple end representing low activity, and the other colors representing intermediate levels). . . . A scan of a slice of brain thus graphically indicates which brain areas were active and inactive during the time interval of the scan.

Functional magnetic resonance imaging (commonly written fMRI) measures brain blood-flow patterns and metabolic changes. Although almost a dozen kinds of imaging technologies exist, fMRI is currently perhaps the most important for cognitive neuroscience researchers. fMRI permits scientists to identify specific brain regions that are active when the subject is carrying out a task, such as reading a text, making a decision, or moving a finger. Scientists can thus compare the brain anatomy and activity of people who read well and poorly, or who make appropriate and inappropriate decisions. Much of what we've learned recently about cognition has been accomplished with fMRI technology.

Positron emission tomography (PET) is another important imaging technology. Scientists using PET insert a small amount of radioactively tagged glucose (or another appropriate compound) into the bloodstream of the experimental subject. Because glucose is the brain's principal food, the PET scans of subjects will reveal the brain areas with the most glucose (that are thus the most active) when, for example, the subjects are asked to say the first verb that comes to mind when they hear a specific noun—such as *cut* or *slice* when they hear the noun *knife*.

Emerging major advances in EEG technology may provide the best initial and potential venue for educational researchers. EEG is the least invasive, cheapest, and most portable of the imaging technologies. For example, because fMRI uses powerful magnets and PET uses radioactive isotopes, and both require expensive equipment in specialized laboratory settings, their use in educational research has been limited by ethical and financial considerations. Conversely, EEG measures electrical brain waves via electrodes placed on the skull, and so it's no more invasive than a blood pressure sleeve. Furthermore, the electrodes can now be placed inside a cap where they send wireless signals to a nearby computer, so a researcher could eventually observe brain activity in non-laboratory settings, such as within a classroom.

———————— o ————————

Brain sciences. The scientific disciplines that focus on understanding the brain and its cognitive processes and that seek to remedy brain maladies.

Recent advances in research technology have helped the thousands of brain scientists to expand dramatically the types and amount of research discoveries and clinical applications. The number of specialized areas in the brain sciences is large and increasing, but the following four perhaps relate the most to issues that educators confront:

Neuroscience focuses on the scientific study of the nervous system's organization and development at both the cellular and systems levels. Its focus is more on research than on clinical applications.

Cognitive neuroscience focuses on how brain biology gives rise to emotion, attention, thought, and behavior. The term emerged in the late 1970s and is increasingly supplementing the term *psychology*, which historically was focused principally on behavior. Cognitive neuroscientists study many of the teaching and learning issues that are of importance to educators.

Neurology focuses on the medical diagnosis and treatment of nervous systems disorders.

Psychiatry focuses on the medical diagnosis and treatment of mental disorders.

———————— o ————————

Cerebellum. The relatively small two-hemisphere structure tucked under the cerebral hemispheres right behind the brainstem—the little bump at the lower back of our head.

The cerebellum is massively interconnected with the rest of our brain. Scientists long thought that the cerebellum's principal task was to smoothly coordinate automatic movement programs by modifying our brain's basic motor and balance decisions, but they now consider the cerebellum to also be an important support system for various other cognitive functions, such as to monitor and fine-tune unconscious sensory input (and especially touch).

Think of a computer-nerd friend who provides analogous support when you need to install some hardware/software or fix a glitch. You could probably do it by yourself, albeit awkwardly, but it's so nice to have your friend there to smooth your efforts—someone who understands the nuances in the instructions, who can easily and correctly connect things.

Cerebellum means *little brain* in Latin, but the deeply folded, elegantly organized, and densely packed cerebellum is 11 percent of our brain's weight, and about the area of one of the cerebral hemispheres when it's spread out. Further it has more neurons than the rest of our brain.

The principal input into the cerebellum is processed by the 10 billion tiny granule cells, one of the smallest types of neuron in our brain (packed 6 million per square millimeter). Conversely, all cerebellar output is processed by Purkinje cells, one of the largest types of neurons in our brain. Three other types of neurons—stellate, basket, and Golgi cells—modulate the input/output activity of granule and Purkinje cells.

○

Cerebral cortex. The outer deeply folded surface of the cerebrum that processes conscious sensory, thought, decision, and motor functions. The principal divisions of the cerebral cortex are the occipital, parietal, temporal, and frontal lobes, and the hemispheres.

Our brain organizes its trillion+ neurons and glial cells into (1) a relatively small subcortical area (the brainstem, cerebellum, and surrounding systems) whose modular structures innately regulate and coordinate such basic survival processes as circulation, respiration, and movement, and (2) the large surrounding six layer sheet of deeply folded neural tissue called the cerebral cortex. The cerebral cortex encompasses 77 percent of our brain, and it processes learned rational behaviors that emerge out of the challenges we confront. The unfolded cortex is slightly larger than the size and thickness of a stack of six sheets of 12×18 inch construction paper.

The six layers of the cortex are principally populated by pyramidal and stellate (or granule) neurons. Pyramidal neurons have a pyramid shaped cell body and long axon/dendrite extensions that extend well beyond their immediate cortical area. Star-shaped stellate (or granule) neurons have shorter axon/dendrite extensions, and so connect principally with nearby neurons. Incoming information enters into layer four; internal processing of the information occurs in layers one to three; and the outgoing response leaves from layers five and six.

The cortex is composed principally of hundreds of millions of highly interconnected hair-thin (100 neuron) minicolumns that extend vertically through the six cortical layers (called the gray matter). Each minicolumn is specialized to process a very specific unit of information (such as to recognize a horizontal line or a specific tone). One hundred adjacent minicolumns combine into a unit to form a macrocolumn (about the thickness of the lead in a pencil) that can process more complex functions related to the minicolumns it incorporates (perhaps to help differentiate between the cello and flute version of a tone). Thousands of related macrocolumns form one of the 50+ anatomically and functionally distinct Brodmann areas that each hemisphere contains. [The German neuroanatomist Korbinian Brodmann's pioneering way of organizing the cerebral cortex into distinct regions based on structural variations in neurons and on their organization within the cortex.

Brodmann identified fifty-two distinct numbered areas in 1909, and this system is still substantially used, although other scientists have further subdivided many of the original Brodmann areas into more than two hundred areas. Brain imaging technology is now providing a better view of the functional organization of the cortex, where various cognitive tasks are processed.]

The axons in columnar neurons extend down the column through the cortical layers into the white matter, a dense web of axon connections beneath the gray matter. The axons eventually leave the white matter to connect with dendrites in neurons in a related nearby column or to project into a column or brain nucleus elsewhere in our brain.

Thus, discrete columnar brain areas and systems process basic limited cognitive functions. These are incorporated into larger, specialized, widely distributed but highly interconnected areas and systems that collaborate on complex cognitive tasks. For example, our visual system has about 30 separate columnar subsystems that process such visual properties as shape, depth, color, quantity, and movement. The subsystem that responds to the color red processes it on every red object we see, and the subsystem that responds to circular shapes processes balls/CDs/tires/

doughnuts/etc. Several of these subsystems will combine to process our perception of a single red ball rolling across a table.

Two simple metaphors will help [in understanding] the division and organization of our brain's hundreds of processing systems, many of which are innately dedicated to a specific important task—and most of which aren't active at any given time.

A *library metaphor*. Think of a 100-neuron column (in the gray matter) as containing the information in a 100-page book, and its axonal white matter (that connects with other neurons) as the bibliography that connects the information in that book to other books. Further, think of the entire cerebral cortex as a library, the columns as library books, and the some 100 Brodmann areas that encompass the cerebral cortex as the various library areas (that contain books and other information on history, science, etc.).

Library shelf areas are thus assigned to a given category of books—fiction in one library area, science in another, etc. A student would generally gather information from several books in a given area while preparing a report on that topic, and would ignore library areas and books unrelated to the research topic. Our brain similarly efficiently gathers the information it needs from brain areas specialized to provide the needed information or function and doesn't activate other unrelated areas.

Important library topics have more shelf space devoted to them than less important topics, but the library's shelf space can be reorganized to accommodate an expanding collection of books in a category. Dedicated (or modular) neuronal systems can similarly recruit neurons from less-dedicated surrounding areas if they need more power to process their task. We can observe this developing spatial inequality in the larger amount of motor cortex space dedicated to coordinating movement in a person's dominant arm/hand as compared to the other, or in the expansion of neuronal space devoted to left hand digital capabilities when a right handed person becomes a violin student.

A *kitchen metaphor*. A kitchen is a room where food is received, stored, and processed (and a brain similarly receives, integrates, and stores information arriving from inside and outside our body). A kitchen is filled with provisions and utensils suitable for a wide variety of menus, but most aren't being used at any given time. A cook planning to cook carrots uses only a peeler, knife, pan, water faucet, seasonings, and stove—not potatoes, the toaster, or other kitchen provisions or utensils. A recipe is a record of which of many kitchen provisions and utensils are used to prepare the food (and a brain scan similarly records which brain areas are involved in an activity).

In a kitchen a few key ingredients and utensils are used in almost all food production activity—food staples such as salt and onions, utensils for cutting and heating (and a few key brain systems and functions are similarly central to much of what we do).

Finally, kitchens often contain dull knives, broken equipment, and under/over-ripe food that can affect the proper preparation of a menu (and our brain can contain immature and malfunctioning systems that reduce the overall effectiveness of cognitive activity).

o

Cerebral hemispheres. The two major divisions of the cerebrum, separated by the deep longitudinal cerebral fissure into the right and left hemispheres, and connected by the underlying corpus callosum and anterior commisure.

Most of our conscious thought and action are processed in the two cerebral hemispheres. They have different processing assignments but typically function as an integrated efficient unit because they are so highly interconnected. Think of a married couple who have determined the primary responsibility for each of various household tasks, but who constantly discuss possible solutions to challenges that involve the family as a unit.

Responding to looming dangers and opportunities is an important cognitive task. The fundamental organizing principle for the right and left hemispheres emerges out of an important question a brain must answer before deciding how to respond to a challenge: Have I confronted this problem before?

The right hemisphere (in most humans) is organized principally to process novel challenges, and the left hemisphere to process knowledge and effective routines developed during previous similar challenges. For example, we process strange faces principally in our right hemisphere, and familiar faces in the left. Musically naive people process music principally in their right hemisphere, trained musicians in the left.

The initial solution to a novel challenge doesn't necessarily have to be the best solution—just something that works enough to keep us alive. We then save that solution as a memory, recall and edit it for use the next time we confront a similar problem, and then save that solution as a memory. Think of the similar way in which we save the successful drafts of a manuscript until it becomes just what we want it to be.

Although both hemispheres are active in processing most cognitive functions, the relative level of involvement thus shifts from the right to the left hemisphere over time and with increased competence. The right hemisphere is thus organized to rapidly and creatively respond to a novel challenge, but the more linear organization of the left hemisphere eventually translates the successful initial responses into an efficient established routine that is activated whenever the challenge reoccurs.

It makes sense. Grammatical language is an efficient established procedure to enhance communication within a socially complex species, so it's not surprising that considerable left hemisphere space is devoted to it. A dependent infant uses whatever (right hemisphere) nonverbal communication skills it can creatively muster to get the help it needs, but happily spends much of its childhood mastering the much more efficient existing cultural (left hemisphere) language template that we pass from generation to generation.

Each hemisphere is divided into four lobes. The three lobes in the back half receive and analyze incoming sensory information (occipital/sight, temporal/hearing, and parietal/touch), and integrate it into a perceptual map of the current challenges—the right hemisphere focusing on novel and the left hemisphere on familiar elements. The frontal lobe determines a response strategy—the right hemisphere again focusing on creative solutions to novel challenges, the left hemisphere on activating established routines.

We can thus think of the cerebral hemispheres as efficiently equipped to recognize (sensory lobes) and respond (frontal lobes) to novel (right hemisphere) and familiar (left hemisphere) challenges.

———————— o ————————

Cerebrum. The combined right and left hemisphere regions in the large upper forebrain part of our brain. The cerebrum contains the top cerebral cortex layer of cells (gray matter) and the underlying network of connections among cellular systems (white matter). Some brain scientists also include the diencephalon as a part of the cerebrum, so it's somewhat confusing.

———————— o ————————

Meme. The cultural equivalent of a biological gene.

A gene contains and transmits the cross-generation biological information an organism needs to develop and maintain itself. A meme is the cultural equivalent of a gene—a bit of replicated information that spreads through a society via imitation, teaching, and learning. Memes can range from trivial jokes, tunes, and slogans to such useful information as how to acquire and prepare food and shelter. Like genes, memes can evolve over time (such as in clothing fashions) and pass from one generation to the next (such through books, films, recordings).

Animals that have a relatively short life span and live within a narrow ecological niche are born with innate survival and reproduction strategies. They typically die when they confront an environmental challenge beyond their innate capabilities. Variant members of their species that can somehow meet the challenges will survive, and so pass on the genetic characteristics that enhanced their success. The concept of *learning* for such species is thus principally an evolutionary process in which subsequent generations gradually adapt to environmental change.

Humans need a supplementary strategy. We have a long, interdependent life span and can live almost anywhere. We thus confront many complex challenges that would be impossible to encode genetically (such as recognizing individuals, recalling restaurants, playing a piano, and constructing clothing). Because we're born with an immature brain, most of our survival strategies aren't innate, but must be learned throughout life, and especially during our extended juvenile stage. Brain processes that enhance learning are thus essential to human life. Mirror neurons, memory, and memes are key elements of this complex system.

Memetic information is probably stored in memory networks where it's principally used while solving personal problems, but it can also be transmitted to others via imitation and language. It's also possible that many people will store a specific meme within a same or related brain location and configuration.

A memory network is a neuronal configuration that can represent an idea, object, or event. Think of the *Happy Birthday* song. A birthday will activate the memory network, but it's also possible for other networks in our brain to trigger the network internally, even though no birthday is being celebrated (and you're probably mentally singing the *Happy Birthday* song right now).

Yet just as it's possible to construct a protein by expressing the information in a gene without destroying the gene in the process, it's similarly possible to transmit the information in our memory into other brains via language or behavior without destroying our own memory. It's a replication of information, not a gift. The *Happy Birthday* song thus becomes a meme whose evolutionary travels among culturally related brains are analogous to the spread of genetic information within a species.

○

REFERENCES

Aungur, R. (2002). *The electric meme: A new theory of how we think*. New York: Free Press.

Blackmore, S. (1999). *The meme machine.* New York: Oxford University Press.

———————— o ————————

Mirror neurons. Neurons in the premotor cortex and possibly elsewhere that activate both when observing a specific action in another person (such as a smile) and also when carrying out the same action. They are the neuronal substrate of mimicry.

The development of a smoothly controlled motor system is a major childhood priority.

. . . How infants begin their mastery of complex motor behaviors is a fascinating developmental phenomenon. Consider a behavior that most parents observe. If you stick out your tongue to an observant infant shortly after birth, the probability is high that she will reciprocate the behavior.

Sticking out our tongue is an uncommon act for humans, and it requires the activation of a complex motor neuron sequence. Our tongue is an important muscle system that facilitates eating and speech, so we normally keep it inside our mouth. An infant could randomly fire the appropriate motor neurons for tongue protection, but that's not what occurs when an infant sticks out her tongue in immediate mimicry of a parent's action. How can an infant possibly master such a complex motor act immediately after observing it?

The remarkable mirror neuron system explains the modeling-mimicking process that is central to much human learning. Initial studies focused on a left hemisphere area that regulates speech production in humans (Broca's area). The discovery of mirror neurons might provide the same powerful unifying framework for our understanding of teaching and learning that the discovery of DNA did for our understanding of genetics.

A smoothly coordinated motor sequence involves the typically unconscious preparation for a movement followed by the actual movement. For example, while my left index finger is typing the *c* in *cat*, my left little finger is getting ready to type *a* and my left index finger will shortly move up to the top row to type the *t*. The result is a single seamless typing action—*cat*.

The motor cortex plays a key role in activating such muscles. It's a narrow ear-to-ear band of neural tissue, with specific segments dedicated to regulating specific groups of body muscles. The premotor area directly in front of the motor cortex primes the next movements in a motor sequence.

Neurons in the premotor area that fire in preparation for upcoming movements also fire when we observe someone else carry out that action.

Common brain regions thus process both the perception and production of a movement. The infant's observation of her parent's projecting tongue fires the premotor neurons that represent her tongue, and this priming activates the related motor cortex neurons that project her tongue out in mimicry.

We experience this mimicking phenomenon most commonly when we see someone yawn, and then typically have to stifle our own. Because infants must learn many movements, they don't inhibit the mimicking of movements they observe. For them, it's "monkey see, monkey do" (and it's interesting that the initial mirror neuron research was done on monkeys).

Our mirror neurons won't fire at the mere observation of a hand or mouth—only when it's carrying out a goal-directed action. Furthermore, they will respond to a hand but not to a tool that's grasping or moving an object (because body parts and not tools are represented in our motor and premotor areas).

Mirror neurons may thus facilitate the preliminary motor neuron simulation, priming, programming, and rehearsing that occurs in children, and this process obviously enhances our eventual mastery of complex motor behaviors and our ability to "read" the minds of others. For example, inferring the potential movements of others is an essential skill in many games in which players try to fake out opponents. Mirror neuron stimulation may also explain why so many people enjoy observing the movements of virtuoso athletes, dancers, and musicians. It allows us to represent actions mentally that we can't mimic physically. . . . Scientists are also exploring the relationship between mirror neuron activity and our ability to imagine our own planned actions, be empathetic, and develop articulate speech. Mirror neurons may thus eventually help to explain many teaching and learning mysteries in which modeling provides children with an effective behavioral pattern to follow; they may also help to explain disabilities (such as autism) in which children can't "read" the minds of others.

_____ o _____

REFERENCE

Meltzoff, A., & Prinz, W. (2002). *The imitative mind: Development, evolution, and brain bases.* Cambridge: Cambridge University Press. (Note especially chapter 14 by the principal discoverers of mirror neurons, Giacomo Rizzolatti and Vittorio Gallesse, "From Mirror Neurons to Imitation: Facts and Speculations," pp. 247–266.)

PART TWO

THE BRAIN IN THE CLASSROOM

THE BRAIN-BASED LEARNING DEBATE

4

NEUROSCIENCE AND EDUCATION

Usha Goswami

Neuroscience is a relatively new discipline encompassing neurology, psychology, and biology. It has made great strides in the last 100 years, during which many aspects of the physiology, biochemistry, pharmacology, and structure of the vertebrate brain have been understood. Understanding of some of the basic perceptual, cognitive, attentional, emotional, and mnemonic functions is also making progress, particularly since the advent of the cognitive neurosciences, which focus specifically on understanding higher level processes of cognition via imaging technology. Neuroimaging has enabled scientists to study the human brain at work in vivo, deepening our understanding of the very complex processes underpinning speech and language, thinking and reasoning, reading and mathematics. It seems timely, therefore, to consider how we might implement our increased understanding of brain development and brain function to explore educational questions.

THE STUDY OF LEARNING unites education and neuroscience. Neuroscience as broadly defined investigates the processes by which the brain learns and remembers, from the molecular and cellular levels right through to brain systems (for example, the system of neural areas and pathways underpinning our ability to speak and comprehend language). This focus on learning and memory can be at a variety of levels. Understanding cell signaling and synaptic mechanisms (one brain cell connects to another via a synapse) is important for understanding learning, but so is examination of the functions of specific brain structures such as the hippocampus by natural lesion studies or by invasive methods. Brain cells (or neurons) transmit information via electrical signals, which pass from cell to cell via the synapses, triggering the release of neurotransmitters (chemical messengers). There are around 100 billion neurons in the brain, each with massive connections to other neurons. Understanding the ways in which neurotransmitters work is a major goal of neuroscience. Patterns of neural activity are thought to correspond to particular mental states or mental representations. Learning broadly comprises changes in connectivity, either via changes in potentiation at the synapse or via the strengthening or pruning of connections. Successful teaching thus directly affects brain function, by changing connectivity.

Clearly, educators do not study learning at the level of the cell. Successful learning is also dependent on the curriculum and the teacher, the context provided by the classroom and the family, and the context of the school and the wider community. All of these factors of course interact with the characteristics of individual brains. For example, children with high levels of the MAOA gene (monoamine oxidize A) who experience maltreatment and adverse family environments seem to be protected from developing antisocial behaviors (Caspi et al., 2002), possibly via moderating effects on their neural response to stress. Diet also affects the brain. A child whose diet is poor will not be able to respond to excellent teaching in the same way as a child whose brain is well-nourished. It is already possible to study the effects of various medications on cognitive function. Methylphenidate (Ritalin), a medication frequently prescribed for children with ADHD (Attention Deficit Hyperactivity Disorder), has been shown to improve stimulus recognition in medicated children (in terms of attention to auditory and visual stimuli as revealed by neuroimaging; see Seifert, Scheuerpflug, Zillessen, Fallgater, & Warnke, 2003). Neuroimaging techniques also offer the potential to study the effects of different diets, food additives, and potential toxins on educational performance.

Teaching

It is notable, however, that neuroscience does not as yet study teaching. Successful teaching is the natural counterpart of successful learning, and is described as a "natural cognition" by Strauss (2003). Forms of teaching are found throughout the animal kingdom, usually related to ways of getting food. However, the performance of *intentional acts* to increase the knowledge of others (teaching with a "theory of mind") does seem to be unique to humans, and is perhaps essential to what it means to be a human being (Strauss, Ziv, & Stein, 2002). The identification and analysis of successful pedagogy is central to research in education, but is currently a foreign field to cognitive neuroscience. There are occasional studies of the neural changes accompanying certain types of highly focused educational programs (such as remedial programs for teaching literacy to dyslexic children; see below), but wider questions involving the invisible mental processes and inferences made by successful teachers have not begun to be asked. Strauss suggests that questions such as whether there are specialized neural circuits for different aspects of teaching may soon be tractable to neuroimaging methods, and this is a thought-provoking idea. Teaching is a very specialized kind of social interaction, and some of its aspects (reading the minds of others, inferring their motivational and emotional states) are after all already investigated in cognitive neuroscience.

Used creatively, therefore, cognitive neuroscience methods have the potential to deliver important information relevant to the design and delivery of educational curricula as well as the quality of teaching itself. Cognitive neuroscience may also offer methods for the early identification of special needs, and enable assessment of the delivery of education for special needs. At the same time, however, it is worth noting that "neuromyths" abound. Some popular beliefs about what brain science can actually deliver to education are quite unrealistic. Although current brain science technologies offer exciting opportunities to educationists, they complement rather than replace traditional methods of educational enquiry.

A Quick Primer on Brain Development

Many critical aspects of brain development are complete prior to birth (see Johnson, 1997, for an overview). The development of the neural tube begins during the first weeks of gestation, and "proliferative zones" within the tube give birth to the cells that compose the brain. These cells migrate to the different regions where they will be employed in the mature brain prior to birth. By 7 months gestation almost all of the neurons that will comprise the mature brain have been formed. Brain development following birth consists almost exclusively of the growth of axons, synapses, and dendrites (fiber connections): this process is called synaptogenesis. For visual and auditory cortex, there is dramatic early synaptogenesis, with maximum density of around 150 percent of adult levels between 4 and 12 months followed by pruning. Synaptic density in the visual cortex returns to adult levels between 2 and 4 years. For other areas such as prefrontal cortex (thought to underpin planning and reasoning), density increases more slowly and peaks after the first year. Reduction to adult levels of density is not seen until some time between 10 and 20 years. Brain metabolism (glucose uptake, an approximate index of synaptic functioning) is also above adult levels in the early years, with a peak of about 150 percent somewhere around 4–5 years.

By the age of around 10 years, brain metabolism reduces to adult levels for most cortical regions. The general pattern of brain development is clear. There are bursts of synaptogenesis, peaks of density, and then synapse rearrangement and stabilization with myelinization, occurring at different times and rates for different brain regions (that is, different sensitive periods for the development of different types of knowledge). Brain volume quadruples between birth and adulthood, because of the proliferation of connections, not because of the production of new neurons. Nevertheless, the brain is highly plastic, and significant new connections frequently form in adulthood in response to new learning or to environmental insults (such as a stroke). Similarly, sensitive periods are not all-or-none. If visual input is lacking during early development, for example, the critical period is extended (Fagiolini & Hensch, 2000). Nevertheless, visual functions that develop late (for example, depth perception) suffer more from early deprivation than functions that are relatively mature at birth (such as color perception, Maurer, Lewis, & Brent 1989). Thus more complex abilities may have a lower likelihood of recovery than elementary skills. One reason may be that axons have already stabilized on target cells for which they are not normally able to compete, thereby causing irreversible reorganization. It is important to realize that there are large individual differences between brains. Even in genetically identical twins, there is striking variation in the size of different brain structures, and in the number of neurons that different brains use to carry out identical functions. This individual variation is coupled with significant localization of function. . . . Although adult brains all show [the same] basic structure, it is thought that early in development a number of possible developmental paths and end states are possible. The fact that development converges on the same basic brain structure across cultures and gene pools is probably to do with the constraints on development present in the environment. Most children are exposed to very similar constraints despite slightly different rearing environments.

Large differences in environment, such as being reared in darkness or without contact with other humans, are thankfully absent or rare. When large environmental differences occur, they have notable effects on cognitive function. For example, neuroimaging studies show that blind adults are faster at processing auditory information than sighted controls, and that congenitally deaf adults are faster at processing visual information in the peripheral field than hearing controls (for example, Neville & Bavelier, 2000;

Neville, Schmidt, & Kutas, 1983; Röder, Rösler, & Neville, 1999). Nevertheless, neurons themselves are interchangeable in the immature system, and so dramatic differences in environment can lead to different developmental outcomes. For example, the area underpinning spoken language in hearing people (used for auditory analysis) is recruited for sign language in deaf people (visual/spatial analysis) (Neville et al., 1998). Visual brain areas are recruited for Braille reading (tactile analysis) in blind people (see Röder & Neville, 2003). It has even been reported that a blind adult who suffered a stroke specific to the visual areas of her brain consequently lost her proficient Braille reading ability, despite the fact that her somatosensory perception abilities were unaffected (Jackson, 2000). It has also been suggested that all modalities are initially mutually linked, as during early infancy auditory stimulation also evokes large responses in visual areas of the brain, and somatosensory responses are enhanced by white noise (for example, Neville, 1995). If this is the case, a kind of "synesthesia" could enable infants to extract schemas that are independent of particular modalities, schemas such as number, intensity, and time (see Röder & Neville, 2003). If this mutual linkage extends into early childhood, it may explain why younger children respond so well to teaching via multi-sensory methods.

Neuroimaging Tools for Developmental Cognitive Neuroscience

Neuroimaging studies are based on the assumption that any cognitive task makes specific demands on the brain which will be met by changes in neural activity. These changes in activity affect local blood flow which can be measured either directly (PET) or indirectly (fMRI). Dynamic interactions among mental processes can be measured by ERPs [event-related potentials].

PET (positron emission tomography) relies on the injection of radioactive tracers, and is not suitable for use with children. Brain areas with higher levels of blood flow have larger amounts of the tracer, allowing pictures of the distribution of radiation to be created and thereby enabling the localization of different neural functions. fMRI (functional magnetic resonance imaging) also enables the localization of brain activity.

This technique requires inserting the participant into a large magnet (like a big tube), and works by measuring the magnetic resonance signal generated by the protons of water molecules in neural cells. When blood flow to particular brain areas increases, the distribution of water in the brain tissue also changes. This enables measurement of a BOLD (blood oxygenation level dependent) response which measures changes in the oxygenation state of hemoglobin associated with neural activity. The change in BOLD response is the outcome measure in most fMRI studies. It is very noisy inside the magnet and participants are given headphones to shield their ears and a panic button (the magnet is claustrophobic). Because of these factors, it has been challenging to adapt fMRI for use with children (who also move a lot, impeding scanning accuracy). However, with the advent of specially adapted coils and less claustrophobic head scanners, such studies are growing in number.

A different and widely used neuroimaging technique that can be applied to children is that of the event related potential (ERP). ERPs enable the timing rather than localization of neural events to be studied. Sensitive electrodes are placed on the skin of the scalp and then recordings of brain activity are taken. Recording of the spontaneous natural rhythms of the brain is called EEG (electroencephalography). ERP refers to systematic deflections in electrical activity that may occur to precede, accompany, or follow experimenter-determined events. ERP rhythms are thus time-locked to specific events designed to study cognitive function. The usual technique is for the child to watch a video while wearing a headcap (like a swimming cap) that holds the electrodes. For visual ERP studies, the video is delivering the stimuli; for auditory ERP studies, the linguistic stimuli form a background noise and the child sits engrossed in a silent cartoon. The most usual outcome measures are (i) the latency of the potentials, (ii) the amplitude (magnitude) of the various positive and negative changes in neural response, and (iii) the distribution of the activity. The different potentials (characterized in countless ERP studies) are called N100, P200, N400, and so on, denoting negative peak at 100 ms, positive peak at 200 ms, and so on. The amplitude and duration of single ERP components such as the P200 increase until age 3 to 4 years (in parallel with synaptic density), and then decrease until puberty. ERP latencies decrease within the first years of life (in parallel with myelinization) and reach adult levels in late childhood. ERP studies have provided extensive evidence on the time course of neural processing and are sensitive to millisecond differences. The sequence of observed potentials and their amplitude and duration are used to understand the underlying cognitive processes.

Selected Studies from Cognitive Neuroscience with Interesting Implications for Education

How valuable is cognitive neuroscience to educational psychologists? Current opinions vary (Bruer, 1997; Byrnes & Fox, 1998; Geary, 1998; Geake & Cooper, 2003; Mayer, 1998; Schunk, 1998; Stanovich, 1998), but in general the consensus is moving away from early views that neuroscience is irrelevant because it only confirms what we already knew. The eventual answer will probably be that it is very valuable indeed. The tools of cognitive neuroscience offer various possibilities to education, including the early diagnosis of special educational needs, the monitoring and comparison of the effects of different kinds of educational input on learning, and an increased understanding of individual differences in learning and the best ways to suit input to learner. I will now describe briefly some recent neuroscience studies in certain areas of cognitive development, and give a flavor of how their methods could contribute to more specifically educational questions.

Language

Despite sharing 98.5 percent of our genome with chimpanzees, we humans can talk and chimps cannot. Interestingly, genes expressed in the developing brain may hold part of the answer. For example, a gene called FOXP2 differs in mouse and man by three amino acid differences, two of which occurred after separation from the common human-chimp ancestor about 200,000 years ago (Marcus & Fisher, 2003). This gene is implicated in a severe developmental disorder of speech and language that affects the control of face and mouth movements, impeding speech. Neurally, accurate vocal imitation appears to be critical for the development of speech (Fitch, 2000). Hence when linguistic input is degraded or absent for various reasons (for example, being hearing impaired, being orally impaired), speech and language are affected. Studies of normal adults show that grammatical processing relies more on frontal regions of the left hemisphere, whereas semantic processing and vocabulary learning activate posterior lateral regions of both hemispheres. For reasons that are not yet well understood, the brain systems important for syntactic and grammatical processing are more vulnerable to altered language input than the brain systems responsible for semantic and lexical functions. ERP studies show that when English is acquired late due to auditory deprivation or late immigration to an English-speaking country, syntactic abilities do not develop at the same rate or to the same extent (Neville, Coffey, Lawson, Fischer, Emmorey, & Bellugi, 1997). Late learners do not rely on left hemisphere systems for grammatical processing, but use both hemispheres (Weber-Fox & Neville, 1996). ERP studies also show that congenitally blind people show bilateral representation of language functions (Röder, Rösler, & Neville 2000). Blind people also process speech more efficiently (Hollins, 1989), for example, they speed up cassette tapes, finding them too slow, and still comprehend the speech even though the recording quality suffers.

Reading

Neuroimaging studies of both children and adults suggest that the major systems for reading alphabetic scripts are lateralized to the left hemisphere. These studies typically measure brain responses to single word reading using fMRI or ERPs. Reviews of such studies conclude that alphabetic/orthographic processing seems mainly associated with occipital, temporal, and parietal areas (for example, Pugh et al., 2001). The occipital-temporal areas are most active when processing visual features, letter shapes, and orthography. The inferior occipital-temporal area shows electrophysiological dissociations between words and nonwords at around 180 ms, suggesting that these representations are not purely visual but are linguistically structured. Activation in temporo-occipital areas increases with reading skill (for example, Shaywitz et al., 2002), and is decreased in children with developmental dyslexia.

Phonological awareness (the ability to recognize and manipulate component sounds in words) predicts reading acquisition across languages, and phonological processing appears to be focused on the temporo-parietal junction. This may be the main site supporting letter-to-sound recoding and is also implicated in spelling disorders.

Dyslexic children, who typically have phonological deficits, show reduced activation in the temporo-parietal junction during tasks such as deciding whether different letters rhyme (for example, P, T = yes, P, K = no). Targeted reading remediation increases activation in this area (for example, Simos et al., 2002). Finally, recordings of event-related magnetic fields (MEG) in dyslexic children suggest that there is atypical organization of the right hemisphere (Heim, Eulitz, & Elbert, 2003). This is consistent with suggestions that compensation strategies adopted by the dyslexic brain require greater right hemisphere involvement in reading.

Although to date neuroimaging studies have largely confirmed what was already known about reading and its development from behavioral studies, neuroscience techniques also offer a way of distinguishing between different cognitive theories (for example, whether dyslexia has a visual basis or a linguistic basis in children). Neuroimaging techniques also offer a potential means for distinguishing between deviance and delay when studying developmental disorders. For example, our preliminary studies of basic auditory processing in dyslexic children using ERPs suggest that the phonological system of the dyslexic child is immature rather than deviant

(Thomson, Baldeweg, & Goswami, in preparation). Dyslexic children show remarkable similarity in N1 response to younger reading level controls, while showing much larger N1 amplitudes than age-matched controls. Finally, PET studies have shown that the functional organization of the brain differs in literate and illiterate adults (Castro-Caldas, Petersson, Reis, Stone-Elander, & Ingvar, 1998). Portuguese women in their sixties who had never learned to read because of lack of access to education were compared with literate Portuguese women from the same villages in word and nonword repetition tasks. It was found that totally different brain areas were activated during nonword repetition for the illiterate versus literate participants. Learning to read and write in childhood thus changes the functional organization of the adult brain.

Mathematics

For mathematics, cognitive neuroscience is beginning to go beyond existing cognitive models. It has been argued that there is more than one neural system for the representation of numbers. A phylogenetically old "number sense" system, found in animals and infants as well as older participants, seems to underpin knowledge about numbers and their relations (Dehaene, Dehaene-Lambertz, & Cohen, 1998). This system, located bilaterally in the intraparietal areas, is activated when participants perform tasks such as number comparison, whether the comparisons involve Arabic numerals, sets of dots, or number words. Because mode of presentation does not affect the location of the parietal ERP components, this system is thought to organize knowledge about number quantities. Developmental ERP studies have shown that young children use exactly the same parietal areas to perform number comparison tasks (Temple & Posner, 1998). A different type of numerical knowledge is thought to be stored verbally, in the language system (Dehaene, Spelke, Pinel, Stanescu, & Tsirkin, 1999). This neural system also stores knowledge about poetry and overlearned verbal sequences, such as the months of the year. Mathematically, it underpins counting and rote-acquired knowledge such as the multiplication tables. This linguistic system seems to store "number facts" rather than compute calculations. Many simple arithmetical problems (for example, $3 + 4$, 3×4) are so overlearned that they may be stored as declarative knowledge. More complex calculation seems to involve visuospatial regions (Zago et al., 2001), possibly attesting to the importance of visual mental imagery in multi-digit operations (an internalized and sophisticated form of a number line; see Pesenti, Thioux, Seron, & De Volder, 2000). Finally, a distinct parietal-premotor area is activated during finger counting and also calculation.

This last observation may suggest that the neural areas activated during finger counting (a developmental strategy for the acquisition of calculation skills) eventually come to partially underpin numerical manipulation skills in adults. If this were the case, then perhaps finger counting has important consequences for the developing brain, and should be encouraged in school. In any event, neuroimaging techniques offer ways of exploring such questions. They can also be used to discover the basis of dyscalculia in children. For example, dyslexic children often seem to have associated mathematical difficulties. If dyslexia has a phonological basis, then it seems likely that the mathematical system affected in these children should be the verbal system underpinning counting and calculation. Dyslexic children with mathematical difficulties may show neural anomalies in the activation of this system, but not in the activation of the parietal and premotor number systems. Children with dyscalculia who do not have reading difficulties may show different patterns of impairment. Knowledge of the neural basis of their difficulties could then inform individual remedial curricula.

Direct Effects of Experience

Although it is frequently assumed that specific experiences have an effect on children, neuroimaging offers ways of investigating this assumption directly. The obvious prediction is that specific experiences will have specific effects, increasing neural representations in areas directly relevant to the skills involved. One area of specific experience that is frequent in childhood is musical experience. fMRI studies have shown that skilled pianists (adults) have enlarged cortical representations in auditory cortex, specific to piano tones. Enlargement was correlated with the age at which musicians began to practice, but did not differ between musicians with absolute versus relative pitch (Pantev et al., 1998). Similarly, MEG studies show that skilled violinists have enlarged neural representations for their left fingers, those most important for playing the violin (Elbert, Pantev, Wienbruch, Rockstroh, & Taub, 1996). Clearly, different sensory systems are affected by musical expertise depending on the nature of the musical instrument concerned. ERP studies have also shown use-dependent functional reorganization in readers of braille.

Skilled braille readers are more sensitive to tactile information than controls, and this extends across all fingers, not just the index finger (Röder, Rösler, Hennighausen, & Nacker, 1996). The neural representations of muscles engaged in braille reading are also enlarged. Finally, it is interesting to note that London taxi drivers who possess "the knowledge" [an intimate acquaintance with the streets in London] show enlarged hippocampus formations (Maguire et al., 2000). The hippocampus is a small brain area thought to be involved in spatial representation and navigation. In London taxi drivers, the posterior hippocampi were significantly larger than those of controls who did not drive taxis. Furthermore, hippocampal volume was correlated with the amount of time spent as a taxi driver. Again, localized plasticity is found in the adult brain in response to specific environmental inputs. Plasticity in children, of course, is likely to be even greater. Our growing understanding of plasticity offers a way of studying the impact of specialized remedial programs on brain function. For example, on the basis of the cerebellar theory of dyslexia, remedial programs are available that are designed to improve motor function. It is claimed that these programs will also improve reading. Whether this is in fact the case can be measured directly via neuroimaging. If the effects of such remedial programs are specific, then neuroimaging should reveal changes in motor representations but not in phonological and orthographic processing. If the effects generalize to literacy (for example, via improved automaticity), then changes in occipital, temporal, and parietal areas should also be observed.

Sleep and Cognition

The idea that sleep might serve a cognitive function dates from at least the time of Freud, with his analysis of dreams. Recent neuroimaging studies suggest indeed that rapid eye movement (REM) sleep is not only associated with self-reports of dreaming but is important for learning and memory. Maquet and colleagues (2000) used PET to study regional brain activity during REM sleep following training on a serial reaction time task. During task learning, volunteer students were trained to press one of six marked keys on a computer in response to associated visual signals on the computer screen. Training lasted for four hours, from 4:00 P.M. until 8:00 P.M. The participants were then scanned during sleep. Controls were either scanned when awake while receiving the training, or were scanned when asleep following no training. It was found that the brain areas most active in the trained awake group when performing the task were also most active during REM sleep in the trained participants. They were not active during sleep in the untrained participants. Hence certain regions of the brain (in occipital and premotor cortex) were actually reactivated during sleep. It seems that REM sleep either allows the consolidation of memories or the forgetting of unnecessary material (or both together). When tested again on the computer task on the following day, significant improvement in performance was found to have occurred. Although the cellular mechanisms underlying this are not understood, it seems likely that memory consolidation relies on augmented synaptic transmission and eventually on increased synaptic density—the same mechanisms that structure the developing brain. Again, this suggests substantial plasticity even in adulthood, supporting educational emphases on life-long learning.

Emotion and Cognition

It is increasingly recognized that efficient learning does not take place when the learner is experiencing fear or stress. Stress can both help and harm the body. Stress responses can provide the extra strength and attention needed to cope with a sudden emergency, but inappropriate stress has a significant effect on both physiological and cognitive functioning. The main emotional system within the brain is the limbic system, a set of structures incorporating the amygdala and hippocampus. The "emotional brain" (LeDoux, 1996) has strong connections with frontal cortex (the major site for reasoning and problem solving). When a learner is stressed or fearful, connections with frontal cortex become impaired, with a negative impact on learning. Stress and fear also affect social judgments, and responses to reward and risk. One important function of the emotional brain is assessing the value of information being received. When the amygdala is strongly activated, it interrupts action and thought, and triggers rapid bodily responses critical for survival. It is suggested by LeDoux that classroom fear or stress might reduce children's ability to pay attention to the learning task because of this automatic interruption mechanism. To date, however, neuroimaging studies of the developmental effects of stress on cognitive function are sparse or non-existent. In the educational arena, studying the role of stress (and emotional affect generally) in classroom learning seems an area ripe for development. Simple ERP measures of attentional processes, such as those used by Seifert et al. (2003) to study children with ADHD receiving Ritalin, could easily be adapted for such purposes.

Neuromyths

The engaging term *neuromyths,* coined by the OECD [Organization for Economic Cooperation and Development] report on understanding the brain (OECD, 2002), suggests the ease and rapidity with which scientific findings can be translated into misinformation regarding what neuroscience can offer education.

The three myths given most attention in the OECD report are (1) the lay belief in hemispheric differences ("left brain" versus "right brain" learning), (2) the notion that the brain is only plastic for certain kinds of information during certain "critical periods" and that therefore education in these areas must occur during the critical periods, and (3) the idea that the most effective educational interventions need to be timed with periods of synaptogenesis.

Regarding neuromyth 1, the left brain/right brain claims probably have their basis in the fact that there is some hemispheric specialization in terms of the localization of different skills. For example, many aspects of language processing are left-lateralized (although not, as we have seen, in blind people or in those who emigrate in later childhood to a new linguistic community). Some aspects of face recognition, in contrast, are lateralized to the right hemisphere. Nevertheless, there are massive cross-hemisphere connections in the normal brain, and both hemispheres work together in every cognitive task so far explored with neuroimaging, including language and face recognition tasks.

Regarding neuromyth 2, optimal periods for certain types of learning clearly exist in development, but they are sensitive periods rather than critical ones. The term *critical period* implies that the opportunity to learn is lost forever if the biological window is missed. In fact, there seem to be almost no cognitive capacities that can be "lost" at an early age. As discussed earlier, some aspects of complex processing suffer more than others from deprivation of early environmental input (for example, depth perception in vision, grammar learning in language), but nevertheless learning is still possible. It is probably better for the final performance levels achieved to educate children in, for example, other languages during the sensitive period for language acquisition. Nevertheless, the existence of a sensitive period does not mean that adults are unable to acquire competent foreign language skills later in life.

Neuromyth 3 concerning synaptogenesis may have arisen from influential work on learning in rats. This research showed that rodent brains form more connections in enriched and stimulating environments (for example, Greenough, Black, & Wallace, 1987). As discussed earlier, any kind of specific environmental stimulation causes the brain to form new connections (recall the enlarged cortical representations of professional musicians and the enlarged hippocampi of London taxi drivers). These demonstrations do not mean that greater synaptic density *predicts* a greater capacity to learn, however.

Other neuromyths can also be identified. One is the idea that a person can either have a "male brain" or a "female brain." The terms "male brain" and "female brain" were coined to refer to differences in *cognitive* style rather than biological differences (Baron-Cohen, 2003). Baron-Cohen argued that men were better "systemizers" (good at understanding mechanical systems) and women were better "empathizers" (good at communication and understanding others). He did not argue that male and female brains were radically different, but used the terms *male* and *female brain* as a psychological shorthand for (overlapping) cognitive profiles.

Another neuromyth is the idea that "implicit" learning could open new avenues educationally. Much human learning is "implicit," in the sense that learning takes place in the brain despite lack of attention to/conscious awareness of what is being learned (for example, Berns, Cohen, & Mintun, 1997, but see Johnstone & Shanks, 2001). Almost all studies of implicit learning use *perceptual* tasks as their behavioral measures (for example, the participant gets better at responding appropriately to "random" letter strings in a computer task when the "random" strings are actually generated according to an underlying "grammar" or rule system which can be learned). There are no studies showing implicit learning of the *cognitive* skills underpinning educational achievement.

These skills most likely require effortful learning and direct teaching.

Conclusions

Clearly, the potential for neuroscience to make contributions to educational research is great. Nevertheless, bridges need to be built between neuroscience and basic research in education. Bruer (1997) suggested that cognitive psychologists are admirably placed to erect these bridges, although he also cautioned that while neuroscience has learned a lot about neurons and synapses, it has not learned nearly enough to guide educational practice in any meaningful way. This view is perhaps too pessimistic. Cognitive developmental neuroscience has established a number of neural "markers" that can be used to assess development, for example, of the language system. These markers may be useful for investigating educational questions. Taking ERP signatures of language processing as a case in point, different parameters are robustly associated with semantic processing (for example, N400), phonetic processing (for example, mis-match negativity or MMN), and syntactic processing (for example, P600). These parameters need to be investigated longitudinally in children. Certain patterns may turn out to be indicative of certain developmental disorders. For example, children at risk for dyslexia may show immature or atypical MMNs to phonetic distinctions (Csepe, 2003). Children with SLI (specific language impairment) may have generally immature auditory systems, systems resembling those of children 3–4 years younger than them (Bishop & McArthur, in preparation). Characteristic ERPs may also change in response to targeted educational programs. For example, the MMN to phonetic distinctions may become sharper (as indexed by faster latencies) in response to literacy tuition in phonics (see Csepe, 2003).

If this were to be established across languages, education would have a neural tool for comparing the efficiency of different approaches to the teaching of initial reading. For example, one could measure whether the MMN to phonetic distinctions sharpened in response to literacy tuition based on whole language methods. This is only one example of the creative application of currently available neuroscience techniques to important issues in education. Educational and cognitive psychologists need to take the initiative, and think outside the box about how current neuroscience techniques can help to answer outstanding educational questions.

REFERENCES

Baron-Cohen, S. (2003). *The essential difference: Men, women and the extreme male brain.* London: Penguin/Allen Lane.

Berns, G. S., Cohen, J. D., & Mintun, M. A. (1997). Brain regions responsive to novelty in the absence of awareness. *Science, 276,* 1272–1275.

Bishop, D.V.M., & McArthur, G. (in preparation). *Using event-related potentials to study auditory processing in children with language and literacy impairments.*

Bruer, J. T. (1997). Education and the brain: A bridge too far. *Educational Researcher, 26*(8), 4–16.

Byrnes, J. P., & Fox, N. A. (1998). The education relevance of research in cognitive neuroscience. *Educational Psychology Review, 10*(3), 297–342.

Caspi, A., McClay, J., Moffitt, T. E., Mill, J., Martin, J., Craig, I. W., et al. (2002). Role of genotype in the cycle of violence in maltreated children. *Science, 297,* 851–854.

Castro-Caldas, A., Petersson, K. M., Reis, A., Stone-Elander S., & Ingvar, M. (1998). The illiterate brain: Learning to read and write during childhood influences the functional organization of the adult brain. *Brain, 121,* 1053–1063.

Csepe, V. (2003). Auditory event-related potentials in studying developmental dyslexia. In V. Csepe (Ed.), *Dyslexia: Different brain, different behavior* (pp. 81–112). Hingham, MA: Kluwer Academic.

Dehaene, S., Dehaene-Lambertz, G., & Cohen, L. (1998). Abstract representations of numbers in the animal and human brain. *Trends in Neuroscience, 21*(8), 355–611.

Dehaene, S., Spelke, E., Pinel, P., Stanescu, R., & Tsirkin, S. (1999). Sources of mathematical thinking: Behavioral and brain-imaging evidence. *Science, 284*, 970–974.

Elbert, T., Pantev, C., Wienbruch, C., Rockstroh, B., & Taub, E. (1996). Increased cortical representation of the fingers of the left hand in string players. *Science, 270*, 305–307.

Fagiolini, M., & Hensch, R. K. (2000). Inhibitory threshold for critical-period activation in primary visual cortex. *Nature, 404*, 183–186.

Fitch, W. T. (2000). The evolution of speech: A comparative review. *Trends in Cognitive Sciences, 4*(7), 258–267.

Geake, J., & Cooper, P. (2003). Cognitive neuroscience: Implications for education? *Westminster Studies in Education, 26*(1), 7–20.

Geary, D. C. (1998). What is the function of mind and brain? *Educational Psychology Review, 10*(4), 377–387.

Greenough, W. T., Black, J. E., & Wallace, C. S. (1987). Experience and brain development. *Child Development, 58*, 539–559.

Heim, S., Eulitz, C., & Elbert, T. (2003). Altered hemispheric asymmetry of auditory P100m in dyslexia. *European Journal of Neuroscience, 17*, 1715–1722.

Hollins, M. (1989). *Understanding blindness.* Mahwah, NJ: Erlbaum.

Jackson, S. (2000). Seeing what you feel. *Trends in Cognitive Sciences, 4*, 257.

Johnson, M. H. (1997). *Developmental cognitive neuroscience.* Cambridge, MA: Blackwell.

Johnstone, T., & Shanks, D. R. (2001). Abstractionist and processing accounts of implicit learning. *Cognitive Psychology, 42*, 61–112.

LeDoux, J. (1996). *The emotional brain.* New York: Simon & Schuster.

Maguire, E. A., Gadian, D. S., Johnsrude, I. S., Good, C. D., Ashburner, J., Frackowiak, R. S., et al. (2000). Navigation related structural change in the hippocampi of taxi drivers. *Proceedings of the National Academy of Sciences of the United States of America, 97*(8), 4398–4403.

Maquet, P., Laureys, S., Peigneux, P., Fuchs, S., Petiau, C., Phillips, C., et al. (2000). Experience-dependent changes in cerebral activation during human REM sleep. *Nature Neuroscience, 3*(8), 831–836.

Marcus, G. F., & Fisher, S. E. (2003). FOXP2 in focus: What can genes tell us about speech and language? *Trends in Cognitive Sciences, 7*(6), 257–262.

Maurer, D., Lewis, T. L., & Brent, H. (1989). The effects of deprivation on human visual development: Studies in children treated with cataracts. In F. J. Morrison, C. Lord, & D. P. Keating (Eds.), *Applied developmental psychology* (pp. 139–227). Orlando, FL: Academic Press.

Mayer, R. E. (1998). Does the brain have a place in educational psychology? *Educational Psychology Review, 10*(4), 389–396.

Neville, H. J. (1995). Developmental specificity in neurocognitive development in humans. In M. S. Gazzaniga (Ed.), *The cognitive neurosciences* (pp. 219–231). Cambridge, MA: MIT Press.

Neville, H. J., & Bavelier, D. (2000). Specificity and plasticity in neurocognitive development in humans. In M. S. Gazzaniga (Ed.), *The cognitive neurosciences* (pp. 83–98). Cambridge, MA: MIT Press.

Neville, H. J., Bavelier, D., Corina, D., Rauschecker, J., Karni, A., Lalwani, A., et al. (1998). Cerebral organization for language in deaf and hearing subjects: Biological constraints and effects of experience. *Proceedings of the National Academy of Sciences of the United States of America, 95,* 922–929.

Neville, H. J., Coffey, S. A., Lawson, D. S., Fischer, A., Emmorey, K., & Bellugi, U. (1997). Neural systems mediating American Sign Language: Effects of sensory experience and age of acquisition. *Brain and Language, 57,* 285–308.

Neville, H. J., Schmidt, A., & Kutas, M. (1983). Altered visual-evoked potentials in congenitally deaf adults. *Brain Research, 266,* 127–132.

OECD. (2002). *Understanding the brain: Towards a new learning science.* Available online from oecd.org.

Pantev, C., Oostenveld, R., Engelien, A., Ross, B., Roberts, L. E., & Hike, M. (1998). Increased auditory cortical representation in musicians. *Nature, 393,* 811–814.

Pesenti, M., Thioux, M., Seron, X., & De Volder, A. (2000). Neuroanatomical substrates of arabic number processing, numerical comparison, and simple addition: A PET study. *Journal of Cognitive Neuroscience, 12*(3), 461–479.

Pugh, K. R., Mencl, W. E., Jenner, A. R., Katz, L., Frost, S. J., Lee, J. R., et al. (2001). Neurobiological studies of reading and reading disability. *Journal of Communication Disorders, 34,* 479–492.

Röder, B., & Neville, H. (2003). Developmental functional plasticity. In J. Grafman & I. H. Robertson (Eds.), *Handbook of neuropsychology* (2nd ed., Vol. 9, pp. 231–270). Oxford: Elsevier Science.

Röder, G., Rösler, F., Hennighausen, E., & Nacker, F. (1996). Event related potentials during auditory and somatosensory discrimination in sighted and blind human subjects. *Cognitive Brain Research, 4,* 77–93.

Röder, G., Rösler, F., & Neville, H. J. (1999). Effects of interstimulus interval on auditory event-related potentials in congenitally blind and normally sighted humans. *Neuroscience Letters, 264,* 53–56.

Röder, G., Rösler, F., & Neville, H. J. (2000). Event-related potentials during language processing in congenitally blind and sighted people. *Neuropsychologia, 38,* 1482–1502.

Schunk, D. H. (1998). An educational psychologist's perspective on cognitive neuroscience. *Educational Psychology Review, 10*(4), 411–417.

Seifert, J., Scheuerpflug, P., Zillessen, K. E., Fallgater, A., & Warnke, A. (2003). Electrophysiological investigation of the effectiveness of methylphenidate in children with and without ADHD. *Journal of Neural Transmission, 110*(7), 821–829.

Shaywitz, B., Shaywitz, S., Pugh, K., Mencl, W., Fulbright, R., Skudlarski, P., et al. (2002). Disruption of posterior brain systems for reading in children with developmental dyslexia. *Biological Psychiatry, 52,* 101–110.

Simos, P. G., Fletcher, J. M., Bergman, E., Breier, J. I., Foorman, B. R., Castillo, E. M., et al. (2002). Dyslexia-specific brain activation profile becomes normal following successful remedial training. *Neurology, 58,* 1203–1213.

Stanovich, K. E. (1998). Cognitive neuroscience and educational psychology: What season is it? *Educational Psychology Review, 10*(4), 419–426.

Strauss, S. (2003). Teaching as a natural cognition and its implications for teacher education. In D. Pillemer & S. White (Eds.), *Developmental psychology and the social changes of our time.* Cambridge: Cambridge University Press.

Strauss, S., Ziv, M., & Stein, A. (2002). Teaching as a natural cognition and its relations to preschoolers' developing theory of mind. *Cognitive Development, 17,* 1473–1787.

Temple, E., & Posner, M. I. (1998). Brain mechanisms of quantity are similar in 5-year-old children and adults. *Proceedings of the National Academy of Sciences of the United States of America, 95,* 7836–7841.

Thomson, J., Baldeweg, T., & Goswami, U. (in preparation). *Auditory event-related potentials during rise time processing in dyslexic and typically-developing children.*

Weber-Fox, C. M., & Neville, H. J. (1996). Maturational constraints on functional specialization for language processing: ERP and behavioral evidence in bilingual speakers. *Journal of Cognitive Neuroscience, 8,* 231–256.

Zago, L., Pesenti, M., Mellet, E., Crivello, F., Mazoyer, B., & Tzourio-Mazoyer, N. (2001). Neural correlates of simple and complex mental calculation. *Neuro-Image, 13,* 314–327.

5

IN SEARCH OF . . .
BRAIN-BASED EDUCATION

John T. Bruer

WE HAVE ALMOST survived the Decade of the Brain. During the 1990s, government agencies, foundations, and advocacy groups engaged in a highly successful effort to raise public awareness about advances in brain research. Brain science became material for cover stories in our national newsmagazines. Increased public awareness raised educators' always simmering interest in the brain to the boiling point. Over the past five years, there have been numerous books, conferences, and entire issues of education journals devoted to what has come to be called brain-based education.

Brain-based educators tend to support progressive education reforms. They decry the factory model of education, in which experts create knowledge, teachers disseminate it, and students are graded on how much of it they can absorb and retain. Like many other educators, brain-based educators favor a constructivist, active learning model. Students should be actively engaged in learning and in guiding their own instruction. Brain enthusiasts see neuroscience as perhaps the best weapon with which to destroy our outdated factory model.[1]

---

[1]Renate Nummela Caine and Geoffrey Caine, *Making Connections: Teaching and the Human Brain* (New York: Addison-Wesley, 1994); idem, "Building a Bridge Between the Neurosciences and Education: Cautions and Possibilities," *NASSP Bulletin*, vol. 82, 1998, pp. 1–8; Eric Jensen, *Teaching with the Brain in Mind* (Alexandria, Va.: Association for Supervision and Curriculum Development, 1998); and Robert Sylwester, *A Celebration of Neurons* (Alexandria, Va.: Association for Supervision and Curriculum Development, 1995).

They argue that teachers should teach for meaning and understanding. To do so, they claim, teachers should create learning environments that are low in threat and high in challenge, and students should be actively engaged and immersed in complex experiences. No reasonable parent or informed educator would take issue with these ideas. Indeed, if more schools taught for understanding and if more teachers had the resources to do so, our schools would be better learning environments.

However, there is nothing new in this critique of traditional education. It is based on a cognitive and constructivist model of learning that is firmly rooted in more than 30 years of psychological research. Whatever scientific evidence we have for or against the efficacy of such educational approaches can be found in any current textbook on educational psychology.[2] None of the evidence comes from brain research. It comes from cognitive and developmental psychology; from the behavioral, not the biological, sciences; from our scientific understanding of the mind, not from our scientific understanding of the brain.

To the extent that brain-based educators' recipe for school and classroom change is well grounded in this behavioral research, their message is valuable. Teachers should know about short- and long-term memory; about primacy/recency effects; about how procedural, declarative, and episodic memory differ; and about how prior knowledge affects our current ability to learn. But to claim that these are brain-based findings is misleading.

While we know a considerable amount from psychological research that is pertinent to teaching and learning, we know much less about how the brain functions and learns.[3] For nearly a century, the science of the mind (psychology) developed independently from the science of the brain (neuroscience). Psychologists were interested in our mental functions and capacities—how we learn, remember, and think. Neuroscientists were interested in how the brain develops and functions. It was as if psychologists were interested only in our mental software and neuroscientists only in our neural hardware. Deeply held theoretical assumptions in both fields supported a view that mind and brain could, and indeed should, be studied independently.

---

[2]See, for example, Michael Pressley and C. B. McCormick, *Advanced Educational Psychology for Educators, Researchers, and Policymakers* (New York: HarperCollins, 1995).

[3]John T. Bruer, *Schools for Thought: A Science of Learning in the Classroom* (Cambridge, Mass.: MIT Press, 1993); and idem, "Education and the Brain: A Bridge Too Far," *Educational Researcher,* November 1997, pp. 4–16.

It is only in the past 15 years or so that these theoretical barriers have fallen. Now scientists called cognitive neuroscientists are beginning to study how our neural hardware might run our mental software, how brain structures support mental functions, how our neural circuits enable us to think and learn. This is an exciting and new scientific endeavor, but it is also a very young one. As a result we know relatively little about learning, thinking, and remembering at the level of brain areas, neural circuits, or synapses; we know very little about how the brain thinks, remembers, and learns.

Yet brain science has always had a seductive appeal for educators.[4] Brain science appears to give hard biological data and explanations that, for some reason, we find more compelling than the soft data that come from psychological science. But seductive appeal and a very limited brain science database are a dangerous combination. They make it relatively easy to formulate bold statements about brain science and education that are speculative at best and often far removed from neuroscientific fact. Nonetheless, the allure of brain science ensures that these ideas will often find a substantial and accepting audience. As Joseph LeDoux, a leading authority on the neuroscience of emotion, cautioned educators at a 1996 brain and education conference, "These ideas are easy to sell to the public, but it is easy to take them beyond their actual basis in science."[5]

And the ideas are far-ranging indeed. Within the literature on the brain and education one finds, for example, that brain science supports Blooms Taxonomy, Madeline Hunter's effective teaching, whole-language instruction, Vygotsky's theory of social learning, thematic instruction, portfolio assessment, and cooperative learning.

The difficulty is that the brain-based education literature is very much like a docudrama or an episode of "In Search of . . ." in which an interesting segment on Egyptology suddenly takes a bizarre turn that links Tutankhamen with the alien landing in Roswell, New Mexico. Just where did the episode turn from archaeological fact to speculation or fantasy? That is the same question one must constantly ask when reading about brain-based education.

---

[4]Susan F. Chipman, "Integrating Three Perspectives on Learning," in Sarah L. Friedman, Kenneth A. Klivington, and R. W. Peterson, eds., *The Brain, Cognition, and Education* (Orlando, Fla.: Academic Press, 1986), pp. 203–232.
[5]*Bridging the Gap Between Neuroscience and Education: Summary of a Workshop Cosponsored by the Education Commission of the States and the Charles A. Dana Foundation* (Denver: Education Commission of the States, 1996), p. 5.

Educators, like all professionals, should be interested in knowing how basic research, including brain science, might contribute to improved professional practice. The danger with much of the brain-based education literature, as with an episode, is that it becomes exceedingly difficult to separate the science from the speculation, to sort what we know from what we would like to be the case. If our interest is enhancing teaching and learning by applying science to education, this is not the way to do it. Would we want our children to learn about the Exodus by watching "In Search of Ramses' Martian Wife?"

We might think of each of the numerous claims that brain-based educators make as similar to an "In Search of . . ." episode. For each one, we should ask, "Where does the science end and the speculation begin?" I cannot do that here. So instead I'll concentrate on two ideas that appear prominently in brain-based education articles: the educational significance of brain laterality (right brain versus left brain) and the claim that neuroscience has established that there is a sensitive period for learning.

Left Brain, Right Brain: One More Time

"Right brain versus left brain" is one of those popular ideas that will not die. Speculations about the educational significance of brain laterality have been circulating in the education literature for 30 years. Although repeatedly criticized and dismissed by psychologists and brain scientists, the speculation continues.[6] David Sousa devotes a chapter of *How the Brain Learns* to explaining brain laterality and presents classroom strategies that teachers might use to ensure that both hemispheres are involved in learning.[7] Following the standard line, the *left hemisphere* is the logical hemisphere, involved in speech, reading, and writing. It is the analytical hemisphere that evaluates factual material in a rational way and that understands the literal interpretation of words. It is a serial processor that tracks time and sequences and that recognizes words, letters, and numbers. The *right hemisphere* is the intuitive, creative hemisphere. It gathers information more from images than from words. It is a parallel processor well suited for

---

[6]Chipman, op. cit.; Howard Gardner, *Art, Mind, and Brain: A Cognitive Approach to Creativity* (New York: Basic Books, 1982); Mike Rose, "Narrowing the Mind and Page: Remedial Writers and Cognitive Reductionism," *College Composition and Communication,* vol. 39, 1988, pp. 267–302; and Jerre Levy, "Right Brain, Left Brain: Fact and Fiction," *Psychology Today,* May 1985, p. 38.
[7]David A. Sousa, *How the Brain Learns: A Classroom Teacher's Guide* (Reston, Va.: National Association of Secondary School Principals, 1995).

pattern recognition and spatial reasoning. It is the hemisphere that recognizes faces, places, and objects.

According to this traditional view of laterality, left-hemisphere-dominant individuals tend to be more verbal, more analytical, and better problem solvers. Females, we are told, are more likely than males to be left-hemisphere dominant. Right-hemisphere-dominant individuals, more typically males, paint and draw well, are good at math, and deal with the visual world more easily than with the verbal. Schools, Sousa points out, are overwhelmingly left-hemisphere places in which left-hemisphere-dominant individuals, mostly girls, feel more comfortable than right-hemisphere-dominant individuals, mostly boys. Hemispheric dominance also explains why girls are superior to boys in arithmetic—it is linear and logical, and there is only one correct answer to each problem—while girls suffer math anxiety when it comes to the right-hemisphere activities of algebra and geometry. These latter disciplines, unlike arithmetic, are holistic, relational, and spatial and also allow multiple solutions to problems.

Before we consider how, or whether, brain science supports this traditional view, educators should be wary of claims about the educational significance of gender differences in brain laterality. There are tasks that psychologists have used in their studies that reveal gender-based differences in performance. Often, however, these differences are specific to a task. Although males are superior to females at mentally rotating objects, this seems to be the only spatial task for which psychologists have found such a difference.[8] Moreover, when they do find gender differences, these differences tend to be very small. If they were measured on an IQ-like scale with a mean of 100 and a standard deviation of 15, these gender differences amount to around five points. Furthermore, the range of difference within genders is broad. Many males have better language skills than most females; many females have better spatial and mathematical skills than most males. The scientific consensus among psychologists and neuroscientists who conduct these studies is that whatever gender differences exist may have interesting consequences for the scientific study of the brain, but they have no practical or instructional consequences.[9]

Now let's consider the brain sciences and how or whether they offer support for some of the particular teaching strategies Sousa recommends.

[8]M. C. Linn and A. C. Petersen, "Emergence and Characterization of Sex Differences in Spatial Ability: A Meta-Analysis," *Child Development,* vol. 56, 1985, pp. 1470–1498.

[9]Sally Springer and Georg Deutsch, *Left Brain, Right Brain* (New York: W. H. Freeman, 1993).

To involve the right hemisphere in learning, Sousa writes, teachers should encourage students to generate and use mental imagery: "For most people, the left hemisphere specializes in coding information verbally while the right hemisphere codes information visually. Although teachers spend much time talking (and sometimes have their students talk) about the learning objective, little time is given to developing visual cues." To ensure that the left hemisphere gets equal time, teachers should let students "read, write, and compute often."[10]

What brain scientists currently know about spatial reasoning and mental imagery provides counterexamples to such simplistic claims as these. Such claims arise out of a folk theory about brain laterality, not a neuroscientific one.

Here are two simple spatial tasks: (1) determine whether one object is above or below another, and (2) determine whether two objects are more or less than one foot apart. Based on our folk theory of the brain, as spatial tasks both of these should be right-hemisphere tasks. However, if we delve a little deeper, as psychologists and neuroscientists tend to do, we see that the information-processing or computational demands of the two tasks are different.[11] The first task requires that we place objects or parts of objects into broad categories—up/down or left/right—but we do not have to determine how far up or down (or left or right) one object is from the other. Psychologists call this *categorical* spatial reasoning. In contrast, the second task is a spatial *coordinate* task, in which we must compute and retain precise distance relations between the objects.

Research over the last decade has shown that categorical and coordinate spatial reasoning are performed by distinct subsystems in the brain.[12] A subsystem in the brain's *left* hemisphere performs categorical spatial reasoning. A subsystem in the brain's *right* hemisphere processes coordinate spatial relationships. Although the research does point to differences in the information-processing abilities and biases of the brain hemispheres, those differences are found at a finer level of analysis than "spatial reasoning." It makes no sense to claim that spatial reasoning is a right-hemisphere task.

Based on research like this, Christopher Chabris and Stephen Kosslyn, leading researchers in the field of spatial reasoning and visual imagery,

---

[10]Sousa, pp. 95, 99.

[11]Christopher F. Chabris and Stephen M. Kosslyn, "How Do the Cerebral Hemispheres Contribute to Encoding Spatial Relations?" *Current Directions in Psychology,* vol. 7, 1998, pp. 8–14.

[12]Ibid.

claim that any model of brain lateralization that assigns conglomerations of complex mental abilities, such as spatial reasoning, to one hemisphere or the other, as our folk theory does, is simply too crude to be scientifically or practically useful. Our folk theory can neither explain what the brain is doing nor generate useful predictions about where novel tasks might be computed in the brain.[13] Unfortunately, it is just such a crude folk theory that brain-based educators rely on when framing their recommendations.

Visual imagery is another example. From the traditional, folk-theoretic perspective, generating and using visual imagery is a right-hemisphere function. Generating and using visual imagery is a complex operation that involves, even at a crude level of analysis, at least five distinct mental subcomponents: (1) to create a visual image of a dog, you must transfer long-term visual memories into a temporary visual memory store; (2) to determine if your imagined dog has a tail, you must zoom in and identify details of the image; (3) to put a blue collar on the dog requires that you add a new element to your previously generated image; (4) to make the dog look the other way demands that you rotate your image of the dog; and (5) to draw or describe the imagined dog, you must scan the visual image with your mind's eye.

There is an abundance of neuroscientific evidence that this complex task is not confined to the right hemisphere. There are patients with brain damage who can recognize visual objects and draw or describe visible objects normally, yet these patients cannot answer questions that require them to generate a mental image. ("Think of a dog. Does it have a long tail?") These patients have long-term visual memories, but they cannot use those memories to generate mental images. All these patients have damage to the rear portion of the left hemisphere.[14]

Studies on split-brain patients, people who have had their two hemispheres surgically disconnected to treat severe epilepsy, allow scientists to present visual stimuli to one hemisphere but not the other. Michael Gazzaniga and Kosslyn showed split-brain patients a lower-case letter and then asked the patients whether the corresponding capital letter had any curved lines.[15] The task required that the patients generate a mental image of the capital letter based on the lower-case letter they had seen. When the stimuli were presented to the patients' left hemispheres, they

[13]Ibid.

[14]Martha Farah, *Visual Agnosias* (Cambridge, Mass.: MIT Press, 1991).

[15]Stephen M. Kosslyn et al., "A Computational Analysis of Mental Image Generation: Evidence from Functional Dissociations in Split-Brain Patients," *Journal of Experimental Psychology: General,* vol. 114, 1985, pp. 311–341.

performed perfectly on the task. However, the patients made many mistakes when the letter stimuli were presented to the right hemisphere. Likewise, brain-imaging studies of normal adult subjects performing imagery tasks show that both hemispheres are active in these tasks.[16] Based on all these data, brain scientists have concluded that the ability to generate visual imagery depends on the left hemisphere.

One of the most accessible presentations of this research appears in *Images of Mind,* by Michael Posner and Mark Raichle, in which they conclude, "The common belief that creating mental imagery is a function of the right hemisphere is clearly false."[17] Again, different brain areas are specialized for different tasks, but that specialization occurs at a finer level of analysis than "using visual imagery." Using visual imagery may be a useful learning strategy, but if it is useful it is not because it involves an otherwise underutilized right hemisphere in learning.

The same problem also subverts claims that one hemisphere or the other is the site of number recognition or reading skills. Here is a simple number task, expressed in two apparently equivalent ways: What is bigger, two or five? What is bigger, 2 or 5? It involves recognizing number symbols and understanding what those symbols mean. According to our folk theory, this should be a left-hemisphere task. But once again our folk theory is too crude.

Numerical comparison involves at least two mental subskills: identifying the number names and then comparing the numerical magnitudes that they designate. Although we seldom think of it, we are bilingual when it comes to numbers. We have number words—e.g., one, two to name numbers, and we also have special written symbols, Arabic numerals—e.g., 1, 2. Our numerical bilingualism means that the two comparison questions above place different computational demands on the mind/brain. Using brain-recording techniques, Stanislaus Dehaene found that we identify number words using a system in the brain's left hemisphere, but we identify Arabic numerals using brain areas in both the right and left hemispheres. Once we identify either the number words or the Arabic digits as symbols for numerical quantities, a distinct neural subsystem in the brain's right hemisphere compares magnitudes named by the two number symbols.[18]

---

[16]Stephen M. Kosslyn et al., "Two Types of Image Generation: Evidence for Left and Right Hemisphere Processes," *Neuropsychologia,* vol. 33, 1995, pp. 1485–1510.

[17]Michael I. Posner and Mark E. Raichle, *Images of Mind* (New York: Scientific American Library, 1994), p. 95.

[18]Stanislaus Dehaene, "The Organization of Brain Activations in Number Comparison," *Journal of Cognitive Neuroscience,* vol. 8, 1996, pp. 47–68.

Even for such a simple number task as comparison, both hemispheres are involved. Thus it makes no neuroscientific sense to claim that the left hemisphere recognizes numbers. Brain areas are specialized, but at a much finer level than "recognizing numbers." This simple task is already too complex for our folk theory to handle. Forget about algebra and geometry.

Similar research that analyzes speech and reading skills into their component processes also shows that reading is not simply a left-hemisphere task, as our folk theory suggests. Recognizing speech sounds, decoding written words, finding the meanings of words, constructing the gist of a written text, and making inferences as we read all rely on subsystems in both brain hemispheres.[19]

There is another different, but equally misleading, interpretation of brain laterality that occurs in the literature of brain-based education. In *Making Connections,* Renate Caine and Geoffrey Caine are critical of traditional brain dichotomizers and warn that the brain does not lend itself to such simple explanations. In their view, the results of research on split brains and hemispheric specialization are inconclusive—"both hemispheres are involved in all activities"—a conclusion that would seem to be consistent with what we have seen in our brief review of spatial reasoning, visual imagery, number skills, and reading.

However, following the folk theory, they do maintain that the left hemisphere processes parts and the right hemisphere processes wholes. In their interpretation, the educational significance of laterality research is that it shows that, within the brain, parts and wholes always interact. Laterality research thus provides scientific support for one of their principles of brain-based education: the brain processes parts and wholes simultaneously. Rather than number comparison or categorical spatial reasoning, the Caines provide a more global example: "Consider a poem, a play, a great novel, or a great work of philosophy. They all involve a sense of the 'wholeness' of things and a capacity to work with patterns, often in timeless ways. In other words, the 'left brain' processes are enriched and supported by 'right brain' processes."[20]

For educators, the Caines see the two-brain doctrine as a "valuable metaphor that helps educators acknowledge two separate but simultaneous tendencies in the brain for organizing information. One is to reduce information to parts; the other is to perceive and work with it as a whole

---

[19]Mark Jung Beeman and Christine Chiarello, "Complementary Right- and Left-Hemisphere Language Comprehension," *Current Directions in Psychology,* vol. 7, 1998, pp. 2–7.

[20]Caine and Caine, p. 37.

or a series of wholes."[21] Effective brain-based educational strategies overlook neither parts nor wholes, but constantly attempt to provide opportunities in which students can make connections and integrate parts and wholes. Thus, the Caines number among their examples of brain-based approaches whole-language instruction,[22] integrated curricula, thematic teaching, and cooperative learning.[23] Similarly, because we make connections best when new information is embedded in meaningful life events and in socially interactive situations, Lev Vygotsky's theory of social learning should also be highly brain compatible.[24] To the extent that one would want to view this as a metaphor, all I can say is that some of us find some metaphors more appealing than others.

To the extent that this is supposed to be an attempt to ground educational principles in brain science, the aliens have just landed in Egypt.

Where did things go awry? Although they claim that laterality research in the sense of hemispheric localization is inconclusive, the Caines do maintain the piece of our folk theory that attributes "whole" processing to the right hemisphere and "part" processing to the left hemisphere. Because the two hemispheres are connected in normal healthy brains, they conclude that the brain processes parts and wholes simultaneously. It certainly does—although it probably is not the case that wholes and parts can be so neatly dichotomized. For example, in visual word decoding, the right hemisphere seems to read words letter by letter—by looking at the parts—while the left hemisphere recognizes entire words—the visual word forms.[25]

But again, the parts and wholes to which the brain is sensitive appear to occur at quite a fine-grained level of analysis—categories versus coordinates, generating versus scanning visual images, identifying number words versus Arabic digits. The Caines' example of part/whole interactions—the left-hemisphere comprehension of a text and the right-hemisphere appreciation of wholeness—relates to such a highly complex task that involves so many parts and wholes at different levels of analysis that it is trivially true that the whole brain is involved. Thus, their appeal to brain science suffers from the same problem Kosslyn identified in the attempts to use crude theories to understand the brain. The only brain categories that the Caines appeal to are parts and wholes. Then they attempt to

---

[21]Ibid., p. 91.
[22]Ibid., pp. 9, 48, 91.
[23]Ibid., pp. 127–130.
[24]Ibid., pp. 47–48.
[25]Beeman and Chiarello, op. cit.

understand learning and exceedingly complex tasks in terms of parts and wholes. This approach bothers neither to analyze the brain nor to analyze behaviors.

The danger here is that one might think that there are brain-based reasons to adopt whole-language instruction, integrated curricula, or Vygotskian social learning. There are none. Whether or not these educational practices should be adopted must be determined on the basis of the impact they have on student learning. The evidence we now have on whole-language instruction is at best inconclusive, and the efficacy of social learning theory remains an open question. Brain science contributes no evidence, pro or con, for the brain-based strategies that the Caines espouse.

The fundamental problem with the right-brain versus left-brain claims that one finds in the education literature is that they rely on our intuitions and folk theories about the brain, rather than on what brain science is actually able to tell us. Our folk theories are too crude and imprecise to have any scientific, predictive, or instructional value. What modern brain science is telling us— and what brain-based educators fail to appreciate—is that it makes no scientific sense to map gross, unanalyzed behaviors and skills—reading, arithmetic, spatial reasoning—onto one brain hemisphere or another.

Brains Like Sponges: The Sensitive Period

A new and popular, but problematic, idea found in the brain-based literature is that there is a critical or sensitive period in brain development, lasting until a child is around 10 years old, during which children learn faster, easier, and with more meaning than at any other time in their lives. David Sousa presented the claim this way in a recent commentary in *Education Week*, titled "Is the Fuss About Brain Research Justified?"

> As the child grows, the brain selectively strengthens and prunes connections based on experience. Although this process continues throughout our lives, it seems to be most pronounced between the ages of 2 and 11, as different development areas emerge and taper off. . . . These so-called windows of opportunity represent critical periods when the brain demands certain types of input to create or consolidate neural networks, especially for acquiring language, emotional control, and learning to play music. Certainly, one can learn new information and skills at any age. But what the child learns during that window period will strongly influence what is learned after the window closes.[26]

---

[26]David A. Sousa, "Is the Fuss About Brain Research Justified?" *Education Week*, December 16, 1998, p. 35.

In a recent *Educational Leadership* article, Pat Wolfe and Ron Brandt prudently caution educators against any quick marriage between brain science and education. However, among the well-established neuroscientific findings about which educators can be confident, they include, "Some abilities are acquired more easily during certain sensitive periods, or 'windows of opportunity.'" Later they continue, "During these years, [the brain] also has a remarkable ability to adapt and reorganize. It appears to develop some capacities with more ease at this time than in the years after puberty. These stages once called 'critical periods' are more accurately described as 'sensitive periods' or 'windows of opportunity.'"[27] Eric Jensen, in *Teaching with the Brain in Mind,* also writes that "the brain learns fastest and easiest during the school years."[28]

If there were neuroscientific evidence for the existence of such a sensitive period, such evidence might appear to provide a biological argument for the importance of elementary teaching and a scientific rationale for redirecting resources, restructuring curricula, and reforming pedagogy to take advantage of the once-in-a-lifetime learning opportunity nature has given us. If teachers could understand when sensitive periods begin and end, the thinking goes, they could structure curricula to take advantage of these unique windows of opportunity. Sousa tells of an experienced fifth-grade teacher who was upset when a mother asked the teacher what she was doing to take advantage of her daughter's windows of opportunity before they closed. Unfortunately, according to Sousa, the teacher was unaware of the windows-of-opportunity research. He warns, "As the public learns more about brain research through the popular press, scenes like this are destined to be repeated, further eroding confidence in teachers and in schools."[29]

This well-established neuroscientific "finding" about a sensitive period for learning originated in the popular press and in advocacy documents. It is an instance where neuroscientists have speculated about the implications of their work for education and where educators have uncritically embraced that speculation. Presenting speculation as fact poses a greater threat to the public's confidence in teachers and schools than does Sousa's fifth-grade teacher.

During 1993, the *Chicago Tribune* ran Ron Kotulak's series of Pulitzer Prize–winning articles on the new brain science. Kotulak's articles later

---

[27]Pat Wolfe and Ron Brandt, "What Do We Know from Brain Research?" *Educational Leadership,* November 1998, p. 12.
[28]Jensen, p. 32.
[29]Sousa, "Is the Fuss About Brain Research Justified?" p. 35.

appeared as a book titled *Inside the Brain: Revolutionary Discoveries of How the Mind Works*. Kotulak, an esteemed science writer, presented the first explicit statement that I have been able to find on the existence of a sensitive period between ages 4 and 10, during which children's brains learn fastest and easiest.[30] Variations on the claim appear in the Carnegie Corporation of New York's 1996 publication, *Years of Promise: A Comprehensive Learning Strategy for America's Children,* and in *Building Knowledge for a Nation of Learners,* published by the Office of Educational Research and Improvement of the U.S. Department of Education.[31]

A report released in conjunction with the April 1997 White House Conference on Early Brain Development stated, "[B]y the age of three, the brains of children are two and a half times more active than the brains of adults—and they stay that way throughout the first decade of life. . . . This suggests that young children—particularly infants and toddlers—are biologically primed for learning and that these early years provide a unique window of opportunity or prime time for learning."[32]

If the sensitive period from age 4 to age 10 is a finding about which educators can be confident and one that justifies the current fuss about brain science, we would expect to find an extensive body of neuroscientific research that supports the claim. Surprisingly, brain-based enthusiasts appeal to a very limited body of evidence.

In Kotulak's initial statement of the sensitive-period claim, he refers to the brain-imaging work of Dr. Harry Chugani, M.D., at Wayne State University: "Chugani, whose imaging studies revealed that children's brains learned fastest and easiest between the ages of 4 and 10, said these years are often wasted because of lack of input."[33]

Years of Promise, the Carnegie Corporation report, cites a speech Kotulak presented at a conference on Brain Development in Young Children, held at the University of Chicago on June 13, 1996. Again referring to Chugani's work, Kotulak said that the years from 4 to about 10 "are

---

[30]Ronald Kotulak, *Inside the Brain: Revolutionary Discoveries of How the Mind Works* (Kansas City: Andrews McMeel, 1996), p. 46.

[31]*Years of Promise: A Comprehensive Learning Strategy for America's Children* (New York: Carnegie Corporation of New York, 1996), pp. 9–10; and Office of Educational Research and Improvement, *Building Knowledge for a Nation of Learners* (Washington, D.C.: U.S. Department of Education, 1996).

[32]Rima Shore, *Rethinking the Brain: New Insights into Early Development* (New York: Families and Work Institute, 1997), pp. 21, 36.

[33]Kotulak, p. 46.

the wonder years of learning, when a child can easily pick up a foreign language without an accent and learn a musical instrument with ease."[34] *Years of Promise* also cites a review article published by Dr. Chugani that is based on remarks he made at that Chicago conference.[35] *Rethinking the Brain,* a report based on the Chicago conference, also cites the same sources, as does the U.S. Department of Education document. What's more, Wolfe, Brandt, and Jensen also cite Chugani's work in their discussions of the sensitive period for learning.

A 1996 article on education and the brain that appeared in *Education Week* reported, "By age 4, Chugani found, a child's brain uses more than twice the glucose that an adult brain uses. Between the ages 4 and 10, the amount of glucose a child's brain uses remains relatively stable. But by age 10, glucose utilization begins to drop off until it reaches adult levels at age 16 or 17. Chugani's findings suggest that a child's peak learning years occur just as all those synapses are forming."[36]

To be fair, these educators are not misrepresenting Chugani's views. He has often been quoted on the existence and educational importance of the sensitive period from age 4 until age 10.[37] In a review of his own work, published in *Preventive Medicine,* Chugani wrote: "The notion of an extended period during childhood when activity-dependent [synapse] stabilization occurs has recently received considerable attention by those individuals and organizations dealing with early intervention to provide 'environmental enrichment' and with the optimal design of educational curricula. Thus, it is now believed by many (including this author) that the biological 'window of opportunity' when learning is efficient and easily retained is perhaps not fully exploited by our educational system."[38]

---

[34]Ronald Kotulak, "Learning How to Use the Brain," 1996, available on the Web at http://www.newhorizons.org/ofc_21cliusebrain.html.

[35]Harry T. Chugani, "Neuroimaging of Developmental Nonlinearity and Developmental Pathologies," in R. W. Thatcher et al., eds., *Developmental Neuroimaging* (San Diego: Academic Press, 1996), pp. 187–195.

[36]Debra Viadero, "Brain Trust," *Education Week,* September 18, 1996, pp. 31–33.

[37]*Better Beginnings* (Pittsburgh: Office of Child Development, University of Pittsburgh, 1997); A. DiCresce, "Brain Surges," 1997, available on the Web at www.med.wayne.edu/wmp97/brain.htm; and Lynell Hancock, "Why Do Schools Flunk Biology?" *Newsweek,* February 19, 1996, pp. 58–59.

[38]Harry Chugani, "A Critical Period of Brain Development: Studies of Cerebral Glucose Utilization with PET," *Preventive Medicine,* vol. 27, 1998, pp. 184–188.

Oddly, none of these articles and reports cite the single research article that provides the experimental evidence that originally motivated the claim: a 1987 *Annals of Neurology* article.[39] In that 1987 article, Chugani and his colleagues, M. E. Phelps and J. C. Mazziota, report results of PET (positron emission tomography) scans on 29 epileptic children, ranging in age from five days to 15 years. Because PET scans require the injection of radioactive substances, physicians can scan children only for diagnostic and therapeutic purposes; they cannot scan "normal, healthy" children just out of scientific curiosity. Thus the 1987 study is an extremely important one because it was the first, if not the only, imaging study that attempted to trace brain development from infancy through adolescence.

The scientists administered radioactively labeled glucose to the children and used PET scans to measure the rate at which specific brain areas took up the glucose. The assumption is that areas of the brain that are more active require more energy and so will take up more of the glucose. While the scans were being acquired, the scientists made every effort to eliminate, or at least minimize, all sensory stimulation for the subjects. Thus they measured the rate of glucose uptake when the brain was (presumably) not engaged in any sensory or cognitive processing. That is, they measured resting brain-glucose metabolism.

One of their major findings was that, in all the brain areas they examined, metabolic levels reached adult values when children were approximately 2 years old and continued to increase, reaching rates twice the adult level by age 3 or 4. Resting glucose uptake remained at this elevated level until the children were around 9 years old. At age 9, the rates of brain glucose metabolism started to decline and stabilized at adult values by the end of the teenage years. What the researchers found, then, was a "high plateau" period for metabolic activity in the brain that lasted from roughly age 3 to age 9.

What is the significance of this high plateau period? To interpret their findings, Chugani and his colleagues relied on earlier research in which brain scientists had counted synapses in samples of human brain tissue to determine how the number and density of synaptic connections change in the human brain over our life spans. In the late 1970s, Peter Huttenlocher of the University of Chicago found that, starting a few months after birth

---

[39]Harry T. Chugani, M. E. Phelps, and J. C. Mazziota, "Positron Emission Tomography Study of Human Brain Function Development," *Annals of Neurology*, vol. 22, 1987, pp. 487–497.

and continuing until age 3, various parts of the brain formed synapses very rapidly.[40] This early, exuberant synapse growth resulted in synaptic densities in young children's brains that were 50 percent higher than the densities in mature adult brains. In humans, synaptic densities appear to remain at these elevated levels until around puberty, when some mechanism that is apparently under genetic control causes synapses to be eliminated or pruned back to the lower adult levels.

With this background, Chugani and his colleagues reasoned as follows. There is other evidence suggesting that maintaining synapses and their associated neural structures accounts for most of the glucose that the brain consumes. Their PET study measured changes in the brain's glucose consumption over the life span. Therefore, they reasoned, as the density and number of synapses wax and wane, so too does the rate of brain-glucose metabolism. This 1987 PET study provides important indirect evidence about brain development, based on the study of living brains, that corroborates the direct evidence based on counting synapses in samples of brain tissue taken from patients at autopsy. In the original paper, the scientists stated an important conclusion: "Our findings support the commonly accepted view that brain maturation in humans proceeds at least into the second decade of life."[41]

However, if you read the 1987 paper by Chugani, Phelps, and Mazziota, you will not find a section titled "The Relationship of Elevated Brain Metabolism and Synaptic Densities to Learning." Neither Chugani nor any of his co-authors have studied how quickly or easily 5-year-olds learn as opposed to 15-year-olds. Nor have other neuroscientists studied what high synaptic densities or high brain energy consumption means for the ease, rapidity, and depth of learning.

To connect high brain metabolism or excessive synaptic density with a critical period for learning requires some fancy footwork or maybe more

---

[40]Peter R. Huttenlocher, "Synaptic Density in Human Frontal Cortex Developmental Changes of Aging," *Brain Research*, vol. 163, 1979, pp. 195–205; Peter R. Huttenlocher et al., "Synaptogenesis in Human Visual Cortex Evidence for Synapse Elimination During Normal Development," *Neuroscience Letters*, vol. 33, 1982, pp. 247–52; Peter R. Huttenlocher and Ch. de Courten, "The Development of Synapses in Striate Cortex of Man," *Human Neurobiology*, vol. 6, 1987, pp. 1–9; and Peter R. Huttenlocher and A. S. Dabholkar, "Regional Differences in Synaptogenesis in Human Cerebral Cortex," *Journal of Comparative Neurology*, vol. 387, 1997, pp. 167–178.

[41]Chugani, Phelps, and Mazziota, p. 496.

accurately, sleight of hand. We know that from early childhood until around age 10, children have extra or redundant synaptic connections in their brains. So, the reasoning goes, during this high plateau period of excess brain connectivity, the individual is given the opportunity to retain and increase the efficiency of connections that, through repeated use during a critical period, are deemed to be important, whereas connections that are used to a lesser extent are more susceptible to being eliminated.[42] This, of course, is simply to assume that the high plateau period is a critical period.

Linking the critical period with learning requires an implicit appeal to another folk belief that appears throughout the history of the brain in education literature. This common assumption is that periods of rapid brain growth or high activity are optimal times, sensitive periods, or windows of opportunity for learning.[43] We get from Chugani's important brain-imaging results to a critical period for learning via two assumptions, neither of which is supported by neuroscientific data, and neither of which has even been the object of neuroscientific research. The claim that the period of high brain connectivity is a critical period for learning, far from being a neuroscientific finding about which educators can be confident, is at best neuroscientific speculation.

Chugani accurately described the scientific state of affairs in his *Preventive Medicine* review. He *believes,* along with some educators and early childhood advocates, that there is a biological window of opportunity when learning is easy, efficient, and easily retained. But there is no neuroscientific evidence to support this belief. And where there is no scientific evidence, there is no scientific fact.

Furthermore, it would appear that we have a considerable amount of research ahead of us if we are to amass the evidence for or against this belief. Neuroscientists have little idea of how experience before puberty affects either the timing or the extent of synaptic elimination. While they have documented that the pruning of synapses does occur, no reliable studies have compared differences in final adult synaptic connectivity with differences in the experiences of individuals before puberty. Nor do they know whether the animals or individuals with greater synaptic

[42]Chugani, "Neuroimaging of Developmental Nonlinearity," p. 187.

[43]Herman T. Epstein, "Growth Spurts During Brain Development: Implications for Educational Policy and Practice," in S. Chall and A. F. Mirsky, eds., *Education and the Brain* (Chicago: University of Chicago Press, 1978), pp. 343–370; and Chipman, op. cit.

densities in adulthood are necessarily more intelligent and developed. Neuroscientists do not know if prior training and education affect either loss or retention of synapses at puberty.[44]

Nor do neuroscientists know how learning is related to changes in brain metabolism and synaptic connectivity over our lifetimes. As the developmental neurobiologist Patricia Goldman-Rakic told educators, "While children's brains acquire a tremendous amount of information during the early years, most learning takes place after synaptic formation stabilizes."[45] That is, a great deal, if not most, learning takes place after age 10 and after pruning has occurred. If so, we may turn into efficient general learning machines only after puberty, only after synaptic formation stabilizes and our brains are less active.

Finally, the entire discussion of this purported critical period takes place under an implicit assumption that children actually do learn faster, more easily, and more deeply between the ages of 4 and 10. There are certainly critical periods for the development of species-wide skills, such as seeing, hearing, and acquiring a first language, but critical periods are interesting to psychologists because they seem to be the exception rather than the rule in human development. As Jacqueline Johnson and Elissa Newport remind us in their article on critical periods in language learning, "In most domains of learning, skill increases over development."[46]

When we ask whether children actually do learn more easily and meaningfully than adults, the answers we get are usually anecdotes about athletes, musicians, and students of second languages. We have not begun to look at the rate, efficiency, and depth of learning across various age groups in a representative sample of learning domains. We are making an assumption about learning behavior and then relying on highly speculative brain science to explain our assumption. We have a lot more research to do.

---

[44]Patricia S. Goldman-Rakic, Jean-Pierre Bourgeois, and Pasko Rakic, "Synaptic Substrate of Cognitive Development: Synaptogenesis in the Prefrontal Cortex of the Nonhuman Primate," in N. A. Krasnegor, G. R. Lyon, and P. S. Goldman-Rakic, *Development of the Prefrontal Cortex: Evolution, Neurobiology, and Behavior* (Baltimore: Paul H. Brooks, 1997), pp. 27–47.

[45]*Bridging the Gap*, p. 11.

[46]Jacqueline S. Johnson and Elissa L. Newport, "Critical Period Effects on Universal Properties," *Cognition,* vol. 39, 1991, p. 215.

So, despite what you read in the papers and in the brain-based education literature, neuroscience has not established that there is a sensitive period between the ages of 4 and 10 during which children learn more quickly, easily, and meaningfully. Brain-based educators have uncritically embraced neuroscientific speculation.

The pyramids were built by aliens—to house Elvis.

A February 1996 article in *Newsweek* on the brain and education quoted Linda Darling-Hammond: "Our school system was invented in the late 1800s, and little has changed. Can you imagine if the medical profession ran this way?"[47] Darling-Hammond is right. Our school system must change to reflect what we now know about teaching, learning, mind, and brain. To the extent that we want education to be a research-based enterprise, the medical profession provides a reasonable model. We can only be thankful that members of the medical profession are more careful in applying biological research to their professional practice than some educators are in applying brain research to theirs.

We should not shrug off this problem. It is symptomatic of some deeper problems about how research is presented to educators, about what educators find compelling, about how educators evaluate research, and about how professional development time and dollars are spent. The "In Search of . . ." series is a television program that provides an entertaining mix of fact, fiction, and fantasy. That can be an amusing exercise, but it is not always instructive. The brain-based education literature represents a genre of writing, most often appearing in professional education publications, that provides a popular mix of fact, misinterpretation, and speculation. That can be intriguing, but it is not always informative. "In Search of . . ." is no way to present history, and the brain-based education literature is not the way to present the science of learning.

---

[47]Hancock, p. 59.

6

LEARNING NOT BY CHANCE

ENRICHMENT IN THE CLASSROOM

Marian C. Diamond
Janet Hopson

Learning is not attained by chance,
it must be sought for with ardor and
attended to with diligence.

—Abigail Adams, in a letter to her son,
John Quincy Adams, May 8, 1780

"ONE CHILD IN OUR DISTRICT," says Claudia Pogreba, principal of Woodway Elementary School in Edmonds, Washington, "well, his story gives me goosebumps." The boy, whose mother had been a heavy drinker during his fetal development, had "a very negative attitude toward school and was making poor decisions." These "decisions"—to misbehave with teachers, start fights with other children, and to cut classes—were landing him in the principal's office regularly. He and Pogreba were developing a relationship—one desired by neither party—based on his disruptive behavior. Just as the situation was growing worse, Pogreba explains, the boy "got hooked on the newspaper." Woodway schoolchildren publish their own newspaper, complete with advertisements from nearby retailers. "He started designing ads for local businesses," says Pogreba, "using graph paper to figure out space and area. He was good at what he did and took it very seriously. He also started conducting interviews for stories." Soon, she recalls, "he was making appointments with me to lay out ads and plan sales campaigns. Our relationship went from troubled to very positive." The boy, now in middle school, remains enthusiastic. He still values his applied experience on the newspaper, but, more generally, he has come to see reading, math, and formerly abstract school subjects as practical tools for his own success.

Sue Preckwinkle's fourth grade reading class at Dubois Elementary School is doing better than ever. The school is part of District 186 in Springfield, Illinois, and its staff has been teaching reading a particularly successful way for nearly ten years. In the mid 1980s, an education professor from the University of Illinois contacted the district's reading coordinator with a bold new idea for reading instruction. The idea was called "reciprocal teaching," and in it, a group of children help each other learn to read.

At that time, Springfield grade school students generally sat in rows, read an entire assigned story like "The Chocolate Touch" by Patrick Catling, then tried to write out or say answers to questions in class. Nearly half the children struggled with that approach, Preckwinkle recalls, but "reciprocal teaching really helped, and today, we are getting much better results."

Now, Dubois schoolchildren sit in small "literature circles" and read a passage from a story. Then they discuss it together in ways peculiar to the "reciprocal" method. In the past, says Preckwinkle, "the children had much more trouble with reading comprehension." Now, they can read "The Chocolate Touch," follow the escapades of boy protagonist John Midas as he turns everything he touches to chocolate—from his toothpaste to his trumpet to his mother—and build reading skills at the same time. "Working in a group is nonthreatening," she says. "The slower readers have better models to follow and they all have the thrill of sharing a story with someone their own age."

Education Meets the Brain

These educational success stories would have been impossible without recent research into the brain and its thinking process—or so say proponents. In a field noted for buzzwords and bandwagons, some educators have in recent years been touting the science of deliberate enrichment, including discoveries from the Diamond lab at U.C. Berkeley, to stimulate their students' development. They call many of the new educational theories and techniques "brain-based education," and this approach is generating some real benefits, as well as a lot of dollars for a few entrepreneurs. Certain teachers swear by "brain-based" methods, while others see them as time-tested techniques with new labels. Still others choose a different approach and dismiss "brain-based" as so much hooey. Regardless, there are excellent reasons for teachers, school districts, and parents to jump on *some* band-wagon: traditional American school approaches seem to work poorly for a large percentage of students, and nationwide, the majority of graduates are facing employment in the new millennial information age without the requisite skills. Can the lessons from deliberate enrichment experiments and other kinds of brain research be successfully applied to mass education? If not, what else can educators do to address the gap between what most graduating seniors know and what society expects of them?

Education in a Fix

The days when confident parents sent carefree children off to the public schoolhouse in search of a fine education are long past in many communities. Most people will agree that American public education is in trouble without being able to cite any of the facts that prove it:

○ In 1983, the National Commission on Excellence in Education sent out an alarm call with its report *A Nation at Risk*. Among its conclusions were these: American students ranked in last place in seven of nineteen international achievement tests, and ranked below second place in each of the other twelve. Thirteen percent of U.S. teens are functionally illiterate. And three-quarters of recent recruits to the armed services read below the ninth grade level.[1]

○ After a decade of sweeping and costly educational reforms following that 1983 report, the picture had changed only slightly. More students were taking rigorous course loads, but science and math scores had barely inched upward after a precipitous fall in the early 1970s and a nearly fifteen-year depression. History scores have continued to fall; on the history section of a recent exam called the National Assessment of Educational Progress, only 40 percent of high school seniors could show a basic knowledge of American history, including why the Pilgrims emigrated to New England.[2]

---

[1]Milton Goldberg and James Harvey, "A Nation at Risk: The Report of the National Commission on Excellence in Education," *Phi Delta Kappa* (September 1983): 14–19.

[2]Lynell Hancock and Pat Wingert, "A Mixed Report Card," *Newsweek* (January 13, 1995): 69.

o   Educational goals set in 1990 for the coming decade by then-President George Bush and fifty state governors have gone largely unmet: drugs are more prevalent in the schools now than in 1990. There now are fewer teachers with undergraduate or graduate degrees in the subjects they are teaching than in 1990. And there has been no increase in the percentage of students graduating from high school (86 percent). Schools do, however, seem to be a bit safer, judging by the percentage of tenth graders accosted or injured at school (40 percent in 1991 versus 36 percent in 1994).[3]

o   Executives from the nation's largest corporations told a governors' conference in April 1996 that American high school graduates lack the skills they need to succeed in business. Large corporations can train graduates in specific vocational skills, an IBM executive said at the conference, but "what is killing us is having to teach them to read and to compute and to communicate and to think."[4]

o   When math researchers tested American preschool children against their counterparts in Japan, they detected virtually no difference in the children's understanding of numbers and counting at ages three and four. By the end of grade school, however, according to UCLA educational researcher James Stigler, the *lowest-scoring* Japanese children are solving arithmetic problems with more success than the *highest-scoring American* elementary school pupils.

o   The largest state in the union, California, has more than 10 percent of the nation's enrolled elementary and high school students. Within ten years, the current 5.8 million California schoolchildren are expected to be replaced by 6.8 million, and will require nearly 100,000 extra teachers, 6,000 new schools, and an additional $15 billion just to provide education at the current level. That level, unfortunately, is far from adequate, at least if you judge by student performance: a state-administered test of fourth, eighth, and tenth graders in 1995 showed that six out of ten California students scored below the "basic" level in reading. This tied with Louisiana for the worst grade school reading scores in the nation.[5] Writing and math scores were nearly as low, according to State Superintendent of Schools Delaine Eastin, who called the results "alarming."

---

[3]Rene Sanchez, "Schools Falling Short of Ambitious Goals," *Washington Post*, reprinted in *San Francisco Chronicle* (November 10, 1995): A2.
[4]Paul Gray, "Debating Standards," *Time* (April 8, 1996): 40.
[5]Louis Freedburg, "U.S. Schools Bracing for Huge Influx," *San Francisco Chronicle* (August 22, 1996): Al. Also, Nanette Asimov, "Alarming Statewide Test Results," *San Francisco Chronicle* (April 5, 1995): Al. And, Robert B. Gunnison and Greg Lucas, "Plan to Boost Reading Scores," *San Francisco Chronicle* (July 28, 1996): Al.

o The National Association of Scholars (NAS) reports that the top fifty U.S. colleges and universities have slashed their basic "liberal arts" prerequisites. In 1964, the NAS reports, 60 percent of these top schools required history courses, 90 percent required physical or biological science courses, and 82 percent required math. Today, only 2 percent require history, 34 percent require science, and 12 percent require math. The college school year has also shrunk by 20 percent from 191 days to 156 days.[6]

o Understandably, many Americans have lost confidence in their schools. Fully half of those polled no longer trust the public schools and think private schools do a better job at maintaining discipline in class, keeping students safe, upholding high academic standards, and teaching honesty, reliability, and other traditional values.[7]

The question, "What's wrong with American education?" has been addressed and answered hundreds of times by school boards, special commissions, federal studies, educators, and authors. A much more fascinating question concerns "Why?"—Why do American schools fail to provide most children with a real understanding of basic facts, and the ability to apply standard literacy skills to real-world situations?

. . . One primary explanation [is that] American students spend far fewer hours in school than their counterparts in Europe and Asia, and far more time watching television, hanging out, dating, and working part-time jobs. Typical fifth graders in Taipei, for example, do thirteen hours of homework per week compared to the four hours per week on average that fifth graders perform in Minneapolis.[8] Some American parents keep close tabs on their children's schoolwork and homework, but more do not; this lack of concern itself erodes school performance by suggesting that homework is the child's prerogative and is unimportant.

Wherever educational researchers have looked, however, it's been clear that homework pays off, even for struggling students, and even for a subject like math. A researcher from the University of California at San Diego, Julian Betts, recently reported his findings on a study of extra math homework.[9] After tracking 6,000 junior high and high school students for over seven years, he discovered that an additional thirty

---

[6]Debra J. Saunders, "Dumbing Down America from the Top," *San Francisco Chronicle* (March 13, 1996): A16.

[7]Tamara Henry, "Public Attitudes Seem to Favor Private Schools," *USA Today* (October 11, 1995): 4A.

[8]Jonathan Marshall, "How Homework Really Pays Off," *San Francisco Chronicle* (May 20, 1996): C2.

[9]Marshall (1996).

minutes of math homework per night in grades seven through eleven raised the students' scores by the equivalent of nearly two letter grades. What's more, extra homework produced results far more effectively than hiring more teachers with math degrees or reducing class size. And the homework could even go ungraded; the benefits accrued from the student's mental efforts alone, regardless of feedback. (Returned homework papers were all the more helpful, however.)

Another reason for the American educational system's relatively poor showing is the diversity of the collective student body: Japanese teachers usually address racially and economically homogeneous groups of students in a single national language. Some American teachers have that luxury, but here diversity is the rule, not the exception. Taking just one medium-sized school system as an example, San Francisco Unified School District serves nearly 64,000 students of nine "ethnicities": Hispanic, Caucasian, African-American, Chinese, Japanese, Korean, American Indian, Filipino, and "other," including mainly Europeans, Middle Easterners, and Southeast Asians. San Francisco teachers deliver their lessons primarily in English, Chinese, and Spanish, but a visitor can hear Tagalog, Vietnamese, Cambodian, Russian, and several other languages spoken in the schools, depending on the children's native tongues. Students and their parents speak at least fifty-seven languages in their homes, says Dr. Roger Brindle, program evaluator for the San Francisco schools, and this informal tabulation may actually underestimate the diversity. "There are one hundred spoken dialects of Chinese, alone," he says, and many of these are represented in San Francisco households. While San Francisco is admittedly one of America's most multi-cultural cities, other Pacific Rim municipalities, including Los Angeles and Seattle, have similar patterns, as do New York, Miami, Houston, and cities in many other regions.

Not only are millions of American children studying their school lessons in English as a second language, but they are simultaneously learning about a mainstream American culture they may not be part of. Despite our democratic ethos, a child's home life is strongly correlated with his or her achievement in school.[10] Research shows that students tend to score higher on standardized tests:

---

[10]David W. Grissner et al., "Student Achievement and the Changing American Family" (Rand/MR-488-LE. Santa Monica, CA, 1994), pp. 105–106. Also, Bruce Bower, "Talkative Parents Make Kids Smarter," *Science News* (August 17, 1996): 100. And Leah Garchik, "Family's Effect on Scholarship," *San Francisco Chronicle* (August 27, 1996), reporting a study on divorce and academic achievement by Jennifer Gerner and Dean Lillard of Cornell University.

○ When the family is intact (parents not divorced)

○ The more education their parents attained

○ The higher the family income

○ The smaller the family's size

○ The older the mother at the child's birth

○ The more the parents talked to them as infants and toddlers

Since nearly half of all schoolchildren have divorced parents and less than one-third have parents with college degrees, these correlations predict an uphill battle for the majority of students, and in fact, this matches the statistics. All of this said, biology is not destiny and neither is family background; many students do well despite gender, family income, native language, parents' educational level, and the rest. The maverick variable is *motivation*, and some students have it in abundance. Motivation is itself central to a third explanation for the American education system's relatively poor showing: many of our traditional teaching methods depend on a child's inner motivation to pay attention and complete assignments. Yet they often do little to bolster that inner drive and, in fact, in some ways actively erode it.

James Stigler, an educational scholar at the University of California at Los Angeles, has compared the way Japanese and American math teachers operate in their classrooms and has discovered startling differences. (The American approach is familiar to most of us, and encompasses most academic subjects, not just math, Stigler's focus.) The American math teacher stands at a podium or near the chalkboard, lectures and demonstrates how to work a particular kind of problem—say, simple one-digit subtraction—then assigns a sample problem for the students to solve in class. After a few minutes, the teacher will lead the class through the problem they just attempted, and pose questions about each step in the solution as students try to guess the right answers and say what the teacher wants to hear. The American teacher acts as an authority, a source of knowledge, a supplier of right answers, and a corrector of wrong ones.

The Japanese math teacher, by contrast, works in a very different way, according to Stigler. He or she will begin by posing a new kind of problem—double-digit multiplication, let's say—then wait for a "painfully long time" while students struggle with 43×57, or whatever the sample problem may be, on their own. Eventually, the teacher will solicit ideas from the group on how to solve the problem, acting as a discussion moderator to draw out the students' own explanations, rationales, and supporting arguments. Japanese teachers refuse to be authorities in the classroom, Stigler observes, even when students present blatantly wrong solutions. Instead, they steer the discussion toward a collective agreement of what makes sense to the students and how to relate it to earlier procedures like addition or subtraction, and not toward a single correct answer.

Stigler recently borrowed a day's math lesson from a Japanese teacher and presented the material to two American fourth grades: one in the classic Japanese style and one in the typical American style. He then tested both classes for how well they understood the lesson he taught. Both groups were equally good at picking out the relevant events—the tips and steps needed to work the problem. The American students taught Japanese-style, however, could also distinguish and discard irrelevant events, while the students taught American-style could not. This shows, says Stigler, that the Japanese-style lesson required *thinking* while the American one required mostly memorization and guesswork. Guessing-what-the-teacher-wants is a motivating game only when you play it consistently well. After a few wrong answers, it's safer to clam up, whether you understand a lesson or not.

Methodological differences like these help explain why American grade school students have fallen so far behind their Japanese counterparts by the end of elementary school. But there is more. Not only is learning collaborative in Japan, teaching is too. American teachers choose their own lesson plans and teaching methods and use them autonomously and largely unobserved. All Japanese teachers, on the other hand, observe and are observed by their colleagues, Stigler says. Classroom teachers in that nation have daily meetings and publish thousands of articles to discuss *what works best* for teaching students. Their philosophy, Stigler explains, is that you can't improve a process by inspecting the products. If you ran an assembly line, you could sort out and throw away 20 percent of the widgets as defective, but still not know which mechanism was stamping out the defective products unless you searched for it directly. In the same way, only by looking at what goes on in the classroom, say Japanese educators, can you separate what works from what doesn't. (Despite their students' high productivity, Japanese educators are not entirely satisfied with their system. A 1996 report in *Science* magazine states that the majority of Japanese teachers worry about their schoolchildren having too little free time and exhibiting too little creativity.)[11]

---

[11]Hiroo Imura, "Science Education in Japan," *Science* 274 (1996): 15.

In the U.S., several factors predispose our traditional methods using the teacher as an autonomous authority: (1) An ethos of intellectual freedom combined with the democratic notion that all teachers are equally competent. (2) A workday packed with monitoring lunchrooms and playgrounds as well as educating students. (3) Very little time allotted for teachers' meetings and collaborations. Add to these, says Stigler, our nation's small, poorly funded educational research effort, and the result is too often classroom lessons based on memorization and "regurgitation" that fail to teach real understanding to any but the brightest and most highly motivated.

Our American system of mass education from kindergarten through senior high school year imposes a heavy expectation: that every child will spend at least twelve years successfully following an academic path. In England, Europe, and many other "First World" industrial societies, students are tested as young teenagers and channeled toward either a rigorously academic college-preparatory high school or a trade school with fewer intellectual demands. Since a high school diploma is considered the minimum entry credential for most American jobs, it seems reasonable that our nation would develop teaching methods that successfully motivate our diverse population to stay in school, to learn effectively, and to remember what they learned.

According to many American educators, however, including James Stigler and John Bruer, president of the James S. McDonnell Foundation in St. Louis, we spend far too little trying to invent and test new ways of teaching, and what we do spend is often focused on producing educational theory (of the sort that procures tenure) rather than innovative new classroom methods. Both of these, they say, help explain our students' poor academic showing. The foundation Bruer heads is one of the few private groups that fund research into better teaching methods, and for years, their role has been growing as federal research dollars have dwindled. Yet school enrollments are climbing beyond the 50 million mark, Bruer points out, and the average instructional investment is $5,000 per child. This makes K through 12 education "a $250 billion business. If you took 5 percent of that figure [to devote to research], it would be $12 billion," Bruer says, "but that dwarfs what we actually spend on educational research now." It would be hard to name any $250 billion industry that devotes less money than education to developing improved techniques, he observes. Plus, Bruer adds, successful new ideas often fail to reach classroom teachers. "Dedicating a small percentage of the total educational budget to disseminating good ideas to teachers in the field could have a huge impact."

Bruer's foundation has funded some remarkably successful projects (described below) that increase students' real understanding and motivation.

Other techniques lumped under the rubric of "brain-based education" are also exciting students and teachers across the country. But the reform of such a giant enterprise proceeds ponderously, and for now, because of America's relatively restricted hours of school and homework, our diversity of student backgrounds, and our traditional teaching methods, test scores continue to reflect our problems as much as our solutions.

A Fix for Education

Some astute educational historian probably predicted that in the 1990s—the government-proclaimed "Decade of the Brain"—we would see an educational reform movement based on brain research. Democracy and mass education have been interlocked for most of American history, and the impetus for changes in public education spring from the same social and scientific movements that have shaped democracy's changing form.

Thomas Jefferson tried in 1779 to establish free elementary school education for colonial children. He was defeated, though, by elitist foes who saw schooling as the responsibility only of the church or of wealthy private families. By the 1840s, as state governments solidified and carved out their authorities, "common schools" (public elementary schools) cropped up in Massachusetts, Connecticut, Rhode Island, Pennsylvania, New York, and Michigan, and in a flood of states thereafter. Along with the nineteenth-century push toward democracy came the earliest public high schools and universities and the demand for enrollments by females and African-Americans.[12]

In the early twentieth century, the juggernaut of industrialization brought wave after wave of educational reform: John Dewey's progressivism, with the founding of experimental schools and softer discipline. Maria Montessori's child-centered education, freeing children from "adult suppression" to explore their own interests and creativity. Robert Hutchins's antivocationalism—a back-to-the-classics retro movement, followed in the 1930s by the plain cloth of "essentialism," with reprises in the 1950s and 1980s.

Educational movements have also mirrored the social reforms of the mid- to late-twentieth century: the push for equal education regardless of sex, race, ethnicity, or physical disabilities. The storm over bilingual instruction. School prayer and creationism. Busing. Compensatory education. Tracking versus "mainstreaming." Finally, the massive educational

---

[12]"History of Education," *Encyclopedia Britannica*, Macropedia, Vol. 18 (1992).

enterprise has reflected society's love-hate relationship with science and technology. This started in the 1950s with *Sputnik* and the scare over our international competitiveness in those areas. And it progressed through the anti-science backlash of the 1960s, the surge of interest in environment and ecology in the 1970s, the demand by women and minorities for better access to science education and jobs in the 1980s, the upsurge of computers in education in the late 1980s and early 1990s, and today, the ascendancy of the brain.

Teachers—especially those laboring during the social and scientific turmoil of the last half century—have shown a tendency to jump on ideological bandwagons. And with good reason. Teachers are an overworked, underpaid, highly dedicated lot, discouraged by the sieve-like memories of many students and the obvious absence of true subject understanding despite everyone's hardest efforts. They are as disturbed as parents and administrators by lagging scores and half-baked literacy, and they are understandably searching for the key, the method, the Right Answer. In the late 1960s and 1970s, for example, there was a flowering of excitement around so-called right-brain, left-brain studies. These suggested new ways of differentiating and reaching artistic, intuitive right-brained learners from analytic, verbal left-brained types.

When shoehorning a seamless spectrum of students into these two categories didn't work overly well, teachers looked for something better. By then, the "triune brain" theory was catching on. This is the idea that humans have a primitive reptilian brain wrapped with an emotional mammalian brain and encrusted with our convoluted neocortex, seat of human intelligence. The interactions of these three cranial species, according to triune theory, can help explain learning and behavior.

By the early 1980s, Howard Gardner had published in *Frames of Mind* his theory about the seven different kinds of intelligence we all possess in large or small measure, and that seemed to many to be an even better way of categorizing students, fathoming their scholastic foibles, and helping them absorb information. In a more recent book, *The Unschooled Mind: How Children Think and How Schools Should Teach,* Gardner described a school curriculum he developed with colleagues at Harvard— a program based heavily on apprenticeships and practical, hands-on training for youngsters. Other educators spun entire school designs off their own interpretations of Gardner's theory, including the Key School in Indianapolis.

By 1990, a pair of education professors from Southern California, Renate Nummela Caine and Geoffrey Caine, published a book on "brain-based" learning called *Making Connections: Teaching and the Human*

Brain. This work laces together various theories and bits of research on behavior, cognition, and brain function into a prescription for educating today's students. It starts with brain anatomy and the Diamond lab's work on plasticity, then touches on gender and hemispheric differences in the brain; human memory research; the triune brain; stress, emotions, and learning; and multiple intelligences. Along the way, it shows how all of these threads can be stitched into a detailed strategy employing hands-on, active involvement and promising better motivation, better retention, and better understanding for students. Within a few years, brain-based education had become a lucrative enterprise for some, complete with competing authors, videos, consultants, in-service training seminars, toll-free 800 numbers and operators waiting to take your order. One can't help but wonder whether education comes in any variety other than "brain-based," whether this is a well-meaning fad that will help a few students in a few places; leave the majority at approximately the same level of confusion; and be replaced in time by some other catchphrase like "whole-body" or "whole-spirit" education; or none of the above.

The school principal who led this chapter, Claudia Pogreba of Edmonds, Washington, has seen educational bandwagons roll in and out during her twenty-some years in the field. Pogreba is well-versed in the "brain-based" tenets, having read the books, heard the consultants, attended the seminars, discussed the ideas with her staff, and presented them to local parents. And she happens to believe quite firmly that they work, *really work*, and represent an educational movement that will last. The story of the troubled boy who found meaning on the Woodway school newspaper was just one of the examples Pogreba offered over lunch on a frigid Seattle day in 1996, when the schools were shut down by icy roads.

Pogreba, a soft-spoken woman with powerful conviction, explains that "another boy was really struggling in class with reading, and was extremely discouraged by school. He signed up—the only boy—to take part in a school drama production and won the role of the king in Cinderella. He had to learn to dance the waltz with a girl who played Cinderella, and he did a really nice job. Everyone was impressed by his effort, and most importantly, his attitude toward school became positive, not negative." Still another boy, a native Spanish speaker, she recalls, refused to speak much English at school and was not learning very effectively. "After he signed up to work in our commercial art venture," Pogreba says, "he started taking school more seriously and believing that it had a purpose. Before long, he was using English more and starting to learn more in class."

The newspaper, dramatic workshop, and commercial art venture Pogreba described are part of a program she and the teachers on her staff call the Woodway Elementary Micro-Community. Two afternoons per week (perhaps three or more in the future) children in grades four to six leave their normal classrooms and take part in one of seven "micro ventures" taught by Woodway teachers, counselors, and experts from the community:

- An illustrated monthly newspaper
- A multimedia production team that creates slide shows and video features
- A dramatic arts group that stages plays
- A team that tutors other students, mediates student conflicts, and learns about stock market investing
- An art venture that generates flyers, posters, programs, and other graphic designs
- A team devoted to improving school life
- An economic team that learns about how to start and run small businesses

Pogreba was instrumental in organizing this set of "immersion" workshops to help children apply academic skills to simulated life situations. She learned about grade school microcommunities in part by visiting an elementary school in Lowell, Massachusetts, which had operated a similar program since 1982. "The microcommunity model hasn't caught on widely," Pogreba says, "because it's a philosophy, not a kit you order, and it is developed through the interests of a school's individual staff members." Planning the Woodway workshops took the staff hundreds of hours, and convincing skeptical parents took many more. One of Pogreba's fellow principals in the Edmonds district, Harriet Green from Lynndale School, who also lunched with us on that cold Seattle Monday, explained further. Both parents and teachers are "very reluctant to give up what they have always done. 'Drill and practice and memorizing did it for me,' they say, 'so why change?' But once Woodway school launched a pilot microcommunity program, 'The parents overwhelmingly supported it,' Pogreba added. 'They said their kids were talking about it and making connections between math and other topics.'"

Some of the fear of math learning was lessened in the Edmonds district even before they introduced the microcommunity plan. "Math is very hands-on and developmentally appropriate, as we teach it. Lots of applications of math concepts," Pogreba explains. "An integration of materials to develop number sense, lots of emphasis on seeking out patterns, and what I think is phenomenal, an emphasis on journaling."

Green explains "journaling." The child "will jot down, 'How did I figure this out?' 'What was I thinking when I did it?' 'How did I get my answer?' 'What did I do in math today?' and the result is an understanding of the subject that also incorporates visualization and language development." "How could that be more aligned with brain research?" Pogreba joins in, rhetorically. In fact, in Edmonds, Washington, as in many districts around the country, elementary education barely resembles the classroom experiences of most adults raised in the 1930, 1940s, or 1950s.

"You don't see many desks in rows anymore," says Green, "and you seldom hear a teacher say, 'That's the wrong answer.'" Instead, she says, "You'll hear, 'Tell me why you think that.' Or, 'What made you give that answer?' What's more," she goes on, "instead of saying, 'I'm going to have all the kids reading on the same page of the same book,' the planning goes more like, 'We're going to be reading such and such a story and I'm going to want a lot of activities that build on it. Some will appeal to some kids' learning styles and interests and some will appeal to others. So I am going to put puppet making on one table to go with the story, and on another, a series of questions where the kids have to write answers. And I'm going to put a tape of the story over here, and paints over there for making a mural about the story.'"

Pogreba credits some of the changeover to a paid consultant from California who presented "brain-based" education theory to the Edmonds district several years ago.[13] The teachers there were already using many innovative techniques, Pogreba explains, and the seminars "substantiated that our focus was developmentally correct." Harriet Green, however, a serious woman with strong opinions, is more skeptical. "We had to make some leaps to put things together between brain research, education, teaching, and the community. Simply to say that the brain research we just learned about—dealing with rat studies—means that you should react to your children this way and do this kind of stimulating environment stuff is a leap!"

There is a tendency, Green says, "to want to have a research base for what we've already known were great teaching practices. Kids learn and retain things when they are actively involved . . . that's how I define 'brain-based education.' You could call it 'teaching to the multiple intelligences,' or before that, that 'everybody has their own unique learning style,' and when teachers teach the same ways to everybody, they're not reaching some students."

---

[13]Patricia Wolfe and Marny Sorgen, "Mind, Memory, and Learning: Implications for the Classroom" (80 Crest Road, Fairfax, CA 94930) (1990).

Green uses a personal anecdote to explain learning styles. "I was the model student," she says. "I went through high school as a great memorizer and I gave teachers back exactly what they wanted. I got A's on my tests. I made maximum honor roll. And I went to college and played the same game and graduated magna cum laude." Green's husband, by contrast, "was a self-taught learner. He read what he was interested in but he didn't care much to read what was assigned unless he happened to be interested in it." Today, she goes on, "He and I talk history, and for all the A-pluses I got in my history courses, I remember nothing. And furthermore, I remembered nothing the day after the test! But my husband remembers everything there is to know about history and can talk about it intelligently because it was driven by his own interest. I think that tells you a lot about what we are trying to do in education now. Yeah, the old way worked, sort of. I learned a process—put down the two and carry the one. But I had no idea what I was doing: If I forgot to move one number over, I had an absurd answer and didn't even notice! Those stellar teachers along the way that we all remember—they may not have called what they were doing 'brain-compatible' or using 'multiple intelligences.' But they knew how to grab a kid's learning style . . . and they did it intuitively."

While the labels may not impress principal Harriet Green, the learning strategies that are being called "brain-based"—hands-on, collaborative, open-ended, applied—certainly do. When we asked whether these innovative approaches produce better learners, better prepared for life, she was quick to respond. "I don't have a doubt in my mind, but it depends on what your measure is. If it is how successful they are going to be in the real world, definitely. If it's how well they perform on standardized tests, not necessarily. If your measure is how turned-on they are to what they are learning, absolutely. But if it's how well they can spout back information, probably not."

A Science of Learning Based on Classroom Results

For some educators, like John Bruer of the James S. McDonnell Foundation, "brain-based" education is not just a label, it's a "huge leap." Bruer's organization reviews and funds educational research, and while he thinks "how the brain works to support cognitive function is a very interesting question, we are decades away from having any understanding of brain function that would contribute to classroom learning." Right now, he says, "there is a lot of bad neuroscience being peddled in the educational market-place." In spite of the powerful evidence showing that experience changes the brain, Bruer insists the link with classroom performance is missing. "I don't know of a neuroscientific result that one can implement in the classroom and show that it is *for those reasons* that children's educational outcome was improved." Some of the techniques being recommended under the "brain-based" rubric, Bruer continues, do work, "but what it's got to do with the brain is a leap of faith."

Bruer criticizes educators who think that "doing something different is by definition doing something better. And it's just not true!" When a physician is confronted by a drug company salesman with a new product, "He should ask, 'Okay, how much better will my patients do if I buy this drug from your company than they are doing now?' A good physician will think that way," Bruer insists, "but educators seldom do." As a result, he says, teachers are susceptible to "the guru of the week who goes in to a school on a Wednesday afternoon or a Saturday morning to talk to teachers for three or four hours and it's wonderful and pleasant," but fails to "amount to any significant change in teacher behavior."

Bruer advocates a new "science of learning" based on how learners process and use information, not on "synapses and arborization and neurotransmitters." Rather than focus on "cellular, molecular things," he argues, educational researchers—at least for now—should stick to techniques with a proven foundation in the science of cognition (how we think) and with verifiable results in the classroom.

The number line games developed by Robbie Case and Sharon Griffin are prime examples in Bruer's recent book, *Schools for Thought: A Science of Learning in the Classroom*. Teaching these games, he says, is an educational technique with a quantifiable outcome in student test scores as well as in a real understanding of the subject that they can apply in other situations. Another example is "reciprocal teaching," the approach to reading instruction Sue Preckwinkle uses for her fourth graders in Springfield, Illinois. John Bruer also cites a seventh-grade boy named Charles with an IQ of 70 and a third-grade reading level.[14] After three weeks of reciprocal reading lessons, the boy had advanced nearly two years on standardized reading tests, and the gains lasted long after the remedial lessons ended. In the reciprocal technique, children work together in groups to summarize a short passage they just read, to create questions about the subject matter, to clarify any misunderstandings and talk about the gist of the story (with the teacher's guidance), and then finally to predict what the next part of the story or book will say.

---

[14]John T. Bruer, "The Mind's Journey from Novice to Expert," *American Educator* (Summer 1993): 6–15, 38–46.

Charles and Sue Preckwinkle's fourth graders are just a few of the beneficiaries; the new technique is now widely used in Springfield, Illinois, and in a number of other school districts nationally. Everywhere it's applied, reading comprehension and retention seem to go up dramatically.

Bruer points to a third example of an educational technique with proven results based on cognitive science—how the mind learns. A physics teacher named Jim Minstrell working at Mercer Island High School in Washington State created a new way to teach physics concepts so that students could absorb, remember, and apply them. Minstrell sets up an experiment such as placing a ten-pound bag of sugar on a scale beneath a glass dome. Next he asks students to predict whether the weight will change if he pumps all of the air from the dome. By doing this, Minstrell discovered that all students come to physics with preconceptions about what objects weigh and how they move, fall, and behave in various circumstances based on their own observations throughout childhood. Minstrell also found that these preconceptions are not highly individualized and instead, fall into just a few groupings.

In the weight-in-a-vacuum experiment, every one of his students predicts one of just four outcomes: that the weight will double; stay at ten pounds; fall to zero; or fluctuate by an ounce or two. Minstrell leads a discussion during which students defend their guesses. Then he pumps the air from the jar, reveals that the weight remains at exactly ten pounds, and explains why. Using this approach (which is, coincidentally, very similar to the Japanese method for teaching math), Minstrell allows each student to discover his or her own beliefs and amend them based on new observations of the physical world (during the experiment). Other approaches Minstrell has tried leave the students' naive misconceptions in place; when they finish the physics course, they quickly forget the thin veneer of memorized concepts and fall back on their original guesses. Minstrell calls his method the "Cognitive Approach," and reports that Mercer Island students taught this way scored substantially higher on math and physics tests than similar students at a sister school who learned science and math with traditional techniques.

John Bruer, a leader in the funding of educational research (and whose foundation supports Minstrell's work) comments, "The challenge for the educator is to make a bridge from a child's informal learning that occurs outside of school to the formal demands that school presents. I don't think that brain research and glucose metabolism or whatever has a whole lot to say about that." But, he concedes, "I don't want to discount [brain research] because eventually we will know much more. In twenty years, it's conceivable we will understand the brain circuitry involved in reading, for example, and how learning to read changes neural circuitry as the skills mature."

Since today's students and teachers can scarcely wait twenty years for a neuroscience of learning to emerge with proof enough for the highly meticulous, what's the best alternative? The behavioral strategies of cognitive education researchers for teaching math, reading, science, and other subjects are surely an important start, and the McDonnell Foundation in St. Louis is trying hard to spread the word to teachers. But the enthusiasm Claudia Pogreba, Sue Preckwinkle, and many other educators feel about techniques based on brain research cannot be ignored, even if the "brain-based" label and the notions behind it seem like a great leap to some.

Ironically, the student involvement and motivation at the core of the "brain-based" model is decades, even centuries old. The microcommunity Pogreba helped organize at Woodway School in Edmonds, Washington, is based on a similar ten-year-long experiment at Lowell School in Massachusetts. It, in turn, drew ideas from Peninsula School in Menlo Park, California, which began an "open participation plan" in the 1930s, following John Dewey's philosophies.[15] For many years, Howard Gardner and his colleagues at Harvard have been applying the multiple intelligences idea in a student-participation program based on the apprenticeships employed since antiquity in societies all over the world. And English educator John Abbott of the Education 2000 Trust seconds the idea of apprenticeships in a recent article. Students want "more contact with adults other than parents and teachers," Abbott writes, and society does young people "a grave disservice by separating the world of learning from the world of work." Students need "interaction with ideas and the environment," he concludes, "if they are to develop a sense of general purpose, self-esteem, and an understanding of the essential interconnectedness of all forms of human endeavor."[16]

Call this educational movement "brain-based," if you like; the key factor is motivation. And that is also what deliberate enrichment is about: pursuing activities that are fun, interesting, even exciting to a child and that provide challenge and stimulation while requiring active involvement.

Abigail Adams had no inkling of future controversies when she wrote that "learning is not attained by chance" and must be "sought for with ardor and attended to with diligence." It is obvious from the disputes surrounding modern education, however, and from the disappointing

---

[15]Mary Anne Raywid, "Why Do These Kids Love School?" *Phi Delta Kappan* (April 1992): 631–633.

[16]John Abbott, "Children Need Communities, Communities Need Children," *American Journal of Educational Leadership* (May 1995).

performance of most American students, that a successful learning environment cannot be attained by chance or tradition, and that the lecture-memorization drill-test model of the past is largely unsuccessful for children. We adults may have learned our numbers that way, our reading, vocabulary, history, and science. But it was surely our own ardor and diligence, our own inner drive to learn that propelled us. How much better it would have been for us to have had these immersion-participation-application approaches, these apprenticeships, collaborative learning groups, and microcommunities! And how much better it will be for arousing motivation in our children—regardless of intelligence and learning type—and at building contexts for true understanding. We can hardly continue educating "by chance" and then expect young people to perform in a rapidly evolving information era.

Students must see a reason for applying their ardor and diligence beyond college entrance exams and future earning power. These may work for older children, but will seldom motivate youngsters just starting to learn basic subjects. A participatory school where children see a direct application for their learning tools—like the boy designing newspaper ads or the child learning about commercial art in English—is a place for fun, motivation, and enrichment. Since we know how to do this from working models like the Peninsula, Lowell, and Edmonds schools, why wait twenty years? With the chance to create more enchanted minds and with the terrible costs of mental deprivation, perhaps a leap is justified while other kinds of educational research continue. To return to medical metaphors, a physician might know that researchers are testing a new and highly effective drug and that it will be available in a few years. But he or she would rarely, if ever, withhold the best available alternative in the meantime. Should we do any less for our children?

7

MIND AND BRAIN

John D. Bransford
Ann L. Brown
Rodney R. Cocking

AS THE POPULAR PRESS has discovered, people have a keen appetite for research information about how the brain works and how thought processes develop (*Newsweek*, 1996, 1997; *Time*, 1997a, 1997b). Interest runs particularly high in stories about the neuro-development of babies and children and the effect of early experiences on learning. The fields of neuroscience and cognitive science are helping to satisfy this fundamental curiosity about how people think and learn.

In considering which findings from brain research are relevant to human learning or, by extension, to education, one must be careful to avoid adopting faddish concepts that have not been demonstrated to be of value in classroom practice. Among these is the concept that the left and right hemispheres of the brain should be taught separately to maximize the effectiveness of learning. Another is the notion that the brain grows in holistic "spurts," within or around which specific educational objectives should be arranged: as discussed in this chapter, there is significant evidence that brain regions develop asynchronously, although any specific educational implications of this remain to be determined. Another widely held misconception is that people use only 20 percent of their brains—with different percentage figures in different incarnations—and should be able to use more of it. This belief appears to have arisen from the early neuroscience finding that much of the cerebral cortex consists of "silent areas" that are not activated by sensory or motor activity. However, it is now known that these silent areas mediate higher cognitive functions that are not directly coupled to sensory or motor activity.

Advances in neuroscience are confirming theoretical positions advanced by developmental psychology for a number of years, such as the importance of early experience in development (Hunt, 1961). What is new . . . is the *convergence* of evidence from a number of scientific fields. As the sciences of developmental psychology, cognitive psychology, and neuroscience, to name but three, have contributed vast numbers of research studies, details about learning and development have converged to form a more complete picture of how intellectual development occurs. Clarification of some of the mechanisms of learning by neuroscience has been advanced, in part, by the advent of non-invasive imaging technologies, such as positron emission tomography (PET) and functional magnetic resonance imaging (fMRI). These technologies have allowed researchers to observe human learning processes directly.

This chapter reviews key findings from neuroscience and cognitive science that are expanding knowledge of the mechanisms of human learning. Three main points guide the discussion in this chapter:

1. Learning changes the physical structure of the brain.

2. These structural changes alter the functional organization of the brain; in other words, learning organizes and reorganizes the brain.

3. Different parts of the brain may be ready to learn at different times.

We first explain some basic concepts of neuroscience and new knowledge about brain development, including the effects of instruction and learning on the brain. We then look at language in learning as an example of the mind-brain connection. Lastly, we examine research on how memory is represented in the brain and its implications for learning.

From a neuroscience perspective, instruction and learning are very important parts of a child's brain development and psychological development processes. Brain development and psychological development involve continuous interactions between a child and the external environment—or, more accurately, a hierarchy of environments, extending from the level of the individual body cells to the most obvious boundary of the skin. Greater understanding of the nature of this interactive process renders moot such questions as how much depends on genes and how much on environment. As various developmental researchers have suggested, this question is much like asking which contributes most to the area of a rectangle, its height or its width (Eisenberg, 1995).

The Brain: Foundation for Learning

Neuroscientists study the anatomy, physiology, chemistry, and molecular biology of the nervous system, with particular interest in how brain activity relates to behavior and learning. Several crucial questions about early learning particularly intrigue neuroscientists. How does the brain develop? Are there stages of brain development? Are there critical periods when certain things must happen for the brain to develop normally? How is information encoded in the developing and the adult nervous systems? And perhaps most important: How does experience affect the brain?

Some Basics

A nerve cell, or neuron, is a cell that receives information from other nerve cells or from the sensory organs and then projects that information to other nerve cells, while still other neurons project it back to the parts of the body that interact with the environment, such as the muscles. Nerve cells are equipped with a cell body—a sort of metabolic heart—and an enormous treelike structure called the dendritic field, which is the input side of the neuron. Information comes into the cell from projections called axons. Most of the excitatory information comes into the cell from the dendritic field, often through tiny dendritic projections called spines. The junctions through which information passes from one neuron to another are called synapses, which can be excitatory or inhibitory in nature. The neuron integrates the information it receives from all of its synapses and this determines its output.

During the development process, the "wiring diagram" of the brain is created through the formation of synapses. At birth, the human brain has in place only a relatively small proportion of the trillions of synapses it will eventually have; it gains about two-thirds of its adult size after birth. The rest of the synapses are formed after birth, and a portion of this process is guided by experience.

Synaptic connections are added to the brain in two basic ways. The first way is that synapses are overproduced, then selectively lost. Synapse overproduction and loss is a fundamental mechanism that the brain uses to incorporate information from experience. It tends to occur during the early periods of development. In the visual cortex—the area of the cerebral cortex of the brain that controls sight—a person has many more synapses at 6 months of age than at adulthood. This is because more and more synapses are formed in the early months of life, then they disappear, sometimes in prodigious numbers. The time required for this phenomenon to run its course varies in different parts of the brain, from 2 to 3 years in the human visual cortex to 8 to 10 years in some parts of the frontal cortex.

Some neuroscientists explain synapse formation by analogy to the art of sculpture. Classical artists working in marble created a sculpture by chiseling away unnecessary bits of stone until they achieved their final form. Animal studies suggest that the "pruning" that occurs during synapse overproduction and loss is similar to this act of carving a sculpture. The nervous system sets up a large number of connections; experience then plays on this network, selecting the appropriate connections and removing the inappropriate ones. What remains is a refined final form that constitutes the sensory and perhaps the cognitive bases for the later phases of development.

The second method of synapse formation is through the addition of new synapses—like the artist who creates a sculpture by adding things together until the form is complete. Unlike synapse overproduction and loss, the process of synapse addition operates throughout the entire human life span and is especially important in later life. This process is not only sensitive to experience, it is actually driven by experience. Synapse addition probably lies at the base of some, or even most, forms of memory. As discussed later in this chapter, the work of cognitive scientists and education researchers is contributing to our understanding of synapse addition.

Wiring the Brain

The role of experience in wiring the brain has been illuminated by research on the visual cortex in animals and humans. In adults, the inputs entering the brain from the two eyes terminate separately in adjacent regions of the visual cortex. Subsequently, the two inputs converge on the next set of neurons. People are not born with this neural pattern. But through the normal processes of seeing, the brain sorts things out.

Neuroscientists discovered this phenomenon by studying humans with visual abnormalities, such as a cataract or a muscle irregularity that deviates the eye. If the eye is deprived of the appropriate visual experience at an early stage of development (because of such abnormalities), it loses its ability to transmit visual information into the central nervous system. When the eye that was incapable of seeing at a very early age was corrected later, the correction alone did not help—the afflicted eye still could not see. When researchers looked at the brains of monkeys in which similar kinds of experimental manipulations had been made, they found that the normal eye had captured a larger than average amount of neurons, and the impeded eye had correspondingly lost those connections.

This phenomenon only occurs if an eye is prevented from experiencing normal vision very early in development. The period at which the eye is sensitive corresponds to the time of synapse overproduction and loss in the visual cortex. Out of the initial mix of overlapping inputs, the neural connections that belong to the eye that sees normally tend to survive, while the connections that belong to the abnormal eye wither away. When both eyes see normally, each eye loses some of the overlapping connections, but both keep a normal number.

In the case of deprivation from birth, one eye completely takes over. The later the deprivation occurs after birth, the less effect it has. By about 6 months of age, closing one eye for weeks on end will produce no effect whatsoever. The critical period has passed; the connections have already sorted themselves out, and the overlapping connections have been eliminated.

This anomaly has helped scientists gain insights into normal visual development. In normal development, the pathway for each eye is sculpted (or "pruned") down to the right number of connections, and those connections are sculpted in other ways, for example, to allow one to see patterns. By overproducing synapses and then selecting the right connections, the brain develops an organized wiring diagram that functions optimally. The brain development process actually uses visual information entering from outside to become more precisely organized than it could with intrinsic molecular mechanisms alone. This external information is even more important for later cognitive development. The more a person interacts with the world, the more a person needs information from the world incorporated into the brain structures.

Synapse overproduction and selection may progress at different rates in different parts of the brain (Huttenlocher and Dabholkar, 1997). In the primary visual cortex, a peak in synapse density occurs relatively quickly. In the medial frontal cortex, a region clearly associated with higher cognitive functions, the process is more protracted: synapse production starts before birth and synapse density continues to increase until 5 or 6 years of age. The selection process, which corresponds conceptually to the main organization of patterns, continues during the next 4–5 years and ends around early adolescence. This lack of synchrony among cortical regions may also occur upon individual cortical neurons where different inputs may mature at different rates (see Juraska, 1982, on animal studies).

After the cycle of synapse overproduction and selection has run its course, additional changes occur in the brain. They appear to include both the modification of existing synapses and the addition of entirely new synapses to the brain. Research evidence (described in the next section) suggests that activity in the nervous system associated with learning experiences somehow causes nerve cells to create new synapses. Unlike the process of synapse overproduction and loss, synapse addition and modification are life-long processes, driven by experience. In essence, the quality of information to which one is exposed and the amount of information one acquires is reflected throughout one's life in the structure of the brain. This process is probably not the only way that information is stored in the brain, but it is a very important way that provides insight into how people learn.

Experiences and Environments for Brain Development

Alterations in the brain that occur during learning seem to make the nerve cells more efficient or powerful. Animals raised in complex environments have a greater volume of capillaries per nerve cell—and therefore a greater supply of blood to the brain—than the caged animals, regardless of whether the caged animal lived alone or with companions (Black et al., 1987). (Capillaries are the tiny blood vessels that supply oxygen and other nutrients to the brain.) In this way experience increases the overall quality of functioning of the brain. Using astrocytes (cells that support neuron functioning by providing nutrients and removing waste) as the index, there are higher amounts of astrocyte per neuron in the complex-environment animals than in the caged groups. Overall, these studies depict an orchestrated pattern of increased capacity in the brain that depends on experience.

Other studies of animals show other changes in the brain through learning (see Exhibit 7.1).

The weight and thickness of the cerebral cortex can be measurably altered in rats that are reared from weaning, or placed as adults, in a large cage enriched by the presence both of a changing set of objects for play and exploration and of other rats to induce play and exploration (Rosenzweig and Bennett, 1978). These animals also perform better on a variety of problem-solving tasks than rats reared in standard laboratory cages. Interestingly, both the interactive presence of a social group and direct physical contact with the environment are important factors: animals placed in the enriched environment alone showed relatively little benefit; neither did animals placed in small cages within the larger environment (Ferchmin et at., 1978; Rosenzweig and Bennett, 1972). Thus, the gross structure of the cerebral cortex was altered both by exposure to opportunities for learning and by learning in a social context.

Exhibit 7.1. Making Rats Smarter

How do rats learn? Can rats be "educated"? In classic studies, rats are place in a complex communal environment filled with objects that provide ample opportunities for exploration and play (Greenough, 1976). The objects are changed and rearranged each day, and during the changing time, the animals are put in yet another environment with another set of objects. So, like their real-world counterparts in the sewers of New York or the fields of Kansas, these rats have a relatively rich set of experiences from which to draw information. A contrasting group of rats is placed in a more typical laboratory environment, living alone or with one or two others in a barren cage—which is obviously a poor model of a rat's real world. These two settings can help determine how experience affects the development of the normal brain and normal cognitive structures, and one can also see what happens when animals are deprived of critical experiences.

After living in the complex of impoverished environments for a period from weaning to rat adolescence, the two groups of animals were subjected to a learning experience. The rats that had grown up in the complex environment made fewer errors at the outset than the other rats; they also learned more quickly not to make any errors at all. In this sense, they were smarter than their more deprived counterparts. And with positive rewards, they performed better on complex tasks than the animals raised in individual cages. Most significant, learning altered the rats' brains: the animals from the complex environment had 20–25 percent more synapses per nerve cell in the visual cortex than the animals from the standard cages (see Turner and Greenough, 1985; Beaulieu and Colonnier, 1987). It is clear that when animals learn, they add new connections to the wiring of their brains—a phenomenon not limited to early development (see, e.g., Greenough et al., 1979).

Does Mere Neural Activity Change the Brain or Is Learning Required?

Are the changes in the brain due to actual learning or to variations in aggregate levels of neural activity? Animals in a complex environment not only learn from experiences, but they also run, play, and exercise, which activates the brain. The question is whether activation alone can produce brain changes without the subjects actually learning anything, just as activation of muscles by exercise can cause them to grow. To answer this question, a group of animals that learned challenging motor skills but had relatively little brain activity was compared with groups that had high levels of brain activity but did relatively little learning (Black et al., 1990). There were four groups in all. One group of rats was taught to traverse an elevated obstacle course; these "acrobats" became very good at the task over a month or so of practice. A second group of "mandatory exercisers" was put on a treadmill once a day, where they ran for 30 minutes, rested for 10 minutes, then ran another 30 minutes. A third group of "voluntary exercisers" had free access to an activity wheel attached directly to their cage, which they used often. A control group of "cage potato" rats had no exercise.

What happened to the volume of blood vessels and number of synapses per neuron in the rats? Both the mandatory exercisers and the voluntary exercisers showed higher densities of blood vessels than either the cage potato rats or the acrobats, who learned skills that did not involve significant amounts of activity. But when the number of synapses per nerve cell was measured, the acrobats were the standout group. Learning adds synapses; exercise does not. Thus, different kinds of experience condition the brain in different ways. Synapse formation and blood vessel formation (vascularization) are two important forms of brain adaptation, but they are driven by different physiological mechanisms and by different behavioral events.

Localized Changes

Learning specific tasks brings about localized changes in the areas of the brain appropriate to the task. For example, when young adult animals were taught a maze, structural changes occurred in the visual area of the cerebral cortex (Greenough et al., 1979). When they learned the maze with one eye blocked with an opaque contact lens, only the brain regions connected to the open eye were altered (Chang and Greenough, 1982). When they learned a set of complex motor skills, structural changes occurred in the motor region of the cerebral cortex and in the cerebellum, a hindbrain structure that coordinates motor activity (Black et al., 1990; Kleim et al., 1996).

These changes in brain structure underlie changes in the functional organization of the brain. That is, learning imposes new patterns of organization on the brain, and this phenomenon has been confirmed by electrophysiological recordings of the activity of nerve cells (Beaulieu and Cynader, 1990). Studies of brain development provide a model of the learning process at a cellular level: the changes first observed in rats have also proved to be true in mice, cats, monkeys, and birds, and they almost certainly occur in humans.

Role of Instruction in Brain Development

Clearly, the brain can store information, but what kinds of information? The neuroscientist does not address these questions. Answering them is the job of cognitive scientists, education researchers, and others who study the effects of experiences on human behavior and human potential. Several examples illustrate how instruction in specific kinds of information can influence natural development processes. This section discusses a case involving language development.

Language and Brain Development

Brain development is often timed to take advantage of particular experiences, such that information from the environment helps to organize the brain. The development of language in humans is an example of a natural process that is guided by a timetable with certain limiting conditions. Like the development of the visual system, parallel processes occur in human language development for the capacity to perceive phonemes, the "atoms" of speech. A phoneme is defined as the smallest meaningful unit of speech sound. Human beings discriminate the "b" sound from the "p" sound largely by perceiving the time of the onset of the voice relative to the time the lips part; there is a boundary that separates "b" from "p" that helps to distinguish "bet" from "pet." Boundaries of this sort exist among closely related phonemes, and in adults these boundaries reflect language experience. Very young children discriminate many more phonemic boundaries than adults, but they lose their discriminatory powers when certain boundaries are not supported by experience with spoken language (Kuhl, 1993). Native Japanese speakers, for example, typically do not discriminate the "r" from the "l" sounds that are evident to English speakers, and this ability is lost in early childhood because it is not in the speech that they hear. It is not known whether synapse overproduction and elimination underlies this process, but it certainly seems plausible.

The process of synapse elimination occurs relatively slowly in the cerebral cortical regions that are involved in aspects of language and other higher cognitive functions (Huttenlocher and Dabholkar, 1997). Different brain systems appear to develop according to different time frames, driven in part by experience and in part by intrinsic forces. This process suggests that children's brains may be more ready to learn different things at different times. But, as noted above, learning continues to affect the structure of the brain long after synapse overproduction and loss are completed. New synapses are added that would never have existed without learning, and the wiring diagram of the brain continues to be reorganized throughout one's life. There may be other changes in the brain involved in the encoding of learning, but most scientists agree that synapse addition and modification are the ones that are most certain.

Examples of Effects of Instruction on Brain Development

Detailed knowledge of the brain processes that underlie language has emerged in recent years. For example, there appear to be separate brain areas that specialize in subtasks such as hearing words (spoken language of others), seeing words (reading), speaking words (speech), and generating words (thinking with language). Whether these patterns of brain organization for oral, written, and listening skills require separate exercises to promote the component skills of language and literacy remains to be determined. If these closely related skills have somewhat independent brain representation, then coordinated practice of skills may be a better way to encourage learners to move seamlessly among speaking, writing, and listening.

Language provides a particularly striking example of how instructional processes may contribute to organizing brain functions. The example is interesting because language processes are usually more closely associated with the left side of the brain. As the following discussion points out, specific kinds of experiences can contribute to other areas of the brain taking over some of the language functions. For example, deaf people who learn a sign language are learning to communicate using the visual system in place of the auditory system. Manual sign languages have grammatical structures, with affixes and morphology, but they are not translations of spoken languages. Each particular sign language (such as American Sign Language) has a unique organization, influenced by the fact that it is perceived visually. The perception of sign language depends on parallel visual perception of shape, relative spatial location, and movement of the hands—a very different type of perception than the auditory perception of spoken language (Bellugi, 1980).

In the nervous system of a hearing person, auditory system pathways appear to be closely connected to the brain regions that process the features of spoken language, while visual pathways appear to go through several stages of processing before features of written language are extracted (Blakemore, 1977; Friedman and Cocking, 1986). When a deaf individual learns to communicate with manual signs, different nervous system processes have replaced the ones normally used for language—a significant achievement.

Neuroscientists have investigated how the visual-spatial and language processing areas each come together in a different hemisphere of the brain, while developing certain new functions as a result of the visual language experiences. In the brains of all deaf people, some cortical areas that normally process auditory information become organized to process visual information. Yet there are also demonstrable differences among the brains of deaf people who use sign language and deaf people who do not use sign language, presumably because they have had different language experiences (Neville, 1984, 1995). Among other things, major differences exist in the electrical activities of the brains of deaf individuals who use sign language and those who do not know sign language (Friedman and Cocking, 1986; Neville, 1984). Also, there are similarities between sign language users with normal hearing and sign language users who are deaf that result from their common experiences of engaging in language activities. In other words, specific types of instruction can modify the brain, enabling it to use alternative sensory input to accomplish adaptive functions, in this case, communication.

Another demonstration that the human brain can be functionally reorganized by instruction comes from research on individuals who have suffered strokes or had portions of the brain removed (Bach-y-Rita, 1980, 1981; Crill and Raichle, 1982). Since spontaneous recovery is generally unlikely, the best way to help these individuals regain their lost functions is to provide them with instruction and long periods of practice. Although this kind of learning typically takes a long time, it can lead to partial or total recovery of functions when based on sound principles of instruction. Studies of animals with similar impairments have clearly shown the formation of new brain connections and other adjustments, not unlike those that occur when adults learn (e.g., Jones and Schallert, 1994; Kolb, 1995). Thus, guided learning and learning from individual experiences both play important roles in the functional reorganization of the brain.

Memory and Brain Processes

Research into memory processes has progressed in recent years through the combined efforts of neuroscientists and cognitive scientists, aided by positron emission tomography and functional magnetic resonance imaging (Schacter, 1997). Most of the research advances in memory that help scientists understand learning come from two major groups of studies: studies that show that memory is not a unitary construct and studies that relate features of learning to later effectiveness in recall.

Memory is neither a single entity nor a phenomenon that occurs in a single area of the brain. There are two basic memory processes: declarative memory, or memory for facts and events which occurs primarily in brain systems involving the hippocampus; and procedural or nondeclarative memory, which is memory for skills and other cognitive operations, or memory that cannot be represented in declarative sentences, which occurs principally in the brain systems involving the neostriatum (Squire, 1997).

Different features of learning contribute to the durability or fragility of memory. For example, comparisons of people's memories for words with their memories for pictures of the same objects show a superiority effect for pictures. The superiority effect of pictures is also true if words and pictures are combined during learning (Roediger, 1997). Obviously, this finding has direct relevance for improving the long-term learning of certain kinds of information.

Research has also indicated that the mind is not just a passive recorder of events; rather, it is actively at work both in storing and in recalling information. There is research demonstrating that when a series of events are presented in a random sequence, people reorder them into sequences that make sense when they try to recall them (Lichtenstein and Brewer, 1980). The phenomenon of the active brain is dramatically illustrated further by the fact that the mind can "remember" things that actually did not happen. In one example (Roediger, 1997), people are first given lists of words: sourcandy-sugar-bitter-good-taste-tooth-knife-honey-photo-chocolate-heart-caketart-pie. During the later recognition phase, subjects are asked to respond "yes" or "no" to questions of whether a particular word was on the list. With high frequency and high reliability, subjects report that the word "sweet" was on the list. That is, they "remember" something that is not correct. The finding illustrates the active mind at work using inferencing processes to relate events. People "remember" words that are implied but not stated with the same probability as learned words. In an act of efficiency and "cognitive economy" (Gibson, 1969), the mind creates categories for processing information. Thus, it is a feature of learning that memory processes make relational links to other information.

In view of the fact that experience alters brain structures and that specific experiences have specific effects on the brain, the nature of "experience" becomes an interesting question in relation to memory

processes. For example, when children are asked if a false event has ever
occurred (as verified by their parents), they will correctly say that it never
happened to them (Ceci, 1997). However, after repeated discussions
around the same false events spread over time, the children begin to
identify these false events as true occurrences. After about 12 weeks of
such discussions, children give fully elaborated accounts of these fictitious
events, involving parents, siblings, and a whole host of supporting "evidence." Repeating lists of words with adults similarly reveals that recalling non-experienced events activates the same regions of the brain as
events or words that were directly experienced (Schacter, 1997). Magnetic resonance imaging also shows that the same brain areas are
activated during questions and answers about both true and false events.
This may explain why false memories can seem so compelling to the individual reporting the events.

In sum, classes of words, pictures, and other categories of information
that involve complex cognitive processing on a repeated basis activate the
brain. Activation sets into motion the events that are encoded as part of
long-term memory. Memory processes treat both true and false memory
events similarly and, as shown by imaging technologies, activate the same
brain regions, regardless of the validity of what is being remembered.
Experience is important for the development of brain structures, and
what is registered in the brain as memories of experiences can include
one's own mental activities.

These points about memory are important for understanding learning
and can explain a good deal about why experiences are remembered well or
poorly. Particularly important is the finding that the mind imposes structure
on the information available from experience. This parallels descriptions of
the organization of information in skilled performance . . . : one of the primary differences between the novice and the expert is the manner in which
information is organized and utilized. From the perspective of teaching, it
again suggests the importance of an appropriate overall framework within
which learning occurs most efficiently and effectively . . .

Overall, neuroscience research confirms the important role that experience plays in building the structure of the mind by modifying the structures
of the brain: development is not solely the unfolding of preprogrammed
patterns. Moreover, there is a convergence of many kinds of research on
some of the rules that govern learning. One of the simplest rules is that
practice increases learning; in the brain, there is a similar relationship
between the amount of experience in a complex environment and the
amount of structural change.

In summary, neuroscience is beginning to provide some insights, if not
final answers, to questions of great interest to educators. There is growing

evidence that both the developing and the mature brain are structurally altered when learning occurs. Thus, these structural changes are believed to encode the learning in the brain. Studies have found alterations in the weight and thickness of the cerebral cortex of rats that had direct contact with a stimulating physical environment and an interactive social group. Subsequent work has revealed underlying changes in the structure of nerve cells and of the tissues that support their function. The nerve cells have a greater number of the synapses through which they communicate with each other. The structure of the nerve cells themselves is correspondingly altered. Under at least some conditions, both astrocytes that provide support to the neurons and the capillaries that supply blood may also he altered. The learning of specific tasks appears to alter the specific regions of the brain involved in the task. These findings suggest that the brain is a dynamic organ, shaped to a great extent by experience—by what a living being does, and has done.

Conclusion

It is often popularly argued that advances in the understanding of brain development and mechanisms of learning have substantial implications for education and the learning sciences. In addition, certain brain scientists have offered advice, often with a tenuous scientific basis, that has been incorporated into publications designed for educators (see, e.g., Sylwester, 1995: Ch. 7). Neuroscience has advanced to the point where it is time to think critically about the form in which research information is made available to educators so that it is interpreted appropriately for practice—identifying which research findings are ready for implementation and which are not.

This chapter reviews the evidence for the effects of experience on brain development, the adaptability of the brain for alternative pathways to learning, and the impact of experience on memory. Several findings about the brain and the mind are clear and lead to the next research topics:

1. The functional organization of the brain and the mind depends on and benefits positively from experience.

2. Development is not merely a biologically driven unfolding process, but also an active process that derives essential information from experience.

3. Research has shown that some experiences have the most powerful effects during specific sensitive periods, while others can affect the brain over a much longer time span.

4. An important issue that needs to be determined in relation to education is which things are tied to critical periods (e.g., some aspects of phonemic perception and language learning) and for which things is the time of exposure less critical.

From these findings, it is clear that there are qualitative differences among kinds of learning opportunities. In addition, the brain·"creates" informational experiences through mental activities such as inferencing, category formation, and so forth. These are types of learning opportunities that can be facilitated. By contrast, it is a bridge too far, to paraphrase John Bruer (1997), to suggest that specific activities lead to neural branching (Cardellichio and Field, 1997), as some interpreters of neuroscience have implied.

REFERENCES

Bach-y-Rita, P. 1980. Brain plasticity as a basis for therapeutic procedures. In *Recovery of Function: Theoretical Considerations for Brain Injury Rehabilitation*, P. Bachy-Rita, ed. Baltimore, MD: University Park Press.

Bach-y-Rita, P. 1981. Brain plasticity as a basis of the development of rehabilitation procedures for hemiplegia. *Scandinavian Journal of Rehabilitation Medicine* 13:73–83.

Beaulieu, C., and M. Colonnier. 1987. Effects of the richness of the environment on the cat visual cortex. *Journal of Comparative Neurology* 266:478–494.

Beaulieu, C., and M. Cynader. 1990. Effect of the richness of the environment on neurons in cat visual cortex. I. Receptive field properties. *Developmental Brain Research* 53:71–81.

Bellugi, U. 1980. Clues from the similarities between signed and spoken language. In *Signed and Spoken Language: Biological Constraints on Linguistic Form*, U. Bellugi and M. Studdert -Kennedy, eds. Weinheim, Germany: Venlag Chemie.

Black, J. E., K. R. Isaacs, B. J. Anderson, A. A. Alcantara, and W. T. Greenough. 1990. Learning causes synaptogenesis, whereas motor activity causes angiogenesis, in cerebellar cortex of adult rats. *Proceedings of the National Academy of Sciences U.S.A.* 87:5568–5572.

Black, J. E., A. M. Sirevaag, and W. T. Greenough. 1987. Complex experience promotes capillary formation in young rat visual cortex. *Neuroscience Letters* 83:351–355.

Blakemore, C. 1977. *Mechanics of the Mind*. Cambridge, UK: Cambridge University Press.

Bruer, J. T. 1997. Education and the brain: A bridge too far. *Educational Researcher* 26(8)(November):4–16.

Cardellichio, T., and W. Field. 1997. Seven strategies to enhance neural branching. *Educational Leadership* 54(6)(March).

Ceci, S. J. 1997. Memory: Reproductive, Reconstructive, and Constructive. Paper presented at the Symposium: Recent Advances in Research on Human Memory, National Academy of Sciences, Washington, DC.

Chang, F. L., and W. T. Greenough. 1982. Lateralized effects of monocular training on dendritic branching in adult split-brain rats. *Brain Research* 232:283–292.

Crill, W. E., and M. E. Raichle. 1982. Clinical evaluation of injury and recovery. In *Repair and Regeneration of the Nervous System,* J. G. Nicholls, ed. New York: Springer-Verlag.

Eisenberg, L. 1995. The social construction of the human brain. *American Journal of Psychiatry* 152:1563–1575.

Ferchmin, P. A., E. L. Bennett, and M. R. Rosenzweig. 1978. Direct contact with enriched environment is required to alter cerebral weights in rats. *Journal of Comparative and Physiological Psychology* 88:360–367.

Friedman, S. L., and R. R. Cocking. 1986. Instructional influences on cognition and on the brain. Pp. 319–343 in *The Brain, Cognition, and Education,* S. L. Friedman, K. A. Klivington, and K. W. Peterson, eds. Orlando, FL: Academic Press.

Gibson, E. J. 1969. *Principles of Perceptual Learning and Development.* New York: Appleton-Century-Crofts.

Greenough, W. T. 1976. Enduring brain effects of differential experience and training. Pp. 255–278 in *Neural Mechanisms of Learning and Memory,* M. R. Rosenzweig and E. L. Bennett, eds. Cambridge, MA: MIT Press.

Greenough, W. T., J. M. Juraska, and F. R. Volkmar. 1979. Maze training effects on dendritic branching in occipital cortex of adult rats. *Behavioral and Neural Biology* 26:287–297.

Hunt, J. M. 1961. *Intelligence and experience.* New York: Ronald Press.

Huttenlocher, P. R., and A. S. Dabholkar. 1997. Regional differences in synaptogenesis in human cerebral cortex. *Journal of Comparative Neurology* 387:167–178.

Jones, T. A., and T. Schallert. 1994. Use-dependent growth of pyramidal neurons after neocortex damage. *Journal of Neuroscience* 14:2140–2152.

Juraska, J. M. 1982. The development of pyramidal neurons after eye opening in the visual cortex of hooded rats: A quantitative study. *Journal of Comparative Neurology* 212:208–213.

Kleim, J. A., E. Lussnig, E. R. Schwarz, T. A. Comery, and W. T. Greenough. 1996. Synaptogenesis and Fos expression in the motor cortex of the adult rat following motor skill learning. *Journal of Neuroscience* 16:4529–4535.

Kolb, B. 1995. *Brain Plasticity and Behavior.* Hillsdale, NJ: Erlbaum.

Kuhl, P. K. 1993. Innate predispositions and the effects of experience in speech perception: The native language magnet theory. Pp. 259–274 in

Developmental Neurocognition: Speech and Face Processing in the First Year of Life, B. deBoysson-Bardies, S. deSchonen, P. Juscyzyk, P. McNeilage, and J. Morton, eds. Dordrecht, NL: Kluwer Academic Publishers.

Lichtenstein, E. H., and W. F. Brewer. 1980. Memory for goal-directed events. *Cognitive Psychology* 12:415–445.

Neville, H. J. 1984. Effects of early sensory and language experience on the development of the human brain. In *Neonate Cognition: Beyond the Blooming Buzzing Confusion,* J. Mehler and R. Fox, eds. Hillsdale, NJ: Erlbaum.

Neville, H. J. 1995. Effects of Experience on the Development of the Visual Systems of the Brain on the Language Systems of the Brain. Paper presented in the series Brain Mechanisms Underlying School Subjects, Part 3. University of Oregon, Eugene.

Newsweek. 1996. How kids are wired for music, math, and emotions, by E. Begley. *Newsweek* (February 19):55–61.

Newsweek. 1997. How to build a baby's brain, by E. Begley. *Newsweek* (Summer special issue):28–32.

Roediger, H. 1997. Memory: Explicit and Implicit. Paper presented at the Symposium, Recent Advances in Research on Human Memory, National Academy of Sciences, Washington, DC.

Rosenzweig, M. R., and E. L. Bennett. 1972. Cerebral changes in rats exposed individually to an enriched environment. *Journal of Comparative and Physiological Psychology* 80:304–313.

Rosenzweig, M. R., and E. L. Bennett. 1978. Experiential influences on brain anatomy and brain chemistry in rodents. Pp. 289–330 in *Studies on the Development of Behavior and the Nervous System: Vol. 4. Early Influences,* G. Gottlieb, ed. New York: Academic Press.

Schacter, D. L. 1997. Neuroimaging of Memory and Consciousness. Paper presented at the Symposium, Recent Advances in Research on Human Memory, National Academy of Sciences, Washington, DC.

Squire, L. R. 1997. Memory and Brain Systems. Paper presented at the Symposium: Recent Advances in Research on Human Memory, National Academy of Sciences, Washington, DC.

Sylwester, R. 1995. *A Celebration of Neurons: An Educator's Guide to the Human Brain.* Association for Supervision and Curriculum Development, Alexandria, VA.

Time. 1997a. The day-care dilemma, by J. Collins. *Time* (February 3):57–97.

Time. 1997b. Fertile minds, by J. M. Nash. *Time* (February 3):49–56.

Turner, A. M., and W. Greenough. 1985. Differential rearing effects on rat visual cortex synapses. I. Synaptic and neuronal density and synapses per neuron. *Brain Research* 328:195–203.

PART THREE

THE THINKING BRAIN

MEMORY, COGNITION, AND INTELLIGENCE

8

LEARNING AND REMEMBERING

Sarah-Jayne Blakemore
Uta Frith

Different Types of Learning and Memory

One of the contributions to education that neuroscience is capable of making is illuminating the nature of learning itself. It is unlikely that there is one single all-purpose type of learning for everything. In terms of brain structures involved, learning mathematics differs from learning to read, which differs from learning to play the piano. Each memory system relies on a different brain system and develops at a slightly different time. Remembering who you are differs from remembering where you are.

Episodic memories of particular events or episodes in your life, for example, your first day at school or your most recent birthday, are processed in different brain areas from *semantic memories* of names, numbers, dates, and facts. These two types of memory are distinct from *procedural memory* for skills like tying shoelaces and walking. These types of memory, and more still, are processed separately in the brain and, as we shall see, they can exist in isolation from one another. Learning can be *implicit* or *explicit*. That is, we may sometimes be unaware that we are learning, and on other occasions we may be highly aware.

Implicit Forms of Memory

Different memory systems rely on different brain systems and develop at different times. The most basic type of memory is one that we are not even aware of and which we have little control over. This type of memory is called *a conditioned response*. You might have heard of the Russian physiologist Ivan Pavlov whose experiments with dogs early in the last century established the psychological theory of the *conditioned response*. Pavlov's dogs salivated whenever they heard a bell that they had previously learned to associate with being given food. This is a type of conditioned response, over which the dogs had no control.

Conditioning can also occur if a certain food makes you sick. After that, just the smell or thought of the food can make you feel ill, and you will usually avoid eating that particular food. Just one bad experience with the food can make you avoid it forever. Through evolution this has been built into the brain. It is, after all, a matter of life and death. If you cannot learn to avoid poisonous foods, you could be in trouble.

A well known conditioned response that has been studied in humans is called the "eye-blink response." A small puff of air to the eye causes the eye to blink; if a tone is played at the same time as the puff of air, after a few trials the tone alone will elicit an eye-blink. The brain has learned to associate a tone with an irritating puff of air. Such conditioned responses are believed to be controlled, at least in part, by the *cerebellum*. Even very young babies show conditioned responses.

A similar type of memory is called *conditional learning*. This occurs when an action is learned in order to produce a response. Babies start to develop conditional learning from about three months. Three-month-old babies will quickly learn that kicking a mobile animates it, or that crying usually results in the immediate appearance of a parent!

Leading on from this is memory for motor skills and movement, which is called *procedural memory*. This ability relies on the *basal ganglia*. These deep brain structures are not fully developed at birth, but by about three months of age they are already functioning. At the same age, infants start to show procedural learning. They slowly begin to learn that grasping a toy in a certain way allows them to hold and manipulate it, for example. Gradually the procedures they naturally learn become more sophisticated and include crawling, standing, and eventually walking. These are all very complicated things for the brain to learn, and it is hardly surprising that such a large proportion of the brain is dedicated to learning and carrying out movement skills like these. The brain regions involved are largely different from those responsible for learning facts and remembering events.

It is clear that babies can learn without awareness right from the start. Children tacitly know a lot about the world they live in well before they can talk about it. In adults too, much knowledge appears to be implicit. Try explaining exactly how to ride a bike without getting on one. There are many components to riding a bike that we simply cannot describe. This is an example of implicit procedural memory, but we probably learn all sorts of facts and sequences implicitly too. These implicitly learned pieces of information might contribute to feelings of instinctiveness when, for some reason, we choose one thing over another without really knowing why.

Teaching often involves making implicit or procedural knowledge explicit. Teachers have to explain how to read, how to paint, and how to play the violin, for example. Knowing how or when to make rules explicit is likely to be an important determinant of effective teaching. When can explicit teaching replace implicit learning? Is a degree of prior implicit learning always helpful? It is possible that a reciprocal dialectic between implicit learning and explicit teaching most efficiently supports learning.

The Power of Implicit Learning

Many years of research on implicit learning have shown that people are able to learn information in the absence of awareness. The brain can process and store information without us knowing about it. In explicit learning, we learn information consciously and know very well that we have learned it. Some tasks rely on explicit learning. It is interesting to speculate that some individuals may thrive more on explicit learning than others.

Implicit memory is typically seen when we experience a vague sense of familiarity. Objects, people, or facts identified as familiar are also often preferred, even though we might not know why. Many psychological experiments have studied this remarkable ability. It has been shown that people can learn complex rules by being exposed to sequences that adhere to the rules, without having any explicit notion of the rules or of having learned them. However, some people may know part of the rules or have feelings of recognition when they are shown the rules.

In a typical experiment, volunteers are shown a sequence of many hundreds of letters and are told that there are various "rules" to which the letter sequence adheres. For example, the sequence:

HDSSOHDFSSAHD

adheres to the rules: H is followed by D; S is always repeated once and the second S is followed by a vowel; vowels are followed by H.

Volunteers are not told about any of these rules but, after being simply exposed to many strings of letters that conform to the rules, people tend to pick up the regularities. This is shown in increasingly faster reaction times, which suggest that after a while it is possible to anticipate the next item in the sequence. When letters are introduced that break the rule, reaction times are slowed at that point.

Although participants in these experiments usually claim not to have a clue and often find the experiment frustrating—it feels as though each answer is a complete guess—their answers actually reveal that they have acquired the rules. Volunteers in these experiments are, needless to say, usually amazed by their own results.

So what is happening in the brain when we learn something at this unconscious, implicit, level? Using *positron emission tomography (PET; . . .)*, Jonathan Cohen and colleagues at the University of Pittsburgh mapped the brain regions that are responsive to implicit learning of sequences. Volunteers performed the task that we just described. They had no idea of learning anything.

Once the participants were trained, they were scanned. When there was a subtle change in the nature of the sequence, this resulted in blood flow increases in a network of brain regions including the left *premotor* area and *anterior cingulate,* and part of the basal ganglia on the right. Blood flow decreases at the rule break were observed in the right *prefrontal cortex.* These changes suggest that these regions are responsive to the rule break, which can occur without awareness. The brain notices things that you do not.

Learning and Remembering Skills

Procedural learning of a skill, such as riding a bike or throwing a cricket ball, differs from learning facts and remembering events. Amnesic patients who have suffered damage to their *hippocampus* will thereafter be unable to retain memories of new events in their lives. However, they are often able to learn new procedural skills and they retain skills they acquired before their brain damage.

A severely amnesic patient known as Clive, who has been monitored by neuropsychologists for many years, suffered severe damage to his hippocampus caused by encephalitis. Before his illness Clive used to conduct a top level choir at a college in Cambridge [England]. Clive's ability to lay down short-term memories has been all but wiped out. He has no memory for events that happened more than five minutes earlier, although he can recognize his wife and knows who he is. He has retained memories from before his encephalitis. He just cannot lay down new memories. His wife describes Clive "as if he is no longer conscious." Clive himself writes a diary, and every entry begins something like, "I am conscious for the very first time," and Clive duly scribbles out the previous entry in which he said something similar. What he seems to be lacking, therefore, is the continuity of consciousness from moment to moment.

Despite having had a detrimental effect on his short-term memory for events, the encephalitis did not seem to affect Clive's memory for motor skills. He is able to play the piano as beautifully as he could before damage to his hippocampus occurred, even though he has no memory of having played the piano before, or of the college in which he worked for so many years. He can conduct a choir just as perfectly as before his illness, although he has no memory of ever having seen the choristers previously or ever having conducted before in his life. Neither has he forgotten his language and he can talk and write in perfectly grammatical sentences. The asymmetry of his memory abilities is astounding.

Amnesic patients are often able to acquire new skills, despite not explicitly remembering being taught the skill. Their memories are implicit or subconscious. This is because in these patients, like in Clive, the *basal ganglia* remain intact. The basal ganglia are still capable of procedural learning and maintaining previously acquired movement skills. Amnesic patients have no trouble walking or talking, motor skills that are acquired by the basal ganglia. People with selective damage to the hippocampus can also learn new skills, such as riding a bicycle or playing the piano, even though they are unable to lay down the explicit memories of being taught such skills.

The opposite pattern is seen in people with Parkinson's disease, whose basal ganglia function abnormally. Such people normally have good memory for episodes and facts, but they appear to be unable to learn new skills. So here we have a *double dissociation* between learning facts and learning motor skills. This has been confirmed by recent functional imaging studies, which have demonstrated activity in the hippocampus but not in the basal ganglia when new facts are learned, and activity in the basal ganglia but not in the hippocampus when new motor skills are learned.

Working Memory

A memory system that starts to develop in the first year of life is *working memory*. This is the system that allows us to hold and manipulate information "online." We rely on working memory constantly during our waking lives because it allows us to keep in mind information while doing something else. Without working memory it would be impossible to have a conversation, read this sentence, add up numbers in your head, or dial a phone number. Working memory has been likened to an erasable mental blackboard that allows you to hold information briefly in your mind and manipulate it, be it words, menu prices, or a phone number.

In 1971, Joaquin Fuster at the University of California in Los Angeles, obtained results with monkeys suggesting that a small region in the *prefrontal cortex* plays a role in storing memories for a short time. In one experiment, monkeys were first shown two identical objects—one on the right and the other on the left. On top of one of the objects was a piece of apple, which the monkey could eat. After the monkey had eaten the apple, the two objects were hidden from view for up to 60 seconds before being shown once again to the monkey. The monkey could then reach for the object previously associated with the food by remembering its location.

During these 60 seconds neurons in the prefrontal cortex were highly active. They were not active before, when the objects were presented, or afterward, when the monkey made a choice. Patricia Goldman-Rakic, at Yale University, expanded this work in the 1980s. Her experiments revealed that groups of prefrontal cells are dedicated to specific memory tasks and that by recording the activity of a particular prefrontal neuron, the next action a monkey was about to perform could be predicted.

The prefrontal cortex continues to develop throughout childhood and into adolescence. . . . So, while infants show a basic capacity for short-term and working memory, this capacity continues to be refined throughout childhood. The development of prefrontal cortex and the progress in performance on memory tests go hand in hand. It is likely that some tasks, which seem negligible to adults, are in fact quite taxing for children.

Doing Two Things at Once

People often have to carry out more than one task at a time and this makes demands on working memory, typically requiring the switching between information appropriate for one or the other task. Even just comparing numbers across two columns that are in a different order requires this sort of memory: you need to keep the place in column one to return to it, after you have dealt with the place of the information in column two. Patients with frontal lobe damage tend to be disproportionately impaired at doing two things simultaneously. This suggests a frontal lobe role in these aspects of working memory.

A recent brain-imaging study by Susan Courtney and colleagues at Johns Hopkins University in Baltimore compared brain activity when participants performed two tasks simultaneously with brain activity when each task was performed alone. This experiment confirmed that the prefrontal cortex plays a crucial role in doing two things at once. Neither of the two tasks, a spatial rotation task and a semantic judgment task, produced significant activation of prefrontal cortex when performed alone; only when they were combined was activation of this area observed. Since the frontal lobes are later maturing structures of the brain . . . , it may be possible to adjust task demands during teaching according to the neurological maturity during development. If little Jack seems extremely forgetful, it may not be that he cannot remember facts or events. It may be that he finds it hard to keep in mind simultaneously the instruction to do several tasks at once.

Memory for the Future

Even if we are not actually doing two things at once, we often have to remember to do something in the future while we are in the middle of doing something completely different. You might be in the middle of having a conversation with someone when an internal alarm bell rings: you had previously unconsciously set this clock to remember to make a phone call. So you need to interrupt your conversation for a while but get back to it after the call. Or you might be cooking a meal and all the while you are trying not to forget to put the garbage out in the next 30 minutes or you'll miss the garbage collection. Remembering to do one thing at a future time when you are engaged in some other activity is called *prospective memory*. We use it all the time, and some scientists, including Paul Burgess and Tim Shallice at the University of London, have argued that this ability is unique to humans.

In experiments on prospective memory, Paul Burgess and his colleagues have found that bearing in mind an intention to do something in the future interferes with the task at hand. In one experiment, volunteers were shown two numbers on either side of a screen. Imagine you are taking part as a volunteer in this experiment. You are required to press one of two keys on a computer keyboard—a key on the left (A) if the number on the left is bigger, or a key on the right (L) when the number on the right is bigger. On some trials, you are told to carry on doing this task, but in addition, to look out for whether the two numbers are both even, in which case you have to press a different key altogether (the space bar). Although it is easy to remember this instruction and easy to do the task, people are slower in these types of trials, even when two even numbers never appear.

What is going on in the brain in this kind of task? Damage to the frontal lobes seriously impairs prospective memory performance. Patients with frontal damage simply do not remember to do the second task at the right point in time. Brain-imaging experiments have shown that a specific part of the frontal lobes, called *frontopolar cortex* at the front of the brain, just behind the forehead, is activated when your internal alarm bell is set to remind you to do something while you are absorbed in an ongoing task. This part of the brain seems to be key to remembering to do something in the future.

Memory for Events

There is another kind of memory that involves the *frontal cortex* and the hippocampus. This is called *episodic memory,* and it is the type of memory that is lost, among other things, in patients with Alzheimer's disease. Clive, whom we described earlier, is an extreme case. Episodic memories are memories of events that have occurred with you as main actor or witness in a specific time and place.

The hippocampus starts to mature from late infancy. Although babies and young children are constantly acquiring information and laying down new memories, they seem to do this implicitly, that is, without keeping a record in their mind of when and how they acquired the information. Young children, even when they can speak, cannot tell you much when you ask them about an event. This phenomenon is known as *childhood amnesia.* Three year olds seem unable to remember how they learned about something even when the events took place only moments before. After the age of three, children become better at remembering specific events and episodes, how they occurred, and when they happened.

You might think at first that you would surely remember something where you yourself took part, or were a witness. Memories of events we have witnessed, or participated in, form an important part of our lives and yet, as we all know, such memories are unreliable and can be lost. In old age, people tend to forget that they have just told you that they have been to see the doctor, for instance, and sure enough, they will say it again and again. They cannot remember where they last put their glasses down. We might imagine a record keeper in the mind who continuously keeps track of what you say, do, or observe with interest. This record normally prevents you from repeating yourself, and from forgetting a personally important event but, in old age, it gets sluggish. Of course, memory problems in old age are very varied and not all people suffer to the same extent. However, it seems that the brain system involved in episodic memory is not only quite slow in developing at the beginning of life, but is also the one that is first to fade.

Episodic memories (e.g., what you had for breakfast this morning) are stored in different brain areas from semantic memories (e.g., who is the current president of the USA or what people typically have for breakfast). People with profound amnesia cannot remember episodes they personally experienced—even what they were doing just a few minutes ago—but, as in the case of Clive, they can retain their semantic knowledge and can still talk. It is possible to some extent to make up for a poor episodic memory by using a fact-type memory instead. So you might rehearse what you had for breakfast like a shopping list, and you can then recite it if asked. Although the different types of memory are distinguishable by the brain, what we actually recall might well be a mixture, drawing on different systems of memory. Our conscious mind is unaware of the intricate workings of the neural systems that sustain these memories.

Disorders of Memory in Childhood

Developmental disorders often have a genetic origin but other causes exist as well, for instance, damage to the brain at a very young age. Such damage may not even be noticed at the time. One example of this is developmental disorder of memory, which was not recognized until very recently. Faraneh Varga-Khadem at the University of London found that some babies who are born prematurely and, for various reasons, at that time had received an excessive dose of oxygen sustained damage to the hippocampus. The hippocampus is measurably smaller in these cases. As we have just mentioned, the hippocampus is crucially important to remember what happened when, who did what, and so on.

Varga-Khadem and her colleagues found that the children who had hippocampal damage were not conspicuous in many respects. They did well at school and seemed to perform well on IQ tests. However, when asked what they did the day before, they were unable to answer. Yet they could answer memory questions of the type: "What is the capital of Turkey?" and "What is your address?" This type of semantic memory has a different brain basis, probably in the *entorhinal cortex* and *temporal lobes*, and this was intact.

The hippocampal damage was subtle but it had profound effects on the children as they grew up and tried to adjust. They were unable to remember appointments or assignments, and they did not have a normal continuous memory of what happened to them in the past. They remembered facts, but not when and how they had learned these facts. Yet compensation was possible to some extent. We have already alluded to the fact that you can turn memories that are normally treated as episodes into facts that you acquire like any other knowledge. So you can recite, when asked, what you had for breakfast, even if you do not recall having had breakfast.

For a teacher it might be important to know that learning facts, such as mathematical equations and historical dates, relies on different brain regions from remembering events that you were personally involved in. Children are not necessarily equally good at all of them, and this may not be just a matter of being less interested in some skills than in others.

Brain Basis of Teaching

We know a little of what goes on in the brain when we learn, but hardly anything about what goes on in the brain when we teach. We believe that in the future neuroscience will eventually illuminate the nature of teaching. Teaching is one of the most species-specific capacities that we can list for humans, although some rudimentary forms of implicit teaching may exist in other species. At a minimum, teaching may just mean providing people with the right opportunities and encouraging them to take up these opportunities. An analogy may be a mother duck who takes the young ducklings to the water: as soon as she sets in herself, the ducklings follow her. The teaching that a human mother provides goes much further. She has to teach the child all sorts of complex things, such as how to greet strangers and how to wash their hands. The teaching that a professional teacher provides goes further still. We can learn things within a lifetime that were originally unique inventions and the accumulated work of many generations. Thus, writing and number systems, navigational maps, astronomy, law and so on are transmitted through explicit teaching and specialist teachers.

We need to go back here to *theory of mind,* or *mentalizing. . . . Mentalizing* has a distinct brain basis and can be considered at least to some extent an innate module. It is one of the cognitive capacities that is abundant in humans and appears to be critical to our social interactions and communications. It also appears to be a prerequisite for purposeful teaching. At the very least, to be effective, the teacher has to estimate the appropriate state of knowledge of the student: the teacher needs to make some assumption about what the student knows already and what he or she needs to be told to advance their understanding further. The teacher also needs to estimate the degree of interest that the student brings to the task, and their receptiveness to teaching.

Successful teaching is based on many of the same component skills as in ordinary two-way communication. You do not wish to bore another person. Neither can you always assume that they know the background to what you are talking about. So you need to judge what they already know about a topic. You want the other person to listen to you carefully and you need to alert them that you have something useful and new to teach them.

You may be very ambitious and as a public speaker you may wish to change the other people's attitudes and beliefs. This needs rhetorical skills, which have been studied in great detail since antiquity. They involve many artful devices, such as exaggeration, repetition, and irony. All this relies on the fine-tuning of your ability to read others' minds. You need to know others' existing attitudes and beliefs. Your success depends on your mastery of persuasive techniques, such as flattery, promised rewards, or threats. The teacher's task may not be too dissimilar. Both tasks rely on our ability to attribute feelings and beliefs to others and to manipulate them so as to produce the desired outcome. Teachers and learners have reciprocal roles and mutually help each other. Studying this by observing two people in two scanners simultaneously presents a methodological challenge. This challenge is currently being tackled.

The ability to learn is vastly more ancient and automatic than the ability to teach. All animals learn; very few teach. It may well turn out that teaching has a long way to go yet to reach its optimum potential. In the future, it should be possible to establish systematic programs of research that reveal, in terms of brain activity, the complex interactions that must arise between factors such as teaching style and learning type.

9

WHO OWNS INTELLIGENCE?

Howard Gardner

THE THEORY OF multiple intelligences has helped break the psychometricians' century-long stranglehold on the subject of intelligence. While we may continue to use the words *smart* and *stupid,* and while IQ tests may persist for certain purposes, the monopoly of those who believe in a single general intelligence has come to an end. Brain scientists and geneticists are documenting the incredible differentiation of human capacities, computer programmers are creating systems that are intelligent in different ways, and educators are freshly acknowledging that their students have distinctive strengths and weaknesses.

. . . I have laid out a position that challenges the psychometric consensus. I have proposed a set of several intelligences, each resting on its own neurological substrate, each of which can be nurtured and channeled in specific ways, depending on a particular society's values. I have listed the criteria for an intelligence and shown how these can be evoked in evaluating potential new intelligences. But where does one draw the line? Are my criteria the right ones? In the future, the new dimensions and boundaries of intelligence will likely be thrashed out on a pivotal battlefield. Now that the Scylla of the psychometricians has been overcome, we risk succumbing to the Charybdis of "anything goes"— emotions, morality, and creativity all being absorbed into the "new intelligence." The challenge is to chart a concept of intelligence that reflects new discoveries and understandings and yet can withstand scrutiny.

The Stretch and Limits of Multiple Intelligences

One can think of intelligence as an elastic band. For many years no one effectively challenged its definition, and the band seemed to have lost its elasticity. Some of the new definitions of intelligence have expanded the band and renewed its resilience, even while incorporating the earlier work on intelligence that is still germane. Other definitions have expanded the band to the snapping point, rendering unusable the earlier foundational study of intelligence.

Until now, the term *intelligence* has been largely limited to linguistic and logical capacities, although (as I've argued) humans can process other elements as diverse as the contents of space, music, or their own and others' psyches. Like the elastic band, conceptions of intelligence need to encompass these diverse contents—and stretch even more. We must move beyond solving existing problems and look more at the capacities of human beings to *fashion products* (like works of art, scientific experiments, classroom lessons, organization plans) that draw on one or more intelligences.

As long as intelligences are restricted to the processing of "contents in the world," we avoid epistemological problems. So it should be. The concept of "intelligence" should not be expanded to include personality, motivation, will, attention, character, creativity, and other valued human capacities. If we conflate intelligence with creativity, . . . we can no longer distinguish between the expert (the person highly skilled in a domain) and the creator (one who expands a domain in new and unexpected ways). We would also fail to recognize that creative individuals stand out particularly in terms of their restless temperament and personality, whereas experts efficiently process informational content and accept the status quo.

Consider also what would happen if we stretched intelligence to include good or evil attitudes and behaviors. By making that incursion into morality, we would confront human values within a culture. Granted, a few values probably can be expressed generically enough so that they command universal respect: One promising candidate is the Golden Rule (in its biblical version, in other religions' versions, or in the contemporary version introduced by the sociologist Amitai Etzioni: Respect the mores of your society).[1] However, most other values—even such seemingly

---

[1]The Golden Rule is discussed in A. Etzioni, *The New Golden Rule* (New York: Basic Books, 1996).

unproblematic ones as the rejection of theft, killing, or lying—turn out to be specific to cultures or subcultures.

If we conflated morality and intelligence, we would need to deal with widely discrepant views of what is good and bad, and why—vexing questions about abortion, capital punishment, holy wars, marriage between relatives, patriotism, treatment of strangers, and more. Consider too that people who score high on tests of moral reasoning often act immorally outside the test situations, even as courageous and self-sacrificing people turn out to be unremarkable on tests of moral reasoning.[2] Many of those who hid Jews or other persecuted people during World War II lacked education or sophistication. In contrast, eight of the fourteen men who laid plans to implement the Final Solution held doctoral degrees from major European universities.[3]

Furthermore, Adolf Hitler and Joseph Stalin probably knew full well which situations were considered moral in their culture, but they either did not care (Stalin commented, "How many divisions does the Pope have?" and Hitler extolled the Big Lie) or embraced their own peculiar codes ("Wiping out a generation is a necessary, indeed inevitable, move if you are committed to the establishment of a Communist state." Or "Eliminating Jews is the moral imperative in quest of an Aryan society.")

The notion of an "emotional intelligence" proves problematic in certain respects.[4] Unlike language or space, emotions are not "contents" to be processed. Rather, cognition has evolved so that we can make sense of human beings (self and others) who have and experience emotions. Emotions do accompany cognition, and they may well prove more salient under certain circumstances; they accompany our interactions with others, our listening to music, and our efforts to solve mathematical puzzles. Calling *some* intelligences emotional implies that other intelligences are not, and that implication flies in the face of experience and empirical data. Further problems arise when we conflate emotional intelligence with a certain recommended pattern of behavior—a temptation to which Daniel Goleman sometimes succumbs in his otherwise admirable *Emotional Intelligence*. Goleman singles out as "emotionally intelligent" people who use their understanding of emotions to make others feel

---

[2]Moral reasoning tests are compared with moral behaviors in A. Colby and W. Damon, *Some Do Care* (New York: Free Press, 1992).

[3]On the men who laid the plans to implement the Final Solution, see D. Patterson, *When Learned Men Murder* (Bloomington, Ind.: Phi Delta Kappan Educational Foundation, 1996).

[4]See D. Goleman, *Emotional Intelligence* (New York: Bantam, 1995).

better, solve conflicts, or cooperate in home or work situations. I certainly cherish such people, but we cannot assume that being emotionally intelligent means those skills will be used for socially desirable ends.

For these reasons, I prefer the term *emotional sensitivity*, which applies to those who are sensitive to emotions in themselves and others—that is, individuals who exhibit the personal intelligences (in my own terminology). Presumably, clinicians and salespeople excel in sensitivity to others; poets and mystics, in sensitivity to the melodies of their own psyches. And there are others—autistic or psychopathic persons, for example—who seem completely deaf to the emotional realm. I insist, however, on a strict distinction between being emotionally sensitive and being a "good" or "moral" person, since someone who is sensitive to others' emotions may still manipulate, deceive, or create hatred. I call, then, for a delineation of intelligence that includes the full range of contents to which human beings are sensitive, but excludes such valued but separate human traits as creativity, morality, and emotional appropriateness. This delineation makes scientific and epistemological sense; it reinvigorates but does not break the elastic band; and it helps resolve two remaining struggles: how to assess intelligences and how to connect intelligences to other virtues.

The Assessment of Intelligences

All societies want to place the most appropriate people in positions of importance, but the most desirable niches often have far more candidates than can be accommodated. Hence, some forms of assessment are almost inevitable. Once we restrict the definition of *intelligence* to human information-processing and product-making capacities, we can use and supplement the established technology of assessment. We can continue to use paper-and-pencil or computer-adapted techniques, while simultaneously looking at a broader range of capacities, such as sensitivity to musical patterns or the understanding of people's motivations. And we can avoid ticklish, and possibly unanswerable, questions about the assessment of values and morality. But even with a limited definition of intelligence, important questions remain about which assessment path to follow. Here I hold strong views. I consider it a fool's errand to embrace the search for a "pure" intelligence—whether general intelligence, musical intelligence, or interpersonal intelligence. I do not believe that such alchemical cognitive essences actually exist; they are an outcome of our penchant for creating (and then attributing reality to) terminology rather than searching for determinable, measurable entities. Moreover, the correlations that have been found between allegedly "pure measures" (like certain brain-wave patterns that purport to measure intelligence directly) and the skills we actually value in the world (like mathematical problem solving and good writing) are too modest to be useful.

What matters is the use of intelligences, individually and in concert, to carry out tasks valued by a society. Accordingly, we should be assessing people's success in carrying out valued tasks that presumably involve certain intelligences. For example, instead of testing musical intelligence by looking at evoked cortical responses when someone is listening to pure tones, we should teach people to sing songs, play instruments, or compose or transform melodies, and then determine how well they have mastered these tasks. By the same token, we should not search for immaculate emotional sensitivity—for example, with tests of galvanic skin response to a word or photograph. Rather, we should observe people in real-life situations where *they* have to be sensitive to the aspirations and motives of others. For example, we can see how someone handles a fight between two teenagers or convinces a supervisor to change an undesirable policy. These are realistic contexts for assessing mastery of the emotional realm.

Increasingly, we have another assessment option: simulations. We are now in a position to use technologies that not only can present realistic situations or problems but can also measure performance through virtual realities, and even "intelligently" select subsequent steps in light of responses on earlier phases of the simulations. Thus, presenting a student with an unfamiliar tune on a computer and having him learn the tune, transpose it, and orchestrate it can reveal much about his intelligence in musical matters. Similarly, we can learn about interpersonal or emotional sensitivity by simulating human interactions and asking people to judge the shifting motivations of each actor. For example, subjects can give their running reactions to members of a jury who are attempting to reach a verdict on a sensitive case. Or one can create an interactive hypermedia program—for example, a program that features members of an organization as they are grappling with a major change in corporate strategy—and ask respondents to react to the virtual (or "real") people's moves even as those moves are being altered by the program.

An increase in the breadth, or elasticity, of our concept of intelligence, then, should open the possibility for innovative forms of assessment that are far more authentic than the classical short-answer examinations. Why settle for an IQ test or an SAT, on which the items are at best remote "proxies" for the ability to design experiments, write essays, critique musical performances, or resolve a dispute? Why not instead ask people to *do* the things—either in person or on-line? As long as we do not open the Pandora's box of values and subjectivity, we can continue to use established insights and technologies judiciously. Of course, if we used the psychometricians' traditional armamentaria, we could create an instrument to test any conceivable virtue (or vice), including morality, creativity, and emotional intelligence. Indeed, since Goleman's landmark book, there have been dozens of efforts to create tests for emotional intelligence. But such instruments are far more likely to satisfy the test makers' desires for reliability (that is, each testee would get roughly the same score on two separate administrations of an instrument) than the need for validity (that is, the test measures the trait it purports to measure, such as emotional sensitivity within one's family or at the workplace).

These kinds of instruments are questionable for two reasons: First, it is too difficult to agree on what it means to be emotionally intelligent—consider the different interpretations that might be given by Jesse Helms and Jesse Jackson, or Margaret Thatcher and Margaret Mead. Second, "scores" on such tests are more likely to reveal test-taking savvy (people's skills in language and logical inference) than fundamental emotional acuity.

We are at a turning point. A tight view of assessment is likely to produce reliable instruments that correlate well with one another but do not broaden the sample of talents to be surveyed or the range of individuals who will stand out. A subtler view opens up many new and exciting possibilities. We will be able to look directly at the skills and capacities we value, and we will give people a variety of ways to demonstrate what they know and what they can do. Rather than just selecting one kind of a person, we may help to place many kinds of people in positions well matched to their skills and aspirations. If assessment is to be reinvented, such innovations point the way.

Connecting Intelligences to Other Virtues

While broadening the definition of intelligence, I have steadfastly argued that the expansion of the band must be regulated. We cannot hijack the word *intelligence* so that it becomes all things to all people—the psychometric equivalent of the Holy Grail. Yet the problem remains: How, in a post-Aristotelian, post-Confucian era, one in which psychometrics still looms large, should we think about the virtuous human being—the human being who is justly admired because of his or her personal qualities? One promising approach is to recognize that intelligences, creativity, and morality—to mention just three commonly recognized virtues—are separate. Each may require its own measurement or assessment, and certain species or subspecies of these virtues will prove far easier to assess objectively than others. Indeed, with respect to creativity and morality, we are more likely to rely on overall judgments by disinterested experts than on any putative test battery. At the same time, we might well look for people who combine attributes: people who have musical *and* interpersonal intelligence, who are psychometrically intelligent *and* creative in the arts, who combine emotional sensitivity *and a* high standard of moral conduct.

Consider that selective colleges pay much attention to scholastic performance, as measured by the College Entrance Examination Board and secondary school grades; but they also weigh other features, and sometimes a student with lower test scores but high value in citizenship or motivation is chosen over one who has "aced" the tests. Admissions officers do not confound these virtues (indeed, they may use different "scales" and issue different "grades"), but they recognize the attractiveness of candidates who exemplify two or more of these desirable traits.

We probably will never recreate an Eden where intellectual and ethical values commingle, and we should recognize that these virtues can be separate. Indeed, despite the appeal of the Confucian or Grecian hero, these virtues are often all too remote from one another. Thus, when we attempt to aggregate the virtues, through phrases like "emotional intelligence," "creative intelligence," or "moral intelligence," we should realize that we are expressing a wish rather than describing a probable reality. Despite this caution, it is important to recognize that there are powerful models— people who successfully exemplify two or more cardinal human virtues. In the recent past, one can without reservation name the scientist Niels Bohr, the writer Rachel Carson, the athlete Arthur Ashe, the statesman George Marshall, and the musicians Louis Armstrong, Pablo Casals, and Ella Fitzgerald. In our own time, few would challenge the singling out of Nelson Mandela.

Examining lives like these reveals human possibilities. Young people learn primarily from the examples of powerful adults around them, ones who are admirable as well as ones who are simply glamorous. Sustained attention to admirable examples may well increase the incidence of people who will eventually link capacities now considered scientifically and epistemologically separate.

Firsthand acquaintance with exemplary models probably constitutes the first step in becoming a person of multiple virtues, but exposure is not enough. Capacities must be trained. Threats to morality and decency must be identified and confronted. We need practice, with feedback, in handling morally charged situations, dilemmas that pull us in competing directions. We must learn from others but also recognize that we must sometimes go our own way. And ultimately, we must be ready to serve as role models for younger people.

The British novelist E. M. Forster counseled: "Only connect." Some expansionists in the territory of intelligence have prematurely claimed connections that do not exist. But it is within our power to help forge connections that are important for our physical and psychic survival. Just how the precise borders of intelligence are drawn is a question we can leave to scholars. But the imperative to broaden the definition of intelligence responsibly goes well beyond the academy. Who "owns" intelligence promises to be an even more critical issue in the twenty-first century than it has been in this era of the IQ test.

Remaining Puzzles: The Research Agenda

The first half of the twentieth century was the period of physics; the second, the period of molecular biology and genetics. Few doubt that the [twenty-first] century will highlight the study of the brain and mind. And, of course, exploring the nature of intelligence will be an important part of the research agenda. The research of the coming years will explore three major areas—each with two main thrusts.

The Basic Sciences of Intelligence

While intelligence has belonged largely to psychology, I see it increasingly being explored by other disciplines. On the one hand, those who work at the cellular and genetic levels are asking which genes control which aspects of intellectual functioning and how the genes work together to produce intelligent behavior. On the other hand, there is a growing interest in, and knowledge of, the ways human intelligence is applied in different social and cultural contexts.[5]

We already know of genes or gene clusters that code for specific cognitive abilities like reading and spatial capacities, and there may be others that are critical in the attainment of high IQ-test scores. The interest in the structure of specific human abilities is magnified by new imaging techniques; we now can examine the neural structures involved

---

[5]Identifying the genes for general intelligence: M. J. Chorney, K. Chorney et al., "A Quantitative Trait Locus Associated with Cognitive Ability in Children," *Psychological Science*, 9, no. 3 (May 1998): 159–66.

in particular aspects of language (like reading, naming, and learning foreign languages), music (like rhythm and tonal perception), and even the understanding of people's minds, which proves crucial in interpersonal intelligence. At the other end of the scientific spectrum, within our own society, ethnographic investigators are studying different work settings and trying to determine which intelligences people use alone and in concert to accomplish important tasks. Studies of the building of a computer and of the navigation of a huge carrier reveal, for example, that no single individual understands the entire process; rather, this type of intelligent behavior depends upon capacities distributed across numerous individuals.[6]

Cross-cultural studies continue to challenge our notions of human intellect. We look at contemporary societies and note the different emphases placed, for example, on sensitivity to others, on the capacity to cooperate with strangers, or on various putative psychic capacities like meditation or healing. And retrospectively we can also study intelligences of an earlier era. The archaeologist Stephen Mithen, for example, has described the naturalist and technological intelligences that may have been important for the forerunners of *Homo sapiens* 250,000 to 500,000 years ago.[7]

These lines of study help us appreciate the limitations of singular views of intelligence, formulated largely in terms of the capacities needed to exist in a certain kind of European or American school one century ago.

The Operations of Intelligences

Information-processing techniques and computer simulations offer powerful ways of learning how people perform specific tasks, from understanding a foreign language to creating a piece of music. Such studies not only will facilitate the development of software that excels at these tasks but also will suggest the kind of training that can improve the performance of ordinary (and extraordinarily talented or impaired) people. It is equally important to understand those capacities that extend beyond the operations of single intelligences or subintelligences. Cognitively oriented

---

[6]Intelligences used in concert: E. Hutchins, "The Social Organization of Distributed Intelligence," in *Perspectives in Socially Shaped Cognition*, ed. L. B. Resnick, J. M. Levine, and D. Teasley (Washington D.C.: American Psychological. 283–307); T. Kidder, *The Soul of a New Machine* (Boston: Little, Brown, 1981).

[7]The forerunners of *Homo sapiens* are discussed in S. Mithen, *The Prehistory of the Mind* (London: Thames & Hudson, 1996).

researchers will probe in two directions. They will investigate the ways in which particular intelligences work together, in general or on specific tasks. And they will explore those capacities that seem to cut across different intelligences—the making of metaphors and analogies, the capacity to synthesize information, the emergence of wisdom. Unfortunately, MI [multiple intelligence] theory has not made much progress in explicating the nature of these transintellectual capacities. And these capacities have also eluded investigators from other psychological camps. It is probably true that some capacities, like the making of metaphors, will turn out to be part of the basic cognitive equipment of all human beings, while others, like the capacity to synthesize different bodies of information, require a culture that has cultivated these encyclopedic skills over a long period.

Shifting Demands

Two 1997 events symbolize tidal shifts in world culture: the defeat of chess champion Gary Kasparov by the IBM "Deep Blue" computer program proved once and for all that a machine could be "smarter" than the cleverest human performer in a domain long cherished by the intelligentsia. And the cloning of the sheep Dolly by the Scottish scientist Ian Wilmut and his colleagues demonstrated the potential to engage in the most profound experiments of genetic engineering.[8] Some people would like to turn their backs on these events, because they fear a world in which machines dominate human beings or because they don't want to see people play God by controlling the genetic options of future generations. I share these reservations, though I doubt whether it is possible to prevent human beings from exploring such possibilities. However impressive, Dolly and Deep Blue are products of technology; they are neither good nor evil in themselves. We humans, operating individually and as a corporate body, must judge how the technology that spawned these "creatures" should be used or not used.

Many of us would welcome a society in which drudgery is eliminated because robots carry out mindless work. But a society freed of much human labor can turn in two opposite directions. We might be freed to exercise higher powers of mind in the arts or in other creative spheres, or we might surrender to the pursuit of mind-numbing entertainment, either benign (like television comedies or soap operas) or malignant (the bread and circuses held in amphitheaters during the decline of Rome).

---

[8]On the cloning of the sheep Dolly, see G. Kolata, *Clone: The Road to Dolly and the Path Ahead* (New York: Morrow, 1998).

As a species, we remain free to become smart or stupid, moral or immoral, in various ways.

The options offered by genetic engineering are even sharper. Even those who are repelled by the idea of cloning or more aggressive forms of eugenics understand the appeal of testing for the lethal gene of, say, Huntington's chorea and, if possible, turning it off. But the decisions first exercised in the realm of bodily disease will sooner or later reverberate in the corridors of personality and intellect. We have to ask whether we want to eliminate the genes that give rise to dyslexia, and we may have to ask whether we will tolerate genetic engineering aimed at producing individuals who excel at mathematics, chess, music making, or the less appealing capacity to manipulate others. The identification of new intelligences and a superior understanding of how they operate will stimulate geneticists to probe the biological underpinning of these capacities and, by the same token, geneticists' discoveries will alert us to the possibility of new or different configurations among human intellectual capacities.

No single authority has the right to make decisions in crucial realms like artificial intelligence or genetic engineering. But this does not mean that the opposite is true: that these decisions do not belong to anybody or that marketplace forces should be allowed to determine what is done. We cannot have a society in which people abdicate personal responsibility, dismiss the need to debate issues, and reject outright approaches that might be reasonable. Human societies can and must participate actively in decisions that affect the health and well-being of the planet. The primary responsibility rests upon those who actually work in fields like engineering or genetics. They know the field best and therefore have the potential to discern misapplications before those become clear to outsiders. But because intimacy is rarely correlated with disinterestedness, I place an equal burden of responsibility on those who work in neighboring fields, who have enough familiarity to make informed judgments, and also can take a neutral or broader stance. We must not remove responsibility from those who are closest to the action. But ordinary citizens sometimes have better instincts than those whose lives are immersed in a discipline. The problem is that ordinary citizens are typically poorly informed and so are easy prey to misrepresentations and deceptions.

I place hope in four groups: better-trained journalists who can clarify options for the public, political leaders who have studied the issues and are able to explain them, ordinary citizens who are willing to inform themselves about the issues enough to share the decision-making burden with experts, and leaders or "trustees" of domains who will put aside their own ambitions to promote a wider good. Unfortunately, rewards in our society today favor none of these options. Yet the stakes could not be higher: if we do not make the most informed decisions—I might even say the most *intelligent* decisions—about our genetic and cultural destinies, we may find it has become too late.

For the next millennium, I nominate a new virtue: *species humility*. In the past, we honored those (like St. Francis) who were humble, even as we scorned leaders and groups guilty of hubris. But we are now one, inextricably bound world, and the unimaginable, in many forms, has become possible. As a species, we must somehow arrive at decisions about what we will do and what we will not, about which Pandora's boxes to open and which to keep shut. We have eliminated smallpox and polio, and we stand on the verge of eliminating biological warfare and land mines. Perhaps we can also agree not to manipulate the intellectual capacities of future generations.

Greater Individuation: A Challenge for the Future

A wondrous feature of life is that we humans differ from one another, and, despite the homogenization of the world, our differences show no sign of declining. Indeed, the opposite is the case. Humans evolved to live in small groups, with similar experiences from one day to the next and from one generation to the next. In such milieus, the number of "models for living" were small. We now live in a global village, with rapid change and constant contact with thousands of others. The more experiences we have, the more media we are exposed to, the more people we interact with, the greater the differences that are likely to emerge. Diversity is the order of the millennium.

If the past millennium ushered in greater democracy, this one should usher in greater individuation—individuation, not in the sense of selfishness or self-seeking, but in the sense of knowledge about and respect for each individual. We already can know a great deal about individuals, and we are learning even more from genetics, psychology, and other behavioral and biological sciences. Information widely available in databases will allow us to determine how we resemble and differ from one another and will empower us to make more judicious life decisions.

We cannot avoid moral issues. Individual information can be used to manipulate us; intelligent programmed agents can serve us what they *think* we want or what they *want us* to want. And there is no guarantee that we will make sensible use of information about ourselves. In certain spheres we will not want to dote on our individuality; we hope, for example, that everyone will honor the laws of driving and will show civility to each other on the road. But when it comes to learning, using our minds well, and informing others and being informed by others, there need be no limitations. Knowledge need not be competitive; we can all increase our own knowledge and the knowledge of others without end, without the peril of zero-sum situations. Indeed, information about our own minds and the minds of others can be mobilized to broaden our understandings in myriad ways and to open up new vistas.

Everyone acknowledges the importance of science and technology, but it is also important to remember the necessity for the arts and the humanities. The sciences deal with general principles, universal laws, and broad predictions; the arts and humanities deal with individuality. We learn about seminal historical figures in their individuality; we explore the psyches of diverse (and often perverse) characters in literature; we gain from artists' and musicians' reflections of their own emotional lives through their works. Every time we are exposed to a new individual—in person or in spirit—our own horizons broaden. And the possibilities of experiencing different consciousnesses never diminish. The humanist of classical times said, "Nothing human is alien to me"; and the saga of individual consciousnesses cannot be reduced to formulas or generalizations.

Here, we connect to multiple human intelligences. Granted only our species membership, we are fundamentally alike. Factoring in each person's unique genetic blueprint, we become capable of achieving different potentials, and our different family and cultural milieus ensure that we will eventually become distinct human beings. Because our genes and our experiences are unique and because our brains must figure out meanings, no two selves, no two consciousnesses, no two minds are exactly alike. Each of us is therefore situated to make a unique contribution to the world. In the recognition of our individuality, we may discover our deepest common tie—that we are all joint products of natural and cultural evolution. And we may discover why we must join forces, in a complementary but synergistic way, to make sure that Nature and Culture survive for future generations.

10

THE BALANCE
THEORY OF WISDOM

Robert J. Sternberg

THE CURRENT THEORY VIEWS successful intelligence and creativity as the bases for wisdom. Successful intelligence and creativity are necessary, but not sufficient, conditions for wisdom. Particularly important is tacit knowledge, which is critical to practical intelligence.

The Balance Theory

Wisdom as Successful Intelligence and Creativity Balancing Interests

Wisdom is defined as the application of successful intelligence and creativity as mediated by values toward the achievement of a common good through a balance among (a) intrapersonal, (b) interpersonal, and (c) extrapersonal interests, over (a) short and (b) long terms, in order to achieve a balance among (a) adaptation to existing environments, (b) shaping of existing environments, and (c) selection of new environments, as shown in Figure 10.1.

Thus, wisdom is not just about maximizing one's own or someone else's self-interest, but about balancing various self-interests (intrapersonal) with the interests of others (interpersonal) and of other aspects of the context in which one lives (extrapersonal), such as one's city or country or environment or even God. Wisdom also involves creativity, in that the wise solution to a problem may be far from obvious.

Figure 10.1.

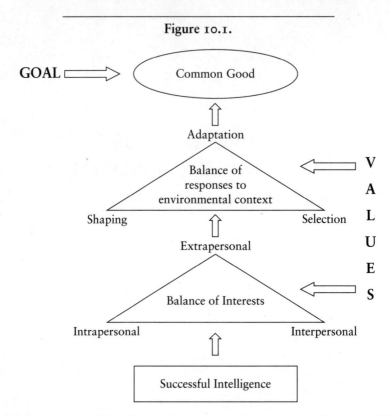

Wisdom as successful intelligence balancing goals, responses, and interests. The individual applies successful intelligence in order to seek a common good. Such application involves balancing of intrapersonal, interpersonal, and extrapersonal interests to adapt to, shape, and select environments. Judgments regarding how to achieve a common good inevitably involve the infusion of values.

An implication of this view is that when one applies successful intelligence and creativity, one may deliberately seek outcomes that are good for oneself and bad for others. In wisdom, one certainly may seek good ends for oneself, but one also seeks common good outcomes for others. If one's motivations are to maximize certain people's interests and minimize other people's, wisdom is not involved. In wisdom, one seeks a common good, realizing that this common good may be better for some than for others. A terrorist may be academically intelligent; he may be practically intelligent; he cannot be wise.

Problems requiring wisdom always involve at least some element of each of intrapersonal, interpersonal, and extrapersonal interests. For example, one might decide that it is wise to take a particular teaching position, a decision that seemingly involves only one person. But many people are typically affected by an individual's decision to take a job—significant others, children, perhaps parents and friends. And the decision always has to be made in the context of what the whole range of available options is. Thus, people have to know what the options are and what they mean. To be wise, one must know what one knows, know what one does not know, know what can be known, and know what cannot be known at a given time or place.

What kinds of considerations might be included under each of the three kinds of interests? Intrapersonal interests might include the desire to enhance one's popularity or prestige, to make more money, to learn more, to increase one's spiritual well-being, to increase one's power, and so forth. Interpersonal interests might be quite similar, except as they apply to other people rather than oneself. Extrapersonal interests might include contributing to the welfare of one's school, helping one's community, contributing to the well-being of one's country, or serving God, and so forth. Different people balance these interests in different ways. At one extreme, a malevolent dictator might emphasize his or her own personal power and wealth; at the other extreme, a saint might emphasize only serving others and God.

Failures in balancing intrapersonal, interpersonal, and extrapersonal interests can have devastating effects. Consider some examples.

Although both Richard Nixon and Bill Clinton, as presidents, were rather self-absorbed, neither was wise. Wisdom involves a balancing not only of the three kinds of interests, but also of three possible courses of action in response to this balancing: adaptation of oneself or others to existing environments; shaping of environments in order to render them more compatible with oneself or others; and selection of new environments. In adaptation, the individual tries to find ways to conform to the existing environment that forms his or her context. Sometimes adaptation is the best course of action under a given set of circumstances. But typically one seeks a balance between adaptation and shaping, realizing that fit to an environment requires not only changing oneself, but changing the environment as well. When an individual finds it impossible or at least implausible to attain such a fit, he or she may decide to select a new environment altogether, leaving, for example, a job, a community, a marriage, or whatever.

Wisdom manifests itself as a series of processes, which are typically cyclical and can occur in a variety of orders. These processes are the meta-components of thought, including (a) recognizing the existence of a problem, (b) defining the nature of the problem, (c) representing information about the problem, (d) formulating a strategy for solving the problem, (e) allocating resources to the solution of a problem, (f) monitoring one's solution of the problem, and (g) evaluating feedback regarding that solution. In deciding about a teaching job, for example, one first has to see both taking the position and not taking it as viable options (problem recognition); then figure out exactly what taking or not taking the position would mean for oneself (defining the problem); then consider the costs and benefits to oneself and others (representing information about the problem); and so forth.

Wisdom is typically acquired by what I have referred to . . . as knowledge-acquisition components (Sternberg, 1985). Its acquisition depends on (a) selectively encoding new information that is relevant for one's purposes in learning about that context; (b) selectively comparing this information to old information to see how the new fits with the old; and (c) selectively combining pieces of information to make them fit together into an orderly whole (Sternberg, Wagner, & Okagaki, 1993).

This treatment of wisdom, which emphasizes the role of tacit knowledge, should not be interpreted to mean that formal knowledge is not or cannot be relevant to wise judgments and decision making. Quite the contrary: Obviously formal knowledge can be and often is extremely relevant to wise judgments and decision making. For example, consider the story of Solomon's judgment regarding the two women claiming to be the mother of the same infant. Stories of wise leadership are often learned in formal settings. But these aspects of knowledge, although relevant to wise judgments, need to be connected to such judgments via tacit knowledge. For example, consider the decision of Nelson Mandela in school to unify his country. But when to apply this knowledge, where to apply it, how to apply it, to whom to apply it, even why to apply it—these are the stuff of tacit knowledge. They are not and cannot be directly taught in school lessons. They are the lessons learned from experience. They can be learned in school, but they are not directly taught out of textbooks or lectures.

Sources of Developmental and Individual Differences in Wisdom

The balance theory suggests a number of sources of developmental and individual differences in wisdom. In particular, there are two kinds of sources, those directly affecting the balance processes and those that are antecedent.

Individual and Developmental Differences
Directly Affecting the Balance Processes

There are seven sources of differences directly affecting the balance processes. Consider, as an example, a teacher who has been instructed by a principal to spend almost all of his time teaching in a way to maximize students' scores on a statewide assessment test, but who believes that the principal is essentially forcing him to abandon truly educating his students.

1. *Goals.* People may differ in terms of the extent to which they seek a common good, and thus in the extent to which they aim for the essential goal of wisdom. They also may differ in terms of what they view as the common good. The teacher may believe it is not in the children's best interest to engage in what he views as mindless drills for a test. The principal, however, may have a different view. The teacher is thus left with the responsibility of deciding what is in the best interests of all concerned.

2. *Balancing Responses to Environmental Contexts.* People may differ in their balance of responses to environmental contexts. Responses always reflect in the interaction of the individual making the judgment and the environment, and people can interact with contexts in myriad ways. The teacher may adapt to the environment and do exactly what the principal has told him to do, or shape the environment and do exactly what he believes he should do, or try to find some balance between adaptation and shaping that largely meets the principal's goals but also largely meets his own. Or the teacher may decide that the environment of the school is sufficiently aversive to his philosophy of teaching that he would prefer to teach elsewhere.

3. *Balancing of Interests.* People may balance interests in different ways. The teacher must decide how to balance his own interests in good teaching and also in staying on good terms with the principal; the children's interests in learning but also doing well on the statewide tests; the parents' interests in having well-educated children; and so on.

4. *Balancing of Short and Long Terms.* People may differ in their emphases. The teacher may believe that, in the long run, a proper education involves much more than preparing for statewide tests, but at the same time realize that, in the short run, the children's scores on the tests will affect their future as well as his future and possibly those of his principal and school.

5. *Acquisition of Tacit Knowledge.* People differ in the extent to which they acquire tacit knowledge. The teacher may bring relatively sophisticated tacit knowledge to solving this problem of how to teach the children, or may bring virtually no tacit knowledge and may have no clear option other than to do what the principal says.

6. *Utilization of Tacit Knowledge.* People differ in how well and how fully they utilize the tacit knowledge they have acquired. The teacher may decide to teach in a way that represents a compromise between his own views and those of the principal, but the way in which this decision is implemented will depend on his knowledge of how to balance the various interests involved in the decision.

7. *Values.* People have different values mediating their utilization of intelligence and creativity in the balancing of interests and responses. Values may vary somewhat across space and time, as well as among individuals within a given cultural context. The teacher's values may require him to diverge at least somewhat from the instructions of the principal. Another teacher's values might lead him to do what the principal says, regardless of how he personally feels. Nevertheless, there seem to be certain core values that are common to the world's great ethical systems and religions. They include values such as honesty, sincerity, reciprocity, compassion, and courage.

These sources of differences produce variations in how wise people are and in how well they can apply their wisdom in different kinds of situations. To the extent that wisdom is typically associated with greater intellectual and even physical maturity, it is presumably because the development of tacit knowledge and of values is something that unfolds over the course of the life span, not in childhood or in the early years of adulthood.

The above sources of individual differences pertain to the balancing processes. Other sources are antecedent to these processes.

Relations of Wisdom to Other Skills

Wisdom is related to other psychological constructs but not identical to any of them. In particular, it is related to knowledge, as well as to analytical, creative, and practical aspects of intelligence, and other aspects of intelligence.

First, wisdom requires knowledge, but the heart of wisdom is tacit, informal knowledge of the kind learned in the school of life, not the kind of explicit formal knowledge taught in schools. One could be a "walking encyclopedia" and show little or no wisdom because the knowledge one needs to be wise is not found in encyclopedias or even, generally, in the type of teaching found in most schools (with the possible exception of those that teach Socratically).

Second, wisdom requires analytical thinking, but it is not the kind of analytical thinking typically emphasized in schools or measured on tests of academic abilities and achievements (discussed in Sternberg, 1980). Rather it is the analysis of real-world dilemmas where clean and neat abstractions often give way to messy and disorderly concrete interests. The kind of abstract analytical thinking that may lead to outstanding performance on a test such as the Raven Matrices, which present figural reasoning items, will be of some but not much use in complex real-world dilemmas such as how to defuse the conflict between India and Pakistan.

An important part of analytical thinking is metacognition. Wisdom seems related to metacognition because the metacomponents involved in wisdom are similar or identical to those that follow from other accounts of metacognition (for example, Campione, Brown, & Ferrara, 1982; Nelson, 1999). Thus, in wisdom, as in other types of thinking, one needs to define problems, formulate strategies to solve problems, allocate resources to the solution of these problems, and so forth. These processes are used in wisdom, as they are in other types of thinking, but in wisdom they are used to balance different types of interests in order to seek a common good.

Third, wise solutions are often creative ones, as King Solomon demonstrated in cleverly determining which of two women was truly the mother of a child. But the kind of crowd-defying, buy-low, sell-high attitude that leads to creative contributions does not in itself lead to wisdom. Creative people often tend toward extremes, although their later contributions may be more integrative (Gardner, 1993). Creative thinking is often brash whereas wise thinking is balanced. This is not to say that the same people cannot be both creative and wise. It is to say, however, that the kinds of thinking required to be creative and wise are different and thus will not necessarily be found in the same person. Moreover, teaching people to think creatively (see, for example, Sternberg & Williams, 1996) will not teach them to think wisely.

Wisdom is also related to creatively insightful thinking. According to Sternberg and Davidson (1982), the three knowledge-acquisition components correspond to three kinds of insights, and these three components of knowledge acquisition are also used in the acquisition of wisdom and other kinds of thinking. Selective comparison insights, for example, are used in analogical problem solving when one solves a current problem by applying information obtained in the past in solving a related kind of problem. For example, deciding whether a military campaign will prove to be another "Vietnam" involves selective comparison: Is the new campaign going to be enough like the Vietnam campaign to lead to a similar disaster?

It is important to note that although wise thinking must be, to some extent, creative, creative thinking (as discussed above) need not be wise. Wise thinking must be creative to some extent because it generates a novel and problem-relevant high-quality solution involving balancing of interests, and novelty and appropriate quality are the two hallmarks of creativity (see essays in Sternberg, 1999a). But a solution can be creative—as in solving a mathematical proof—but have no particular characteristics of wisdom. The proof involves no balancing of interests and no search for a common good. It is simply an intellectual problem involving creative thinking.

Fourth, practical thinking is closer to wisdom than are analytical and creative thinking, but again, it is not the same. Wisdom is a particular kind of practical thinking. It (a) balances competing intrapersonal, interpersonal, and extrapersonal interests, over short and (b) long terms, (c) balances adaptation to, shaping of, and selection of environments, in (d) the service of a common good. Thus, people can be good practical thinkers without being wise but they cannot be wise without being good practical thinkers. Good practical thinking is necessary but not sufficient for the manifestation of wisdom.

Fifth, wisdom also seems to bear at least some relation to constructs such as social intelligence (Cantor & Kihlstrom, 1987; Kihlstrom & Cantor, 2000; Sternberg & Smith, 1985), emotional intelligence (Goleman, 1995; Mayer & Salovey, 1993; Salovey & Mayer, 1990), and interpersonal and intrapersonal intelligences (Gardner, 1983, 1999). There are also differences, however. Social intelligence can be applied to understanding and getting along with others, to any ends, for any purposes. Wisdom seeks out a good through a balancing of interests. Thus, a salesperson who figures out how to sell a worthless product to a customer might do so through using social intelligence to understand the customer's wants, but has not applied wisdom in the process. Emotional intelligence involves understanding, judging, and regulating emotions. These skills are an important part of wisdom. But making wise judgments requires going beyond the understanding, regulation, or judgment of emotions. It requires processing the information to achieve a balance of interests and formulating a judgment that makes effective use of the information to achieve a common good. Moreover, wisdom may require a balance of interpersonal and intrapersonal intelligences, but it also requires an understanding of extrapersonal factors, and a balance of these three factors to attain a common good. Thus wisdom seems to go somewhat beyond these theoretically distinct kinds of intelligences as well. Perhaps the most salient difference among constructs is that wisdom is applied toward the achievement of ends that are perceived as yielding a common good, whereas the various kinds of intelligences may be applied deliberately toward achieving either good ends or bad ones, at least for some of the parties involved. It is interesting that the conception of wisdom proposed here is substantially closer to Chinese than to American conceptions of intelligence (Yang & Sternberg, 1997a, 1997b). One of the words used in Chinese to characterize intelligence is the same as the word used to characterize wisdom. . . .

Developing Wise Thinking

Why Should Wisdom Be Included in the School Curriculum?

The development of wisdom is beneficial because the judgments it yields can improve our quality of life and conduct (Kekes, 1995). Knowledge can and indeed must accompany wisdom. People need knowledge to draw on in rendering judgments—knowledge of human nature, of life circumstances, or strategies that succeed and strategies that fail. Although knowledge is necessary for wisdom, it is not sufficient for it. Merely having knowledge does not entail its use in judging rightly, soundly, or justly. Many highly knowledgeable individuals lead lives that are unhappy. Some of them make decisions that are poor or even reprehensible. [The twentieth] century provides many examples of such decisions.

There are several reasons why schools should seriously consider including instruction in wisdom-related skills in the school curriculum.

First, as noted above, knowledge is insufficient for wisdom and certainly does not guarantee satisfaction or happiness. Wisdom seems a better vehicle for the attainment of these goals.

Second, wisdom provides a mindful and considered way to enter considered and deliberative values into important judgments. One cannot be wise and at the same time impulsive or mindless (Langer, 1997) in one's judgments.

Third, wisdom represents an avenue to creating a better, more harmonious world. Dictators such as Adolf Hitler and Joseph Stalin may have been knowledgeable and may even have been good critical thinkers, at least with regard to the maintenance of their own power. Given the definition of wisdom, however, it would be hard to argue they were wise.

Fourth and finally, students—who will later become parents and leaders—are always part of a greater community and hence will benefit from learning to judge rightly, soundly, or justly on behalf of their community (Ardelt, 1997; Sternberg, 1990, 1998b, 1999b; Varela, 1999).

If the future is plagued with conflict and turmoil, this instability does not simply reside *out there somewhere*; it resides and has its origin *in ourselves*. For all these reasons, we endorse teaching students not only to recall facts and to think critically (and even creatively) about the content of the subjects they learn, but to think wisely about it, too.

Some Past Orientations and Programs Relevant to the Development of Wisdom

What would education that fostered wisdom look like? Three previous programs seem particularly related to the goals of the proposed orientation of teaching for wisdom. All have been proposed by educators with a primarily philosophical orientation. The first program, *Philosophy for Children* (Lipman, 1982; Lipman, Sharp, & Oscanyan, 1980), uses a set of novels to develop analytical-thinking skills in children. Children read the novels and learn to evaluate information in them and to make judgments about the characters in the novels and the kinds of choices they should make in their lives. The second program is Paul's (1987) program, which emphasizes dialogical thinking, or seeing problems from a variety of perspectives. The third program is that of Perkins (1986), which emphasizes understanding of "knowledge by design"—in other words, how knowledge is designed and used to solve problems in the world. Ennis (1987) has provided a taxonomy of critical-thinking skills, many of which are required for wise thinking, and Bransford and Stein (1993), Feuerstein (1980), and Halpern (1996) have all provided systematic courses that teach skills of critical thinking needed for wise thinking. Feuerstein's (1980) program has been the most widely used of this group. Other programs also touch on aspects of the proposed instruction described here (see Reigeluth et al.'s [1999] book on instructional-design theories and models for descriptions of a variety of programs).

It is impossible to speak of wisdom outside the context of a set of values, which in combination may lead one to a moral stance, or, in Kohlberg's (1969, 1983) view, stage. The same can be said of all practical intelligence: behavior is viewed as practically intelligent as a function of what is valued in a societal/cultural context. Values mediate how one balances interests and responses, and collectively contribute even to how one defines a common good. The intersection of wisdom with the moral domain can be seen in the overlap between the notion of wisdom presented here and that of moral reasoning as it applies in the two highest stages (4 and 5) of Kohlberg's (1969) theory. Wisdom also involves caring for others as well as oneself (Gilligan, 1982). At the same time, wisdom is broader than moral reasoning. It applies to any human problem involving a balance of intrapersonal, interpersonal, and extrapersonal interests, whether or not moral issues are at stake.

Sixteen Principles of Teaching for Wisdom Derived from the Balance Theory of Wisdom

There are sixteen principles derived from the balance theory that form the core of how wisdom can be developed in the classroom:

1. Explore with students the notion that conventional abilities and achievements are not enough for a satisfying life. Many people become trapped in their lives and, despite feeling conventionally successful, feel that their lives lack fulfillment. Fulfillment is not an alternative to success, but is an aspect of it that, for most people, goes beyond money, promotions, large houses, and so forth.

2. Demonstrate how wisdom is critical for a satisfying life. In the long run, wise decisions benefit people in ways that foolish decisions never do.

3. Teach students the usefulness of interdependence—a rising tide raises all ships; a falling tide can sink them.

4. Teach role-model wisdom because what you do is more important than what you say. Wisdom is action-dependent and wise actions need to be demonstrated.

5. Have students read about wise judgments and decision making so they understand that there are such means of judging and decision making.

6. Help students to recognize their own interests, those of other people, and those of institutions.

7. Help students to balance their own interests, those of other people, and those of institutions.

8. Teach students that the "means" by which the end is obtained matters, not just the end.

9. Help students learn the roles of adaptation, shaping, and selection, and how to balance them. Wise judgments are dependent in part on selecting among these environmental responses.

10. Encourage students to form, critique, and integrate their own values in their thinking.

11. Encourage students to think dialectically, realizing that both questions and their answers evolve over time, and that the answer to an important life question can differ at different times in one's life (such as whether to go to college).

12. Show students the importance of dialogical thinking, whereby they understand interests and ideas from multiple points of view.

13. Teach students to search for and then try to reach the common good—a good where everyone wins, not only those with whom one identifies.

14. Encourage and reward wisdom.

15. Teach students to monitor events in their lives and their own thought processes about these events. One way to recognize others' interests is to begin to identify one's own.

16. Help students understand the importance of inoculating oneself against the pressures of unbalanced self-interest and small-group interest.

Procedures to Follow in Teaching for Wisdom

There are several procedures a teacher can follow in teaching for wisdom. First, students would read classic works of literature and philosophy (whether Western or otherwise) to learn and reflect on the wisdom of the sages. The rush to dump classic works in favor of modern ones makes sense only if the wisdom the modern works impart equals or exceeds that of the classic works.

Second, students would engage in class discussions, projects, and essays that encourage them to discuss the lessons they have learned from the classic works, and how they can be applied to their own lives and the lives of others. A particular emphasis would be placed on the development of dialogical and dialectical thinking. Dialogical thinking (see Principle 12) involves understanding significant problems from multiple points of view, how others can legitimately conceive of things in a way quite different from one's own. Dialectical thinking (see Principle 11) involves understanding that ideas and the paradigms under which they fall evolve and keep evolving, not only from the past to the present, but from the present to the future (Hegel, 1807/1931; see also Sternberg, 1998c).

Third, students would study not only "truth," as we know it, but values as well. They would not be force-fed a set of values, but would be encouraged to develop their own values.

Fourth, such instruction would place an increased emphasis on critical, creative, and practical thinking in the service of good ends—ends that benefit not only the individual doing the thinking but others as well. All these types of thinking would be valued, not just critical thinking.

Fifth, students would be encouraged to think about how almost everything they study might be used for better or worse ends, and to realize that the ends to which knowledge is put *do* matter.

Finally, teachers would realize that the only way they can develop wisdom in their students is to serve as role models of wisdom themselves. This would, I believe, take a much more Socratic approach to teaching than teachers customarily employ. Students often want large quantities of information spoon-fed or even force-fed to them. They attempt to memorize this material for exams, only to forget it soon thereafter. In a wisdom-based approach to teaching, students will need to take a more active role. But a wisdom-based approach is not tantamount to a constructivist approach to learning. Students have not achieved or even come close to achieving wisdom when they have merely constructed their own learning. They must be able to construct knowledge not only from their own point of view, but from the point of view of others. Constructionism from only a single point of view can lead to egocentric rather than balanced understanding.

Lessons taught to emphasize wisdom would have a rather different character from lessons as they are often taught today. Consider examples.

First, social studies and especially history lessons would look very different. High school American history books typically teach American history from only one point of view, that of the new Americans. Thus Columbus is referred to as having "discovered" America, a strange notion from the standpoint of the many occupants who already lived here when it was "discovered." The conquest of the Southwest and the fall of the Alamo are presented only from the point of view of the new settlers, not from the standpoint of, say, the Mexicans who lost roughly half their territory to the invaders. This kind of ethnocentric and frankly propagandistic teaching would have no place in a curriculum that sought to develop wisdom and an appreciation of the need to balance interests.

Second, science teaching would no longer be about facts presented as though they are the final word. Science is often presented as though it represents the end of a process of evolution of thought rather than one of many midpoints (Sternberg, 1998a). Students can scarcely realize from this kind of teaching that the paradigms of today, and thus the theories and findings that emanate from them, will eventually be superseded, as the paradigms, theories, and findings of yesterday were replaced by those of today. Students would learn that, contrary to the way many textbooks are written, the classical "scientific method" is largely a fantasy rather than a reality and that scientists are as susceptible to fads as are members of other groups.

Third, teaching literature would reflect a kind of balance often absent. Literature is often taught and characters judged in terms of the standards and context of the contemporary U.S. scene today, rather than those of the time and place in which the events took place. From the proposed standpoint, the study of literature must, to some extent, proceed in the context of the study of history. Banning books often reflects the application of certain contemporary standards of which an author from the past never could have been aware.

Fourth, foreign languages would be taught in the cultural context in which they are embedded. Perhaps American students have so much more difficulty learning foreign languages than do children in much of Europe not because they lack the ability but because they lack the motivation. They do not see the need to learn another language whereas, say, a Flemish-speaking child in Belgium does. Americans might be better off if they made more of an attempt wisely to understand other cultures rather than just expecting people from other cultures to understand them. Learning the language of a culture is a key to understanding. Americans might be less quick to impose their cultural values on others if they understood the cultural values of others. It is interesting to speculate on why Esperanto, a language designed to provide a common medium of communication across cultures, has been a notable failure. Perhaps it is because Esperanto is embedded in no culture at all. It is the language of no one.

Culture cannot be taught, in the context of foreign-language learning, in the way it now often is—as an aside divorced from the actual learning of the language. It should be taught as an integral part of the language, as a primary context in which the language is embedded. The vituperative fights we see about bilingual education and about the use of Spanish in the United States or French in Canada are not just, or even primarily, fights about language. They are fights about culture, and they are fights in need of wise resolutions.

Finally, as implied throughout these examples, the curriculum needs to be far more integrated. Literature needs to be integrated with history, science with history and social-policy studies, foreign language with culture. Even within disciplines, far more integration is needed. Different approaches to psychology, for example, are often taught as competing when in fact they are totally compatible. Thus, biological, cognitive, developmental, social, and clinical psychology provide complementary viewpoints on human beings. They do not each claim to be the "right approach." The study of the brain is important, for example, but most of the insights about learning and memory that can be applied to instruction have come from behavioral and cognitive approaches, not from the biological approach.

And some of the insights that have supposedly come from the biological approach—such as "left-brain" and "right-brain" learning—are based on ignorant or outdated caricatures of research in this area rather than on actual findings.

Conclusion

The road to this new approach of teaching for wisdom is found to be a rocky one. First, entrenched structures, whatever they may be, are difficult to change, and wisdom is neither taught in schools nor even discussed. Second, many people will not see the value of teaching something that shows no promise of raising conventional test scores. These scores, which formerly were predictors of more interesting criteria, have now become criteria, or ends in themselves. The society has lost track of why they ever mattered in the first place and they have engendered the same kind of mindless competition we see in people who relentlessly compare their economic achievements with those of others. Third, wisdom is much more difficult to develop than is the kind of achievement that can be developed and readily tested via multiple-choice tests. Finally, people who have gained influence and power in a society via one means are unlikely to want either to give up that power or to see a new criterion established on which they might not rank so favorably. Thus, there is no easy path to wisdom. There never was, and probably never will be.

Wisdom might bring us a world that would seek to better itself and the conditions of all the people in it. At some level, we as a society have a choice. What do we wish to maximize through our schooling? Is it just knowledge? Is it just intelligence? Or is it also wisdom? If it is wisdom, then we need to put our students on a much different course. We need to value not only how they use their outstanding individual abilities to maximize their attainments but also how they use their individual abilities to maximize the attainments of others. We need, in short, to value wisdom.

REFERENCES

Ardelt, M. (1997). Wisdom and life satisfaction in old age. *Journals of Gerontology Series B-Psychological Sciences & Social Sciences, 52B*, 15–27.

Bransford, J. D., & Stein, B. S. (1993). *The IDEAL problem solver: A guide for improving thinking, learning, and creativity* (2nd ed.). New York: Freeman.

Campione, J. C., Brown, A. L., & Ferrara, R. (1982). Mental retardation and intelligence. In R. J. Sternberg (Ed.), *Handbook of human intelligence* (pp. 392–490). New York: Cambridge University Press.

Cantor, N., & Kihlstrom, J. F. (1987). *Personality and social intelligence.* Englewood Cliffs, NJ: Prentice Hall.

Ennis, R. H. (1987). A taxonomy of critical thinking dispositions and abilities. In J. B. Baron & R. J. Sternberg (Eds.), *Teaching thinking skills: Theory and practice* (pp. 9–26). New York: Freeman.

Feuerstein, R. (1980). *Instrumental enrichment: An intervention program for cognitive modifiability.* Baltimore, MD: University Park Press.

Gardner, H. (1983). *Frames of mind: The theory of multiple intelligences.* New York: Basic Books.

Gardner, H. (1993). *Multiple intelligences: The theory in practice.* New York: Basic Books.

Gardner, H. (1999). *Intelligence reframed: Multiple intelligences for the 21st century.* New York: Basic Books.

Gilligan, C. (1982). *In a different voice: Psychological theory and women's development.* Cambridge, MA: Harvard University Press.

Goleman, D. (1995). *Emotional intelligence.* New York: Bantam Books.

Halpern, D. F. (1996). *Thought and knowledge: An introduction to critical thinking* (2nd ed.). Mahwah, NJ: Lawrence Erlbaum Associates.

Hegel, G. W. F. (1931). *The phenomenology of the mind* (2nd ed.; J.D. Baillie, Trans). London: Allen & Unwin (original work published 1807).

Kekes, J. (1995). *Moral wisdom and good lives.* Ithaca, NY: Cornell University Press.

Kihlstrom, J. F., & Cantor, N. (2000). Social intelligence. In R. J. Sternberg (Ed.), *Handbook of intelligence* (2nd ed.)(pp. 359–379). Cambridge, U.K.: Cambridge University Press.

Kohlberg, L. (1969). Stage and sequence: The cognitive-developmental approach to socialization. In G. A. Goslin (Ed.), *Handbook of socialization theory and research* (pp. 347–380). Chicago: Rand McNally.

Kohlberg, L. (1983). *The psychology of moral development.* New York: Harper & Row.

Langer, E. J. (1997). *The power of mindful learning.* Reading, MA: Addison-Wesley Publishing Co, Inc.

Lipman, M. (1982). *Harry Stottlemeier's discovery.* Upper Montclair, NJ: First Mountain Foundation.

Lipman, M., Sharp, A. M., & Oscanyan, F. S. (1980). *Philosophy in the classroom.* Philadelphia, PA: Temple University Press.

Mayer, J. D., & Salovey, P. (1993). The intelligence of emotional intelligence. *Intelligence, 17,* 433–442.

Nelson, T. O. (1999). Cognition versus metacognition. In R. J. Sternberg (Ed.), *The nature of cognition* (pp. 625–641). Cambridge, MA: The MIT Press.

Paul, R. W. (1987). Dialogical thinking: Critical thought essential to the acquisition of rational knowledge and passions. In J. B. Baron & R. J. Sternberg (Eds.), *Teaching thinking skills: Theory and practice* (pp. 127–148). New York: Freeman.

Perkins, D. N. (1986). *Knowledge as design.* Hillsdale, NJ: Lawrence Erlbaum Associates.

Reigeluth, C. M. et al. (Eds.). (1999). *Instructional-design theories and models: A new paradigm of instructional theory, Vol. II.* Mahwah, NJ: Lawrence Erlbaum Associates.

Salovey, P., & Mayer, J. D. (1990). Emotional intelligence. *Imagination, Cognition, and Personality, 9,* 185–211.

Sternberg, R. J. (1980). Sketch of a componential subtheory of human intelligence. *Behavioral and Brain Sciences, 3,* 573–584.

Sternberg, R. J. (1985). *Beyond IQ: A triarchic theory of human intelligence.* New York: Cambridge University Press.

Sternberg, R. J. (Ed.). (1990). *Wisdom: Its nature, origins, and development.* New York: Cambridge University Press.

Sternberg, R. J. (1998a). Abilities are forms of developing expertise. *Educational Researcher, 27,* 11–20.

Sternberg, R. J. (1998b). A balance theory of wisdom. *Review of General Psychology, 2,* 347–365.

Sternberg, R. J. (1998c). The dialectic as a tool of teaching psychology. *Teaching of Psychology, 25,* 177–180.

Sternberg, R. J. (1999a). *Handbook of creativity.* New York: Cambridge University Press.

Sternberg, R. J. (1999b). The theory of successful intelligence. *Review of General Psychology, 3*, 292–316.

Sternberg, R. J., & Davidson, J. E. (Eds.). (1982, June). The mind of the puzzler. *Psychology Today, 16*, 37–44.

Sternberg, R. J., & Smith, C. (1985). Social intelligence and decoding skills in non-verbal communication. *Social Cognition, 2*, 168–192.

Sternberg, R. J., Wagner, R. K., & Okagaki, L. (1993). Practical Intelligence: The nature and role of tacit knowledge in work and at school. In H. Reese & J. Puckett (Eds.), *Advances in lifespan development* (pp. 205–227). Hillsdale, NJ: Lawrence Erlbaum Associates.

Sternberg, R. J., & Williams, W. M. (1996). *How to develop student creativity.* Alexandria, VA: Association for Supervision and Curriculum Development.

Varela, F. J. (1999). *Ethical know-how: Action, wisdom, and cognition.* Stanford, CA: Stanford University Press.

Yang, S., & Sternberg, R. J. (1997a). Conceptions of intelligence in ancient Chinese philosophy. *Journal of Theoretical and Philosophical Psychology, 17*(2), 101–119.

Yang, S., & Sternberg, R. J. (1997b). Taiwanese Chinese people's conceptions of intelligence. *Intelligence, 25*(1), 21–36.

11

REMEMBRANCE OF EMOTIONS PAST

Joseph LeDoux

*Every man has reminiscences which he would not tell to
everyone but only to his friends. He has other matters in his
mind which he would not reveal even to his friends, but only
to himself, and that in secret. But there are other things which
a man is afraid to tell even to himself, and every decent man
has a number of such things stored away in his mind.*

Fyodor Dostoevsky, *Notes from the Underground*[1]

BICYCLING. SPEAKING ENGLISH. The Pledge of Allegiance. Multiplication by 7s. The rules of dominoes. Bowel control. A taste for spinach. Immense fear of snakes. Balancing when standing. The meaning of "halcyon days." The words to "Subterranean Homesick Blues." Anxiety associated with the sound of a dentist drill. The smell of banana pudding.

What do all of these have in common? They are each things I've learned and stored in my brain. Some I've learned to do, or learned to expect; others are remembered personal experiences; and still others are just rote facts.

For a long time, it was thought that there was one kind of learning system that would take care of all the learning the brain does. During the

---

[1]Dostoyevsky (1864), quoted in Erdelyi (1985).

behaviorist reign, for example, it was assumed that psychologists could study any kind of learning in any kind of animal and find out how humans learn the things we learn. This logic was not only applied to those things that humans and animals both do, like finding food and avoiding danger, but also to things that humans do easily and animals do poorly if at all, like speaking.

It is now known that there are multiple memory systems in the brain, each devoted to different memory functions. The brain system that allowed me to learn to hit a baseball is different from the one that allows me to remember trying to hit the ball and failing, and this is different still from the system that made me tense and anxious when I stepped up to the plate after having been beaned the last time up. Though these are each forms of long-term memory (memory that lasts more than a few seconds), they are mediated by different neural networks. Different kinds of memory, like different kinds of emotions and different kinds of sensations, come out of different brain systems.

In this chapter we are going to be concerned with two learning systems that the brain uses to form memories about emotional experiences. The separate existence of these two kinds of memories in the brain is nicely illustrated by considering a famous case study in which one of these systems was damaged, but the other continued to function normally.

Is That a Pin in Your Hand or Are You Just Glad to See Me?

In the early part of [the twentieth] century, a French physician named Edouard Claparede examined a female patient who, as a result of brain damage, had seemingly lost all ability to create new memories.[2] Each time Claparede walked into the room he had to reintroduce himself to her, as she had no recollection of having seen him before. The memory problem was so severe that if Claparede left the room and returned a few minutes later, she wouldn't remember having seen him.

One day, he tried something new. He entered the room, and, as on every other day, he held out his hand to greet her. In typical fashion she shook his hand. But when their hands met, she quickly pulled hers back, for Claparede had concealed a tack in his palm and had pricked her with it. The next time he returned to the room to greet her, she still had no recognition of him, but she refused to shake his hand. She could not tell him why she would not shake hands with him, but she wouldn't do it.

---

[2]Claparede (1911).

Claparede had come to signify danger. He was no longer just a man, no longer just a doctor, but had become a stimulus with a specific emotional meaning. Although the patient did not have a conscious memory of the situation, subconsciously she learned that shaking Claparede's hand could cause her harm, and her brain used this stored information, this memory, to prevent the unpleasantness from occurring again.

These instances of memory sparing and loss were not easily interpreted in Claparede's time and until recently were thought of as reflecting the survival and breakdown of different aspects of one learning and memory system. But modern studies of the brain mechanisms of memory have given us a different view. It now seems that Claparede was seeing the operation of two different memory systems in his patient—one involved in forming memories of experiences and making those memories available for conscious recollection at some later time, and another operating outside of consciousness and controlling behavior without explicit awareness of the past learning.

Conscious recollection is the kind of memory that we have in mind when we use the term "memory" in everyday conversation: to remember is to be conscious of some past experience, and to have a memory problem (again, in everyday parlance) is to have difficulty with this ability. Scientists refer to conscious recollections as declarative or explicit memories.[3] Memories created this way can be brought to mind and described verbally. Sometimes we may have trouble dredging up the memory, but it is potentially available as a conscious memory. As a result of brain damage, Claparede's patient had a problem with this type of memory.

But the patient's ability to protect herself from a situation of potential danger by refusing to shake hands reflects a different kind of memory system. This system forms implicit or nondeclarative memories about dangerous or otherwise threatening situations. Memories of this type . . .

---

[3]*Declarative memory* and *explicit memory* are both terms that are used to distinguish conscious recollection from memories that are based on unconscious processes. The two terms, however, come from somewhat different kinds of research. Declarative memory came out of research aimed at understanding the function of the temporal lobe memory system, which we'll have much to say about. In contrast, explicit memory came out of research on the psychology of memory more than the neural basis of memory. Here, the two terms will used interchangeably to refer to conscious memory and to distinguish memory that involves conscious recollection from memory that is based on unconscious processes, as conscious memory is now clearly established to be a function of the temporal lobe memory system.

are created through the mechanisms of fear conditioning—because of its association with the painful pinprick, the sight of Claparede became a *learned trigger* of defensive behavior (a conditioned fear stimulus). . . . Conditioned fear responses involve implicit or unconscious processes in two important senses: the learning that occurs does not depend on conscious awareness and, once the learning has taken place, the stimulus does not have to be consciously perceived in order to elicit the conditioned emotional responses. We may become aware that fear conditioning has taken place, but we do not have control over its occurrence or conscious access to its workings. Claparede's patient shows us something similar: as a result of brain damage, she had no conscious memory of the learning experience through which the conditioned fear stimulus implicitly acquired the capacity to protect her from being pricked again.

Through brain damage we can thus see the operation of an implicit emotional memory system in the absence of explicit conscious memory of the emotional learning experience. Normally, though, in the undamaged brain, explicit memory and implicit emotional memory systems are working at the same time, each forming their own special brand of memories. So if you met Claparede today and he was, after all these years, still up to his old tricks, you would form an explicit conscious memory of being pricked by the old codger, as well as an implicit or unconscious memory. We are going to call the implicit, fear-conditioned memory an "emotional memory" and the explicit declarative memory a "memory of an emotion." Having already explored how fear conditioning works, we will now examine the neural organization of the explicit or declarative memory system, and also take a look at interactions between this conscious memory network and the unconsciously functioning fear conditioning system.

Henry Mnemonic: The Life and Times of Case H.M.

Karl Lashley, the father of modern physiological psychology and one of the most influential brain researchers in the first half of the twentieth century, conducted an extensive series of investigations attempting to find the locus of memory in the rat brain.[4] His conclusion, that memory is not

---

[4]Lashley (1950). In this book, Lashley concluded that memory was not localized to any one system of the brain. This conclusion has turned out to be completely wrong. How did one of the most careful researchers in the history of brain science make such a big mistake? Lashley, like most researchers of his day, assumed that any task that measured a change in behavior at some point in time

mediated by any particular neural system but is instead diffusely distributed in the brain, was widely accepted. By mid-century researchers had
quit looking for the location of memory in the brain—it seemed that this
was a fruitless and even a misguided quest. However, the tides began to
shift when a young man suffering from an extreme case of epilepsy was
operated on in Hartford, Connecticut, in 1953.[5]

Known to legions of brain scientists and psychologists as H.M.,[6] this
patient has single-handedly, though unwittingly, shaped the course of
research on the brain mechanisms of explicit (conscious) memory over
the past forty years. At the time of the operation he was twenty-seven
and had been experiencing convulsive epileptic attacks since sixteen. All
attempts to control the seizures with medications available at the time
had failed. Because of the severity and intractability of his epilepsy, H.M.
was deemed an appropriate candidate for a radical, last-resort, experimental procedure in which the brain tissue containing the major sites or
"foci" of the disease are removed. In his case, it was necessary to remove
large regions of the temporal lobes on both sides of his brain.

Measured by the extent to which its medical goal was achieved, the
surgery was a great success—the epileptic seizures came to be controllable
by anticonvulsant medications. On the other hand, there was one unfortunate and unanticipated consequence. H.M. lost his memory. More specifically, he lost his capacity to form explicit, declarative, or conscious
long-term memories. However, the distinction between explicit and
implicit memories did not arise until much later, and in fact was based in
part on the studies of H.M. So we will forsake the distinction for a while
until we've considered H.M. and his problems in more detail.

---

as a result of some earlier experience was as good as any other task in measuring memory. He chose to use various maze learning tasks in his quest to find
memory in the brain. We now know that these mazes can be solved in many
different ways—a blind animal, for example, can use touch or smell cues. The
fact that the maze problems had multiple solutions meant that multiple memory
systems were engaged in the learning. As a result, no one brain lesion would
interfere with performance. Lashley was thus led to the false conclusion that
memory is widely distributed because he used behavioral tasks that called
into play multiple memory systems located in different brain regions. We now
interpret this in terms of the existence of multiple memory systems in the brain.
[5]Scoville and Milner (1957).
[6]It is unusual in studies of patients to refer to them by their initials in order to
protect their identity. It is fairly commonly known, though, that H.M.'s first
name was Henry.

H.M.'s memory disorder, his amnesia, has been studied and written about extensively over the years. Neal Cohen and Howard Eichenbaum, two leading memory researchers, recently summarized H.M.'s condition: "Now, nearly 40 years after his surgery, H.M. does not know his age or the current date; does not know where he is living; does not know the current status of his parents (who are long deceased); and does not know his own history."[7] And Larry Squire, another leader in the field, describes it this way: "Although his epileptic condition was markedly improved, he could accomplish little, if any, new learning. . . . His impairment in new learning is so pervasive and severe that he requires constant supervisory care. He does not learn the names or faces of those who see him regularly. Having aged since his surgery, he does not now recognize a photograph of himself."[8] But probably the most straightforward and telling characterization of H.M.'s condition appeared in the first publication that described his unfortunate state. William Scoville, the surgeon, and Brenda Milner, the psychologist who studied H.M. initially, noted that H.M. forgot the events of daily life as quickly as they occurred.[9]

One of the facts that was clear from Milner's studies was that H.M.'s memory problem had nothing to do with a loss of intellectual ability. H.M.'s IQ after the surgery was in the normal range, in fact on the high side of normal, and remained there over the years. The black holes of knowledge in his mind did not reflect some general breakdown in his ability to think and reason. He was not stupid. He simply couldn't remember.

In many ways, H.M.'s memory deficit was quite similar to the disorder in Claparede's patient. However, for two reasons, H.M. is a more important case for understanding memory. The first is that H.M. was extensively examined from the mid-1950s until only a few years ago. Probably no patient in the history of neurology has been studied in such detail and over such an extended period. Throughout, he was a willing and able subject, but in recent years, as age took its toll, he became less capable of participating in these studies. The result of all this work is that we know exactly which aspects of his memory were compromised. The second reason that H.M. has been so important for understanding memory is that we know the location of the damage in his brain. His lesion was the result of a precise surgical removal (rather than an accident of nature). The surgical record thus indicates where the damage is. It has also been

[7]N. J. Cohen and H. Eichenbaum (1993).
[8]Squire (1987).
[9]Scoville and Milner (1957).

possible to look inside his skull with modern brain imaging techniques and confirm the location of the damage. By combining this exacting neurological information about the locus of brain damage with the detailed information about which aspects of memory are disturbed and intact, researchers studying H.M. have obtained important insights into the way memory is organized in the brain.[10]

The Long and the Short of It

Today, it is widely accepted that memory can be divided into a short-term store, which lasts seconds, and a long-term one lasting from minutes to a lifetime.[11] What you are conscious of now is what is momentarily in your short-term memory (especially what is called working memory, a special kind of short-term memory. . .), and what goes into your short-term memory is what can go into your long-term memory.[12] This distinction had been around since the late nineteenth century, having been proposed (with different terms) by William James (who else?),[13] but the most conclusive evidence that short- and long-term memory are really different processes mediated by distinct brain systems probably came from Milner's early studies of H.M.

Although H.M. seemed to forget almost everything that happened to him (he was unable to form long-term memories), he could nevertheless hold on to information for a few seconds (he had short-term memory). For example, if he was shown a card with a picture on it and the card was put away, he could say what was on the card if he was asked immediately, but if a minute or so passed he was completely unable to say

---

[10][The following] section is based on descriptions of H.M. found in several publications: Scoville and Milner (1957); Squire (1987); N. J. Cohen and H. Eichenbaum (1993).

[11]There is also an intermediate store that has been discovered through studies in which drugs are used to interfere with storage and through studies of animals lacking certain chemicals in their nervous systems.

[12]There are patients in whom aspects of short-term memory (STM) are interfered with (they perform poorly on the digit span test, a measure of STM) but they can form long-term memories of other things. However, STM is itself modular and it is unlikely that you could have a long-term memory of some stimulus that you failed to have an STM of.

[13]James (1890). James distinguished primary versus secondary memory, which roughly correspond to what we have in mind when we talk about short- and long-term memory today, although there are some subtle differences in the concepts.

what he had seen, or even whether he had seen anything. From the results of many kinds of tests, it became clear that removal of regions of the temporal lobe in H.M. interfered with long- but not short-term memory, suggesting that the formation of long-term memories is mediated by the temporal lobe, but that short-term memory involves some other brain system.[14]

H.M. has also taught us that the brain system involved in forming new long-term memories is different from the one that stores old long-term memories. H.M. could remember events from his childhood and early adult life quite well. In fact, his memory of things before the operation was good, up to a couple of years prior to the surgery. Consequently, Milner pointed out that H.M. had a very severe anterograde amnesia (an inability to put new information into long-term memory) but only a mild retrograde amnesia (an inability to remember things that happened before the surgery). H.M.'s major deficit was thus one of depositing new learning into the long-term memory bank, rather than withdrawing information placed there earlier in life.

The findings from H.M. thus clearly distinguished short-term and long-term memory, and also suggested that long-term memory involves at least two stages, an initial one requiring the temporal lobe regions that were removed, and a later stage involving some other brain regions, most likely areas of the neocortex.[15] The temporal lobe is needed for forming long-term memories, but gradually, over years, memories become independent of this brain system. These are powerful concepts that remain central to our understanding of the brain mechanisms of memory.

In Search of a Model

The areas of the temporal lobe that were damaged in H.M. included major portions of the hippocampus and amygdala, and surrounding transitional areas. Some of these were areas that MacLean had identified as components of the limbic system, which . . . was supposed to constitute the emotional system of the brain. H.M. provided some of the first difficulties for the limbic system theory of emotion, suggesting that some

---

[14]Short-term memory is now often thought of as a working memory system and is believed to involve the prefrontal cortex. For a discussion of the role of the prefrontal cortex in temporary memory processes, see Fuster (1989); Goldman-Rakic (1993).

[15]Squire, Knowlton, and Musen (1993); Teyler and DiScenna (1986); McClelland, McNaughton, and O'Reilly (1995).

regions of the limbic system are involved at least as much in cognitive functions (like memory) as in emotion.

Although several temporal lobe regions were damaged in H.M., the view emerged that damage to the hippocampus was primarily responsible for the memory disorder. Other patients were operated on, in addition to H.M., and when these were all considered together it seemed that the extent of the memory disorder was directly related to the amount of the hippocampus that had been removed. On the basis of these observations, the hippocampus emerged as the leading candidate brain region for the laying down of new memories. Surgeons now make every effort to leave the hippocampus and related brain regions intact, at least on one side of the brain, when operating on the temporal lobes so that devastating effects on memory can be prevented.

By the late 1950s, the task at hand for memory researchers seemed clear and straightforward: turn to studies of experimental animals to figure out how the hippocampus accomplishes its mnemonic job. In animal studies, memory is tested not by asking the subject whether he or she remembers, but by determining whether behavioral performance is affected by prior learning experiences. Countless studies of the effects of hippocampectomy (hippocampal removal) on memory were performed in a variety of animals. The results were inconsistent and disappointing. Lesions sometimes interfered with the ability of animals to remember what they learned, and sometimes did not. It seemed that either the human and nonhuman brain have different mechanisms of memory, or that the researchers had just not found the right way to test memory in animals.

But in the early 1970s David Gaffan, an Oxford psychologist, came up with a way of testing memory in monkeys that proved to be a reliable measure of hippocampal-dependent functions.[16] It was a task called delayed nonmatching to sample. The monkey was shown a stimulus, say a toy soldier. The stimulus was then removed. After a delay, two stimuli appeared, the toy soldier and a toy car of about the same size. The monkey could get a treat (like a raisin or Fruit Loop) by picking the stimulus that had not appeared before (the stimulus that did not match the sample), which in this case was the car. If the sample (the soldier) was picked, no treat followed.

Having a sweet tooth, monkeys are very willing to play these kinds of games. Normal monkeys do fine, even at relatively long delays between

---

[16]Gaffan (1974).

the sample and the two test stimuli. Monkeys with hippocampal damage also perform reasonably well at short delays. But as the delay increases, they perform miserably—they respond randomly to the two stimuli, choosing the stimulus that matches the sample as often as the nonmatch.[17] This breakdown at the long delays cannot be due to a simple failure to learn the rule (pick the stimulus that does not match the sample). They learn the rule before the hippocampus is removed, so they already know it and just have to apply it to the stimuli that appear in a particular test. Most important, they use the rule well at short delays. The problem is really one of holding on to the memory of the sample long enough to choose the nonmatching item.

Delayed nonmatching to sample does not exactly resemble the kinds of tasks used to test memory in amnesic or normal humans.[18] Humans are given verbal instructions about how to perform the task, whereas animals are given weeks or months of behavioral training so that they can learn the rule. Humans are typically tested on verbal material or are required to give verbal responses even with nonverbal test stimuli. Animals always express their memory through behavioral performance. Humans are not given sweets every time they get an answer right. The important thing about delayed nonmatching to sample was thus not that it perfectly corresponded to the kinds of tests used to reveal memory problems in H.M. but that it proved to be a reliable means of revealing a hippocampal-dependent memory in animals. For this reason, delayed nonmatching to sample became the gold standard for modeling human temporal lobe amnesia in monkeys.

Delayed nonmatching to sample was also tried in studies of other species, particularly rats, and was found to be a good way of testing hippocampal-dependent memory in these animals as well.[19] But through studies of rats, other kinds of tasks were also discovered that reliably implicated the hippocampus. These mostly involved various forms of learning and memory that depend on the use of spatial cues. In one task, rats are tested in a maze in which different alleys radiate out from a central platform.[20] The rat is put in the center and has to choose one of the alleys. His job is to remember which alleys he's not gone down before. If he picks one of the previously unvisited alleys, he gets a treat. If he goes down a previously visited one, he gets nothing. The only way to solve this task is to use

---

[17]Zola-Morgan and Squire (1993); Murray (1992); Mishkin (1982).
[18]Iversen (1976); N. J. Cohen and H. Eichenbaum (1993).
[19]N. J. Cohen and H. Eichenbaum (1993).
[20]Olton, Becker, and Handleman (1979).

spatial cues, such as the location of an alley with respect to the location of other items in the room in which the maze is. In another task, rats are put into a tank containing milky water.[21] They are decent swimmers, but don't really care for it, and will swim to safety as soon as possible. Initially, there is a platform above the water. Once they've learned where it is, the platform is submerged just below the surface. The rats have to remember where the platform was and use spatial cues around the room to guide their swim to safety. Lesions of the hippocampus interfere with spatial memory in both the radial maze and the water maze.

By the late 1970s, the ducks seemed to be lining up. Studies of animals and humans were finally both pointing to the hippocampus as a key player in the game of memory. But then Mortimer Mishkin of the National Institute of Mental Health noted a problem with this neat and tidy story about the role of the hippocampus in memory and amnesia.[22] He pointed out that all of the patients, including H.M., who became amnesic as a result of temporal lobe lesions had damage to the amygdala as well as the hippocampus. Might the amygdala also be important? Mishkin tested this idea by examining the effects of combined lesions of the hippocampus and amygdala versus separate lesions of these two areas in monkeys. The findings seemed crystal clear. Damage to the amygdala and hippocampus together was more detrimental than damage to either alone on delayed nonmatching to sample. The idea that limbic areas, like the amygdala and hippocampus, are more involved in emotion than cognition was already challenged by the discovery that the hippocampus contributes to cognition (memory). The possibility that the amygdala was part of the memory system blurred this distinction between cognitive and emotional functions of limbic areas even more.

Other researchers, however, did not fully accept the view that the amygdala was part of the memory system, and by the late 1980s the tide was shifting back toward the hippocampus as the core of the long-term memory system. Larry Squire, Stuart Zola-Morgan, and David Amaral of San Diego examined a patient with a severe memory disorder, not unlike H.M.'s.[23] Not too long afterward, the patient died, and the brain was made available for analysis. This patient turned out to have a pure hippocampal lesion. There was no detectable damage anywhere else. This selective lesion resulted from anoxia, a reduction in oxygen supply to the

---

[21]Morris (1984); Morris et al (1982).
[22]Mishkin (1978).
[23]Zola-Morgan, Squire, and Amaral (1986).

brain, which especially affects cells in the hippocampus. Amnesia, it seemed, could result from damage to only the hippocampus.

Why, then, did the combined hippocampal and amygdala lesion produce more of a deficit on delayed nonmatching to sample than the hippocampal lesions alone in monkeys? The San Diego team next took on this issue. They noted that in the process of removing the amygdala, surgeons often damage cortical areas that provide an important linkage between the neocortex and the hippocampus. Perhaps Mishkin's effect was not due to amygdala damage but to an interruption of the flow of information back and forth between the neocortex and the hippocampus. The San Diego researchers figured out how to remove the amygdala without disturbing the cortical areas related to the hippocampus. This pure amygdala lesion had no effect on delayed nonmatching to sample.[24] Importantly, though, the pure amygdala lesion did produce the emotional concomitants of the Kluver-Bucy syndrome, especially reduced fear.[25] The role of the hippocampus in memory seemed rescued, and the burden of cognition was again lifted from the amygdala.

What, then, is the relative contribution of the hippocampus as opposed to those pesky cortical areas surrounding the amygdala and hippocampus? Mishkin and Betsy Murray showed that damage to the surrounding cortex also produces deficits in delayed nonmatching to sample; in fact, these lesions produced more of a deficit than the hippocampal damage.[26] On the basis of this finding, Murray and Mishkin questioned the premier role of the hippocampus in memory and argued instead that the surrounding cortex is particularly crucial. Other researchers, however, point out that this is too strong a conclusion to base solely on delayed nonmatching to sample, which may not be the magic bullet that it has been made out to be.[27] After all, there is pretty solid evidence that pure hippocampal damage in humans can lead to amnesia (recall the anoxia case above). Delayed nonmatching to sample may be a better test of the function of the surrounding cortex than of the hippocampus, which would suggest that these two areas each contribute uniquely to memory.[28]

This debate over the details will no doubt continue. However, most researchers in the field are in agreement about the broad outline of how

---

[24]Zola-Morgan, Squire, and Amaral (1989).
[25]Zola-Morgan et al. (1991).
[26]Meunier et al (1993); Murray (1992).
[27]Squire, Knowlton, and Musen (1993); Zola-Morgan and Squire (1993); Eichenbaum, Otto, and Cohen (1994); N. J. Cohen and H. Eichenbaum (1993).
[28]Eichenbaum, Otto, and Cohen (1994).

the temporal lobe memory system works.[29] Sensory processing areas of the cortex receive inputs about external events and create perceptual representations of the stimuli. These representations are then shuttled to the surrounding cortical regions, which, in turn, send further processed representations to the hippocampus. The hippocampus then communicates back with the surrounding regions, which communicate with the neocortex. The maintenance of the memory over the short run (a few years) requires that the temporal lobe memory system be intact, either because components of this system store the memory trace or because the trace is maintained by interactions between the temporal lobe system and the neocortex. Gradually, over years, the hippocampus relinquishes its control over the memory to the neocortex, where the memory appears to remain as long as it is a memory, which may be a lifetime.

This model of memory, which has emerged from studies of amnesic animals and humans, gives us a way of understanding the mental changes that take place over time in Alzheimer's disease.[30] The disease begins its attack on the brain in the temporal lobe, particularly in the hippocampus, thus explaining why forgetfulness is the first warning sign. But the disease eventually creeps into the neocortex, suggesting why, as the disease progresses, all aspects of memory (old and new) are compromised, along with a variety of other cortically dependent cognitive functions. Without years of research on amnesia in both humans and animals, the cognitive dissolution that occurs as Alzheimer's disease spreads through the forebrain would not be so readily interpreted. And having these insights about how the disease is compromising the mind and brain in tandem may be one of the best aids in figuring out approaches to preventing, arresting, or reversing the cognitive meltdown that occurs.

Pockets of Memory

In the early days, H.M. failed to form new long-term memories in the vast majority of memory tasks that he was given.[31] It did not matter so much whether he was tested with words, pictures, or sounds, he could not remember. His memory problem was, accordingly, described as a "global amnesia." The few odd things that he could retain seemed, at first, like isolated, unrelated snippets of memory. However, as more and more findings came in from different kinds of memory tests, it became

---

[29]Zola-Morgan and Squire (1993); N. J. Cohen and H. Eichenbaum (1993); McClelland, McNaughton, and O'Reilly (1995); Murray (1992).
[30]DeLeon et al (1989); Parasuramna and Martin (1994).
[31]Milner (1962).

clear that there were well-defined pockets of memory sparing in H.M. As a result of these discoveries, temporal lobe amnesia is no longer considered to be a global memory disorder affecting all forms of new learning. By figuring out what kinds of learning functions are spared and disrupted in amnesia, researchers have been able to characterize the contribution of the temporal lobe system to memory.

One of the first observations of spared learning resulted when Milner asked H.M. to try to copy a picture of a star while only watching a mirror reflection of his hand.[32] This required that he learn to control his hand on the basis of the abnormal (visually reversed) feedback coming to his brain about where his hand was in space. He did poorly the first time, but with practice he improved, and he retained the ability to express the improved performance over time. Suzanne Corkin of MIT then found that H.M. also improved with practice in another manual skill learning task—one in which he was required to keep a handheld stylus on a small dot that was spinning around on a turntable.[33] As with the mirror drawing task, the more times he did it the better he got. Interestingly, and importantly, on both manual skill learning tasks, he improved in spite of the fact that he had no conscious memory of the earlier experiences that led to the improved performance. These findings suggested that the learning and remembrance of manual skills might be mediated by some system other than the temporal lobe system.

Neal Cohen later examined whether spared skill learning ability in amnesia might extend to what is called cognitive skills, the ability to get better at doing mental tasks.[34] He showed that the ability of amnesics to read mirror images of words improved with practice (e.g., "egral" is the mirror image of "large"). He also showed that the patients could learn some complicated rule-based strategies required to solve certain mathematical problems or puzzles. One much discussed instance is a puzzle game called the Tower of Hanoi. To solve this problem, discs of different sizes have to be moved in a certain way between three pegs without ever letting a smaller peg be under a larger one. Even normal subjects have difficulty finding the "optimal" solution to the puzzle. However, with lots of practice, the amnesic patients, including H.M., were able to achieve

---

[32]Milner (1965).
[33]Corkin (1968).
[34]D. H. Cohen (1980); N. J. Cohen and Squire (1980); N. J. Cohen and Corkin (1981).

this solution. As with the other learning tasks, they had no recollection of playing the game.

Research by Elizabeth Warrington and Larry Weiskrantz in England showed that "priming" is preserved in amnesic patients.[35] Like the other instances of spared learning and memory in amnesia, priming involves the demonstration of learning by the effects of prior experience on later behavioral performance rather than by the subject's knowledge of the prior learning. For example, in one version of priming, the subject is given a list of words. Later, if asked to recall the items that were on the list, amnesic patients perform miserably. However, if instead of being asked to recall the items they are given fragments of words and asked to complete them, like normal subjects they do better on the fragments that go with words in the study list than they do for fragments that have no match in the study list.

Weiskrantz and Warrington also showed that the classical conditioning of eyeblink responses is preserved in amnesia.[36] In this task, a tone is paired with an aversive stimulus (usually an air puff to the eye). After hundreds of trials, the tone elicits eyelid closure immediately before the onset of the air puff. This precisely timed response protects the delicate tissues of the eye from the air puff. Amnesic patients show normal eyeblink conditioning. This is not surprising given the fact that we now know from animal studies that eyeblink conditioning involves circuits in the brain stem and is unaffected by removal of all brain tissue above the midbrain.[37] The patients nevertheless later have no memory of having seen the conditioning apparatus.

The Multiplicity of Memory

What do all these spared learning and memory functions have in common, and how do they differ from the functions that are disrupted in temporal lobe amnesia? Cohen and Squire put all of the findings together and came up with an answer.[38] They proposed that damage to the temporal lobe memory system interferes with the ability to consciously recollect, but leaves intact the ability to learn certain skills. They called these two processes declarative and procedural memory. A similar dichotomy was

---

[35]Warrington and Weiskrantz (1973).
[36]Weiskrantz and Warrington (1979).
[37]Steinmetz and Thompson (1991).
[38]N. J. Cohen and Squire (1980); Squire and Cohen (1984); Squire, Cohen, and Nadel (1984).

offered by Daniel Schacter of Harvard, who distinguished between explicit and implicit memory.[39] Conscious awareness of the basis of performance occurs in explicit memory, but in implicit memory performance is guided by unconscious factors. Skill learning, priming, and classical conditioning are all examples of implicit or procedural learning. These are each intact in temporal lobe amnesia and involve brain areas other than the temporal lobe memory system. Other memory dichotomies have been proposed over the years,[40] but the distinction between conscious, explicit, declarative memory, on the one hand, and unconscious, implicit, procedural memory, on the other, has had the greatest impact on current thinking and will be emphasized here.

The distinction between explicit and implicit memory is dramatically illustrated by a study performed by Squire and his colleagues.[41] They showed that amnesics could be made to either succeed or fail a memory test, simply by changing the instructions—some instructions took the patients down the explicit memory path, which gave rise to failure, whereas other instructions led them on a successful stroll through implicit memory land. In all conditions the stimuli were the same, and only the memory instruction changed. The subjects were first given a list of words to study. Then a few minutes later, they received one of three sets of instructions: recall as many words as you can from the list; use the following cues to help you remember as many words on the list as you can; or, say the first word that comes to mind when you see the following cues. The cues in the latter two conditions were three-letter stems of words that had been on the list: MOT for MOTEL, ABS for ABSENT, INC for INCOME, and so on. Each stem could come from many other words: MOT could be from MOTHER or MOTLEY as well as MOTEL. Not surprisingly, the amnesics did poorly when they had to recall without any cues. They also did poorly when told to use the cues to help them remember the words. But they were as good as normal subjects when the instruction was to say the first word that comes to mind after seeing a cue. In the latter case, the cues were primes rather than recall aids. When performing the priming task, and thus using an implicit memory system, they functioned fine, but damage to the temporal lobe memory system prevented them from consciously recalling the items, even with the aid of cues. Howard Eichenbaum, in studies of rats, found something similar: depending on the

---

[39]Schacter and Graf (1986).
[40]Tulving (1983); O'Keefe and Nadel (1978); Olton, Becker, and Handleman (1979); Mishkin, Malamut, and Bachevalier (1984).
[41]Graf, Squire, and Mandler (1984).

instructions given to rats (through training experiences), he showed that it was possible to make a learning situation either dependent upon or independent of the hippocampus.[42]

Cohen and Squire were quick to point out that explicit, declarative memory is mediated by a single memory system, the temporal lobe memory system, but that there are multiple implicit or procedural memory systems. Thus, the brain system that mediates priming is different from the systems involved in skill learning or classical conditioning. Further, different forms of classical conditioning are also mediated by different neural systems—eyeblink conditioning by brain stem circuits and fear conditioning by the amygdala and its connections. The brain clearly has multiple memory systems, each devoted to different kinds of learning and memory functions.

In retrospect, the multiplicity of memory systems should have been apparent from the fact that it was so hard to find memory tasks that depend on the hippocampus in animals. Although a few such tasks were found, the vast majority of the memory tasks used to study animal memory are performed just fine in the absence of the hippocampus. If performance on some tasks depends on the hippocampus and performance on others does not, it must be the case that memory is not a unitary phenomenon and that different memory systems exist in the brain. But in the 1960s and 1970s, there wasn't a clear framework for understanding these variable effects. They led to confusion rather than clarity. The idea of multiple memory systems helped it all make sense.

So What Does the Hippocampus Represent?

We can get a pretty good idea about what makes the hippocampus so important for its brand of memory by examining the kinds of inputs that the hippocampus receives from the neocortex.[43] As we mentioned above, the major link between the hippocampus and the neocortex is the transition cortex. This region receives inputs from the highest stages of neocortical processing in each of the major sensory modalities. So once a cortical sensory system has done all that it can do with a stimulus, say a sight or a sound, it ships the information to the transition region, where the different sensory modalities can be mixed together. This means that in the transition circuits we can begin to form representations of the world that are no longer just visual or auditory or olfactory, but that

---

[42]N. J. Cohen and H. Eichenbaum (1993).
[43]Amaral (1987).

include all of these at once. We begin to leave the purely perceptual and enter the conceptual domain of the brain. The transition region then sends these conceptual representations to the hippocampus, where even more complex representations are created.

One of the first clues as to the way the hippocampus accomplishes its job came from a study performed in the early 1970s by John O'Keefe at University College, London.[44] He found that cells in the hippocampus of a rat became very active when the rat moved into a certain part of a test chamber. The cells then became inactive when the rat moved elsewhere. He found lots of these cells, and each one became active in a different place. O'Keefe called these "place cells." The chamber was topless and rats could see out into the room. O'Keefe showed that the firing of the cells was controlled by the rat's sense of where it was in the room, for if the various cues around the room were removed, the firing patterns changed dramatically. Importantly, though, the place cells were not strictly responding to visual stimuli, since they maintained their "place fields" (the location where they became active) in complete darkness. O'Keefe and colleague Lynn Nadel published an influential book in 1978 called *The Hippocampus as a Cognitive Map* in which they proposed that the hippocampus forms sensory-independent spatial representations of the world.[45] One important function of these spatial representations, according to O'Keefe and Nadel, is to create a context in which to place memories. Context makes memories autobiographical, locating them in space and time, and this, they say, accounts for the role of the hippocampus in memory. They proposed an early multiple memory system account that distinguished a locale (spatial) memory system mediated by the hippocampus from several other systems mediated by other brain regions. O'Keefe and Nadel were mainly concerned with the locale system and made no attempt to identify the brain systems underlying the other forms of learning.

O'Keefe's observations, and the book with Nadel, created a whole industry devoted to understanding the role of the hippocampus in processing spatial cues. The demonstration of hippocampal-dependent memory in the radial maze[46] and the water maze[47] were direct outgrowths of the place cell findings, and many experiments were conducted to figure out exactly how the hippocampus encodes space. In addition to O'Keefe's

---

[44]O'Keefe (1976).
[45]O'Keefe and Nadel (1978).
[46]Olton, Becker, and Handleman (1979).
[47]Morris et al. (1982).

continued research,[48] particularly notable has been the work of Bruce McNaughton and Carol Barnes in Tucson,[49] the late David Olton in Baltimore,[50] Richard Morris in Edinburgh,[51] and Jim Ranck, John Kubie, and Bob Muller in Brooklyn.[52]

But not all investigators have accepted the idea that the hippocampus is a spatial machine. Howard Eichenbaum, for example, questions the role of the hippocampus in spatial processing per se, arguing that what the hippocampus is especially good at and important for is creating representations that involve the multiple cues at once, with space being a particular example of this rather than the primary instance of it.[53] Others, like Jerry Rudy and Rob Sutherland, have argued that the hippocampus creates representations that involve configurations (blends) of cues that transcend the individual stimuli making up the configuration.[54] This differs from Eichenbaum's hypothesis, which argues that the hippocampal representation involves the relation between individual cues rather than a representation in which the cues are fused into a newly synthesized configuration.

More work is needed to choose between spatial, configural, and relational hypotheses. The ultimate verdict will rest with the one that eventually explains how the sights, smells, and sounds of an experience, as well as the arrangement of all of the various stimuli and events in space and time, are represented in the hippocampus.

When Paul MacLean was putting forth his limbic system theory, he proposed that the hippocampus was an ideal place for emotion to reside. He suggested that because of its primitive, simple architecture, the hippocampus wouldn't be able to make fine distinctions between stimuli and would easily mix things up.[55] This, MacLean suggested, might account for the irrationality and confusion of our emotional life. But today, the pendulum has swung in the other direction. The hippocampus is thought to have an exquisite design that leads to sophisticated computational

---

[48]O'Keefe (1993).

[49]McNaughton and Barnes (1990); Barnes et al. (1995); Wilson and McNaughton (1994).

[50]Olton, Becker, and Handleman (1979).

[51]Morris (1984); Morris et al. (1982).

[52]Kubie, Muller, and Bostock (1990); Kubie and Ranck (1983); Muller, Ranck, and Taube (1996).

[53]Eichenbaum, Otto, and Cohen (1994).

[54]Rudy and Sutherland (1992).

[55]MacLean (1949, 1952).

power[56] rather than a primitive organization that leads to confusion. The hippocampus has indeed come to be thought of as a key link in one of the most important cognitive systems of the brain, the temporal lobe memory system.

Tweedledee and Tweedledum: Emotional Memories and Memories of Emotions

Let's now explore the implications of the distinction between explicit and implicit memory for our understanding of how memories are formed in an emotional situation. Suppose you are driving down the road and have a terrible accident. The horn gets stuck on. You are in pain and are generally traumatized by the experience. Later, when you hear the sound of a horn, both the implicit and explicit memory systems are activated. The sound of the horn (or a neural representation of it), having become a conditioned fear stimulus, goes straight from the auditory system to the amygdala and implicitly elicits bodily responses that typically occur in situations of danger: muscle tension (a vestige of freezing), changes in blood pressure and heart rate, increased perspiration, and so on. The sound also travels through the cortex to the temporal lobe memory system, where explicit declarative memories are activated. You are reminded of the accident. You consciously remember where you were going and who you were with. You also remember how awful it was. But in the declarative memory system, there is nothing different about the fact that you were with Bob and the fact that the accident was awful. Both are just facts, propositions that can be declared, about the experience. The particular fact that the accident was awful is not an emotional memory. It is a declarative memory about an emotional experience. It is mediated by the temporal lobe memory system and it has no emotional consequences itself. In order to have an aversive emotional memory, complete with the bodily experiences that come with an emotion, you have to activate an emotional memory system, for example, the implicit fear memory system involving the amygdala (see Figure 11.1).

There is a place, though, where explicit memories of emotional experiences and implicit emotional memories meet—in working memory and its creation of immediate conscious experience. The sound of the horn, through the implicit emotional memory system, opens the floodgates of

---

[56]McClelland, McNaughton, and O'Reilly (1995); Gluck and Myers (1995).

Figure 11.1. Brain Systems of Emotional Memory and Memory of Emotion

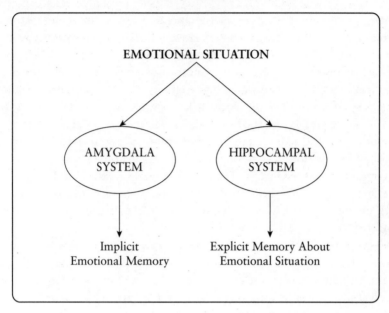

It is now common to think of the brain as containing a variety of different
memory systems. Conscious, declarative or explicit memory is mediated by the
hippocampus and related cortical areas, whereas various unconscious or
implicit forms of memory are mediated by different systems. One implicit
memory system is an emotional (fear) memory system involving the amygdala
and related areas. In traumatic situations, implicit and explicit systems function
in parallel. Later, if you are exposed to stimuli that were present during trauma,
both systems will most likely be reactivated. Through the hippocampal system
you will remember who you were with and what you were doing during the
trauma, and will also remember, as a cold fact, that the situation was awful.
Through the amygdala system the stimuli will cause your muscles to tense up,
your blood pressure and heart rate to change, and hormones to be released,
among other bodily and brain functions. Because these systems are activated
by the same stimuli and are functioning at the same time, the two kinds of
memories seem to be part of one unified memory function. Only by taking
those systems apart, especially through studies of experimental animals, but
also through important studies of rare human cases, are we able to understand
how memory systems are operating in parallel to give rise to independent
memory functions.

emotional arousal, turning on all the bodily responses associated with fear and defense. The fact that you are aroused becomes part of your current experience. This fact comes to rest side by side in consciousness with your explicit memory of the accident. Without the emotional arousal elicited through the implicit system, the conscious memory would be emotionally flat. But the corepresentation in awareness of the conscious memory and the current emotional arousal give an emotional flavoring to the conscious memory. Actually, these two events (the past memory and the present arousal) are seamlessly fused as a unified conscious experience of the moment. This unified experience of the past memory and the arousal can then potentially get converted into a new explicit long-term memory, one that will include the fact that you were emotionally aroused last time you remembered the accident. In this case the memory of the accident did not lead to the emotional arousal. The implicit arousal of emotion gave emotional coloration to the explicit memory (see Figure 11.2).

Nevertheless, we know from personal experience that conscious memories can make us tense and anxious, and we need to account for this as well. All that is needed for this to occur is a set of connections from the explicit memory system to the amygdala. There are in fact abundant connections from the hippocampus and the transition regions, as well as many other areas of the cortex, to the amygdala.

It is also possible that implicitly processed stimuli activate the amygdala without activating explicit memories or otherwise being represented in consciousness. Unconscious processing of stimuli can occur either because the stimulus itself is unnoticed or because its implications are unnoticed. For example, suppose the accident described above happened long ago and your explicit memory system has since forgotten about many of the details, such as the fact that the horn had been stuck on. The sound of a horn now, many years later, is ignored by the explicit memory system. But if the emotional memory system has not forgotten, the sound of the horn, when it hits the amygdala, will trigger an emotional reaction. In a situation like this, you may find yourself in the throes of an emotional state that exists for reasons you do not quite understand. This condition of being emotionally aroused and not knowing why is all too common for most of us, and was, in fact, the key condition for which the Schachter-Singer theory of emotion tried to account. But in order for emotion to be aroused in this way, the implicit emotional memory system would have to be less forgetful than the explicit memory system. Two facts suggest that this may be the case. One is that the explicit memory system is notoriously forgetful and inaccurate. . . . The other is that

Figure 11.2. Intersection of Explicit Memory and Emotional Arousal in Immediate Conscious Experience

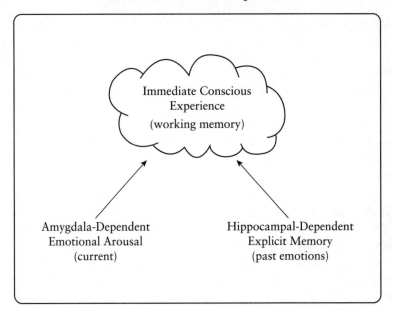

The outcome of activity in the explicit memory system of the hippocampus is a conscious awareness of stored knowledge or personal experiences. The outcome of activity in the amygdala is the expression of emotional (defensive) responses. But we also become conscious of the fact that we are emotionally aroused, allowing us to fuse, in consciousness, explicit memories of past situations with immediate emotional arousal. In this way, new explicit memories that are formed about past memories can be given emotional coloration as well.

conditioned fear responses exhibit little diminution with the passage of time. In fact, they often increase in their potency as time wears on, a phenomenon called "the incubation of fear."[57] It is possible to decrease the potency of a conditioned response by presenting the learned trigger, the CS, over and over again without the US. However, so-called extinguished responses often recur on their own, and even when they don't they can be brought back to life by stressful events.[58] Observations like these have led us to conclude that conditioned fear learning is particularly resilient, and in fact may represent an indelible form

[57]Eysenck (1979).
[58]Jacobs and Nadel (1985).

of learning. This conclusion has extremely important implications for understanding certain psychiatric conditions.

Infantile Amnesia

The idea of separate systems devoted to forming implicit emotional memories and explicit memories of emotions is relevant for understanding infantile amnesia, our inability to remember experiences from early childhood, roughly before age three. Infantile amnesia was first discussed by Freud, who noted that there had not been enough astonishment of the fact that by the time a child is two he can speak well and is at home with complicated mental situations, but if he is later told of some remark made during this time, he will have no memory of it.[59]

Lynn Nadel, together with Jake Jacobs, proposed that the key to infantile amnesia was the relatively prolonged period of maturation that the hippocampus goes through.[60] In order to be fully functional, a brain region has to grow its cells and get them connected with other cells in the various regions with which it communicates. It seems to take the hippocampus a bit longer than most other brain regions to get its act together. So Jacobs and Nadel proposed that we don't have explicit memories of early childhood because the system that forms them is not ready to do its job. Other brain systems, though, must be ready to do their learning and remembering sooner, since children learn lots of things during this amnesic time, even if they don't have conscious memories of the learning.

Jacobs and Nadel were particularly interested in the way that early trauma, though not remembered, might have lasting, detrimental influences on mental life. They proposed that the system that forms unconscious memories of traumatic events might mature before the hippocampus. They did not identify what this unconscious system for traumatic learning and memory was, but we now know, of course, that this system crucially involves the amygdala and its connections.

Although there is a dearth of biological research on the developmental maturation of the amygdala, behavioral studies suggest that the amygdala does indeed mature before the hippocampus. Jerry Rudy and his colleagues at the University of Colorado examined the age at which rats could learn hippocampal-dependent versus amygdala-dependent tasks.[61] They found that the amygdala task was acquired earlier in life than the

[59]Freud (1966).
[60]Jacobs and Nadel (1985).
[61]Rudy and Morledge (1994).

hippocampal task. The amygdala appears to be functionally mature before the hippocampus.

The separate function and differential maturation of the amygdala has important implications for understanding psychopathological conditions.

REFERENCES

Amaral, D. G. (1987). Memory: Anatomical organization of candidate brain regions. In *Handbook of physiology. Section 1: The nervous system. Vol. 5: Higher functions of the brain,* F. Plum, ed. (Bethesda, MD: American Physiological Society), pp. 211–294.

Amaral, D. G., Price, J. L., Pitkanen, A., and Carmichael, S. T. (1992). Anatomical organization of the primate amygdaloid complex. In *The amygdala: Neurobiological aspects of emotion, memory, and mental dysfunction,* J. P. Aggleton, ed. (New York: Wiley-Liss), pp. 1–66.

Barnes, C. A., Erickson, C. A., Davis, S., and McNaughton, B. L. (1995). Hippocampal synaptic enhancement as a basis for learning and memory: A selected review of current evidence from behaving animals. In *Brain and memory: Modulation and mediation of neuroplasticity,* J. L. McGaugh, N. M. Weinberger, and G. Lynch, eds. (New York: Oxford University Press), pp. 259–276.

Claparede, E. (1911). Recognition and "me-ness." In *Organization and pathology of thought* (1951), D. Rapaport, ed. (New York: Columbia University Press), pp. 58–75.

Cohen, D. H. (1980). The functional neuroanatomy of a conditioned response. In *Neural mechanisms of goal-directed behavior and learning,* R. F. Thompson, L. H. Hicks, and B. Shvyrkov, eds. (New York: Academic Press), pp. 283–302.

Cohen, N. J. (1980). *Neuropsychological evidence for a distinction between procedural and declarative knowledge in human memory and amnesia* (San Diego: University of California Press).

Cohen, N. J., and Corkin, S. (1981). The amnesic patient H.M.: Learning and retention of cognitive skills. *Society for Neuroscience Abstracts 7,* 517–518.

Cohen, N. J., and Eichenbaum, H. (1993). *Memory, amnesia, and the hippocampal system* (Cambridge: MIT Press).

Cohen, N. J., and Squire, L. (1980). Preserved learning and retention of pattern-analyzing skill in amnesia: Dissociation of knowing how and knowing that. *Science, 210,* 207–209.

Corkin, S. (1968). Acquisition of motor skill after bilateral medial temporal lobe excision. *Neuropsychologia 6,* 255–265.

DeLeon, M. J., George, A. E., Stylopoulos, L. A., Smith, G., and Miller, D. C. (1989). Early marker for Alzheimer's disease: The atrophic hippocampus. *Lancet* September 16, 672–673.

Dostoyevsky, F. (1864). *Notes from the underground* (New York: Dell).

Eichenbaum, H., Otto, T., and Cohen, N. J. (1994). Two functional components of the hippocampal memory system. *Behavioral and Brain Sciences 17,* 449–518.

Erdelyi, M. (1985). *Psychoanalysis: Freud's cognitive psychology* (New York: Freeman).

Eysenck, H. J. (1979). The conditioning model of neurosis. *Behavioral and Brain Sciences 2,* 155–199.

Freud, S. (1966). *Introductory letters on psychoanalysis,* Standard Edition, J. Strachey, ed. (New York: Norton).

Fuster, J. M. (1989). *The prefrontal cortex* (New York: Raven).

Gaffan, D. (1974). Recognition impaired and association intact in the memory of monkeys after transaction of the fornix. *Journal of Comparative and Physiological Psychology 86,* 1100–1109.

Gluck, M. A., and Myers, C. E. (1995). Representation and association in memory: A neurocomputational view of hippocampal function. *Current Directions in Psychological Science 4,* 23–29.

Goldman-Rakic, P. S. (1993). Working memory and the mind. In *Mind and brain: Readings from Scientific American magazine,* W. H. Freeman, ed. (New York; Freeman), pp. 66–77.

Graf, P., Squire, L. R., and Mandler, G. (1984). The information that amnesic patients do not forget. *Journal of Experimental Psychology: Learning, Memory and Cognition 10,* 164–178.

Iversen, S. (1976). Do temporal lobe lesions produce amnesia in animals? *International Review of Neurobiology 19,* 1–49.

Jacobs, W. J., and Nadel, L. (1985). Stress-induced recovery of fears and phobias. *Psychological Review 92,* 512–531.

James, W. (1890). *Principles of psychology* (New York: Holt).

Kubie, J., and Ranck, J. (1983). Sensory-behavioral correlates of individual hippocampal neurons in three situations: Space and context. In *The neurobiology of the hippocampus,* W. Seifert, ed. (New York: Academic Press).

Kubie, J. L., Muller, R. U., and Bostock, E. (1990). Spatial firing properties of hippocampal theta cells. *Journal of Neuroscience 10*(4), 1110–1123.

Lashley, K. S. (1950). In search of the engram. *Symposia of the Society for Experimental Biology 4,* 454–482.

MacLean, P. D. (1949). Psychosomatic disease and the "visceral brain": Recent developments bearing on the Papez theory of emotion. *Psychosomatic Medicine 11,* 338–353.

MacLean, P. D. (1952). Some psychiatric implications of physiological studies on frontotemporal portion of limbic system (visceral brain). *Electroencephalography and Clinical Neurophysiology 4*, 407–418.

McClelland, J. L., McNaughton, B. L., and O'Reilly, R. C. (1995). Why there are complementary learning systems in the hippocampus and neocortex: Insights from the successes and failures of connectionist models of learning and memory. *Psychological Review 102*, 419–457.

McNaughton, B. L., and Barnes, C. A. (1990). From cooperative synaptic enhancement to associative memory: Bridging the abyss. *Seminars in the Neurosciences 2*, 403–416.

Meunier, M., Bachevalier, J., Mishkin, M., and Murray, E. A. (1993). Effects on visual recognition of combined and separate ablations of the entorhinal and perihinal cortex in rhesus monkeys. *Journal of Neuroscience 13*, 5418–5432.

Milner, B. (1962). Les trouble de la mémoire accompagnant des lésions hippocampiques bilaterales. In *Physiologie de l'hippocampe*, P. Plassouant, ed. (Paris: Centre de la Recherche Scientifique).

Milner, B. (1965). Memory disturbances after bilateral hippocampal lesions in man. In *Cognitive process and brain*, P. M. Milner and S. E. Glickman, eds. (Princeton: Van Nostrand).

Mishkin, M. (1978). Memory in monkeys severely impaired by combined but not separate removal amygdala and hippocampus. *Nature 273*, 297–298.

Mishkin, M. (1982). A memory system in the monkey. *Philosophical Transactions of the Royal Society, London, Series B: Biological Sciences 298*, 85–95.

Mishkin, M., Malamut, B., and Bachevalier, J. (1984). Memories and habits: Two neural systems. In *The neurobiology of learning and memory*, J. L. McGaugh, G. Lynch, and N. M. Weinberger, eds. (New York: Guilford).

Morris, R. G. M. (1984). Development of a water-maze procedure for studying spatial learning in the rat. *Journal of Neuroscience Methods 11*, 47–60.

Morris, R. G. M., Garrard, P., Rawlins, J. N. P., and O'Keefe, J. (1982). Place navigation impaired in rats with hippocampal lesions. *Nature 273*, 297–298.

Muller, R., Ranck, J., and Taube, J. (1996). Head direction cells: Properties and functional significance. *Current Opinion in Neurobiology 6*, 196–206.

Murray, E. A. (1992). Medial temporal lobe structures contributing to recognition memory: The amygdaloid complex versus the rhinal cortex. In J. P. Aggleton, ed. *The Amygdala: Neurobiological Aspects of Emotion, Memory, and Mental Dysfunction.* (New York: Wiley-Liss).

O'Keefe, J. (1976). Place units in the hippocampus of the freely moving rat. *Experimental Neurology 51*, 78–109.

O'Keefe, J. (1993). Hippocampus, theta, and spatial memory. *Current Opinion in Neurobiology 3*, 917–924.

O'Keefe, J., and Nadel, L. (1978). *The hippocampus as a cognitive map* (Oxford: Clarendon Press).

Olton, D., Becker, J. T., and Handleman, G. E. (1979). Hippocampus, space and memory. *Behavioral and Brain Sciences 2*, 313–365.

Parasuramna, R., and Martin, A. (1994). Cognition in Alzheimer's disease. *Current Opinion in Neurobiology 4*, 237–244.

Rudy, J. W., and Morledge, P. (1994). Ontogeny of contextual fear conditioning rats: Implications for consolidation, infantile amnesia, and hippocampal system function. *Behavioral Neuroscience 108*, 227–234.

Rudy, J. W., and Sutherland, R. J. (1992). Configural and elemental associations and the memory coherence problem. *Journal of Cognitive Neuroscience 4*(3), 208–216.

Schacter, S., and Graf, P. (1986). Effects of elaborative processing on implicit and explicit memory for new associations. *Journal of Experimental Psychology: Learning, Memory, and Cognition 12*(3), 432–444.

Scoville, W. B., and Milner, B. (1957). Loss of recent memory after bilateral hippocampal lesions. *Journal of Neurology and Psychiatry 20*, 11–21.

Squire, L. (1987). *Memory and the brain* (New York: Oxford University Press).

Squire, L. R., and Cohen, N. J. (1984). Human memory and amnesia. In *Neurobiology of learning and memory*, G. Lynch, J. L. McGaugh, and N. M. Weinberger, eds. (New York: Guilford).

Squire, L. R., Cohen, N. J., and Nadel, L. (1984). The medial temporal region and memory consolidation: A new hypothesis. In *Memory consolidation*, H. Eingartner and E. Parker, eds. (Hillsdale, NJ: Erlbaum).

Squire, L. R., Knowlton, B., and Musen, G. (1993). The structure and organization of memory. *Annual Review of Psychology, 44*, 453–495.

Steinmetz, J. E., and Thompson, R. F. (1991). Brain substrates of aversive classical conditioning. In *Neurobiology of learning, emotion and affect*, J. I. Madden, ed. (New York: Raven), pp. 97–120.

Teyler, T. J., and DiScenna, P. (1986). The hippocampal memory indexing theory. *Behavioral Neuroscience 100*, 147–154.

Tulving, E. (1983). *Elements of episodic memory* (New York: Oxford University Press).

Warrington, E., and Weiskrantz, L. (1973). The effect of prior learning on subsequent retention in amnesic patients. *Neuropsychologia 20*, 233–248.

Weiskrantz, L., and Warrington, E. (1979). Conditioning in amnesic patients. *Neuropsychologia 17*, 187–194.

Wilson, M. A., and McNaughton, B. L. (1994). Reactivation of hippocampal ensemble memories during sleep. *Science 265*, 676–679.

Zola-Morgan, S., and Squire, L. R. (1993). Neuroanatomy of memory. *Annual Review of Neuroscience 16*, 547–563.

Zola-Morgan, S., Squire, L. R., Alvarez-Royo, P., and Clower, R. P. (1991). Independence of memory functions and emotional behavior: separate contributions of the hippocampal formation and the amygdale. *Hippocampus 1*, 207–20.

Zola-Morgan, S., Squire, L. R., and Amaral, D. G. (1986). Human amnesia and the medial temporal region: Enduring memory impairment following a bilateral lesion limited to field CA1 of the hippocampus. *Journal of Neuroscience 6*(10), 2950–2967.

Zola-Morgan, S., Squire, L. R., and Amaral, D. G. (1989). Lesions of the amygdala that spare adjacent cortical regions do not impair memory or exacerbate the impairment following lesions of the hippocampal formation. *Journal of Neuroscience 9*, 1922–1936.

PART FOUR

THE FEELING BRAIN

EMOTIONAL AND SOCIAL
FOUNDATIONS

12

WE FEEL, THEREFORE WE LEARN

THE RELEVANCE OF AFFECTIVE AND SOCIAL
NEUROSCIENCE TO EDUCATION

Mary Helen Immordino-Yang
Antonio Damasio

RECENT ADVANCES IN THE neuroscience of emotions are highlighting connections between cognitive and emotional functions that have the potential to revolutionize our understanding of learning in the context of schools. In particular, connections between decision making, social functioning, and moral reasoning hold new promise for breakthroughs in understanding the role of emotion in decision making, the relationship between learning and emotion, how culture shapes learning, and ultimately the development of morality and human ethics. These are all topics of eminent importance to educators as they work to prepare skilled, informed, and ethical students who can navigate the world's social, moral, and cognitive challenges as citizens. In this [chapter], we sketch a biological and evolutionary account of the relationship between emotion and rational thought, with the purpose of highlighting new connections between emotional, cognitive, and social functioning, and presenting a framework that we hope will inspire further work on the critical role of emotion in education.

This work was supported by a grant from the Annenberg Center for Communication at the University of Southern California and by a grant from the Mathers Foundation.

Modern biology reveals humans to be fundamentally emotional and social creatures. And yet those of us in the field of education often fail to consider that the high-level cognitive skills taught in schools, including reasoning, decision making, and processes related to language, reading, and mathematics, do not function as rational, disembodied systems, somehow influenced by but detached from emotion and the body. Instead, these crowning evolutionary achievements are grounded in a long history of emotional functions, themselves deeply grounded in humble homeostatic beginnings. Any competent teacher recognizes that emotions and feelings affect students' performance and learning, as does the state of the body, such as how well students have slept and eaten or whether they are feeling sick or well. We contend, however, that the relationship between learning, emotion, and body state runs much deeper than many educators realize and is interwoven with the notion of learning itself. It is not that emotions rule our cognition, or that rational thought does not exist. It is, rather, that the original purpose for which our brains evolved was to manage our physiology, to optimize our survival, and to allow us to flourish. When one considers that this purpose inherently involves monitoring and altering the state of the body and mind in increasingly complex ways, one can appreciate that emotions, which play out in the body and mind, are profoundly intertwined with thought. And after all, this should not be surprising. Complex brains could not have evolved separately from the organisms they were meant to regulate.

But there is another layer to the problem of surviving and flourishing, which probably evolved as a specialized aspect of the relationship between emotion and learning. As brains and the minds they support became more complex, the problem became not only dealing with one's own self but managing social interactions and relationships. The evolution of human societies has produced an amazingly complex social and cultural context, and flourishing within this context means that only our most trivial, routine decisions and actions, and perhaps not even these, occur outside of our socially and culturally constructed reality. Why does a high school student solve a math problem, for example? The reasons range from the intrinsic reward of having found the solution, to getting a good grade, to avoiding punishment, to helping tutor a friend, to getting into a good college, to pleasing his or her parents or the teacher. All of these reasons have a powerful emotional component and relate both to pleasurable sensations and to survival within our culture. Although the notion of surviving and flourishing is interpreted in a cultural and social framework at this late stage in evolution, our brains still bear evidence of their original purpose: to manage our bodies and minds in the service of living, and living happily, in the world with other people.

This realization has several important implications for research at the nexus of education and neuroscience. It points to new directions for understanding the interface of biology, learning, and culture, a critical topic in education that has proven difficult to investigate systematically (Davis, 2003; Rueda, 2006; Rueda, August, & Goldenberg, 2006). It promises to shed light on the elusive link between body and mind, for it describes how the health and sickness of the brain and body can influence each other. And importantly, it underscores our fundamentally social nature, making clear that the very neurobiological systems that support our social interactions and relationships are recruited for the often covert and private decision making that underlies much of our thought. In brief, learning, in the complex sense in which it happens in schools or the real world, is not a rational or disembodied process; neither is it a lonely one.

Reasoning, Decision Making, and Emotion: Evidence from Patients with Brain Damage

To understand why this is so, we begin with some history, and a problem. Well into the 1980s, the study of brain systems underlying behavior and cognition was heavily dominated by a top-down approach in which the processes of learning, language, and reasoning were understood as high-order systems that imposed themselves upon an obedient body. It is not that emotions were completely ignored or that they were not viewed by some as having a brain basis. Rather, their critical role in governing behavior, and in particular rational thought, was overlooked (Damasio, 1994). Emotions were like a toddler in a china shop, interfering with the orderly rows of stemware on the shelves.

And then an interesting problem emerged. In a research atmosphere in which cognition ruled supreme, it became apparent that the irrational behavior of neurological patients who had sustained lesions to a particular sector of the frontal lobe could not be adequately accounted for by invoking cognitive mechanisms alone. After sustaining damage to the ventromedial prefrontal cortex, these patients' social behavior was compromised, making them oblivious to the consequences of their actions, insensitive to others' emotions, and unable to learn from their mistakes. In some instances, these patients violated social convention and even ethical rules, failing to show embarrassment when it was due and failing to provide appropriate sympathetic support to those who expected it and had received it in the past.

These patients' ability to make advantageous decisions became compromised in ways that it had not been before. In fact, there was a complete separation between the period that anteceded the onset of the lesion, when these patients had been upstanding, reliable, and foresightful citizens, and the period thereafter, when they would make decisions that were often disadvantageous to themselves and their families. They would not perform adequately in their jobs, in spite of having the required skills; they would make poor business deals in spite of knowing the risks involved; they would lose their savings and choose the wrong partners in all sorts of relationships. Why would patients suffering from compromised social conduct also make poor decisions about apparently rational matters, such as business investments?

The traditional way to explain these patients' symptoms had been that something had gone wrong with their logical abilities or their knowledge base, such that they could no longer make decisions in a rational way. But, in fact, with further testing, it became apparent that these patients did not have a primary problem with knowledge, knowledge access, or logical reasoning, as had previously been assumed. To the contrary, they could explain cogently the conventional social and logical rules that ought to guide one's behavior and future planning. They had no loss of knowledge or lowering of IQ in the traditional sense. Instead, it gradually became clear that disturbances in the realm of emotion, which had been viewed as a secondary consequence of their brain damage, could provide a better account of their poor decision making. Those emotional aspects included a diminished resonance of emotional reactions generally as well as a specific compromise of social emotions, such as compassion, embarrassment, and guilt. By compromising the possibility of evoking emotions associated with certain past situations, decision options, and outcomes, the patients became unable to select the most appropriate response based on their past experience. Their logic and knowledge could be intact, but they failed to use past emotional knowledge to guide the reasoning process. Furthermore, they could no longer learn from the emotional repercussions of their decisions or respond emotionally to the reactions of their social partners. Their reasoning was flawed because the emotions and social considerations that underlie good reasoning were compromised (Damasio, Grabowski, Frank, Galaburda, & Damasio, 1994; Damasio, Tranel, & Damasio, 1990, 1991).

In retrospect, these patients provided a first glimpse into the fundamental role of emotion in reasoning and decision making. Missing a brain region that is now understood as needed to trigger a cascade of neurological and somatic events that together comprise a social emotion, such as embarrassment, compassion, envy, or admiration, their social behavior suffered. This is significant in itself, but even more intriguing was the realization that, without the ability to adequately access the guiding intuitions that accrue through emotional learning and social feedback, decision making and rational thought became compromised, as did learning from their mistakes and successes. While these patients can reason logically and ethically about standard cognitive and social problems in a laboratory setting (Saver & Damasio, 1991), out in the real world and in real time, they cannot use emotional information to decide between alternative courses of action. They can no longer adequately consider previous rewards and punishments or successes and failures, nor do they notice others' praise or disapproval. These patients have lost their ability to analyze events for their emotional consequences and to tag memories of these events accordingly. Their emotions are dissociated from their rational thought, resulting in compromised reason, decision making, and learning.

What does this mean for our argument about relevance to education? In addition to these patients, further evidence from psychophysiological and other studies of brain-damaged and normal people has allowed us to propose specific neural mechanisms underlying the role and operation of emotional signaling in normal and abnormal decision making (Bechara, 2005; Bechara & Damasio, 1997; Damasio, 1996). While the details of these neural mechanisms and evidence are beyond the scope of this [chapter], taken as a whole, they show that emotions are not just messy toddlers in a china shop, running around breaking and obscuring delicate cognitive glassware. Instead, they are more like the shelves underlying the glassware; without them cognition has less support.

To recap, the prefrontal patients we have described have social deficits. We have argued that these are fundamentally problems of emotion and therefore manifest as well in the realm of decision making. The relationship between these symptoms is very informative, in that it suggests that hidden emotional processes underlie our apparently rational real-world decision making and learning. Furthermore, this relationship underscores the importance of the ability to perceive and incorporate social feedback in learning.

While the relevance of these insights to educational contexts has not yet been empirically tested, they lead us to formulate two important hypotheses. First, because these findings underscore the critical role of emotion in bringing previously acquired knowledge to inform real-world decision making in social contexts, they suggest the intriguing possibility that emotional processes are required for the skills and knowledge acquired in school to transfer to novel situations and to real life. That is, emotion may play a vital role in helping children decide when and how to apply what they have learned in school to the rest of their lives. Second, the close ties between these patients' decision making, emotion, and social functioning may provide a new take on the relationship between biology and culture. Specifically, it may be via an emotional route that the social influences of culture come to shape learning, thought, and behavior.

While more work on the educational and cultural implications of these findings is warranted, interestingly, and sadly, some further insights into the biological connections between learning, emotion, and social functioning, especially as they relate to our hypothesis about culture, can be gleaned from another group of patients that has been discovered over the past few years. In this group, patients sustained comparable prefrontal damage in early childhood, rather than as adults. As they developed, these children were cognitively normal in the traditional IQ sense, able to use logical reasoning and factual knowledge to solve the kinds of academic problems expected of students. However, while smart in the everyday sense of the word, these children slowly revealed themselves as having varying degrees of psychopathic and antisocial tendencies. They were insensitive to punishment and reward and did not seek approval or social acceptance as typical children do. As adults, they were unable to competently manage their lives, wasting time and squandering resources and engaging in dangerous, antisocial, and aggressive behaviors. By outward appearances, these patients behaved in most ways similarly to the patients described above, who sustained prefrontal damage as adults (Anderson, Bechara, Damasio, Tranel, & Damasio, 1999; Damasio, 2005).

Additional investigation of adult patients with childhood onset of brain damage, though, revealed an intriguing difference between childhood and adult-onset prefrontal brain damage. While both groups can reason about traditional cognitive problems in the structure of the laboratory setting and both have normal IQs in the traditional sense, unlike patients with adult-onset prefrontal damage, childhood-onset patients appear never to have learned the rules that govern social and moral behavior. While adult-onset patients know right from wrong in the lab but are unable to use this information to guide their behavior, childhood-onset patients have apparently not learned right from wrong or the proper rules of social conduct. They do not know the social and ethical rules that they are breaking.

What is happening with these patients, and how is it relevant to the argument at hand? Unlike the often remarkable compensation for linguistic and other capacities after early childhood brain damage, so far the system for social conduct and ethical behavior does not show this kind of compensation. It is not that access in an abstract sense to the rules of social conduct requires intact frontal cortices, as the adult-onset patients show, and it is not that a social or moral conduct center in the brain has been irreparably damaged, as this scenario would not explain changes in general decision making. Instead, the situation is both simpler and more grave. These early-onset prefrontal patients may be suffering from the loss of what we might term the *emotional rudder*. Without the ability to manipulate situations and to mark those situations as positive or negative from an affective point of view, these children fail to learn normal social behavior. In turn, they lose the commensurate decision-making abilities described earlier. Insensitive to others' responses to their actions, these children fail to respond to educators' and others' attempts to teach them normal behavior.

But there is another intriguing piece to be learned from these children regarding the relationship between cognition and emotion and the role of the emotional rudder in learning. As in the adult-onset patients, it is still possible for these patients to have an operating cognitive system that allows them to be smart on certain measures and in certain contexts, solving standard cognitive tasks in a laboratory or structured educational setting without difficulty. In these contexts, their lack of knowledge is confined to the social and moral domains.

And yet, once outside of the structured school setting, their social deficits manifest as a much broader problem. They have the nonsocial knowledge they need, but without the guiding effects of the emotional rudder, they cannot use this information to guide their everyday living, even in nonsocial contexts. What these patients confirm is that the very neurobiological systems that support emotional functioning in social interactions also support decision making generally. Without adequate access to social and cultural knowledge, these children cannot use their knowledge efficaciously. As Vygotsky posited more than three-quarters of a century ago, social and cultural functioning actually does underlie much of our non social decision making and reasoning. Or, more precisely, social behavior turns out to be a special case of decision making and morality to be a special case of social behavior (see Damasio, 2005, for a more complete treatment of this argument). The neurological systems that support decision making generally are the same systems that support social and moral behavior. Without adequate access to emotional, social, and moral feedback, in effect the important elements of culture, learning cannot inform real-world functioning as effectively.

A Physiological and Evolutionary Account of Emotion and Cognition: From Automatic Responses to Morality, Creativity, High Reason, and Culture

In the perspective of the insights described earlier, and of much research in neurobiology and general biology in the two intervening decades, the connection between emotion and cognition is being seen in a very different light. To outline the current position, we shall present a simple scenario. Think of an ant crawling along a sidewalk, carrying a piece of food back to its nest. The ant scurries into a sidewalk crack to avoid being stepped on, then continues industriously on its way. What motivates this ant to preserve its own life? How did it decide, albeit non-consciously and automatically, to carry the piece of food and to turn toward its nest? Clearly, the decisions to hide to avoid being crushed, to carry the food, and to continue in the direction of the nest are primitive instances of cognition, composed of complex packages of innate responses that enable the ant to react advantageously to particular classes of situations. But what is essential to understand is that these and myriads of other primitive examples of cognition, even in the lowly ant, act together in the service of an emotional goal: to maintain and promote homeostasis and thus fitness. In short, the ant behaves the way it does because those behaviors promote its survival and efficiency. (Humans, as conscious beings, perceive that efficiency as well-being and pleasure.) Every action the ant takes is inherently biased toward helping the ant, or its group, do well.

Taking an evolutionary perspective, even the simplest unicellular organism has within the nucleus of its cell a master controller that permits that living organism to maintain itself for a certain span of life and to seek during that period the conditions that will allow it to thrive. Emotions and the mechanisms that constitute them as behaviors, which humans experience as resulting in punishment or reward, pain or pleasure, are, in essence, nature's answer to one central problem, that of surviving and flourishing in an ambivalent world. Put simply, the brain has evolved under numerous pressures and oppressions precisely to cope with the problem of reading the body's condition and responding accordingly and begins doing so via the machinery of emotion. This coping shows up in simple ways in simple organisms and in remarkably rich ways as brains get more complex. In the brains of higher animals and people, the richness is such that they can perceive the world through sensory processing and control their behavior in a way that includes what is traditionally called the mind. Out of the basic need to survive and flourish derives a way of dealing with thoughts, with ideas, and eventually with making plans, using imagination, and creating. At their core, all of these complex and artful human behaviors, the sorts of behaviors fostered in education, are carried out in the service of managing life within a culture and, as such, use emotional strategies (Damasio, 1999).

Emotion, then, is a basic form of decision making, a repertoire of know-how and actions that allows people to respond appropriately in different situations. The more advanced cognition becomes, the more high-level reasoning supports the customization of these responses, both in thought and in action. With evolution and development, the specifications of conditions to which people respond, and the modes of response at their disposal, become increasingly nuanced. The more people develop and educate themselves, the more they refine their behavioral and cognitive options. In fact, one could argue that the chief purpose of education is to cultivate children's building of repertoires of cognitive and behavioral strategies and options, helping them to recognize the complexity of situations and to respond in increasingly flexible, sophisticated, and creative ways. In our view, out of these processes of recognizing and responding, the very processes that form the interface between cognition and emotion, emerge the origins of creativity—the artistic, scientific, and technological innovations that are unique to our species. Further, out of these same kinds of processing emerges a special kind of human innovation: the social creativity that we call morality and ethical thought.

As the childhood-onset prefrontal patients show, morality and ethical decision making are special cases of social and emotional functioning. While the beginnings of altruism, compassion, and other notions of social equity exist in simpler forms in the nonhuman primates (Damasio, 2003; Hauser, 2006), human cognitive and emotional abilities far outpace those of the other animals. Our collective accomplishments range from the elevating and awe inspiring to the evil and grotesque. Human ethics and morality are direct evidence that we are able to move beyond the opportunistic ambivalence of nature; indeed, the hallmark of ethical action is the inhibition of immediately advantageous or profitable solutions in the favor of what is good or right within our cultural frame of reference. In this way, ethical decision making represents a pinnacle cognitive and emotional achievement of humans. At its best, ethical decision making weaves together emotion, high reasoning, creativity, and social functioning, all in a cultural context (Gardner, Csikszentmihaly, & Damon, 2001).

Returning to the example of the ant, our purpose in including this example was not to suggest that human emotions are equivalent to those of the ant or that human behavior can be reduced to simple, nonspecific packages that unfold purely nonconsciously in response to particular situations. Although some aspects of human behavior and emotion could be characterized in this way, such reductionism would be grossly misplaced, especially in an essay about connections to education. Instead, we aimed to illustrate that most, if not all, human decisions, behaviors, thoughts, and creations, no matter how far removed from survival in the homeostatic sense, bear the shadow of their emotive start.

In addition, as the prefrontal patients show, the processes of recognizing and responding to complex situations, which we suggest hold the origins of creativity, are fundamentally emotional and social. As such, they are shaped by and evaluated within a cultural context and, as we described in the previous section, are based upon emotional processing. No matter how complex and esoteric they become, our repertoire of behavioral and cognitive options continues to exist in the service of emotional goals. Neurobiologically and evolutionarily speaking, creativity is a means to survive and flourish in a social and cultural context, a statement that appears to apply from the relatively banal circumstances of daily living to the complex arena of ethical thought and behavior. In beginning to elucidate the neurobiological interdependencies between high reasoning, ethics, and creativity, all of which are fundamentally tied to emotion and critically relevant to education, we hope to provide a new vantage point from which to investigate the development and nurturance of these processes in schools.

Emotional Thought: Toward an Evidence-Based Framework

In general, cognition and emotion are regarded as two interrelated aspects of human functioning. However, while it is perfectly reasonable and in fact necessary to distinguish between these two aspects in studying learning and development (Fischer & Bidell, 1998), the overly stringent preservation of this dichotomy may actually obscure the fact that emotions comprise cognitive as well as sensory processes. Furthermore, the aspects of cognition that are recruited most heavily in education, including learning, attention, memory, decision making, motivation, and social functioning, are both profoundly affected by emotion and in fact subsumed within the processes of emotion. Emotions entail the perception of an emotionally competent trigger, a situation either real or imagined that has the power to induce an emotion, as well as a chain of physiological events that will enable changes in both the body and mind (Damasio, 1994). These changes in the mind, involving focusing of attention, calling up of relevant memories, and learning the associations between events and their outcomes, among other things, are the processes with which education is most concerned. Yes, rational thought and logical reasoning do exist, although hardly ever truly devoid of emotion, but they cannot be recruited appropriately and usefully in the real world without emotion. Emotions help to direct our reasoning into the sector of knowledge that is relevant to the current situation or problem.

In Figure 12.1, we provide a graphical depiction of the neurological relationship between cognition and emotion. In the diagram, we have used the term *emotional thought* to refer to the large overlap between cognition and emotion. Emotional thought encompasses processes of learning, memory, and decision making, in both social and nonsocial contexts. It is within the domain of emotional thought that creativity plays out, through increasingly nuanced recognition of complex dilemmas and situations and through the invention of correspondingly flexible and innovative responses. Both the recognition and response aspects of creativity can be informed by rational thought and high reason. In our model, recognition and response processes are much like the concepts of assimilation and accommodation proposed by Piaget (1952, 1954). However, Piaget focused almost exclusively on cognition and the development

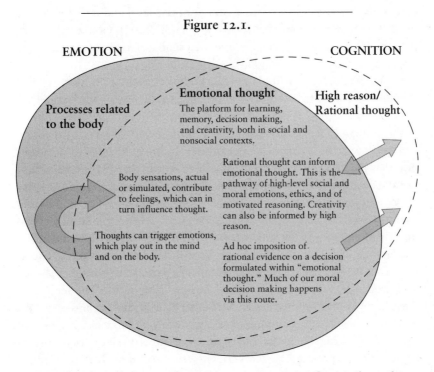

Figure 12.1.

EMOTION   **COGNITION**

Emotional thought   High reason/
Processes related   The platform for learning,   Rational thought
to the body   memory, decision making,
                          and creativity, both in social and
                          nonsocial contexts.

                                              Rational thought can inform
                          Body sensations, actual   emotional thought. This is the
                          or simulated, contribute   pathway of high-level social and
                          to feelings, which can in   moral emotions, ethics, and of
                          turn influence thought.   motivated reasoning. Creativity
                                                       can also be informed by high
                                                       reason.
                          Thoughts can trigger emotions,
                          which play out in the mind   Ad hoc imposition of
                          and on the body.   rational evidence on a decision
                                                        formulated within "emotional
                                                        thought." Much of our moral
                                                        decision making happens
                                                        via this route.

The evolutionary shadow cast by emotion over cognition influences the modern mind. In the diagram, the solid ellipse represents emotion; the dashed ellipse represents cognition. The extensive overlap between the two ellipses represents the domain of emotional thought. Emotional thought can be conscious or nonconscious and is the means by which bodily sensations come into our conscious awareness. High reason is a small section of the diagram and requires consciousness.

of logic, and although he recognized a role for emotion in child development (Piaget, 1981), he did not fully appreciate the fundamentally emotional nature of the processes he described.

In the diagram, high reason and rational thought also contribute to high-level social and moral emotions to form the specialized branch of decision making that is ethics. Motivated reasoning works in a similar manner and refers to the process by which emotional thoughts gain additional significance through the application of rational evidence and knowledge. In the other direction, rational evidence can be imposed upon certain kinds of emotional thought to produce the sort of automatic moral decision making that underlies intuitive notions of good and evil (Greene, Nystrom, Engell, Darley, & Cohen, 2004; Greene, Sommerville, Nystrom, Darley, & Cohen, 2001; Haidt, 2001). For example, in evaluating the morality of incest, experimental evidence suggests that people decide quickly at the subconscious and intuitive level and later impose ad hoc rational evidence on their decision (Haidt, 2001). Conversely, complex moral dilemmas such as whether to send a nation to war are (one hopes) informed by an abundance of rational evidence.

On the left side of the diagram, the bodily aspects of emotion are represented as a loop from emotional thought to the body and back. Here, emotional thoughts, either conscious or nonconscious, can alter the state of the body in characteristic ways, such as by tensing or relaxing the skeletal muscles or by changing the heart rate. In turn, the bodily sensations of these changes, either actual or simulated, contribute either consciously or nonconsciously to feelings, which can then influence thought. (Simulated body sensation refers to the fact that sometimes imagining bodily changes is sufficient; actually tensing the fists, for example, is not necessary.) This is the route by which rational deliberations over, say, a nation's wartime decisions can produce high-level social emotions such as indignation, as well as the bodily social manifestations of these emotions, such as tensed fists, increased heart rate, or loss of appetite. The feeling of these bodily sensations, either consciously or not, can then bias cognitive processes such as attention and memory toward, in this case, aggression. The end result may be an unprovoked argument with one's friend over a topic totally unrelated to the war, the creation of a bleak and angry abstract painting, or a generally tense mood.

In addition to the evidence discussed above, support for these relationships between the body, emotion, and cognition comes mainly from neurobiological and psychophysiological research, in which the induction of emotion, either directly by a stimulus in the environment or indirectly via thoughts or memories, causes mental changes as well as physiological effects on the body. In turn, feelings of emotion rely on the somatosensory systems of the brain. That is, the brain areas associated with interoception (the sensing of body states) are particularly active as people feel emotions such as happiness, fear, anger, or sadness (Damasio et al., 2000).

To conclude, in presenting this model, our goal is not to devalue established notions of cognition and emotion but to provide a biologically based account of this relationship and to begin to specify the nature of the overlap between cognition and emotion in a way that highlights processes relevant to education. These processes include learning, memory, decision making, and creativity, as well as high reason and rational thinking. They also include the influence of the mind on the body and of the body on the mind.

Educational Implications: A Call for Further Research

In teaching children, the focus is often on the logical reasoning skills and factual knowledge that are the most direct indicators of educational success. But there are two problems with this approach. First, neither learning nor recall happens in a purely rational domain, divorced from emotion, even though some of our knowledge will eventually distill into a moderately rational, unemotional form. Second, in teaching students to minimize the emotional aspects of their academic curriculum and function as much as possible in the rational domain, educators may be encouraging students to develop the sorts of knowledge that inherently do not transfer well to real-world situations. As both the early- and late-acquired prefrontal damage patients show, knowledge and reasoning divorced from emotional implications and learning lack meaning and motivation and are of little use in the real world. Simply having the knowledge does not imply that a student will be able to use it advantageously outside of school.

As recent advances in the neurobiology of emotions reveal, in the real world, cognition functions in the service of life-regulating goals, implemented by emotional machinery. Moreover, people's thoughts and feelings are evaluated within a sociocultural context and serve to help them survive and flourish in a social, rather than simply opportunistic, world. While the idea that learning happens in a cultural context is far from new (Tomasello, Carpenter, Call, Behne, & Moll, 2005), we hope that these new insights from neurobiology, which shed light on the nested relationships between emotion, cognition, decision making, and social functioning, will provide a jumping-off point for new thinking on the role of emotion in education. As educators have long known, it is simply not enough for students to master knowledge and logical reasoning skills in the traditional academic sense. They must be able to choose among and recruit these skills and knowledge usefully outside of the structured context of a school or laboratory. Because these choices are grounded in emotion and emotional thought, the physiology of emotion and its consequent process of feeling have enormous repercussions for the way we learn and for the way we consolidate and access knowledge. The more educators come to understand the nature of the relationship between emotion and cognition, the better they may be able to leverage this relationship in the design of learning environments.

In conclusion, new neurobiological evidence regarding the fundamental role of emotion in cognition holds the potential for important innovations in the science of learning and the practice of teaching. As researchers struggle with new directions and techniques for learning about these connections, a biological framework may help to constrain possibilities and generate new hypotheses and research directions. Just as neuroscience is coming to inform other education-related topics and problems (Goswami, 2006), the study of emotions, creativity, and culture is ripe for interdisciplinary collaborations among neuroscientists, psychologists, and educators. After all, we humans cannot divorce ourselves from our biology, nor can we ignore the high-level sociocultural and cognitive forces that make us special within the animal kingdom. When we educators fail to appreciate the importance of students' emotions, we fail to appreciate a critical force in students' learning. One could argue, in fact, that we fail to appreciate the very reason that students learn at all.

REFERENCES

Anderson, S. W., Bechara, A., Damasio, H., Tranel, D., & Damasio, A. R. (1999). Impairment of social and moral behavior related to early damage in human prefrontal cortex. *Nature Neuroscience, 2,* 1032–1037.

Bechara, A. (2005). Decision making, impulse control and loss of willpower to resist drugs: A neurocognitive perspective. *Nature Neuroscience, 8,* 1458–1463.

Bechara, A., & Damasio, H. (1997). Deciding advantageously before knowing the advantageous strategy. *Science, 275,* 1293–1295.

Damasio, A. R. (1994). *Descartes' error: Emotion, reason and the human brain.* New York: Avon Books.

Damasio, A. R. (1996). The somatic marker hypothesis and the possible functions of the prefrontal cortex. *Transactions of the Royal Society (London), 351,* 1413–1420.

Damasio, A. R. (1999). *The feeling of what happens.* New York: Harcourt Brace.

Damasio, A. R. (2003). *Looking for Spinoza: Joy, sorrow and the feeling brain.* Orlando, FL: Harcourt.

Damasio, A. R. (2005). The neurobiological grounding of human values. In J. P. Changeux, A. R. Damasio, W. Singer, & Y. Christen (Eds.), *Neurobiology of human values* (pp. 47–56). London: Springer Verlag.

Damasio, A. R., Grabowski, T. J., Bechara, A., Damasio, H., Ponto, L.L.B., Parvizi, J., & Hichwa, R. D. (2000). Subcortical and cortical brain activity during the feeling of self-generated emotions. *Nature Neuroscience, 3,* 1049–1056.

Damasio, A. R., Tranel, D., & Damasio, H. (1990). Individuals with sociopathic behavior caused by frontal damage fail to respond autonomically to social stimuli. *Behavioral Brain Research, 41,* 81–94.

Damasio, A. R., Tranel, D., & Damasio, H. (1991). Somatic markers and the guidance of behavior: Theory and preliminary testing. In H. S. Levin, H. M. Eisenberg, & A. L. Benton (Eds.), *Frontal lobe function and dysfunction* (pp. 217–229). New York: Oxford University Press.

Damasio, H. (2005). Disorders of social conduct following damage to prefrontal cortices. In J. P. Changeux, A. R. Damasio, W. Singer, & Y. Christen (Eds.), *Neurobiology of human values* (pp. 37–46). London: Springer Verlag.

Damasio, H., Grabowski, T., Frank, R., Galaburda, A. M., & Damasio, A. R. (1994). The return of Phineas Gage: Clues about the brain from the skull of a famous patient. *Science, 264,* 1102–1105.

Davis, H. A. (2003). Conceptualizing the role and influence of student-teacher relationships on children's social and cognitive development. *Educational Psychologist, 38,* 207–234.

Fischer, K. W., & Bidell, T. R. (1998). Dynamic development of psychological structures in action and thought. In R. M. Lerner (Ed.), *Handbook of child psychology: Theoretical models of human development* (5th ed., Vol. 1, pp. 467–561). New York: Wiley.

Gardner, H., Csikszentmihaly, M., & Damon, W. (2001). *Good work: When excellence and ethics meet.* New York: Basic Books.

Goswami, U. (2006). Neuroscience and education: From research to practice? *Nature Reviews Neuroscience, 7,* 406–411.

Greene, J. D., Nystrom, L. E., Engell, A. D., Darley, J. M., & Cohen, J. D. (2004). The neural bases of cognitive conflict and control in moral judgment. *Neuron, 44,* 389–400.

Greene, J. D., Sommerville, R. B., Nystrom, L. E., Darley, J. M., & Cohen, J. D. (2001). An fMRI investigation of emotional engagement in moral judgment. *Science, 293,* 2105–2108.

Haidt, J. (2001). The emotional dog and its rational tail: A social intuitionist approach to moral judgment. *Psychological Review, 108,* 814–834.

Hauser, M. (2006). *Moral minds: How nature designed our universal sense of right and wrong.* New York: HarperCollins.

Piaget, J. (1952). *The origins of intelligence in children* (M. Cook, Trans.). New York: International Universities Press. (Original work published 1936).

Piaget, J. (1954). *The construction of reality in the child* (M. Cook, Trans.). New York: Basic Books. (Original work published 1937).

Piaget, J. (1981). *Intelligence and affectivity: Their relationship during child development* (T. A. Brown & C. E. Kaegi, Eds./Trans.). Palo Alto, CA: Annual Reviews Monograph. (Originally presented as lectures, 1953–1954).

Rueda, R. (2006). Motivational and cognitive aspects of culturally accommodated instruction: The case of reading comprehension. In D. M. McInerney, M. Dowson, & S. V. Etten (Eds.), *Effective schools: Vol. 6: Research on sociocultural influences on motivation and learning* (pp. 135–158). Greenwich, CT: Information Age Publishing.

Rueda, R., August, D., & Goldenberg, C. (2006). The sociocultural context in which children acquire literacy. In D. August & T. Shanahan (Eds.), *Developing literacy in second-language learners: Report of the National Literacy Panel on language-minority children and youth* (pp. 319–340). Mahwah, NJ: Erlbaum.

Saver, J. L., & Damasio, A. R. (1991). Preserved access and processing of social knowledge in a patient with acquired sociopathy due to ventromedial frontal damage. *Neuropsychologia, 29,* 1241–1249.

Tomasello, M., Carpenter, M., Call, J., Behne, T., & Moll, H. (2005). Understanding and sharing of intentions: The origins of cultural cognition. *Behavioral and Brain Sciences, 28,* 675–735.

13

SELECTIONS FROM *WHY ZEBRAS DON'T GET ULCERS*

Robert M. Sapolsky

Selection from "Stress and Memory"

Anxiety: Some Foreshadowing

. . . Moderate and transient stress can enhance the sort of explicit memories that are the purview of the hippocampus. It turns out that stress can enhance another type of memory. This is one relevant to emotional memories, a world apart from the hippocampus and its dull concern with factoids. This alternative type of memory, and its facilitation by stress, revolves around another brain area, the amygdala.

And When Stress Goes On for Too Long

With the "sprinting across the savanna" versus "worrying about a mortgage" dichotomy, we can look at how the formation and retrieval of memories goes awry when stressors become too big or too prolonged.[1] People in the learning and memory business refer to this as an "inverse-U"

---

[1] A general review of the disruptive effects of stress can be found in R. Sapolsky, "Stress and Cognition," in Gazzaniga, M., ed., *The Cognitive Neurosciences,* 3rd ed. (Cambridge, Mass.: MIT Press, 2005).

relationship. As you go from no stress to a moderate, transient amount of stress—the realm of stimulation—memory improves. As you then transition into severe stress, memory declines.

The decline has been shown in numerous studies with lab rats, and with an array of stressors—restraint, shock, exposure to the odor of a cat. The same has been shown when high levels of glucocorticoids are administered to rats instead. But this may not tell us anything interesting. Lots of stress or of glucocorticoids may just be making for a generically messed-up brain. Maybe the rats would now be lousy at tests of muscle coordination, or responsiveness to sensory information, or what have you. But careful control studies have shown that other aspects of brain function, such as implicit memory, are fine. Maybe it's not so much that learning and memory are impaired, as much as the rat being so busy paying attention to that cat smell, or so agitated by it, that it doesn't make much headway solving whatever puzzle is in front of it. And within that realm of explicit memory problems, the retrieval of prior memories seems more vulnerable to stress than the formation of new ones. Similar findings have been reported with non-human primates.

What about humans? Much the same. In a disorder called Cushing's syndrome, people develop one of a number of types of tumors that result in secretion of tons of glucocorticoids. Understand what goes wrong next in a "Cushingoid" patient and you understand half of this book— high blood pressure, diabetes, immune suppression, reproductive problems, the works. And it's been known for decades that they get memory problems, specifically explicit memory problems, known as *Cushingoid dementia*.[2] . . . Synthetic glucocorticoids are often administered to people to control autoimmune or inflammatory disorders. With prolonged treatment, you see explicit memory problems as well.[3] But maybe this is due

---

[2]Memory problems in Cushing's disease: Starkman, M., Gebarski, S., Berent, S., and Schteingart, D., "Hippocampal formation volume, memory dysfunction, and cortisol levels in patients with Cushing's syndrome," *Biological Psychiatry 32* (1992): 756–765. Memory problems in people treated with synthetic glucocorticoids: Keenan, P., Jacobson, M., Soleymani, R., Mayes, M., Stress, M., and Yaldoo, D., "The effect on memory of chronic prednisone treatment in patients with systemic disease," *Neurology 47* (1996): 1396–1403.

[3]Glucocorticoids disrupt memory in healthy humans: Wolkowitz, O., Reuss, V., and Weingartner, H., "Cognitive effects of corticosteroids," *American Journal of Psychiatry 147* (1990): 1297–1310; Wolkowitz, O., Weingartner, H., Rubinow, D., Jimerson, D., Kling, M., Berretini, W., Thompson, K., Breier, A., Doran, A., Reus, V., and Pickar, D., "Steroid modulation of human memory: Biochemical correlates," *Biological Psychiatry 33* (1993): 744–751; Wolkowitz, O., Reus, V.,

to the disease, rather than to the glucocorticoids that were given for the disease. Pamela Keenan of Wayne State University has studied individuals with these inflammatory diseases, comparing those treated with steroidal anti-inflammatory compounds (that is, glucocorticoids) and those getting nonsteroidals; memory problems were a function of getting the glucocorticoids, not of the disease.

As the clearest evidence, just a few days of high doses of synthetic glucocorticoids impairs explicit memory in healthy volunteers. As one problem in interpreting these studies, these synthetic hormones work a bit differently from the real stuff, and the levels administered produce higher circulating glucocorticoid levels than the body normally produces, even during stress. Importantly, stress itself, or infusion of stress levels of the type of glucocorticoid that naturally occurs in humans, disrupts memory as well. As with the nonhuman studies, implicit memory is fine, and it's the recall, the retrieval of prior information, that is more vulnerable than the consolidation of new memories.

There are also findings (although fewer in number) showing that stress disrupts something called "executive function." This is a little different from memory. Rather than this being the cognitive realm of storing and retrieving facts, this concerns what you do with the facts—whether you organize them strategically, how they guide your judgments and decision making. This is the province of a part of the brain called the prefrontal cortex. . . .

Damaging Effects of Stress in Hippocampus

How does prolonged stress disrupt hippocampal-dependent memory? A hierarchy of effects have been shown in laboratory animals:

First, hippocampal neurons no longer work as well. Stress can disrupt long-term potentiation in the hippocampus even in the absence of glucocorticoids

---

Canick, J., Levin, B., and Lupien, S., "Glucocorticoid medication, memory and steroid psychosis in medical illness," *Annals of the New York Academy of Sciences 823* (1997): 81–96; Newcomer, J., Craft, S., Hershey, T., Askins, K., and Bardgett, M., "Glucocorticoid-induced impairment in declarative memory performance in adult human," *Journal of Neuroscience 14* (1994): 2047–2053. Disruptions with naturally high levels of glucocorticoids: Newcomer, J., Selke, G., Melson, A., Hershey, T., Craft, S., Richards, K., and Alderson, A., "Decreased memory performance in healthy humans induced by stress-level cortisol treatment," *Archives of General Psychiatry 56* (1999): 527–533. Stress impairs executive function: Amsten, A., "Stress impairs prefrontal cortical function in rats and monkeys: Role of dopamine Dl and norepinephrine alpha-1 receptor mechanisms," *Progress in Brain Research 126* (2000): 183–192.

(as in a rat whose adrenal glands have been removed), and extreme arousal of the sympathetic nervous system seems responsible for this.[4] Nonetheless, most of the research in this area has focused on the gluco-corticoids. Once glucocorticoid levels go from the range seen for mild or moderate stressors to the range typical of big-time stress, the hormone no longer enhances long-term potentiation, that process by which the con-nection between two neurons "remembers" by becoming more excitable. Instead, glucocorticoids now disrupt the process. Furthermore, similarly high glucocorticoid levels enhance something called *long-term depression,* which might be a mechanism underlying the process of forgetting, the flip side of hippocampal aha-ing.[5]

---

[4]Stress disrupts long-term potentiation and enhances long-term depression: stress levels of glucocorticoids inhibit long-term potentiation: Diamond, D., Bennet, M., Fleshner, M., and Rose, G., "Inverted-U relationship between the level of peripheral corticosterone and the magnitude of hippocampal primed burst potentiation," *Hippocampus 2* (1992): 421; Joels, M., "Steroid hormones and excitability in the mammalian brain," *Frontiers in Neuroendocrinology* 18 (1997): 2. Stress enhances long-term depression: Xu, L., Anwyl, R., and Rowan, M., "Behavioural stress facilitates the induction of long-term depression in the hip-pocampus," *Nature 387* (1997): 497. For a recent demonstration of how forget-ting, and suppressing the formation of new memories, is an active process: Anderson, M., Ochsner, K., Kuhl, B., Cooper, J., Robertson, E., Gabrieli, S., Glover, G., and Gabrieli, J., "Neural systems underlying the suppression of unwanted memories," *Science 303* (2004): 232. Stress disrupts these forms of memory amid preserving implicit memory: Woodson, J., and Macintosh, D., Fleshner, M., and Diamond, D., "Emotion-induced amnesia in rats: Working memory-specific impairment, corticosterone-memory correlation and fear versus arousal effects on memory," *Learning and Memory 10* (2003): 326.

The two receptor systems for glucocorticoids: Reul, J., and de Kloet, E., "Two receptor systems for corticosterone in rat brain: Microdistribution and differen-tial occupation," *Endocrinology 117* (1985): 2505. The relevance of the two receptor systems to memory is discussed in Kim, J. J., and Diamond, D. M."The stressed hippocampus, synaptic plasticity and lost memories," *Nature Reviews Neuroscience 3* (2002): 453–462.

The need for amygdaloid activation for stress to disrupt hippocampal func-tion: discussed in B. Roozendaal, "Glucocorticoids and the regulation of memory consolidation," *Psychoneuroendocrinology 25* (2000): 213–238; J. McGaugh, *Memory and Emotion* (New York: Weidenfeld and Nicolson, 2003). Sex raises glucocorticoid levels without disrupting hippocampal function: Woodson, J., et al., "Emotion-induced amnesia in rats," op. cit.

[5]For a review of long-term depression, see Stevens, C., "Strengths and weak-nesses in memory," *Nature 381* (1996): 471; Nicoll, R., and Malenka, R., "Long-distance long-term depression," *Nature 388* (1997): 427.

How can it be that increasing glucocorticoid levels a little bit (during moderate stressors) does one thing (enhances the potentiation of communication between neurons), while increasing glucocorticoid levels a lot does the opposite? In the mid-1980s, Ron de Kloet of the University of Utrecht in the Netherlands discovered the very elegant answer. It turns out that the hippocampus has large amounts of two different types of receptors for glucocorticoids. Critically, the hormone is about ten times better at binding to one of the receptors (thus termed a "high-affinity" receptor) than the other. What that means is that if glucocorticoid levels only rise a little bit, most of the hormone effect in the hippocampus will be mediated by that high-affinity receptor. In contrast, it is not until you are dealing with a major stressor that the hormone activates a lot of the "low-affinity" receptor. And, logically, it turns out that activation of the high-affinity receptor enhances long-term potentiation, while activation of the low-affinity one does the opposite. This is the basis of the "inverse-U" property mentioned above.

. . . The brain region called the amygdala plays a central role in the types of emotional memories involved in anxiety. But the amygdala is relevant here as well. The amygdala gets highly activated during major stressors and sends a large, influential neuronal projection to the hippocampus. Activation of this pathway seems to be a prerequisite for stress to disrupt hippocampal function.[6] Destroy a rat's amygdala, or sever its connection to the hippocampus, and stress no longer impairs the kind of memory that the hippocampus mediates, even amid the usual high glucocorticoid levels. This explains a finding that harks back to the subject of stress "signatures," and also demonstrates that some activities can represent a challenge to physical allostasis without being psychologically aversive. For example, sex raises glucocorticoid levels in a male rat—without activating the amygdala and without disrupting hippocampal function.

---

[6]Atrophy of hippocampal neuronal connections with stress: Woolley, C. S., Gould, E., and McEwen, B., "Exposure to excess glucocorticoids alters dendritic morphology of adult hippocampal pyramidal neurons," *Brain Research 531* (1990): 225; Magarinos, A., and McEwen, B., "Stress-induced atrophy of apical dendrites of hippocampal CA3c neurons: Comparison of stressors," *Neuroscience 69* (1995): 83; Magarinos, A., and McEwen, B., "Stress-induced atrophy of apical dendrites of hippocampal CA3c neurons: Involvement of glucocorticoid secretion and excitatory amino acid receptors," *Neuroscience 69* (1995): 88; Magarinos, A., McEwen, B., Flugge, G., and Fuchs, E., "Chronic psychosocial stress causes apical dendritic atrophy of hippocampal CA3 pyramidal neurons in subordinate tree shrews," *Journal of Neuroscience 16* (1996): 3534.

Second, neural networks get disconnected. . . . One neuron talks to another, "projects" to it. . . . Those projections are quite literal—long multibranched cables coming out of neurons that form synapses with the multibranched cables of other neurons. These cables (known as *axons* and *dendrites)* are obviously at the heart of neuronal communication and neuronal networks. Bruce McEwen has shown that, in a rat, after as little as a few weeks of stress or of exposure to excessive glucocorticoids, those cables begin to shrivel, to atrophy and retract a bit (Figure 13.1). Moreover, the same can occur in the primate brain. When that happens, synaptic connections get pulled apart and the complexity of your neural networks declines. Fortunately, it appears that at the end of the stressful period, the neurons can dust themselves off and regrow those connections.

This transient atrophy of neuronal processes probably explains a characteristic feature of memory problems during chronic stress. Destroy vast acres of neurons in the hippocampus after a massive stroke or late terminal stage Alzheimer's disease, and memory is profoundly impaired. Memories can be completely lost, and never again will these people remember, for example, something as vital as the names of their spouses. "Weaken" a neural network during a period of chronic stress by retracting some of the complex branches in those neuronal trees, and the memories of

---

Figure 13.1. Neurons of the Hippocampus of a Rat.

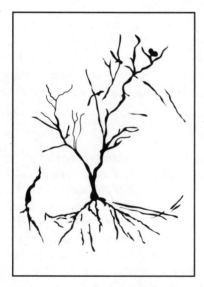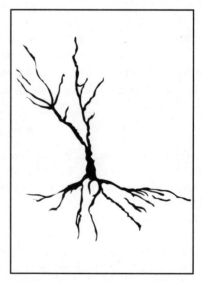

*On the left, healthy neurons; on the right, neurons with their
projections atrophied by sustained stress.*

Toulouse-Lautrec's name are still there. You simply have to tap into more and more associative cues to pull it out, because any given network is less effective at doing its job. Memories are not lost, just harder to access.

Third, the birth of new neurons is inhibited. If you learned your introductory neurobiology any time in the last thousand years, one fact that would be hammered in repeatedly is that the adult brain doesn't make new neurons. In the last decade, it has become clear that this is utterly wrong.[7] As a result, the study of "adult neurogenesis" is now, arguably, the hottest topic in neuroscience.

Two features about such neurogenesis are highly relevant to this chapter. First, the hippocampus is one of only two sites in the brain where these new neurons originate.[8] Second, the rate of neurogenesis can be regulated. Learning, an enriched environment, exercise, or exposure to estrogen all increase the rate of neurogenesis, while the strongest inhibitors identified to date are, you guessed it, stress and glucocorticoids—as little as a few hours of either in a rat.[9]

Two key questions arise. First, when the stress stops, does neurogenesis recover and, if so, how fast? No one knows yet. Second, what does it

---

[7]Actually, the evidence for new neurons in the adult brain was first reported in the 1960s by a handful of heretics who were generally ignored or hounded out of science. The field has finally caught up with them.

[8]The other region supplies new neurons to the olfactory system; for some strange reason, neurons that process odors constantly die off and have to be replaced. It turns out that there is a huge burst in the production of those new olfactory neurons early during pregnancy. They are fully on line just around the time of birth, and the scientists who discovered this speculated that these new olfactory neurons are tagged for the task of imprinting forever on the smell of your offspring (a critical event for mothers of most mammals). And what happens early in pregnancy, when those new olfactory neurons are showing up, but not quite making sense yet? I bet this has something to do with the famed nausea of pregnancy, the food aversions and olfactory sensitivities. This has nothing to do with stress, but it is too cool not to mention. For pregnancy-induced neurogenesis: Shingo, T., et al., "Pregnancy-stimulated neurogenesis in the adult female forebrain mediated by prolactin," *Science* 299 (2003): 117.

[9]Stress inhibits neurogenesis: Gould, E., and Gross, C., "Neurogenesis in adult mammals: Some progress and problems," *Journal of Neuroscience* 22 (2002): 619. This paper is a strong supporter of the idea that there is considerable neurogenesis in the adult hippocampus. The new neurons are needed for certain types of learning: Shors et al., "Neurogenesis in the adult is involved in the formation of trace memories," *Nature* 410 (2001): 372–376. For a review of the field by one of its strongest skeptics, see: Rakic, P., "Neurogenesis in adult primate neocortex: An evaluation of the evidence," *Nature Reviews Neuroscience* 3 (2002): 65–71.

matter that stress inhibits adult neurogenesis? Intrinsic in this question is the larger question of what adult neurogenesis is good for. This is incredibly controversial, an issue that has adversaries practically wrestling each other on the podium during scientific conferences. At one extreme are studies that suggest that under the right conditions, there are tons of neurogenesis in the adult hippocampus, that these new neurons form connections with other neurons, and that these new connections, in fact, are needed for certain types of learning. At the other extreme, every one of these findings is questioned. So the jury's out on this one.

Fourth, hippocampal neurons become endangered. As noted, within seconds of the onset of stress, glucose delivery throughout the brain increases. What if the stressor continues? By about thirty minutes into a continuous stressor, glucose delivery is no longer enhanced, and has returned to normal levels. If the stressor goes on even longer, the delivery of glucose to the brain is even inhibited, particularly in the hippocampus. Delivery is inhibited about 25 percent, and the effect is due to glucocorticoids.[10]

Decreasing glucose uptake to this extent in a healthy, happy neuron is no big deal. It just makes the neuron a little queasy and light-headed. But what if the neuron isn't healthy and happy, and is instead in the middle of a neurological crisis? It's now more likely to die than usual.

Glucocorticoids will compromise the ability of hippocampal neurons to survive an array of insults. Take a rat, give it a major epileptic seizure, and the higher the glucocorticoid levels at the time of the seizure, the more hippocampal neurons will die. Same thing for cardiac arrest, where oxygen and glucose delivery to the brain is cut off, or for a stroke, in which a single blood vessel in the brain shuts down. Same for concussive head trauma, or drugs that generate oxygen radicals. Disturbingly, same

---

[10]An obvious question: over and over I've emphasized how important it is during stress to cut down energy delivery to unessential outposts in your body, diverting it instead to exercising muscle. In the previous section, we added your hippocampus to that list of places that are spoon-fed energy with the onset of a stressor. It seems like that would be a clever area to continue to stoke, as the stressor goes on. Why should glucose delivery eventually be inhibited there? Probably because, as time goes by, you are running more on automatic, relying more on the implicit memory outposts in the brain to do things that involve reflexive movement—the martial arts display you put on to disarm the terrorist or, at least, the coordinated swinging of the softball bat at the company picnic that you've been nervous about. And thus, the decreased glucose delivery to highfalutin brain regions like the hippocampus and cortex may be a means to divert energy to those more reflexive brain regions.

thing for the closest there is to a rat neuron's equivalent of being damaged by Alzheimer's disease (exposing the neuron to fragments of an Alzheimer's-related toxin called *beta-amyloid*). Same for a rat hippocampus's equivalent of having AIDS-related dementia (induced by exposing the neuron to a damaging constituent of the AIDS virus called *gp120*).[11]

My lab and others have shown that the relatively mild energy problem caused by that inhibition of glucose storage by glucocorticoids or stress makes it harder for a neuron to contain the things that go wrong during one of these neurological insults. All of these neurological diseases are ultimately energy crises for a neuron: cut off the glucose to a neuron (hypoglycemia), or cut off both the glucose and oxygen (hypoxia-ischemia), or make a neuron work like mad (a seizure) and energy stores drop precipitously.[12] Damaging tidal waves of neurotransmitters and ions flood into the wrong

---

[11]. . . Stress can indirectly give rise to a stroke or cardiac arrest. But for the other neurological problems noted—seizure, head trauma, AIDS-related dementia, and most important, Alzheimer's disease—there is no evidence that stress or glucocorticoids *cause* these maladies. Instead, the possibility is that they worsen pre-existing cases.

[12]Glucocorticoids inhibit glucose utilization and transport in the hippocampus and in hippocampal neurons and glia: Kadekaro, M., Masonori, I., and Gross, P., "Local cerebral glucose utilization is increased in acutely adrenalectornized rats," *Neuroendocrinology* 47 (1988): 329; Homer, H., Packan, D., and Sapolsky, R., "Glucocorticoids inhibit glucose transport in cultured hippocampal neurons and glia," *Neuroendocrinology* 52 (1990): 57; Virgin, C., Ha, T., Packan, D., Tombaugh, G., Yang, S., Homer, H., and Sapolsky, R., "Glucocorticoids inhibit glucose transport and glutamate uptake in hippocampal astrocytes: Implications for glucocorticoid neurotoxicity," *Journal of Neurochemistry* 57 (1991): 1422.

The concept of neuroendangerment by glucocorticoids is discussed in Sapolsky, R., "Stress, glucocorticoids, and damage to the nervous system: The current state of confusion," *Stress* 1 (1996): 1. Also see Sapolsky, R., *Stress, the Aging Brain, and the Mechanisms of Neuron Death* (Cambridge, Mass.: MIT Press, 1992).

Glucocorticoids worsen the hippocampal damage caused by seizure in the rat: Sapolsky, R., "A mechanism for glucocorticoid toxicity in the hippocampus: Increased neuronal vulnerability to metabolic insults," *Journal of Neuroscience* 5 (1995): 1227; and by lack of oxygen caused by cardiac arrest: Sapolsky, R., and Pulsinelli, W., "Glucocorticoids potentiate ischemic injury to neurons: Therapeutic implications," *Science* 229 (1985): 1397; vulnerability to damage caused by the amyloid fragment of Alzheimer's disease: Behl, C., Lezoualc'h, F., Trapp, T., Widmann, M., Skutella, T., and Holsboer, F., "Glucocorticoids enhance oxidative stress-induced cell death in hippocampal neurons in vitro,"

(continued)

places, oxygen radicals are generated. If you throw in glucocorticoids on top of that, the neuron is even less able to afford to clean up the mess. Thanks to that stroke or seizure, today's the worst day of that neuron's life, and it goes into the crisis with 25 percent less energy in the bank than usual.

Finally, there is now evidence that truly prolonged exposure to stress or glucocorticoids can actually kill hippocampal neurons. The first hints of this came in the late 1960s. Two researchers showed that if guinea pigs are exposed to pharmacological levels of glucocorticoids (that is, higher levels than the body ever normally generates on its own), the brain is damaged. Oddly, damage was mainly limited to the hippocampus. This was right around the time that Bruce McEwen was first reporting that the hippocampus is loaded with receptors for glucocorticoids and no one really appreciated yet how much the hippocampus was the center in the brain for glucocorticoid actions.

Beginning in the early 1980s, various researchers, including myself, showed that this "glucocorticoid neurotoxicity" was not just a pharmacological effect, but was relevant to normal brain aging in the rat.[13]

(continued)   Endocrinology 138 (1997): 101; Goodman, Y., Bruce, A., Cheng, B., and Mattson, M., "Estrogens attenuate and corticosterone exacerbates excitotoxicity, oxidative injury, and amyloid beta-peptide toxicity in hippocampal neurons," Journal of Neurochemistry 66 (1996): 1836; gp120-induced damage in neurons: Brooke, S., Chan, R., Howard, S., and Sapolsky, R., "Endocrine modulation of the neurotoxicity of gp120 implications for AIDS-related dementia complex," Proceedings of the National Academy of Sciences, USA 94 (1997): 9457–9462.

[13]Glucocorticoids as neurotoxic: the first report of glucocorticoid neurotoxicity: Aus der Muhlen, K., and Ockenfels, H., "Morphologische veranderungen in diencephalon and telenceaphlin nach storngen des regelkreises adenohypophyse-nebennierenrinde III. Ergebnisse beim meerschweinchen nach verabreichung von cortison and hydrocortison," Z Zellforsch 93 (1969): 126. The first report of the hippocampus as a glucocorticoid target site: McEwen, B., Weiss, J., and Schwartz, I., "Selective retention of corticosterone by limbic structures in rat brain," Nature 220 (1968): 911. Glucocorticoids and stress and accelerating hippocampal neuron loss: Sapolsky, R., Krey, L., and McEwen, B., "Prolonged glucocorticoid exposure reduces hippocampal neuron number: Implications for aging," Journal of Neuroscience 5 (1985): 1221; Kerr, D., Campbell, L., Applegate, M., Brodish, A., and Landfield, P., "Chronic stress-induced acceleration of electrophysiologic and morphometric biomarkers of hippocampal aging," Journal of Neuroscience 11 (1991): 1316. Removing glucocorticoids or decreasing their secretion delays hippocampal neuron loss: Landfield, P., Baskin, R., and Pitler, T., "Brain-aging correlates: Retardation by hormonal-pharmacological treatments," Science 214 (1981): 581; Meaney, M., Aitken, D., Bhatnager, S., van Berkel, C., and Sapolsky, R., "Effect of neonatal

Collectively, the studies showed that lots of glucocorticoid exposure (in the range seen during stress) or lots of stress itself would accelerate the degeneration of the aging hippocampus. Conversely, diminishing glucocorticoid levels (by removing the adrenals of the rat) would delay hippocampal aging. And as one might expect by now, the extent of glucocorticoid exposure over the rat's lifetime not only determined how much hippocampal degeneration there would be in old age, but how much memory loss as well.

Where do glucocorticoids and stress get off killing your brain cells? Sure, stress hormones can make you sick in lots of ways, but isn't neurotoxicity going a bit beyond the bounds of good taste? A dozen years into studying the phenomenon, we're not yet sure.

Selection from "The View from the Bottom"

Socioeconomic Status, Stress, and Disease

If you want to see an example of chronic stress, study poverty. Being poor involves lots of physical stressors. Manual labor and a greater risk of work-related accidents. Maybe even two or three exhausting jobs, complete with chronic sleep deprivation. Maybe walking to work, walking to the laundromat, walking back from the market with the heavy bag of groceries, instead of driving an air-conditioned car. Maybe too little money to afford a new mattress that might help that aching back, or some more hot water in the shower for that arthritic throb; and, of course, maybe some hunger thrown in as well. . . . The list goes on and on.[14]

---

handling on age-related impairments associated with the hippocampus," *Science* 239 (1988): 766.

Stress and glucocorticoids damage the nonhuman primate hippocampus: Uno, H., Tarara, R., Else, J., Suleman, M., and Sapolsky, R., "Hippocampal damage associated with prolonged and fatal stress in primates," *Journal of Neuroscience* 9 (1989): 1705; Sapolsky, R., Uno, H., Rebert, C., and Finch, C., "Hippocampal damage associated with prolonged glucocorticoid exposure in primates," *Journal of Neuroscience* 10 (1990): 2897; Uno, H., Eisele, S., Sakai, A., Shelton, S., Baker, E., DeJesus, O., and Holden, J., "Neurotoxicity of glucocorticoids in the primate brain," *Hormones and Behavior* 28 (1994): 336.

[14]The poor do have the most stressors: McLeod, J., and Kessler, R., "Socioeconomic status differences in vulnerability to undesirable life events," *Journal of Health, Society and Behavior* 31 (1990): 162; Cohen, S., and Wills, T., "Stress, social support and the buffering hypothesis," *Psychological Bulletin* 98 (1985): 310; Brown, G., and Harris, T., *Social Origins of Depression* (London: Tavistock, 1978).

Naturally, being poor brings disproportionate amounts of psychological stressors as well. Lack of control, lack of predictability: numbing work on an assembly line, an occupational career spent taking orders or going from one temporary stint to the next. The first one laid off when economic times are bad—and studies show that the deleterious effects of unemployment on health begin not at the time the person is laid off, but when the mere threat of it first occurs.[15] Wondering if the money will stretch to the end of the month. Wondering if the rickety car will get you to tomorrow's job interview on time. How's this for an implication of lack of control: one study of the working poor showed that they were less likely to comply with their doctors' orders to take antihypertensive diuretics (drugs that lower blood pressure by making you urinate) because they weren't allowed to go to the bathroom at work as often as they needed to when taking the drugs.

As a next factor, being poor means that you often can't cope with stressors very efficiently.[16] Because you have no resources in reserve, you can never plan for the future, and can only respond to the present crisis. And when you do, your solutions in the present come with a whopping great price later on—metaphorically, or maybe not so metaphorically, you're always paying the rent with money from a loan shark. Everything has to be reactive, in the moment. Which increases the odds that you'll be in even worse shape to deal with the next stressor—growing strong from adversity is mostly a luxury for those who are better off.

Along with all of that stress and reduced means of coping, poverty brings with it a marked lack of outlets. Feeling a little stressed with life and considering a relaxing vacation, buying an exercycle, or taking some classical guitar lessons to get a little peace of mind? Probably not. Or how about quitting that stressful job and taking some time off at home to figure out what you're doing with your life? Not when there's

---

[15]The threat of unemployment disrupts health: Beale, N., and Nethercott, S., "Job-loss and family morbidity: A study of a factory closure," *Journal of the Royal College of General Practitioners* 35 (1985): 510; Cobb, S., and Kasl, S., *Termination: The Consequences of Job Loss*, DHEW-MOSH Publication No.77–224 (Cincinnati, Ohio: U.S. NIOSH, 1977). The study about workers not taking their diuretics because they couldn't go to the bathroom at work: cited in Adler, N., Boyce, T., Chesney, M., Folkman, S., and Syme, S., "Socioeconomic inequalities in health: No easy solution," *Journal of the American Medical Association* 269 (1993): 3140.
[16]The poor don't cope with stressors very efficiently: Hobfoll, S., *Stress, Community and Culture* (New York: Plenum, 1998).

an extended family counting on your paycheck and no money in the bank. Feeling like at least jogging regularly to get some exercise and let off some steam? Statistically, a poor person is far more likely to live in a crime-riddled neighborhood, and jogging may wind up being a hair-raising stressor.

Finally, along with long hours of work and kids to take care of comes a serious lack of social support—if everyone you know is working two or three jobs, you and your loved ones, despite the best of intentions, aren't going to be having much time to sit around being supportive. Thus, poverty generally equals more stressors—and though the studies are mixed as to whether or not the poor have more major catastrophic stressors, they have plenty more chronic daily stressors.

All these hardships suggest that low socioeconomic status (SES— typically measured by a combination of income, occupation, housing conditions, and education) should be associated with chronic activation of the stress-response. Only a few studies have looked at this, but they support this view. One concerned school kids in Montreal, a city with fairly stable communities and low crime. In six- and eight-year-old children, there was already a tendency for lower-SES kids to have elevated glucocorticoid levels. By age ten, there was a step-wise gradient, with low-SES kids averaging almost double the circulating glucocorticoids as the highest-SES kids.[17] Another example concerns people

---

[17]Montreal school kids: Lupien, S., King, S., Meaney, M., and McEwen, B. S., "Child's stress hormone levels correlate with mother's socioeconomic status and depressive state," *Biological Psychiatry* 48 (2000): 976. Lithuanians: Kristnson et al., "Antixoidant stat and mortality from coronary heart disease in Lithuanian and Swedish men," *British Medical Journal* 314 (1997): 629. In a more recent study it was shown that the lower your SES in the British civil service (regardless of gender), the more your glucocorticoid levels rise in anticipation of work in the morning: Kunz-Ebrecht, S., Kirschbaum, C., Marmot, M., and Steptoe, A., "Differences in cortisol awakening response on work days and weekends in women and men from the Whitehall II cohort," *Psychoneuroendocrinology* 29 (2004): 516. Just to complicate things a bit, SES influences glucocorticoid levels during the workday. However, the pattern there is that, among men, the lower your SES (again, in the British civil service), the higher your glucocorticoid levels. In contrast, among women, the higher your SES, the higher your workday glucocorticoid level. See: Steptoe, A., Kunz-Ebrecht, S., Owen, N., Feldman, P., Willemsen, G., Kirschbaum, C., and Marmot, M., "Socioeconomic status and stress-related biological responses over the working day," *Psychosomatic Medicine* 65 (2004): 461–470.

in Lithuania. In 1978, men in Lithuania, then part of the USSR, had the same mortality rates for coronary heart disease as did men in nearby Sweden. By 1994, following the disintegration of the Soviet Union, Lithuanians had four times the Swedish rate. In 1994 Sweden, SES was not related to glucocorticoid levels, whereas in 1994 Lithuania, it was strongly related.

Findings like these suggest that being poor is associated with more stress-related diseases. As a first pass, let's just ask whether low SES is associated with more diseases, period. And is it ever.

The health risk of poverty turns out to be a huge effect, the biggest risk factor there is in all of behavioral medicine—in other words, if you have a bunch of people of the same gender, age, and ethnicity and you want to make some predictions about who is going to live how long, the single most useful fact to know is each person's SES. If you want to increase the odds of living a long and healthy life, don't be poor. Poverty is associated with increased risks of cardiovascular disease, respiratory disease, ulcers, rheumatoid disorders, psychiatric diseases, and a number of types of cancer, just to name a few.[18] It is associated with higher rates of people judging themselves to be of poor health, of infant mortality, and of mortality due to all causes. Moreover, lower SES predicts lower birth weight, after controlling for body size—and we know . . . the lifelong effects of low birth weight . . . , be born poor but hit the lottery when you're three weeks old, spend the rest of your life double-dating with Donald Trump, and you're still going to have a statistical increase in some realms of disease risk for the rest of your life.

Is the relationship between SES and health just some little statistical hiccup in the data? No—it can be a huge effect. In the case of some of

---

[18]As but one example, across the countries of Europe, socioeconomic status accounts for 68 percent of the variance as to who gets a stroke. However, not all diseases are more prevalent among the poor, and, fascinatingly, some are even more common among the wealthy. Melanoma is an example, suggesting that sun exposure in a lounge chair may have different disease risks than getting your neck red from stooped physical labor (or that a huge percentage of poor people laboring away in the sun have a fair amount of melanin in their skin, if you know what I mean). Or multiple sclerosis, and a few other autoimmune diseases and, during its heyday, polio. Or "hospitalism," a pediatric disease of the 1930s in which infants would waste away in hospitals. It is now understood that it was mostly due to lack of contact and sociality—and kids who would wind up in poorer hospitals were less subject to this, since the hospitals couldn't afford state-of-the-art incubators, necessitating that staff actually hold them.

those diseases sensitive to SES, if you cling to the lowest rungs of the socioeconomic ladder, it can mean ten times the prevalence compared with those perched on top.[19] Or stated another way, this translates into a five- to ten-year difference in life expectancy in some countries when

---

[19]A number of writers in the field have noted (even pre-DiCaprio) that there was a strict SES gradient as to who survived on the *Titanic*. The *Titanic* data are discussed in Marmot, M., "Epidemiology of SES and health: Are determinants within countries the same as between countries?" *Annals of the New York Academy of Sciences 896* (1999): 16. Pincus, T., and Callahan, L., "What explains the association between socioeconomic status and health: Primarily access to medical care or mind-body variables?" *Advances 11* (1995): 4; Syme, S., and Berkman, L., "Social class, susceptibility and sickness," *American Journal of Epidemiology 104* (1976): 1; Adler, N., Boyce, T., Chesney, M., Folkman, S., and Syme, S., "Socioeconomic inequalities in health: No easy solution," *Journal of the American Medical Association 269* (1993): 3140; Anderson, N., and Armstead, C., "Toward understanding the association of SES and health; a new challenge for the biopsychosocial approach," *Psychosomatic Medicine 57* (1995): 213; Evans, R., Barer, M., and Marmor, T., *Why Are Some People Healthy and Others Not? The Determinants of Health of Populations* (New York: Aldine de Gruyter, 1994); Antonovsky, A., "Social class and the major cardiovascular diseases," *Journal of Chronic Diseases 21* (1968): 65; Marmot, M., "Stress, social and cultural variations in heart disease," *Journal of Psychosomatic Research 27* (1983): 377; Levenstein, S., Prantera, C., Varvo, V., Arca, M., Scribano, M., Spinella, S., and Berto, E., "Long-term symptom patterns in duodenal ulcer: Psychosocial factors," *Journal of Psychosomatic Research 41* (1996): 465; Hahn, R., Eaker, E., Barker, N., Teutsch, S., Sosniak, W., and Krieger, N., "Poverty and death in the United States," *International Journal of Health Services 26* (1996): 673. Lower birth weight: Stem, A., "Social adversity, low birth weight, and pre-term delivery," *British Medical Journal 295* (1987): 291; Budrys, G., *Unequal Health: How Inequality Contributes to Health or Illness* (Lanham, Md.: Rowman and Littlefield, 2003).

Diseases more prevalent among the wealthy: malignant melanoma and breast cancer: Kitagawa, E., and Hauser, P., *Differential Mortality in the United States* (Cambridge, Mass.: Harvard University Press, 1973). Multiple sclerosis: Pincus, T., and Callahan, L., "What explains the association between socioeconomic status and health: Primarily access to medical care or mind-body variables?" *Advances 11* (1995): 4. Polio: Pincus, T., in Davis, B., ed., *Microbiology, Including Immunology and Molecular Genetics,* 3d ed. (New York: Harper and Row). SES and hospitalism is reviewed in: Sapolsky, R., "How the other half heals," *Discover* (April 1998): 46.

comparing the poorest and wealthiest, and decades' worth of differences when comparing subgroups of the poorest and wealthiest.[20]

Findings such as these go back centuries. For example, one study of men in England and Wales demonstrated a steep SES gradient in mortality in every decade of the twentieth century.[21] This has a critical implication that has been pointed out by Robert Evans of the University of British Columbia: the diseases that people were dying of most frequently a century ago are dramatically different from the most common ones now. Different causes of death, but same SES gradient, same relationship between SES and health. Which tells you that the gradient arises less from disease than from social class. Thus, writes Evans, the "roots [of the SES health gradient] lie beyond the reach of medical therapy."

So SES and health are tightly linked. What direction is the causality? Maybe being poor sets you up for poor health. But maybe it's the other way around, where being sickly sets you up for spiraling down into poverty. The latter certainly happens, but most of the relationship is due to the former. This is demonstrated by showing that your SES at one point in life predicts important features of your health later on.[22] For example, poverty early in life has adverse effects on health forever

---

[20]Five- to ten-year difference in life expectancy: Wilkinson, R., *Mind the Gap: Hierarchies, Health and Human Evolution* (London: Weidenfeld and Nicolson, 2000). Decades of differences: Murray, C. J. L., Michaud, C. M., et al. *U.S. Patterns of Mortality by County and Race: 1965–1994* (Cambridge, Mass.: Burden of Disease Unit, Harvard Center for Population and Development Studies, 1998).

[21]Gradient going back centuries is discussed in: Evans, R., *Interpreting and Addressing Inequalities in Health: From Black to Acheson to Blair to . . . ?* (London: OHE Publications, 2002).

[22]SES predicts health later in life: Lynch, J., Kaplan, G., Pamuk, E., Cohen, R., Heck, K., Balfour, J., and Yen, I., "Income inequality and mortality in metropolitan areas of the United States," *American Journal of Public Health 88* (1998): 1074. Poverty early in life: Hertzman, C., "The biological embedding of early experience and its effects on health in adulthood," *Annals of the New York Academy of Sciences 896* (1999): 85. The nun study: Snowdon, D., Ostwald, S., and Kane, R., "Education, survival and independence in elderly Catholic sisters 1936–1988," *American Journal of Epidemiology 120* (1989): 999; Snowdon, D., Ostwald, S., Kane, R., and Keenan, N., "Years of life with good and poor mental and physical function in the elderly," *Journal of Clinical Epidemiology 42* (1989): 1055. Health and cumulative percentage of life spent poor: Hertzman, op. cit.

after. . . . One remarkable study involved a group of elderly nuns. They took their vows as young adults, and spent the rest of their lives sharing the same diet, same health care, same housing, and so on. Despite controlling for all these variables, in old age their patterns of disease, of dementia, and of longevity were still predicted by the SES status they had when they became nuns more than half a century before.

Thus, SES influences health, and the greater cumulative percentage of your life you've spent poor, the more of an adverse impact on health.[23] Why should SES influence health? A century ago in the United States, or today in a developing country, the answer would be obvious. It would be about poor people getting more infectious diseases, less food, and having an astronomically higher infant mortality rate. But with our shift toward the modern prevalence of slow, degenerative diseases, the answers have shifted as well.

---

[23]What that means is that you're not completely sunk if you're born poor; social mobility helps to some extent.

THE EFFECT OF VIOLENCE AND STRESS IN KIDS' BRAINS

Ronald Kotulak

A NEW KIND OF EPIDEMIC is ravaging our children, scientists warn. It is not caused by germs or poor diet, but by a scourge that is only now being recognized by medicine: brain damage caused by bad experiences.

Such damage, the evidence indicates, can increase the risk of developing a wide variety of ills ranging from aggression, language failure, depression, and other mental disorders to asthma, epilepsy, high blood pressure, immune-system dysfunction, and diabetes.

All of these problems are on the increase as the forces that generate stress—poverty, violence, sexual abuse, family breakup, neglect, drugs, lack of good stimulation, too much of the wrong kind of stimulation—continue to escalate. These kinds of bad experiences, pouring into the brain through the senses—sight, smell, taste, touch, sound—can organize the trillions of constantly active connections between brain cells into diseased networks.

"That puts a lot of importance on parenting because that has a big impact on the way the brain becomes wired," said Christopher Coe, a University of Wisconsin psychologist who has shown that infant monkeys deprived of parenting have deficiencies in key brain structures and suffer from numerous immunological disorders. "There is a social cost if you don't have good parenting. It may be that you stamp an individual for their lifetime, not only in terms of their behavior and emotions, but literally their predisposition for disease."

One of the more astounding discoveries is that the stresses caused by bad experiences can actually affect genes, switching them on or off at the wrong times, forcing them to build abnormal networks of brain-cell connections.

"This means that the environment—external influences from conception onward—has a major role in shaping our individuality by shaping the expression of genes," said neuroscientist Bruce McEwen of Rockefeller University.

Bad experiences affect the brain primarily through stress hormones such as cortisol and adrenaline. Designed to respond to psychological or physical danger, these hormones prepare the body for fight or flight. Normally such changes are smooth: The brain and body are prepared for action when need be and then put back on an even keel when the danger is over.

But when these hormones are overactive as a result of persistent stresses encountered during fetal development or early childhood, they can take over genetic regulation like a band of terrorists. The terrorized genes then set up aberrant networks of connections between brain cells, imprinting how the brain has mislearned: an epileptic seizure instead of a clear signal between cells, a depressive episode instead of a happy thought, a surge of rage instead of a willingness to compromise.

"We can now see how a learning disability could arise from a child's bad experiences," said neuroscientist Michael Merzenich of the University of California at San Francisco. "It's not just by being born with a bad gene or a brain defect but by having a bad learning strategy from infancy. We can see how the brain can become unstable and why that instability should result in a variety of neurological conditions that are common in humans."

How these bad experiences produce their damaging effects is only now beginning to be understood, and it is not without controversy, especially when genes are involved.

"Many people don't want to hear that your brain may be biologically different if you grow up in one environment or another," said Dr. Saul Schanberg, a Duke University biological psychiatrist. "One of those differences may be that [a stressful] environment has caused genes important for survival . . . to become overexpressed, making you more aggressive and violent," he added.

The brain is very resilient and maintains an even course in the face of the most outrageous experiences. That's why most children born in conditions of poverty and violence come out okay. Scientists suspect that the reason some children, regardless of their social or economic status, come out with damaged brains may be that they are genetically more vulnerable to stress. Furthermore, their bad experiences are not neutralized by a caring parent or involved adult.

"The things that are associated with resiliency have to do with protective factors like the quality of home life, the parent-child relationship, or another relationship that provides some security for the child," said Megan Gunnar, a child development psychologist at the University of Minnesota.

Animal experiments clearly show the protective power of a little security, and the brain damage that can occur when it is absent. Newborn animals that are deprived of nurturing by their mothers become dysfunctional and antisocial.

Such damage also occurs before birth, a period in which the fetus was once thought to be protected. For example, rats that are stressed during pregnancy give birth to offspring that are very emotional and reactive.

"They have normal offspring from the standpoint of size and appearance," said Dr. Ned Kalin, chief of psychiatry at the University of Wisconsin at Madison. "But when you look at their development you find that they are hyperresponsive to stress. When you look at their brains you find more adrenaline [a stress hormone]."

On the other hand, Rockefeller University's McEwen and others have found that when they can, in effect, turn up the volume on mothering, newborns grow up in the opposite way: calm, cool, and ready to explore. In their experiments, rat pups are removed from their cages for fifteen minutes a day and then immediately returned.

The difference is that the worried mothers showered attention on the handled rat pups after they were returned to the cage, thereby turning down the amount of stress hormones their young brains would otherwise have been making, McEwen said. "People need to be aware that the brain is doggone vulnerable. If something happens early in life it can have permanent consequences for how a kid develops and learns."

For an increasing number of children, bad experiences are on the rise. The Census Bureau reports that in 1991 there were 14.3 million children living in poverty, an increase of 1 million from 1990.

Violence has become an overwhelming and mind-shattering way of life for many youngsters. A study of more than 1,000 students from poor Chicago neighborhoods found that 74 percent of them had witnessed a murder, shooting, stabbing, or robbery. Nearly half of them were themselves victims of a rape, shooting, stabbing, robbery, or some other violent act.

"The brain responds to experience," said Dr. Richard Davidson, a professor of psychology and psychiatry at the University of Wisconsin. "Children who are raised in impoverished conditions . . . are at high risk for having impoverished brains." (See Figure 14.1.)

The magnitude of the problem was revealed in a recent nationwide study showing that one child in five under age eighteen has a learning,

---

Figure 14.1. Negative Experience and the Brain.

NEGATIVE EXPERIENCE AND THE BRAIN
Brain connections can be damaged by negative experiences, making learning more difficult and sometimes resulting in violent behavior.

MENTAL DISORDERS AND CRIME
A study done by scientists at the University of Montreal shows that substance abusers and subjects with major mental disorders were more likely to be convicted of a crime than those with no disorder or handicap.

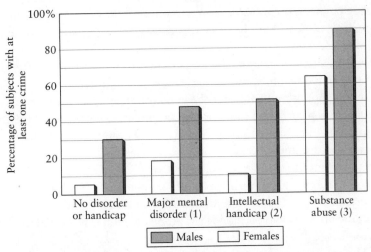

1. Schizophrenia, major depression, paranoia, other psychoses.
2. Attended special classes for intellectual deficiency but were never admitted to a psychiatric ward.
3. Alcohol and/or drug abuse.

"Developmental experiences determine the capability of the brain to do things. If you don't change those developmental experiences, you're not going to change the hardware of the brain and we'll end up building more crime."

– Bruce Perry, neuropsychiatrist

emotional, behavioral, or developmental problem that researchers say can be traced to the continuing dissolution of the two-parent family.

Forty-two percent of U.S. families with children start out with one, two, or three strikes against them, said psychologist Nicholas Zill of Child Trends, Inc., a Washington organization that studies social changes affecting children.

The first strike is lack of education: The mother has not finished high school by the time she has her first baby. The second strike is lack of commitment: The mother and father are unmarried when they have their first child together. The third strike is lack of maturity: The woman is under twenty when she gives birth for the first time. One new family in nine has all three strikes against it.

All these statistics point to the fact that many young parents today may be less prepared to care for children than were their predecessors.

"The biology of our species makes necessary a huge parental investment in order to achieve the fulfillment of each child's potential," said David A. Hamburg, president of the Carnegie Corporation of New York. "For all the atrocities now being committed on our children, we are already paying a great deal . . . in economic inefficiency, loss of productivity, lack of skill, high health care costs, growing prison costs, and a badly ripped social fabric," he said.

New research is redefining the roles of nature and nurture in determining how a child will turn out. In the past, scientists argued that one or the other was more important, but the contemporary view is that both are constantly in play. Such information is beginning to better define the conditions that put children at risk for disease. Finding these children and altering the detrimental experiences as early as possible can change the course of their lives.

Jerome Kagan, a Harvard University psychologist, has been trying to do just that. His studies of middle-class Boston children revealed that about one in three had psychological problems primarily related to a bad environment.

"The causes are always in the biology of the child, either a certain neurochemistry you inherited, structural abnormalities that occurred prenatally, or a bad environment," he said. "And a bad environment— strife at home, abuse, bad peers, lack of role models—is always the most prevalent cause."

Discoveries in the last five years have revolutionized how scientists think about the impact of such negative experiences on brain development. One of the most profound is the finding that environmental stress can activate genes linked to depression and other mental problems.

Research led by Robert Post, chief of the National Institute of Mental Health's biological psychiatry branch, found that stress or drugs of abuse, like cocaine and alcohol, can turn on a gene called C-fos.

The protein made by the C-fos gene attaches to a brain cell's DNA, turning on other genes that make receptors or more connections to other cells. (Receptors are little doorways that sit on a cell's surface to let hormones and other chemical messengers in or out.) The problem is that these new connections and receptors are abnormal. They cause a short circuit in the brain's communication networks that can give rise to seizures, depression, manic-depressive episodes, and a host of mental problems, Post said.

Stress, for instance, through its hormonal intermediaries, turns on genes that leave a memory trace of a bad feeling. Then along comes a lesser stress that triggers the same memory trace and reinforces it. Now, instead of a lousy feeling, the person gets depressed. Finally, after repeated reinforcements, the memory trace takes on a life of its own, firing willy-nilly and producing depression without any outside trigger, Post said.

"The idea that you can learn bad things like depression and epilepsy and that they are encoded through the genes into the physical structure of brain cells is new and exciting," he added. "It provides some of the molecular mechanisms to explain what scientists are beginning to suspect and fear can happen to people who have horrendous developmental experiences."

Such findings already have paid big dividends. Anticonvulsant drugs used to stop epileptic seizures are now routinely used in manic-depressive patients to block the short circuits that precipitate their highs and lows.

Martha Pierson, a neurobiologist at the Baylor College of Medicine in Houston, demonstrated how she has discovered that bad developmental experiences can produce deadly seizures 100 percent of the time in laboratory animals.

She found that if newborn rats, which start hearing on day thirteen, are prevented from hearing sounds for the first two days of this critical period, the connections among their brain cells do not organize into normal patterns. When an animal finally hears a normal sound, it gets an immense input of signals, like being in a garbage can with someone banging on the lid.

"Their brain wiring is scrambled," Pierson said. "They attack anything in sight for five to ten seconds and then go into convulsions. They would die in another seven seconds if you didn't revive them with cardiac massage."

Clearly, the lack of sound during a critical period in development can cause one type of epilepsy. "It means that with bad experiences, you can fail to learn [and] you can develop a disease," she added.

The new findings are helping to explain the big increase in mental problems among America's youth, and to refocus the goals of the National Institute of Mental Health.

"How the brain interacts with the environment, especially during the critical periods of development, has become central to our mission because most mental disorders have their onset in childhood or adolescence," said the institute's former director, Dr. Frederick Goodwin.

An epidemic of mental problems has caught researchers off guard. In the last twenty-five years, Goodwin points out, there has been a doubling of the rates of depression, suicide, crimes of violence, drug abuse, and alcohol abuse.

This dramatic increase comes at a time when the world of many children is unraveling—the divorce rate is doubling, parenting time is reduced because both parents are more likely to be working, the mobility of the population has increased, poverty is growing.

"These trends may be more exaggerated in the inner city but, in fact, they are across the board," Goodwin said. "You only have to look into some of our suburban neighborhoods to see the same problems. It's just that there are more resources available in the suburbs to help these kids."

Understanding how the brain can be damaged as a result of bad experiences gives scientists a new opportunity to prevent the damage and to repair it once it has occurred.

"The question is not only, 'What's wrong with the environment and what can we do about it?' but, 'What makes some kids more vulnerable than others and how can we develop ways to protect them?'" Goodwin said. "That's the new direction we have to go in. If we did that, we'd need fewer prisons."

At the University of Chicago, scientists are tracking down the environmental inputs that may direct a brain down a path of aggression and violence.

The main culprit is stress. Many children are raised in violent, abusive surroundings over which they have no control, said neuropsychiatrist Dr. Bruce Perry, a leader in the work at the University of Chicago, who has since moved to the Baylor College of Medicine. The antidote is giving children a sense of self-worth and teaching them that they are not helpless. "If there's somebody out there who makes you feel like you're special and important, then you can internalize that when you're developing your view of the world," Perry continued. "When you look at children who come out of terrible environments and do well, you find that someone in their lives somehow instilled in them the attitude that they aren't helpless, that they aren't powerless, that they can do something."

Many never get that antidote in time. They often are verbally impoverished on the one hand, but are extremely rich in stressful experiences on the other. They are above average in reading nonverbal cues that tell them when others may be threatening or vulnerable—a capacity that has come to be called "street smart."

But they get into trouble by misinterpreting some of these visual cues, like the student who throws a tantrum or drops out of school because he views a teacher's criticism as aimed at his self-worth rather than as an effort to help him learn. "Their brains are different because of bad environmental experiences," Perry said. "That makes them at risk for the development of a variety of cognitive, behavioral, and emotional problems, and puts them at greater risk for developing certain neuropsychiatric disorders."

Stress hormones ratchet up all of their reactions so that their hearts beat faster, their blood pressure is higher, and they are more impulsive than a normal youngster. And these findings may explain the high rate of hypertension in black males, Perry said. Medical researchers used to think that it was genetic, but now it appears to be caused by stress. "These kids are doubly at risk," explained Perry. "They don't have the opportunities to learn the traditional currency by which we normally get along in our society, and their brain systems that are involved in mood and impulsivity are poorly regulated. As they get older, these kids have fewer coping skills and fewer ways to solve problems. That predisposes them to use aggressive and violent strategies to try to solve problems."

But just as anticonvulsant drugs can control manic-depressive episodes by quelling short circuits in the brain, Perry has found that an antihypertensive drug can reduce aggressive tendencies in these supercharged youngsters as well as lower their blood pressure.

Preliminary results indicate that the drug, called clonidine, blocks much of the action of adrenaline. Adrenaline is a major stress hormone that increases blood pressure, speeds the heartbeat, tightens muscles, and in other ways prepares the body for action in emergencies. When the emergency is over, adrenaline normally recedes and the body calms down. In these children, however, the hormone is kept on high alert.

"They are hyperaroused, impulsive, and have difficulty concentrating," Perry said. "Each of the kids we've tested clonidine on has had a significant reduction in symptoms."

Studies show that every dollar spent on early childhood development programs translates into saving five dollars later in social services, mental health services, prisons, and other programs intended to deal with the aftermath of aggression and violence, he said. "Developmental experiences determine the capability of the brain to do things. If you don't change those developmental experiences, you're not going to change the hardware of the brain and we'll end up building more prisons."

In addition to its link to violence, stress may actually destroy critical brain areas involved in learning and memory. While routine, everyday stress causes no problem, Stanford University scientists have found the first direct evidence that stress hormones produced by long-term negative life experiences can cause the brain to shrink.

Studying a troop of wild baboons in Africa, biologist Robert Sapolsky found that those who were low in the pecking order and who were exposed to constant stress—such as the threat of an attack by the troop's dominant male—had high levels of glucocorticoids, a family of stress hormones of which adrenaline is a member.

When Sapolsky looked at their brains with high-resolution magnetic resonance imaging scans, he found major shrinkage in the hippocampus, an area of the brain that is involved in learning and memory. Exposure to stress hormones caused the connections between brain cells to shrivel up; prolonged exposure killed the cells. This same kind of brain damage was found in laboratory rats exposed to severe stress.

The hippocampus keeps track of facts, such as names, addresses, dates, and events, and lets you know that you know these things. What makes the hippocampus so vulnerable to stress is that it is rich in stress hormone receptors that are normally used to reinforce memories. For these brain cells, excessive stress is like setting off a firecracker in a glass jar.

Major depression can also raise stress hormone levels, and preliminary evidence indicates that it could be damaging brain cells. Brain imaging studies show that people with long-term major depression have a significantly smaller hippocampus than nondepressed people who are the same in every other respect. Similar imaging studies found a smaller hippocampus in adults who suffered from post-traumatic stress disorder as a result of childhood sexual abuse.

The potentially damaging effects of adult stress can also be transferred to newborns. Infants born to mothers who are suffering from major depression tend to have dramatically lower electrical activity in brain areas that regulate joy, happiness, curiosity, and other positive emotions. These children are at greater risk of developing depression the longer their mothers remain depressed. This kind of childhood depression is less genetic than it is environmental. Without the proper emotional input, the infant brain lacks the proper signals that tell it how to wire its positive emotional neural networks. Connections between brain cells that normally are stimulated by joy and pleasure are not reinforced—and they perish.

A study of infants of depressed mothers by Geraldine Dawson of the University of Washington found that about 40 percent of the children had reduced electrical activity in their emotion centers. At three-and-a-half years of age these children were more likely to be withdrawn, aggressive, disobedient, and to have other behavioral problems such as crying and sleep disturbances. The depressed children also had high levels of stress hormones.

Supporting these studies is the research on Cushing's syndrome, a disorder in which a tumor stimulates the adrenal glands to overproduce a complex of stress hormones called glucocorticoids. Brain scans showed that the hippocampus in Cushing's patients shrinks, with shrinkage increasing the longer the condition goes undiagnosed and untreated. When the tumor is removed early, thereby stopping the excessive production of stress hormones, the shrunken brain cells rebound to normal.

The good news about these studies is that the potential threat to memory from prolonged stress and major depression can be reduced and their negative impact on infants prevented. The bad effects can be reduced when a mother's depression is treated through medication or psychotherapy, or a combination of the two; the father is active in raising the child; the child is exposed to other relatives and other caregivers who are upbeat and supportive; and the mother develops a network of caring friends and reduces stress in her life.

PART FIVE

THE LEARNING BRAIN

LANGUAGE, READING, AND MATH

15

THE LITERATE BRAIN

Sarah-Jayne Blakemore
Uta Frith

THE CONSEQUENCES OF literacy for our social, political, and economic lives are enormous. To be deprived of the written word would be an intolerable restriction for most of us, and yet being able to read and write is an artificially taught skill. Being able to read and write for those who are literate is as natural as speaking and listening. In this chapter, we will describe recent brain research on literacy, and show that literacy has profound consequences for the shaping of the human brain.

A Brief History of Writing

Many people hold the invention of writing to be one of the greatest cultural inventions in the history of humankind. Writing started in Sumer, part of Mesopotamia (present-day Iraq), and independently in China, about 5,000 years ago. Its spread throughout all cultures has been rapid, and its spread to individuals has accelerated recently so that universal literacy as a basic human right can be contemplated. The course of the history of writing has not been smooth, and there are different ways of representing language in visible form. Some very ancient examples of writing are pictorial, and the most ancient examples, found in Mesopotamia, were clay models. So if you were trading six sheep with a business partner in another town, you could send an intermediary. He would carry, along with the sheep, a sealed mold which contained six small clay sheep. This method ingeniously allowed both a record of what was transacted and also guarded against dishonesty.

It can readily be imagined that this method could be simplified by reducing clay shapes to simple scratches in clay. These scratches would harden and could represent all sorts of objects and events that could be read a long distance away from where they originated, and what is more, a long time apart. In this way, writing hugely enhanced the ability to transmit knowledge across generations.

Before writing, spoken language existed for tens of thousands of years. Speech, even if well phrased and strong in emotional impact, does not leave a permanent record. Writing does. Speech depends on memory and, while it can be transmitted in song and in epic form, it remains a transient mode of communication. When laws were formulated it was useful to cut them into stone. Thus one of the earliest codes of law, the famous code of the Babylonian King Hammurabi (eighteenth century B.C.), is written in cuneiform writing on hard granite and can be seen today in the Louvre in Paris. The code was respected as a rule book to define criminal offenses and set limits to their punishment. An example is translated as follows: "If any one be too lazy to keep his dam in proper condition, and does not so keep it; if then the dam break and all the fields be flooded, then shall he in whose dam the break occurred be sold for money, and the money shall replace the [grain] which he has caused to be ruined." This was a permanent record for everyone to see as a warning and to refer to if necessary.

However, writing does not convey precisely the same things that speech conveys. It is a code that transmits only certain aspects of language and not others. For instance, written language does not convey the melody or prosody of spoken sentences. Usually it does not convey the stress patterns of words: we have to guess whether to say pro*ject* or *project* and use information from context.

Old Egyptian hieroglyphics and Chinese, for instance, primarily map abstract signs and rudimentary pictures onto language meaning. Other languages have developed writing systems that primarily map visible signs onto the sounds of speech. Here, two very different paths have been taken. Several Indian languages use a syllabary: each syllable that exists in the language has a recognizable symbol. For example, you have individual symbols for ki, ka, ke, ku; bi, ba, be, bu, and so on. This works when the total set of syllables is relatively small, that is, no more than a hundred or so.

As the examples ki, ka, ke, ku and bi, ba, be, bu show, the syllable is capable of being segmented into smaller constituent sounds: consonants and vowels. You can do with far fewer different symbols, say about 20 to 30, to represent as many syllables as you want. Furthermore, you can use these symbols to write down any word from any language, by ear, even if they don't contain the syllables you are used to. You are using tiny speech fragments, *phonemes,* instead. The first big invention of the alphabet was to introduce symbols for consonants, and this is credited to the Phoenicians on the Mediterranean coast. These people had knowledge of Egyptian hieroglyphics but refashioned them to represent the most important speech sounds in their own language.

The Greeks must be credited with the second big invention of the alphabet, the introduction of graphic signs for vowels. This only slightly increased the set of letters in the alphabet and happened around 500 B.C. From then on the alphabet has been adopted by more and more languages while the number of letters has hardly had to be increased. The Romans decreased the number of letters, and the order they used to recite the alphabet is the order we still use today.

The very beginnings of schooling from Greek and Roman times involved learning the alphabet. In around 150 A.D., a fabulously wealthy patron of the arts, Herodes Atticus, who built a theater in Athens that can still be seen today, had a son who had trouble learning the alphabet. This son was considered a good-for-nothing with very poor memory. The father hired 24 slaves for his son, each being given the name of a letter. Presumably, the young Atticus eventually learned their names and at the same time, he learned the alphabet. A major step in his education was thus achieved. Atticus may well have been the first dyslexic recorded in history.

The Legacy of the Alphabet

Learning the alphabet is still the basis of literacy. Even Chinese children are now generally taught the Roman alphabet as a getting-started exercise before the arduous task of gradually learning thousands of symbols. These symbols each have a rich history and represent a mixture of different aspects of language. They are not the same as "words" in the Western sense, but elements of meaning. These elements usually need to be put together in compounds to serve as words. These words allow rich interpretation including historical allusion and puns with other words. Chinese poetry is renowned for containing many layers of meaning, while being highly economical in its written form.

Japanese children have to learn three different writing systems: the Chinese logographic system, referred to as Kanji; the Japanese syllabary, referred to as Kana; and in later school years, the alphabet, referred to as Romaji. Anything less would be considered uncultured! In fact, it would make them not fully literate, as they need to use all systems to understand different literary genres and names of people and places. Given the ease of translating the alphabet into type via a keyboard, many Japanese and Chinese speakers use an alphabetic version of their language by preference.

Even though the alphabetic writing system had such a triumphal history, it is not necessarily the simplest system to learn. Learning to use the alphabet is not equally easy for everybody. The small minority who experience serious difficulty while learning to read and write suffer from dyslexia. They never quite achieve the same degree of effortless reading and writing as the majority of people. Perhaps they would be better off if they could use a writing system that is based on a syllabary. Possibly so, because the intuition of what a syllable is comes easily to almost everybody.

Writing is generally simpler in alphabetic systems since the number of symbols is small, and fortunately, only a few letters are confusing. There are the infamous mirror-reversible letters, b, d and p, q. Almost all children have problems learning and remembering which is which, but get there eventually. The letters are confusing because the brain is used to operating in a three-dimensional world, and operating in the two-dimensional world on paper is a novelty. Think three-dimensionally, and imagine b, d, p, q as solid objects: They are one and the same object rotated in space. Thus, the brain of the young child, when first coming across such shapes, gets into a conflict—a recipe for confusion.

The origin of the letter shapes that we use today goes back to the earliest beginnings of writing when Phoenician and Greek scribes borrowed and modified shapes from Egyptian hieroglyphics. Remarkably little has changed in the shape of letters since the Romans cast them into the form that is particularly suited to stone inscriptions. Many still consider this form as the most beautiful, and the font known as Times New Roman may well be the most widely used in current word processing.

Visible Language in the Brain

Visible language creates a new world of objects, symbols, or letters, which have a lawful relationship to the sound of speech. The mappings between symbols and speech have to be learned, and this learning has a lasting impact on the brain. Thus the brain of the literate person is different from that of the illiterate. Literate people just need to look at print to know what it says. In fact, they decode it automatically, even if they have no intention of reading it. The demonstration that reading is automatic and involuntary is given in the following famous example. The Stroop paradigm was named after a Dutch psychologist who lived in the first half of the twentieth century. He presented people with a list of words written in different colors and asked them to name the color of ink that the words were written in. He measured how long it took them to name the color of the ink for each word. The trick was that sometimes the word was a color name that was different from the color ink it was written in (for example, the word "BLUE" might be written in red ink). When the color of the ink was different from the color the word named, people were slower than if there was no such mismatch. This is because before you name the color of the ink you involuntarily read the word, and the meaning comes to mind unbidden. Once you have learned to read, you cannot help but read words.

In general, it is much faster to read a word than to name a picture. Many people find this astonishing, since as children they were naming pictures well before they were able to read words. Once you can recognize print, the world never looks the same again. When print is in front of your eyes, you are compelled to read it. So is learning to read a kind of "brainwashing"?

Comparing Literate and Illiterate People

If literacy is a kind of brainwashing, then it would follow that the literate and the illiterate brain are organized differently, and this might have consequences for all sorts of things. For instance, literacy may have consequences for how speech is processed, even when it is only heard. However, comparing literate and illiterate people is not easy in places where schooling is not only universal, but compulsory.

Psychologists in Portugal realized that they had the opportunity to study people who are illiterate for historical and sociopolitical reasons. In Portugal, schooling did not become compulsory until the middle of the twentieth century. In remote rural areas in particular, children did not go to school and might even have thought of school as some kind of evil torture that they were glad to escape.

Researchers Luz Cary, José Morais, and their colleagues identified people who were illiterate and had remained illiterate all their working lives. They also identified people who had somehow been able to take advantage of opportunities offered later in life to acquire a moderate amount of reading and writing knowledge. These moderately literate people had remained in the same rural places, doing the same, usually agricultural, jobs. This meant that a fair and stringent comparison between these two groups could be made, a comparison that is truly about the effect of literacy on the brain, and not about the effect of schooling during childhood.

Cary, Morais, and colleagues conducted a number of psychological experiments with these two unusual groups of people. These experiments used spoken language, and sometimes pictures, and they showed a number of surprising differences. The consequences of literacy were particularly strong when it was necessary to break up the sounds of speech, that is, to manipulate *phonemes*. For instance, "what is 'told' without the 't'?" The answer "old" was easy for the literate, but not for the illiterate individuals. This work showed for the first time that the idea of breaking up words into smaller sounds becomes meaningful if one can think of these sounds as letters. After all, it is these phonemes that map directly onto letters.

Think of two groups of children each playing with a toy village. One group has ready-made wooden houses while the other has houses constructed out of Lego bricks. Those who have the Lego brick houses will consider the town as infinitely modifiable, whereas the children with the wooden houses will think of their houses as fixed and whole. For them, the concept of being able to remove pieces from each house and to change the shape of the houses makes no sense.

Brainwashing through literacy is real. Once you have got hold of the principle of the alphabet, your whole perception of speech changes. You are aware that the sounds of words can be broken up and put together again.

Another effect of the alphabetic principle was seen in a study by Alexandre Castro-Caldas and colleagues where again literate and illiterate individuals took part. They were asked to repeat back real words and made-up nonsense words. Everyone could repeat the real words well, and there was no difference between the literate and illiterate group. However, there was an intriguing difference when they repeated nonsense words. The illiterate people tended to turn these into real words. So, for "banona," which does not mean anything, they might say "banana," which has a meaning. Why did they not simply repeat the nonsense words, like the literate group? The literate group were not fazed by nonsense words, because they were already familiar with such entities. After all, the names of the letters are nonsense words, for instance, "eff" and "aitch." Moreover, once you know the alphabetic principle, you have a recipe for making up words that do not exist. When you do not know this principle, made-up words can only be thought of as existing, but unknown, words.

How Different Is the Literate Brain?

These same individuals, then in their sixties, were flown from their rural home in Portugal to the Karolinska Institute in Stockholm to have their brains scanned by Martin Ingvar and colleagues.

When repeating nonwords, the illiterate volunteers activated more strongly the *frontal lobes,* the all-purpose problem-solving areas of the brain, and in particular, those regions that are known to be involved in the retrieval of memories. The literate volunteers activated more strongly the left *temporal lobe,* the area of the brain specifically engaged in language processing. This was expected, because the illiterate people treated the nonsense words like real words, which they had misheard or which they did not know. Hence, they sometimes turned them into real words, and generally searched for such words in their memory. The literate people treated the nonwords, quite nonchalantly, as possible but not real words. There was no need to search their memory or consider turning them into real words.

This unique experiment gave a first direct demonstration of the changes in the brain that are due to literacy. It showed that the literate brain reacts differently even when only listening to speech.

To reiterate, speech sound is a key factor in reading. Skilled readers, who read words automatically, often have the experience that the sound of the word springs to mind unbidden. You might think that reading silently is a purely visual task, but this is not the case. The processes the brain uses when reading silently are remarkably similar to the processes used when reading aloud.

Does the Brain's Reading System Depend on the Language of the Reader?

It is not merely the case that becoming literate changes the brain. The specialized demands of particular languages, such as English, Italian, or French, make specific demands on writing. Even though all these languages use the same alphabet, they have historically developed quite different writing systems.

Theoretically, the alphabet guarantees that you can immediately pronounce a word that is written in another language, but in practice, the writing system of each language involves extra rules for pronunciation. Some writing systems have more complex rules than others. Compare Italian to English, for instance. Italian has a very transparent and regular orthography: what you see is what you say. Sound out letters bit by bit, and the whole word will come out more or less as it should sound: Napoli, Milano, tortellini. In English, by contrast, the correspondence between words and sounds is far from simple and it would be foolish to rely on sounding out letters bit by bit. Where would that get us with "biscuit," "yacht," and "Leicester"? Even worse, the same letter combinations can have very different pronunciations in English. The word "wind," for instance, sounds differently in "The wind was blowing a gale," and "We need to wind up the clock."

With English you have to build up a store of word sounds linked to their precise spelling patterns, or you are lost. What difference does this make to the brain? Remember that even when you read silently, the visual form of the word cannot be divorced from its sound. Some people remember spellings by sounding out what they see—as if it were Italian. For instance, if they see the written word "parliament," they actually hear in their head "par-li-a-ment." Many people, even those who are excellent spellers and don't need to use this particular trick, nevertheless, smile at rhymes of words that are not spelled the same way. For instance:

> There was an old woman of Gloucester,
> Whose parrot two guineas it cost her. (Anon.)

The Reading System of the Brain and Its Fine-Tuning

To study the brain's adaptation to these differences in spelling rules, a European collaborative study was carried out by researchers Eraldo Paulesu in Milan, Jean-François Demonet in Toulouse, and Uta Frith in London. As a first stage, they scanned skilled readers of English and of Italian while reading simple words either aloud or silently. This revealed that the regions that make up the reading system of the brain are exactly the same for Italian and English readers. This system, which has also been demonstrated in studies by other research groups with speakers of English, occupies large areas of the left hemisphere of the brain, the side dedicated to language and speech. This common system is shown in Figure 15.1. The system can be divided into three connected parts, one at the front in the *frontal lobes,* one in the middle in the *parietotemporal cortex,* and one at the back in the *temporal* lobes.

The top figure shows the whole reading system for both languages combined. The middle figure shows the region associated with sound-letter translation being more active in the Italian readers. The lower figure shows the word form area at the back being more active in English readers.

Figure 15.1. The Brain's Reading System in English and Italian.

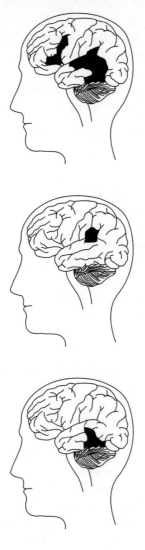

We will come back to these different regions in the next subsection. Figure 15.1 shows the subtle differences found between Italian and English readers. Although the three regions activated were the same, the relative weight given to them during reading was different. The second picture shows the area that was more active for Italian readers. The third picture shows the area that was relatively more active for the English readers. The reading system is fine-tuned to the particular demands of the writing system in question.

In a subsequent study, French-speaking readers were scanned under identical conditions. They activated exactly the same system as the other two language groups, but as far as the fine-tuning was concerned, they sided with the English readers. French, after all, has a rather complex writing system, more akin to English than to Italian. This is especially noticed when trying to spell from dictation. For instance, the sound for *c'est* and *ces* and for *mais* and *mes* is exactly the same.

What Do the Three Regions of the Reading System Do?

A surprising amount is known about the brain's reading system. Over the past 150 years, many patients who suffered brain damage in the left half of the brain, usually as a result of stroke, have been observed. Some of these patients lost their ability to speak; others lost only their ability to read and to write. This knowledge helps us to piece together the function and purpose of the three regions of the reading system. It allows us to understand why these areas, rather than others, have been recruited by the brain for the culturally acquired task of literacy.

The most frontal region is named *Broca's area* in honor of Paul Broca, a French pioneer in neurology. He reported the historically groundbreaking case of "Tan," a man who, after a stroke, could only utter the word "tan" and had otherwise lost his speech completely. Although there are individual differences that make the exact boundaries of Broca's area uncertain, there is full agreement that speech depends on this part of the frontal lobe. In the European study described above, Broca's area was activated both when volunteers read words out aloud and when they read silently. It is as if the brain is prepared to utter the words at a moment's notice.

The middle region of the reading system includes *Wernicke's area* and the *angular gyrus*. The nineteenth-century German neurologist Carl Wernicke was interested in language and its basis in the brain, and found patients who could speak but could not understand language. The area that is damaged in these patients, which lies along the *planum temporale* of the left hemisphere, is known as *Wernicke's area*. The *planum temporale* was of special interest to the American neurologist Norman Geschwind, who in the 1960s noticed that it was bigger on the left than the right in most brains he had the opportunity to study. Numerous studies of patients showed that when this region was damaged, the patient could no longer name letters or translate a written word into speech. This area seems preeminently important for learning the alphabetic code. The *angular gyros*, in the parietal lobe, lies halfway between Wernicke's area and the visual cortex. It has many functions among which is the association of spoken and seen words.

What about the third area, at the base of the left temporal lobe? Wernicke also had patients with damage at the *base* of the left temporal lobe, and these patients had great difficulties spelling and recognizing whole words. They could, nevertheless, still sound out words from their letters. He suggested that this region might control access to a thesaurus, where the spelling, sound, and meaning of each word is stored. Neuroscientist Stanislas Dehaene and his colleague Laurent Cohen in Paris confirmed that the area at the base of the left temporal lobe is indeed concerned with whole words. They call it a *visual word form area.* Cathy Price and colleagues in London have found that this region is also active when people name pictures or sounds, such as "doorbell" or "foghorn."

The Fine-Tuned Reading System

We have seen that the reading system can be divided into three parts and each part has a distinctive role. The frontal part of the reading system, Broca's area, is the brain's basic speech production system. The middle part, Wernicke's area and the angular gyrus, is active during the translation of letters and sounds. The area at the back, the word form area, situated at the bottom of the temporal lobe, is the region involved in storage and retrieval of whole words.

Now, at last, we can explain the differences in the weighting of the different regions of the reading system of Italian, English, and French readers. We can explain this fine-tuning by the exact requirements of the English, French, and Italian writing systems, respectively. In English and French, it is more important to recognize whole word forms than to translate letters to sounds. In Italian, this is less important, because the sound of the whole word is easily derived from the piecemeal translation of letters to sounds. Accordingly, Italian readers activate the translation area more than English and French readers. English and French readers activate the word form area more than Italian readers.

Nevertheless, readers of both languages use both areas, and this suggests that reading relies on more than one process. One fascinating aspect of different alphabetic writing systems is that they have not gone entirely one way or another in a twofold choice: either using the principle of always translating small units of sound to letter ("s-i-t" for "sit"), or using the principle of distinctive spellings for whole words ("cough" and not "c-o-f"). English is a good example of how both these possibilities are mixed together. It turns out that both principles are mixed in most languages, even if not in such a dramatic fashion as in English.

The remarkable automaticity of reading that has been demonstrated with the Stroop paradigm allows readers to do two things at once. They identify the whole word, but at the same time they translate the letters into sounds, piecemeal. It makes sense that one or the other process is weighted a little more heavily according to which writing system is used. Therefore, when learning to read English or French, more work is done by the region responsible for whole word recognition. When learning to read Italian, more work is done by the region that is responsible for letter–sound translation.

Is the Reading System an Add-On to the Speech System?

What is more important, the sound elements of the word, or the sound of the whole word? The skilled reader has a simple answer to this question: obviously both are important. The illiterate person, on the other hand, will go for the whole word sound and may not even know what is meant by sound elements of a word.

The alphabet makes readers aware of something of which they are otherwise unaware: the possibility of cutting up words into tiny sounds. We have already compared this to Lego bricks used in a toy village. We have seen how this allows the combination of sounds without meaning, consonants (b, m) or consonant clusters (sp, str) and vowels (a, o), beginnings of syllables and ends of syllables (str-ing, str-and, h-ing, h-and), and so on. This results in a huge explosion of combinatorial possibilities. In principle, you can write down any made-up word that you can think of.

The same combinatorial explosion underlies speech itself. Unlike in the case of written language, the brain has had millions of years to evolve speech. The processes are deeply embedded and we are entirely unaware of them. The alphabetic system that has come to be the predominant writing system in the world's languages is parasitic on the ancient human speech system. But to master it, we need to become aware of the combinatorial process. . . . This is not equally easy for all readers.

Mixing Colors and Words

The automatic integration of sound and sight is seen not only in reading, but also in a particularly fascinating "condition" called *synesthesia*. People who are synesthetes mix different sensations. It is not really a condition because it happens to people who have no brain abnormality. One person tastes a bitter taste whenever he hears a doorbell. Another can smell strawberries whenever she touches cotton clothing. The most common form of synesthesia involves associating a color with a particular letter or word. Most people with this form of synesthesia associate every letter and every word with a particular color. One synesthetic friend always "sees" the color pink when she hears the letter L or any word beginning with an L, whereas Qs are associated with green for her.

Until recently it was believed that synesthesia is very rare, but more recent estimates suggest that as many as 4 or 5 percent of the population may have some kind of synesthetic experience.

No one knows what causes synesthesia but there are several explanations. One explanation is that the combination of senses is a consequence of childhood associations. In the case of color–word synesthesia, perhaps these people are remembering the colors of the alphabet letters hanging on their walls or the magnetic letters on their fridge from when they were young. But this does not explain why synesthetic people claim really to "see" (not just think of) colors when they read letters.

An alternative idea is that synesthesia is caused by overactive connections between the region of the brain that processes colors, called V4 (visual area 4), and the area of the brain that stores words (the word form area). These two areas lie very close to each other at the back of the brain and it is possible that signals are passed from one region to the other.

Synesthesia is a phenomenon that tells us how rich our experience of written language is. It also gives us a glimpse of the amazing facility of the brain to combine different experiences, and in particular to mix sight and sound. The visual form of the written word immediately evokes the sound of the word, at least in normal readers. We take this for granted, but perhaps it is just as amazing as the ability of synesthetes to evoke a color every time they hear a word.

16

WHY SOME SMART PEOPLE CAN'T READ

Sally Shaywitz

I WANT YOU TO MEET two of my patients, Alex and Gregory. Alex is ten years old, and Gregory, a medical student, just celebrated his twenty-third birthday. Their experiences are typical of children and young adults with dyslexia. You will learn how Alex's and Gregory's seemingly diverse symptoms—trouble reading, absolute terror of reading aloud, problems spelling, difficulties finding the right word, mispronouncing words, rote memory nightmares—represent the expression of a single, isolated weakness. At the same time you will learn that other intellectual abilities—thinking, reasoning, understanding—are untouched by dyslexia. This contrasting pattern produces the paradox of dyslexia: profound and persistent difficulties experienced by some very bright people in learning to read. I am emphasizing the strengths of the dyslexic because there is often a tendency to underestimate his abilities. The reading problem is often glaringly apparent while the strengths may be more subtle and overlooked. Later on I will discuss new insights into dyslexia that tell us that it represents a very isolated weakness; thinking and reasoning are intact and perhaps even enhanced.

Alex

In his first years of life, Alex was so quick to catch on to things that his parents were surprised when he struggled to learn his letters in kindergarten. When shown a letter, he would stare, frown, and then randomly guess.

He couldn't seem to learn the letter names. In first grade he struggled to link letters with their sounds. By the third grade Alex continued to stammer and sputter as he tried to decipher what was on the page in front of him. Language had clearly become a struggle for Alex. He seemed to understand a great deal, yet he was not always articulate. He mispronounced many words, leaving off the beginning *(lephant* for elephant) or the ends of words, or inverting the order within a word *(emeny* for enemy). Alex had trouble finding the exact word he wanted to say even though it seemed he could tell you all about it. One evening he was trying to explain about sharks living in the ocean:

> The water, the water, lots of water, salty water with big fish, it's a lotion. No, no, that's not what I mean. Oh, you know, it's on all the maps, it's a lotion—ocean, that's what it is—a sea, no big sea, it's an ocean, an ocean!

Looking at this handsome, very serious little boy who could spend hours putting together complex puzzles and assembling intricate model airplanes, his father could not believe that Alex had a problem. Alex, however, became increasingly aware of his difficulty reading and asked more and more frequently why all his friends were in a different reading group. He practiced, he tried, but it just never seemed to come out right.

His parents brought him to the Yale Center for evaluation. We learned that Alex was extremely smart, scoring in the gifted range in abstract reasoning and in logic. His vocabulary was also highly developed. Alex could learn, he could reason, and he could understand concepts at a very high level. Despite these strengths, his performance in reading words was dismal; for example, he was able to read only ten out of twenty-four words on a third grade level. What gave Alex the most difficulty, however, was nonsense words (made-up words that can be pronounced; for example, *gem, ruck*). He struggled to decipher these words. Sometimes he used the first letter to generate a response (such as *glim* for *gem, rold* for *ruck*); at other times it seemed as if he just gave up, making seemingly random guesses. In contrast, Alex was able to read a short passage silently and answer questions about it far better than he was able to read and pronounce isolated single words. In reading a passage silently to himself, Alex made good use of clues such as pictures in the book and the surrounding words; he used them to get to the meaning of sentences and passages that contained words he could not read. "I picture what it says," he explained. However, Alex sparkled when asked to *listen* to a story and then respond to a series of questions, scoring significantly above average.

Reading aloud was particularly painful for Alex. He was reluctant to read in front of the class, and it was easy to understand why. His reading was labored; words were mispronounced, substituted, or often omitted entirely. Words that he correctly read in one sentence would be misread in a subsequent sentence. He read excruciatingly slowly and haltingly. Increasingly, Alex would ask to go to the bathroom when it was nearing his turn to read. If called upon, he often acted silly, making the words into a joke or tumbling himself onto the floor and laughing so that he would be sent out of the room.

Poor spelling skills were compounded by his almost illegible handwriting. Letters were large, misshapen, and wobbly. In contrast, Alex's math skills, particularly problem solving and reasoning abilities, were in the superior range. At the close of the testing, Alex diagnosed his own reading problem: "I don't know the sounds the letters make." Furthermore, he told the evaluator that it bothered him that his friends were in a different reading group. Sometimes, he said, this made him very sad. His one wish was to be a better reader, but he didn't know exactly how that would happen.

When I met with Alex's parents, they had many questions: Does he have a problem? If so, what is the nature of the problem? What could be done to help him? Above all, they asked, "Will he be all right?" I reassured them that Alex would not only survive, he would thrive.

Gregory

In the course of my work, I have evaluated for reading disabilities not only hundreds of children but also scores of young adult men and women. Their histories provide a picture of what the future will be for a bright child like Alex who happens to be dyslexic. Gregory was a grown-up Alex. Gregory came to see me after experiencing a series of difficulties in his first-year medical courses. He was quite discouraged.[1]

Although he had been diagnosed as dyslexic in grade school, Gregory had also been placed in a program for gifted students. His native intelligence, together with extensive support and tutoring, had enabled him to graduate from high school with honors and gain admission to an Ivy League college. In college Gregory had worked hard to compensate for his disability and eventually received offers from several top medical schools.

---

[1]Gregory's story appeared in "Dyslexia," *Scientific American* 275 (1996): 98–104.

Now, however, he was beginning to doubt his own ability. He had no trouble comprehending the intricate relationships among physiological systems or the complex mechanisms of disease; indeed, he excelled in those areas that required reasoning skills. More difficult for him was pronouncing long words or novel terms (such as labels used in anatomic descriptions); perhaps his least-well-developed skill was that of rote memorization.

Both Gregory and his professors were perplexed by the inconsistencies in his performance. How could someone who understood difficult concepts so well have trouble with the smaller and simpler details? I explained that Gregory's dyslexia (he was still a slow reader) could account for his inability to name tissue types and body parts in the face of his excellent reasoning skills. His history fit the clinical picture of dyslexia as it has been traditionally defined: an unexpected difficulty learning to read despite intelligence, motivation, and education. Furthermore, I was able to reassure him that because scientists now understand the basic nature of dyslexia, they have been able to devise highly effective strategies to help those with the disorder. I told Gregory that dyslexia reflects a problem within the language system in the brain. The understanding of the central role of language in reading and, particularly, in dyslexia is relatively recent.

Why Alex and Gregory Have Trouble Reading

Explanations of dyslexia that were put forth beginning in the 1920s and that have continued until recently held that defects in the visual system were to blame for the reversals of letters and words thought to typify dyslexia. Eye training was often prescribed to overcome these alleged visual defects. Subsequent research has shown, however, that in contrast to a popular myth, children with dyslexia are not unusually prone to *seeing* letters or words backward and that the deficit responsible for the disorder resides in the language system. These poor readers, like Alex, do have significant difficulty, however, in *naming* the letters, often referring to a *b* as a *d* or reading *saw* as *was*. The problem is a linguistic one, not a visual one.

As noted earlier, dyslexia represents a specific difficulty with reading, not with thinking skills. Comprehending spoken language is often at a very high level, as it was for Alex, as are other higher-level reasoning skills. Dyslexia is a localized problem.

Understanding that dyslexia reflected a language problem and not a general weakness in intelligence or a primary visual impairment represented a major step forward.[2] Further advances have clarified the nature of the language impairment. Dyslexia does not reflect an overall defect in language but, rather, a localized weakness within a specific component of the language system: the phonologic module. The word *phonologic* is derived from the Greek word *phone,* meaning *sound* (as in *phonograph* and *telephone*). The phonologic module is the language factory, the functional part of the brain where the sounds of language are put together to form words and where words are broken down into their elemental sounds.

Over the past two decades a model of dyslexia has emerged that is based on phonological processing—processing the distinctive sounds of language. The phonologic model is consistent both with how dyslexia manifests itself and with what neuroscientists know about brain organization and function. Researchers at the Yale Center and elsewhere have had an opportunity to test and refine this model through reading and, more recently, brain imaging studies. We and other dyslexia researchers have found that the phonologic model provides a cogent explanation as to why some very smart people have trouble learning to read.

The Phonologic Model

To understand how the phonologic model works, you first have to understand how language is processed in the brain. Think of the language system as a graded series of modules or components, each devoted to a particular aspect of language.[3] The operations within the system are rapid and automatic, and we are unaware of them. They are also mandatory. For example, if we are seated at a table in a dining room, we *must* hear what the person at the next table is saying if she is speaking loudly enough. It is nearly impossible to tune language out. That is why it is so difficult to study when others nearby are speaking.

---

[2]Evidence that the difficulty in dyslexia is within the language system is based on findings described by J. Torgesen, R. Wagner, and C. Rashotte in "Longitudinal Studies of Phonological Processing and Reading," *Journal of Educational Psychology* 27 (1994): 276–286, and in J. Fletcher et al., "Cognitive Profiles of Reading Disability: Comparisons of Discrepancy and Low Achievement Definitions," *Journal of Educational Psychology* 86 (1994): 6–23.

[3]Explanations of the modular system can be found in D. Shankweiler and S. Crane, "Language Mechanisms and Reading Disorder: A Modular Approach," *Cognition* 24 (1986): 139–168, and J. A. Fodor, *The Modularity of Mind* (Cambridge, Mass.: MIT Press, 1983).

Scientists have been able to pinpoint the precise location of the glitch within the language system (Figure 16.1). At the upper levels of the language hierarchy are components involved with, for example, semantics (vocabulary or word meaning), syntax (grammatical structure), and discourse (connected sentences). At the lowest level of the hierarchy is the phonologic module, which is dedicated to processing the distinctive sound elements of language. Dyslexia involves a weakness within the language system, specifically at the level of the phonologic module.

The phoneme [defined as the smallest unit of speech that distinguishes one word from another] is the fundamental element of the language system, the essential building block of all spoken and written words. Different combinations of just forty-four phonemes produce the tens of thousands of words in the English language. The word *cat,* for example, consists of three phonemes: *k, aaaa,* and *t.* Before words can be identified, understood, stored in memory, or retrieved from it, they must first be broken down into phonemes by the neural machinery of the brain. Just as proteins must first be broken down into their underlying amino acids before they can be digested, words must first be broken down into their underlying phonemes before they can be processed by the language system. Language is a code, and the only code that can be recognized by the language system and activate its machinery is the phonologic code.

This is critical for both speaking and reading. Let's first consider speaking (Figure 16.2). If I want to say the word *bat,* I will go into my internal dictionary or lexicon deep within my brain and first retrieve and then serially order the appropriate phonemes—*b, aaaa,* and *t*—and then I can say the word *bat.*

Figure 16.1. Pinpointing the Core Weakness in Dyslexia.

**The Language System:
Reading and Speaking**

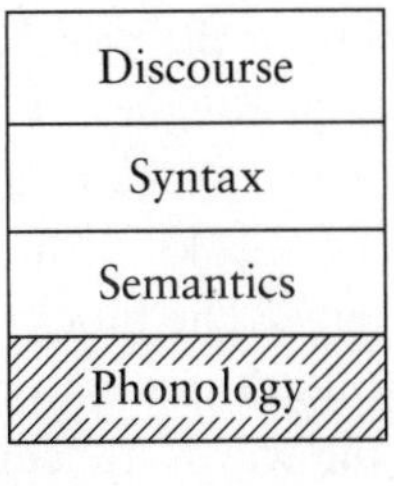

Discourse
Syntax
Semantics
Phonology

Research pinpoints the weakness at the lowest level of the language system.

Figure 16.2. Speaking: Making Words.

SPEAKING

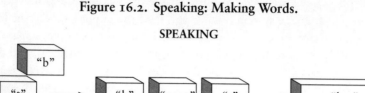

A speaker retrieves and then orders the phonemes to make a word.

In children with dyslexia, the phonemes are less well developed. Think of such a phoneme as a child's carved letter block whose face is so worn that the letter is no longer prominent. As a consequence, such children when speaking may have a hard time selecting the appropriate phoneme and may instead retrieve a phoneme that is similar in sound. Think of Alex's experience in retrieving the word *lotion* when the word he was reaching for was *ocean*. Alex knew exactly what he wanted to say but could not retrieve the exact word, so instead he picked a close but not correct phoneme. Alternatively, a dyslexic might order the phonemes incorrectly, and the result might be, as Alex said, *emeny* instead of *enemy*. Such sound-based confusions are quite common in the spoken language of dyslexics.

Not too long ago I received a note from Pam Stock, a learning disabilities teacher "deep in the trenches" in Maine. I smiled when I read what a bright six-year-old dyslexic boy said on a hot summer day. Looking over at his perspiring mother as she struggled in a traffic jam, he remarked, "You know, Mom, it's not the heat, it's the *humanity.*" (The intended word, of course, was *humidity.*) On another occasion a politician greeting his supporters said, "Welcome to this lovely *recession.*" Of course he meant to say *reception.* In each instance the confusion was a phonologic one (that is, based on the *sound of* the word) and did not reflect a lack of understanding of the meaning of the word in question. Unfortunately, such phonologic slips roll off the tongues of dyslexics fairly regularly and are often incorrectly attributed to a lack of understanding.

Reading is the converse of speaking. In reading we begin with the intact printed word on the page: The blocks representing phonemes are all lined up correctly. The reader's job is to convert the letters into their sounds and appreciate that the words are composed of smaller segments or phonemes (Figure 16.3). Dyslexic children and adults have difficulty

Figure 16.3. Reading: Turning Letters into Sounds.

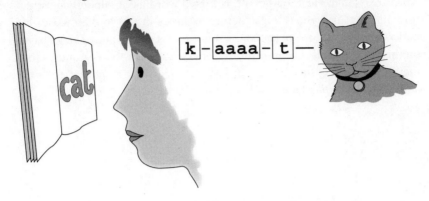

To read, a child converts the letters into sounds or phonemes.

developing an awareness that spoken and written words are comprised of these phonemes or building blocks. Think of the little boy who got his first pair of glasses and then said, "I never knew that building was made of red bricks. I always thought its wall was just one big smudge of red paint." Dyslexics perceive words the same way. While most of us can detect the underlying sounds or phonemes in a word—for example, *k*, *aaaa*, and *t* in *cat*—children who are dyslexic perceive a word as an amorphous blur, without an appreciation of its underlying segmental nature. They fail to appreciate the internal sound structure of words.

The phonologic model tells us the exact steps that must be taken if a child is to go from the puzzlement of seeing letters as abstract squiggly shapes to the satisfaction of recognizing and identifying these letter groups as words. Overall, the child must come to know that the letters he sees on the page represent, or map onto, the sounds he hears when the same word is spoken.

The process of acquiring this knowledge is orderly and follows a logical sequence. First, a child becomes aware that words he hears are not just whole envelopes of sound. Just as the little boy noted the bricks in the wall, the beginning reader starts to notice that words are made up of smaller segments, that words have parts. Next, the child becomes aware of the nature of these segments, that they represent sounds. He realizes, for example, that in the word *cat* there are three segments of sound, *k*, *aaaa*, and *t*. Then the child begins to link letters he sees on paper to what he hears in spoken language. He begins to realize that the letters are related to sounds he hears in words and that the printed word has the same number and the same sequence of phonemes (sounds) as the spoken word.

Finally, he comes to understand that the printed word and the spoken word are related. He knows that the printed word has an underlying structure and that it is the same structure he hears in the spoken word. He understands that both spoken and written words can be pulled apart based on the same sounds, but in print the letters represent these sounds. Once the child has made this linkage, he has mastered what is referred to as *the alphabetic principle*. He is ready to read.

17

WHAT HAPPENS IN THE BRAIN WHEN CHILDREN READ

Patricia Wolfe
Pamela Nevills

Brain Basics

If educators are to make serious progress in solving the reading problems experienced by many children, efforts will need to be based on more than ideological debates on methodologies.

A systematic study of the brain may offer the best hope. Since the 1980s, we have seen a tremendous explosion of research on brain structure and function. We've learned more in the past few years than in all of history. New brain-imaging techniques that show which parts of the brain are active when a person is engaged in various activities have increased tremendously our understanding of how the brain functions. For educators to benefit from this research and begin to apply it in classrooms requires a basic understanding of these structures and their roles. First, we will take a look at the overall structure (macrostructure) of the brain, then we will go a little deeper into the brain and look at the smaller brain structures and systems (microstructure) involved in learning to read a written language.

Macrostructures

The human brain weighs only about 3 pounds, but its light weight belies its importance. All behavior has its roots in the operations of the brain.

A large fissure running from the back (posterior) of the brain to the front (anterior) divides the top of the brain into two hemispheres, a right and a left. Each hemisphere has its own specialties, but the hemispheres work in concert because they are joined by a huge band of nerve fibers called the *corpus callosum*. These specialties will be further delineated as we begin to look at the processes involved in language and reading.

The outer one-quarter-inch-thick layer covering both hemispheres is called the *cerebral cortex*. (*Cortex* is the Latin word for "bark.") Within the cortex lie the abilities that make us uniquely human—the abilities to take in and process sensory data, communicate using language, be aware of what we are thinking (consciousness), recall the past and plan for the future, be aware of our emotions, create theories, move our body parts, and a myriad of other functions, including our ability to read. Each hemisphere is divided into four lobes. See Figure 17.1.

Starting at the very back of the brain are the *occipital lobes,* which are primarily responsible for taking in and interpreting visual stimuli. The cortex covering the occipital lobes is often called the *visual cortex*. Above the occipital lobes at the back of the brain are the *parietal lobes,* which receive tactile information (pressure, temperature, pain, etc.) and are responsible for integrating this information with sights and sounds. The *temporal lobes* are located on the sides of the brain above the ears. The cortex covering them is called the *auditory cortex*. The temporal lobes are responsible for taking in and interpreting auditory stimuli.

Figure 17.1. The Brain with the Four Lobes Attached.

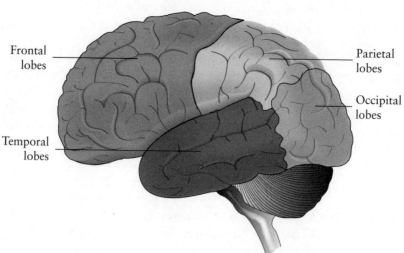

Frontal lobes

Temporal lobes

Parietal lobes

Occipital lobes

Structures within the temporal lobes also control the production of speech and memory. Right behind the forehead and extending back over the top of the brain are the *frontal lobes*. The cortex covering these lobes is referred to as the *association cortex*.

Two individual parts of the cerebral cortex deserve special attention. (See Figure 17.2.) Toward the back of the frontal lobes is a strip of cells called the *motor cortex*. It stretches across the top of the brain like a headband and controls all motor functions except reflexes. Different sections of this strip govern the movements of specific muscles in the body. Immediately behind the motor cortex lies the *somatosensory cortex*. Just as the motor cortex sends messages out to the various muscles in the body about how and when to move, the somatosensory cortex receives information from the environment about temperature, the position of our limbs, sensations of pain, and pressure. As with the motor cortex, each part of the body is represented by a specific area on the surface of the somatosensory cortex.

Microstructures

Almost anything a person does, from moving a hand to picking up a glass to reading a book, requires unbelievable coordination among numerous

Figure 17.2. The Brain Showing the Motor Cortex and Somatosensory Cortex.

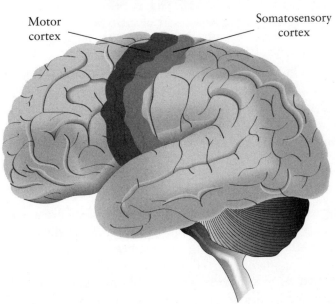

Motor cortex

Somatosensory cortex

small brain structures. As we begin to look at some of these microstructures of the brain, note that although each microstructure is addressed separately, none of them works alone. No one area of the brain is devoted to "comprehension" or "semantics." Rather, every task or function involves an interconnected group of structures. Each area within the group makes a specific contribution to the performance of the task. Therefore, trying to determine the exact functions of a specific part of the brain or the neural pathways involved in language or reading is a challenge.

For years, scientists have worked to understand the brain processes involved in language, but they were limited to studies of the brains of people whose language problems were caused by neurological disease, strokes, or other injuries that often caused some type of *aphasia*. (Aphasia is the partial or complete loss of language abilities following damage to the brain.) During the last two decades of the twentieth century, however, exciting new brain-imaging techniques have allowed scientists to picture the normal brain at work processing language.

Two of the imaging techniques used most frequently by neuroscientists are positron emission tomography (PET) and functional magnetic resonance imaging (fMRI). Simply defined, PET imaging traces the amount of glucose used by the cells of different structures of the brain as a person is engaged in various mental activities. It requires that radioactive glucose be injected into the bloodstream. fMRI, on the other hand, is less invasive as it does not require the injection of any substance. Rather, this imaging technique measures the amount of oxygen being used by the cells. It has the added advantage of showing more precisely where the mental activity is taking place because fMRIs, like regular MRIs, allow scientists to view soft tissue in the body.

Although the way the brain works while normally processing language is not thoroughly understood, most researchers agree that there are several structures and areas central to language. . . . Reading and writing press into use the structures and pathways used to speak and understand language, so we will begin by looking at these structures.

Brain Structures Involved in Language

Language is a kind of code consisting of a set of spoken symbols that represent the words of the language. Once we break the code, we can understand the language. Language is a very complex code, however, requiring us to manipulate all its forms (words, sentences, and intonation) that refer to objects, actions, and thoughts (Caplan, 1995). What goes on in the brain when we select our words, activate the sounds for each word, select the correct order of words to form a sentence (the syntax), and finally determine the proper intonation to convey the meaning?

AUDITORY CORTEX. Much language is generated in response to information coming into the brain from the environment, for example, during a conversation with another person. The first stepping-stone on the language pathway is for the brain to recognize that the stimulus being received is sound. The structures that make this preliminary distinction are the *thalamus* and the *auditory cortex*. The thalamus is the receiving point for all incoming sensory data (with the exception of smell), and its job is to act as a sort of relay station, sending messages to the appropriate part of the cortex for further processing. In this case, the sound stimulus is sent to the primary auditory cortex, which is located in the front of the temporal lobe. The thalamus and the auditory cortex appear to work in concert to determine if the incoming stimulus is language or some other type of sound such as environmental noise, music, or random noise. Once the sounds have been identified as language, the next stepping-stone on the pathway is Wernicke's area.

WERNICKE'S AREA. Named for its discoverer, Austrian neurologist Karl Wernicke, this group of cells is located at the junction of the parietal and temporal lobes in the left hemisphere very near the auditory cortex. (For about nine out of ten right-handed and nearly two-thirds of left-handed people, the major language structures reside in the left hemisphere; Restak, 2001.) The traditional view of Wernicke's area is that it is the semantic processing center and that it plays a significant role in the conscious comprehension of the spoken words by both the listener and the speaker. It appears to contain a sort of lexicon that stores memories of the sounds that make up words. It uses this internal "dictionary" to determine whether the incoming phoneme patterns or words are meaningful.

In this sense, words are not understood until they are processed by Wernicke's area. People who have had damage to this particular area of the brain (called *Wernicke's aphasia)* have no difficulty speaking; however, much of their speech makes no sense. These people also lack the ability to monitor their own speech and do not appear to be aware that they are substituting nonwords for real ones and that to the listener much of what they are saying is meaningless (Carter, 1998). Persons with Wernicke's aphasia also have difficulty comprehending what others are saying to them.

THE ARCUATE FASICULUS AND BROCA'S AREA. Our language pathway is not yet complete. There are two remaining stepping-stones, both controlled by the second major language area of the left hemisphere. The first is the *arcuate fasiculus*. Information leaving Wernicke's area needs to reach the frontal language regions of the brain in order for speech to occur. This feat is accomplished by means of a band of neural fibers called the arcuate fasiculus. Damage to this connecting pathway can result in what is called *conduction aphasia,* where people are not able to repeat what is said to them because the incoming words from Wernicke's area cannot be passed on to the area of the brain responsible for articulation.

The next stepping-stone on the language pathway is called *Broca's area*. This brain region was named for the French neurologist Paul Broca, who first discovered it in the late 1860s. Located in the left hemisphere at the back of the frontal lobe, Broca's area was originally thought to be primarily involved in language production. It has often been referred to as the expressive language center of the brain. Adjoining the section of the motor cortex that controls the jaw, larynx, tongue, and lips, Broca's area appears to convert words into a code to direct the muscle movements involved in speech production. People who have damage to this area (called *Broca's aphasia)* produce a sort of halting, "telegraphic" speech using nouns, verbs, and adjectives while often omitting conjunctions and other parts of speech.

Recent studies have suggested that while it does control production of speech, Broca's area—probably along with some of the surrounding cortical structures—has a second major language function, that of processing syntax, or assembling words into sensible phrases that are grammatically correct. This ability to organize the words is essential for meaning. A string of words becomes a sentence only when appropriate grammatical constructions are in place.

LANGUAGE IN THE RIGHT HEMISPHERE. Although the left hemisphere is nearly always dominant for language processing, this does not mean that the right hemisphere plays no role. Studies of persons with right hemispheric damage and of "split-brain" subjects (persons whose hemispheres cannot communicate with one another because the corpus callosum, the band of fibers connecting the two hemispheres, has been surgically severed) have shown that the right hemisphere can read and understand simple sentences. However, the major role that the right hemisphere seems to play is in the affect given to spoken language. A stroke or lesion in the language areas of the right hemisphere does not affect the ability of a person to speak, but his or her speech is devoid of emotional content. Other right hemispheric functions, such as appreciating humor and metaphor, are also often affected by stroke or trauma.

A CAVEAT. Although the terms *Broca's area* and *Wernicke's area* are commonly used, these language areas are not neat modules with clearly defined borders. A danger exists of overstating the significance of a given cortical area for a particular function, as it may be that each area is involved in more than one language function (Gazzaniga, 1998). The areas of the brain associated with language—its reception, comprehension, processing, and production—are still being studied. As mentioned earlier, it is difficult to map the detailed functions of the language system directly onto the brain's complex anatomical structures. Given these constraints, scientists have, however, produced a tentative architecture of the brain's language pathway that has fairly accurate validity and is useful in our quest to understand what goes on in the brain when we process both spoken and written language (Bear, Conners, & Paradiso, 1996). See Figures 17.3 and 17.4.

Figure 17.3. Diagram of the Language Pathway in the Brain.

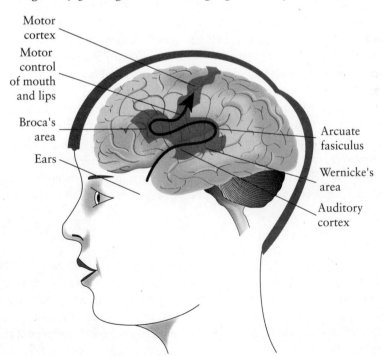

Figure 17.4. The Flow Chart of the Language Pathway.

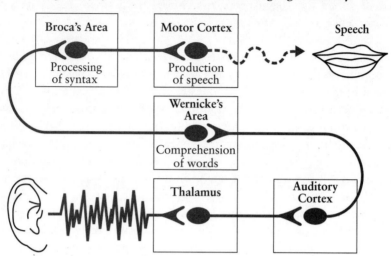

Brain Structures Involved in Reading

One of the miracles of the brain is that engaging in a conversation involves all the brain macrostructures and microstructures just described, but learning how to talk does not require an understanding of them or conscious attention to their processes. While reading these words, fluent readers are not conscious of the structures that are being activated to allow them to process and comprehend the print. However, for some children these processes are not automatic. It is critical for teachers of these children to understand these underlying processes and how they come to be automatic (or don't). Without this understanding, teachers will not be able to comprehend or use the research on dyslexia and other reading research that is being conducted. Therefore, our next step is to examine the structures (in addition to the ones just discussed) that the brain uses to decode and comprehend print.

The Neural Pathway for Reading

As we have discussed, many of the structures used in reading are the same as those used for spoken language. However, print is a relatively recent invention and requires the brain to co-opt structures that were perhaps designed for other purposes. We will look at two additional areas of the brain that are involved in reading: the *visual cortex* and the *angular gyrus*.

VISUAL CORTEX. The human visual system is one of the most studied and best understood areas of the brain. Although a thorough discussion of this system is beyond the scope of this book, a basic understanding is necessary in order to appreciate its role in the reading process. Visual information is contained in the light that is reflected from objects. As light rays enter the eyes, they are transduced, or changed into electrical impulses, and are sent from the eyes through the optic nerves to the thalamus. The job of the thalamus is to relay this information to the primary visual cortex located in the occipital lobes. It is here in the visual cortex that the brain begins the initial step of reading by recognizing the visual pattern of a word (Gazzaniga, 1998). It does this by calling into use an already existing visual feature extraction system for visual stimuli in general. The brain has adapted this system to allow it to process letter strings, as well as other visual features. Even though the features of the word have been extracted, the string of letters has not been perceived as a word. That job falls partially to another structure, the angular gyrus.

ANGULAR GYRUS. Located at the junction of the occipital, parietal, and temporal lobes, the angular gyrus is perfectly situated to be a bridge between the visual word recognition system and the rest of the language processing system. It is here that the letters of the written words are translated into the sounds or *phonemes* of spoken language. Without this transformation, reading and writing would be impossible. Indeed, damage to the angular gyrus disrupts both reading and writing (Carter, 1998). Sally Shaywitz, in discussing the neurobiology of reading and dyslexia, states that the angular gyrus is pivotal in carrying out cross-modal integration (auditory and visual) and mapping the sights of the print onto the phonemic structures of language (Shaywitz, 2003). In essence the angular gyrus, in conjunction with Wernicke's area, is the "hub" where all the relevant information about how a word looks, how it sounds, and what it means is tightly bound together and stored (Shaywitz, 2003). From this point forward, processing of the written word follows pretty much the same pathway as spoken language, going from the angular gyrus to Wernicke's area, across the arcuate fasiculus to Broca's area, and, if reading aloud, to the motor cortex.

We can now add to the diagram the additional structures used in the brain for processing written language. (See Figures 17.5 and 17.6.) Remember that the brain is a parallel processor, and the pathway for reading is not as linear as a drawing makes it appear. Also, the specific task affects which structures (in which hemispheres) will be activated.

Figure 17.5. Diagram of the Reading Pathway in the Brain.

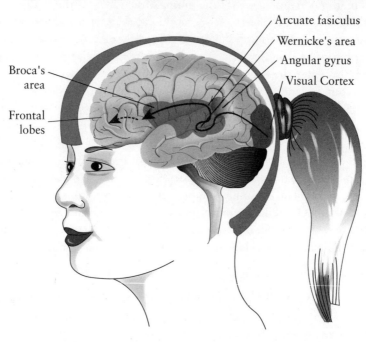

Figure 17.6. The Flow Chart of the Reading Pathway.

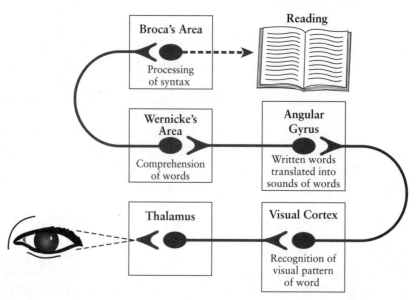

Reading aloud activates different structures from those used in reading silently (Bookheimer, Zeffiro, Blaxton, Gaillard, & Theodore, 1995). Listening to text activates different parts of the brain than does word ordering or syntactic judgments. Which pathways are activated may also depend on how practiced or automatic a task is. However, an understanding of the general functions of the structures involved in processing spoken and written language will allow educators to be more informed consumers of reading research and better able to understand how particular neural deficits affect children's ability to read.

Reading Problems with a Biological Basis

. . . Some of the reasons children fail to learn to read . . . stem from genetic or biological factors. Now that we have examined the structures and pathways the brain uses to read, we can look at what happens when one or more of these systems fails to work normally. People whose reading difficulties stem from neurological sources are called *dyslexic*. *Dyslexia* is a brain disorder that primarily affects a person's ability to read and write (Bloom, Beal, & Kupfer, 2003). This disability is separate from intelligence.

Dyslexic persons generally have normal or above-normal intelligence and their higher-order skills are intact. Their problem is not behavioral, psychological, motivational, or social. Dyslexia appears to be fairly widespread. While reading experts don't all agree on the prevalence of this disorder, Shaywitz believes that it can be found in as many as 17 percent of school-aged children and as many as 40 percent of the adult population (Shaywitz & Shaywitz, 2001). Dyslexia can be either developmental or acquired as the result of some injury to the brain such as trauma, tumor, or stroke. However, what both developmental dyslexia and acquired dyslexia have in common is a disruption in the neural pathways for reading. People do not outgrow dyslexia. Even though as adults they may become more proficient at reading words, they still have difficulty reading unfamiliar words and are not as fluent or automatic in their reading as a nonimpaired reader (Shaywitz & Shaywitz, 2001).

Visual Processing Problems

Because reading begins with visual input, any problem in the visual system can affect the ability to process print. A growing body of research shows that some poor readers may have subtle sensory deficits in visual processing

(Berninger, 2002). These deficits may manifest as poor eye health, poor visual acuity, and/or slower than normal eye movements. Imaging studies of adults with dyslexia conducted at the National Institute of Mental Health (Eden et at., 1996) detected subtle deficits in the visual motion detection area of their brains known as brain region V5/MT. Nonimpaired readers showed robust activity in this area, while persons with dyslexia showed almost no activity. This area of the visual cortex has connections to areas that are active in phonological processing, and it is possible that it plays an important role in the processing of written words.

Although this is a small study and more research needs to be done, Eden et al. believe these findings indicate that dyslexia is a discrete brain disorder and that the source of some reading difficulties may stem from visual deficits rather than problems in the language-related areas. Still other studies are finding that minor differences in how the brain handles the visual processing of images, color, and contrast, as well as fast motion, can impede reading (Eden et al., 1996).

Auditory Processing Problems

Educators are often surprised to learn that in an fMRI or PET scan (which depicts activity levels in the brain) the auditory cortex is active even when a person is reading silently. This occurs because the brain is busy processing all the "sounds" associated with reading, just as it would be if the person were listening to someone speak (Bookheimer et al., 1995). It is not surprising, then, that deficits within the auditory processing areas of the brain are another source of reading problems. These deficits can occur anywhere along the auditory pathway, with the most obvious being a hearing impairment or deafness. Chronic ear infections (chronic otitis media) often lead to intermittent hearing loss in young children and may have a negative effect on language development and, consequently, on reading.

Farther along the auditory pathway, other problems can occur. Recall that, in order to read, children must be able to process the auditory sounds of the language by identifying the sounds (phonemes), linking the phonemes, then associating them to the written words. In English, vowels change relatively slowly, but stop consonants, such as "b" and "p," change more rapidly. Researcher Michael Merzenich and his colleagues at the University of California at San Francisco have discovered that some poor readers do not process these consonant sounds quickly enough (Merzenich et al., 1996). This means that a person with this auditory processing deficit would not be able to clearly distinguish the difference between "bat" and "pat."

Although the original research was conducted with adults, subsequent research has shown that children suffer from the same deficit (Temple et al., 2003). Using a commercially available program (Fast ForWord) that focuses on auditory processing and oral language training, the researchers have been able to train the brains of some dyslexic children to increase the speed and accuracy with which they process rapidly successive and rapidly changing sounds. Brain-imaging scans of these children showed that critical higher-order areas necessary for reading were activated for the first time (Temple et al., 2003). Whether the training results in actual changes in these higher-order areas or if the changes in the basic auditory system are providing information to the higher-order areas is not known at this point (J. Gabrieli, personal communication, April 6, 2003).

Problems in the Language/Reading Pathways

Although many reading difficulties can be attributed to visual or auditory processing deficits, more often the central difficulty appears to be a deficit in the language system. The language pathway of the brain can be conceptualized as a hierarchy of lower- and higher-level skills. At the higher levels are the neural systems that process semantics (the meaning of the language), syntax (organizing words into comprehensible sentences), and discourse (speaking and writing). Underlying these abilities are the lower-level phonological skills dedicated to deciphering the reading code.

In simple terms, the lower levels handle decoding while the higher levels are dedicated to comprehension. This is a reciprocal process. As a person reads, the brain shifts back and forth between decoding and comprehension. As we have seen, scientists are now able to map the neural structures that process both the higher- and the lower-level skills involved in language and reading. Phonological processing occurs in the back of the left hemisphere (in most people) in the angular gyrus and Wernicke's area. The more skilled readers are, the more they activate this region. Higher-level comprehension skills are handled largely by the frontal regions of the left hemisphere in Broca's area and the frontal lobes. Problems or deficits in either of these areas appear to be central to many reading difficulties.

The Glitch in the System

While educators have long known that poor readers have difficulty "sounding out" unfamiliar words or that they read text without comprehension, there has been little research to help them understand why these problems occur. With the advent of brain-imaging technology, this is changing. Sally and Bennett Shaywitz, pediatricians and neuroscientists at the National Institute of Child Health and Human Development (NICHD)—Yale Center for the Study of Learning and Attention, and their colleagues have conducted some of the most illuminating research.

Using fMRI, a noninvasive imaging technique, these researchers studied 144 children by scanning their brains while they read. The children ranged in age from 7 to 18 years. Seventy were dyslexic readers and 74 were nonimpaired readers. What they discovered is that brain activation patterns differed significantly between the two groups.

In nonimpaired readers, there is activity in both the frontal (Broca's area) and the posterior regions (Wernicke's area and the angular gyrus) in the left hemisphere of the brain. However, in the dyslexic readers, there is a relative underactivation in the posterior areas and a relative overactivation in the frontal regions. As Sally Shaywitz states, "It is as if these struggling readers are using the systems in front of the brain to try to compensate for the disruption in the back of the brain" (Shaywitz, 2003, p. 81). In other words, it appears that the dyslexic readers are using the frontal regions as a sort of "alternative backup" to try to decode, because the areas that would normally serve to interpret the written code are not working as they should. This pattern seems to be universal in dyslexics, no matter which language they speak or what their age. An earlier study conducted by the same team of researchers showed that this failure to activate the phonological processing area of the brain continues into adulthood (Shaywitz & Shaywitz, 2001).

This research shows that there is a physiological basis, or "glitch" in the system, for some reading difficulties. As Sally Shaywitz states, "Most likely as the result of a genetically programmed error, the neural system necessary for phonologic analysis is somehow miswired, and a child is left with a phonologic impairment that interferes with spoken and written language" (Shaywitz, 2003, p. 68).

The most recent research led by Bennett and Sally Shaywitz and their colleagues compared the brain scans of 43 young adults who were impaired (dyslexic) readers with 27 nonimpaired readers. These two groups had been followed since elementary school and were from similar socioeconomic backgrounds and had comparable reading skills when they began school. What the researchers discovered was surprising: there appeared to be two distinct types of brain problems in the dyslexic readers. One is predominantly genetic, as reported in the earlier study. These students, as we have seen, appear to have a glitch in their neural circuitry and enlist other parts of their brains to compensate. They can read and comprehend, but they read slowly. "[These] persistently poor readers have a rudimentary system in place, but it's not connected well. They weren't able to develop and connect it right because they haven't had that early stimulation. If you can provide these children early on with effective reading instruction, these children can really learn to read" (Shaywitz et al., 2002).

These exciting new findings have major implications for those who study and teach reading. Researchers, using brain imaging, may be able to validate effective strategies for helping struggling readers as they observe changes that take place in the neural systems for reading as the result of specific reading interventions. . . .

Attention and Memory Systems Involved in Reading

Thus far, we have been examining the physiological structures that the brain has adapted to allow us to read. Attention and memory systems are a bit more difficult to localize in the brain than are the sensory processes. However, an understanding of how the brain's memory systems function is essential to understanding the reading process, since some reading disabilities stem from problems in these areas.

As we have seen, phonemic awareness and phonological awareness are necessary components of reading, but they are not sufficient. In addition, the beginning reader must be able to pay attention to what is being read and needs to have a good memory. What does it mean to pay attention or to have a good memory? Actually, it can mean many things. First, let's look at a model that is commonly used to differentiate among the three major memory systems of the brain.

SENSORY MEMORY. Figure 17.7 depicts how the brain takes in or discards incoming information, manipulates it, and stores it. The first box in the diagram is labeled Sensory Memory and depicts the initial stage of information processing, taking in sensory data, and determining what to keep and what to drop. Sensory memory can be thought of as the brain's attention system. Because much of the sensory stimuli impinging on the body—the feeling of clothing against the body, for example—is not relevant at any given moment, much of the incoming information, perhaps as much as 99 percent, is immediately discarded. This system is obviously critical to reading. Being able to focus on the letters and words rather than on random stimuli is an initial step in becoming a reader.

Many factors influence a child's ability to focus attention. Inattention to a task can be the result of hunger, fatigue, and other physical factors; the emotional state of the child; environmental noise and/or temperature;

Figure 17.7. Diagram of Information Processing Model.

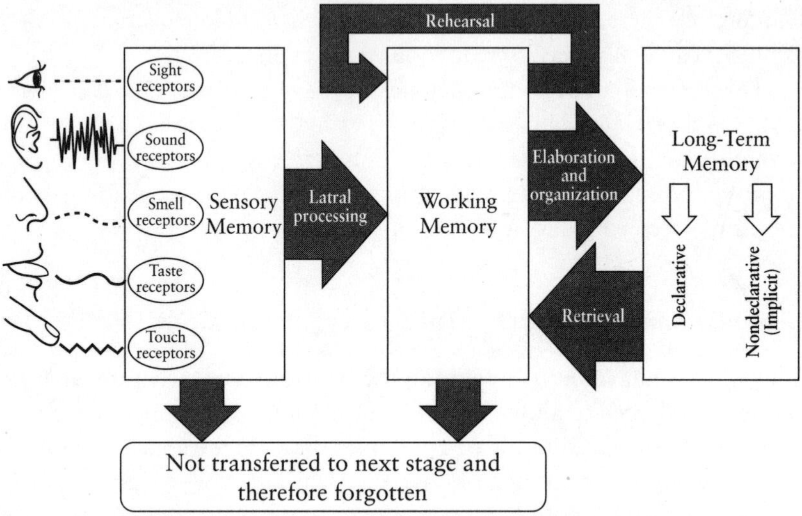

or an inappropriate level of difficulty of the material. Given the right conditions, however, most children have little or no difficulty paying attention to relevant stimuli, but some do. Possibly the most well known, but still poorly understood, biological condition to impact attention is attention deficit/hyperactivity disorder (ADHD).

ADHD is a label given to persons with a neurobiological disorder that interferes with their capacity to attend to tasks and regulate their behavior. Although ADHD and reading disability are distinct disorders, there is good evidence that they often occur together. According to researcher Sally Shaywitz, reading disability is relatively common in children with attention problems. Shaywitz estimates that this occurs in 31 percent of first-grade children, becoming even more frequent as the child grows older. She estimates that over 50 percent of ninth-grade students diagnosed with ADHD have a reading disability (Shaywitz, Fletcher, & Shaywitz, 1994). This disorder is contained to some degree by medication and/or behavioral therapy.

WORKING MEMORY. The filtering of stimuli that occurs in sensory memory happens so quickly that it is an unconscious process. The brain is continuously taking in sensory stimuli, assembling and sorting the data, and directing only some of it to conscious attention. Although conscious processing represents only a small part of information processing, without it readers would not be able to retain the first part of a sentence as they are reading to its end. This short-term, conscious processing is called *working memory*. Working memory allows the brain to hold on to information for a short time, approximately 18 seconds. However, the brain can retain the information longer by rehearsing it. Researcher William Baddeley coined the term "articulatory loop" to describe this type of rehearsal (Baddeley, 1986).

Think about being given several directions at a time or trying to remember a phone number long enough to dial it. Most people probably mentally repeated the directions or the number over and over using their own articulatory loop. This verbal rehearsal or subvocalization appears to be essential for comprehension of what is being read. According to research, skilled readers cannot remember—or comprehend—a complex sentence when they are prevented from subvocalizing its wording (Baddeley, 1979). While children can be observed repeating songs and phrases, this is generally not done with a conscious understanding of the need to rehearse to remember information. This understanding of the need to rehearse information to remember it often does not occur spontaneously until around age 7 or 8. However, children can be taught to do this earlier (Kail, 1984). Younger—and poorer—readers often do not engage in this type of rehearsal. This is especially true for children in homes where parents do not understand the necessity of rehearsal strategies.

It is easy to see how the age of a child or a dysfunctional verbal memory negatively affects reading ability. However, the problem may not necessarily be in the articulatory loop. Other aspects of working memory may be completely normal but still work against the reading process. (Remember that even the brain that works normally was not designed for reading.) In order to understand these, we need to become familiar with several other characteristics of a normal working memory that affect the ability to decode and comprehend print.

The Cocktail Party Effect. In a normal environment, paying attention is generally not difficult. However, when the auditory stimuli increase, such as at a cocktail party, the brain has a problem; it can only pay conscious attention to one train of thought at a time. People can *do* two things at the same time if one is automatic. This phenomenon is familiar. Who hasn't arrived at a familiar location without being aware of driving there? The procedure of driving was so automatic that you were able to think through a problem or plan a meal at the same time you were driving.

Think about children who are still in the process of sounding out unfamiliar words as they are reading. In all likelihood, their train of thought comprehension is lost when they stop to decode. This would also be true of an adult who is learning to read a second language. It is not that the child or adult has a dysfunctional working memory; it is a normal phenomenon of a brain that is focusing on decoding rather than on comprehension. Educators need to be aware of this processing limitation when working with a beginning reader. After the word(s) has been deciphered, it is generally wise to have the child re-read the sentence, checking to make certain that its meaning is understood. Otherwise, children may come to view reading as a sort of "performing art," not realizing that we read for a purpose.

The Capacity of Working Memory. The ability to retain information in working memory is essential for reading. Readers must be able to remember what they have previously read in order to make sense of what they are presently reading. Therefore, it is important to be aware that memory capacity is developmental and that the age of the children determines how much information they can hold on to at a time.

Researcher Pascual-Leone theorizes that the number of items that can be held in working memory varies with age (Pascual-Leone, 1970). According to Pascual-Leone, in a test requiring a subject to recall strings of digits, the typical 5-year-old can recall two digits. The number of digits children can recall accurately increases by 1 every 2 years until a mental age of 15, when the adult capacity of 7 is reached. However, emergent readers are not recalling digits but engaging in the very complex task of learning to read. The capacity of working memory is relative to the requirements of the reading task. These include

○ The amount of effort children are having to invest

○ The speed with which the individual words are decoded

○ Whether children are engaging in verbal rehearsal

○ The length and complexity of the sentences

What this adds to our efforts to understand reading is that the greater effort readers must invest in the individual words, the less processing "space" they will have to recall the preceding words or phrases when it is time to put them all together. The child's brain could be thought of as being on cognitive overload. One research study found that poorer third-grade readers could not remember as many as three words back in a clause (Goldman, Hogaboam, Bell, & Perfetti, 1980).

Chunking as a Way of Increasing the Capacity of Working Memory. Adults have the ability to hold on to seven bits of information. However, it is easy to think of an example of a string of digits longer than seven that can be recalled without difficulty. How does this happen? The answer is in the definition of a bit. When a certain configuration of numbers or letters is processed many times, the brain eventually stores that particular configuration as a single bit of information.

Let's say, for example, that a beginning reader is introduced to an unfamiliar word such as "cap" and is able to read it by pronouncing each letter sound or phoneme. This act requires using three bits of working memory. However, with repeated exposure to the word "cap," it is recognized as a word, not three separate letters, and the reader no longer has to decode it. It has become automatic and is now stored in working memory as one bit or chunk of information.

Michael Pressley (2001) puts it very well in his book *Reading Instruction That Works: The Case for Balanced Teaching.*

> In fact, decoding and comprehension compete for the available short-term capacity. When a reader slowly analyzes a word into component sounds and blends them, a great deal of capacity is consumed, with relatively little left over for comprehension of the word, let alone understanding the overall meaning of the sentence containing the words and the paragraph containing the sentence. In contrast, automatic word recognition consumes very little capacity, and thus frees short-term capacity for the task of comprehending the word and integrating the meaning of the word with the overall meaning of the sentence, paragraph, and text. Consistent with this analysis, uncertain decoders comprehend less than do more rapid, certain decoders [p. 67].

Our ability to chunk information into larger and larger bits is one of the marvelous qualities of our brains that allows us to read fluently and eventually comprehend what we are reading. When we see how the brain links separate bits of information into larger wholes, we see why repeated exposure to a common vocabulary is essential.

Long-Term Memory

Now that we have looked at how the brain encodes incoming information and manipulates it, we are ready to look at the third part of our model, long-term memory. *Long-term memory* explains how the brain stores that information. There are actually two types of long-term memory: declarative and nondeclarative. Declarative memory is just what its name says: recalled information that can be declared, such as names, events, concepts, and other types of learned data. To bring these data to mind requires conscious thought. Nondeclarative memory, on the other hand, consists of habits and skills that have been practiced to the point that they can be performed unconsciously. For this reason, declarative memory is often called *conscious or explicit memory* and nondeclarative labeled *unconscious, procedural, automatic, or implicit memory.*

To read fluently with comprehension requires both declarative and nondeclarative memory skills. At this point, we are more interested in nondeclarative memory as it relates to reading. Our conscious working memory, as we have seen, is limited in the amount of information it can handle. One way to reduce this overload is to get certain procedures or skills to the automatic level. In the case of reading, decoding is what we want to become an automatic or unconscious activity. As has been pointed out, unless this occurs, most or all the space in working memory is used for deciphering the print and little or none is left for the higher-level skills involved in comprehending what is being read. Reading the words in this sentence relies on automatic processing so that the reader can focus on the meaning. However, if this sentence contained an unfamiliar word or one in another language, automatic processing would be disrupted while the reader decoded the word. How do fluent readers reach the point of decoding automaticity? What is necessary to assist the beginning reader in reaching this point?

Obtaining automaticity in any skill is not as much a matter of the person's innate ability or intellectual prowess as it is of the amount and type of practice in the skill. While long, tapered legs might be an asset to becoming an expert gymnast, they would be of little value unless the person practiced long and hard under expert guidance. The same is true of becoming an expert reader. No matter what our IQ, we do not have brains that can remember most words after seeing them once. For readers to obtain automatic word recognition, a great deal of the right kind of practice under expert guidance is also necessary.

First, the grapheme-phoneme (letter-sound) relationships need to be matched and experienced so frequently that they begin to be seen automatically as units. As readers put more and more of these units together into words, the same rehearsal with the words is necessary. (Second-language learners often do the opposite of the procedure. They take the pieces they understand and put them into the language structure.) This is accomplished by frequent retrieval of these words in normal reading activities. Gaining automaticity in reading is not an easy process, but when teachers understand the process and provide beginning readers with many opportunities for rehearsal, it happens with nearly all children.

Understanding the systems in the brain that are involved in learning to read is a necessary, but not sufficient, component in our quest to build a reading brain. We now need to look at how an understanding of brain processes can assist us in determining the best methods to use as we guide children on their journey to becoming readers.

REFERENCES

Baddeley, A. D. (1979). Working memory and reading. In P. Kolers, E. Wrolstad, & H. Bouma (Eds.), *Processing of visible language* (Vol. 1). New York: Plenum Press.

Baddeley, A. D. (1986). *Working memory.* Oxford: Oxford University Press.

Bear, M. F., Conners, B. W., & Paradiso, M. A. (1996). *Neuroscience: Exploring the brain.* Philadelphia: Lippincott/Williams & Wilkins.

Berninger, V. W. (2002). *Revealing the secrets of the brain: Neuropsychologist Virginia Berninger studies brain images before and after instruction for clues to the mystery of learning disabilities* [Online]. Available: http://www.nwrel.org/nwedu/08–03/brain-t.asp.

Bloom, F. E., Beal, M. F., & Kupfer, D. J. (2003). *The Dana guide to brain health.* New York: Free Press.

Bookheimer, S. Y., Zeffiro, T. A., Blaxton, T., Gaillard, W. D., & Theodore, W. H. (1995). Regional cerebral blood flow during object naming and word reading. *Human Brain Mapping, 3*(2), 93–106.

Caplan, D. (1995). *The Harvard Mahoney Neuroscience Institute Letter, 4*(4).

Carter, R. (1998). *Mapping the mind.* Los Angeles: University of California Press.

Center for the Improvement of Early Reading Achievement (CIERA). (2001). *Put reading first: The research building blocks for teaching children to read.* A joint publication with the National Institute for Literacy, the National Institute of Child Health and Human Development, and the U.S. Department of Education. Jessup, MD: National Institute for Literacy.

Eden, G., Van Meter, J., Rumsey, J., Maisog, J., Woods, R., & Zeffiro, T. (1996). Abnormal processing of visual motion in dyslexia revealed by functional brain imaging. *Nature, 382,* 66–69.

Gazzaniga, M. (1998). *The mind's past.* Berkeley: University of California Press.

Goldman, S. R., Hogaboam, T. W., Bell, L. C., & Perfetti, C. A. (1980). Short-term retention of discourse during reading. *Journal of Educational Psychology, 68,* 680–688.

Kail, R. V. (1984). *The development of memory in children.* New York: W.H. Freeman.

Merzenich, M. M., Jenkins, W. M., Johnston, P., Schreiner, C., Miller, S. L., & Tallal, P. (1996). Temporal processing deficits of language-learning impaired children ameliorated by training. *Science, 271,* 77–81.

Pascual-Leone, J. (1970). A maturational model for the transition rule in Piaget's developmental stages. *Acta Psychologica, 32,* 301–345.

Pressley, M. (2001). Comprehension instruction: What makes sense now, what might make sense soon. Reading Online [Online], 5 (2). Available: http://www.readingonline.org/articles/art_index.asp?HREF=/articles/handbook/pressley/Index.html.

Restak, R. (2001). *The secret life of the brain.* Washington, DC: Joseph Henry Press.

Shaywitz, S. (2003). *Overcoming dyslexia: A new and complete science-based program for reading problems at any level.* New York: Alfred A. Knopf.

Shaywitz, S. E., Fletcher, J. M., & Shaywitz, B. A. (1994). Issues in the definition and classification of attention deficit disorder. *Topics in Language Disorders, 14*(4), 1–25.

Shaywitz, S. E., & Shaywitz, B. A. (2001). The neurobiology of reading and dyslexia. *Focus on Basics, 5*(A).

Shaywitz, B. A., Shaywitz, S. E., Pugh, K. R., Mencl, W. E., Fulbright, R. K., Skudlarski, P., Constable, R. T., Marchione, K. E., Fletcher, J. M., Lyon, G. R., & Gore, J. C. (2002). Functional disruption in the organization of the brain for reading in dyslexia. *Biological Psychiatry, 52,* 101–110.

Temple, E., Deutsch, G. K., Poldrac, R. A., Salidis, J., Deutsch, G. K., Miller, S. L., Tallal, P., Merzenich, M. M., & Gabrieli, J. D. (2003). Neural deficits in children with dyslexia ameliorated by behavioral remediation: Evidence from functional MRI. *Proceedings of the National Academy of Science, 100*(5), 2860–2865.

18

SMALL HEADS FOR BIG CALCULATIONS

Stanislas Dehaene

*Two and two make four
four and four make eight
eight and eight make sixteen
Repeat!, says the teacher*

—Jacques Prevert, *Page d'ecriture*

AMBITION, DISTRACTION, UGLIFICATION, AND DERISION. These are the mischievous names the Reverend Charles Lutwidge Dodgson, a mathematics professor better known to us as Lewis Carroll, gave to the four arithmetical operations. Obviously, Carroll did not cherish too many illusions about his pupils' calculation abilities. And perhaps he was right. While children easily acquire number syntax, learning to calculate can be an ordeal. Children and even adults often err in the most elementary of calculations. Who can say that they never get 7×9 or 8×7 wrong? How many of us can mentally compute $113 - 37$ or $100 - 24$ in less than two seconds? Calculation errors are so widespread that far from stigmatizing ignorance, they attract sympathy when they are admitted publicly ("I've always been *hopeless* at math!"). Many of us can almost identify with Alice's plight as she attempts to calculate while traveling through Wonderland: "Let me see: four times five is twelve, and four times six is thirteen, and four times seven is—oh dear! I shall never get to twenty at that rate!"

Why is mental calculation so difficult? In this chapter, we examine the calculation algorithms of the human brain. Although our knowledge of this issue is still far from complete, one thing is certain: Mental arithmetic poses serious problems for the human brain. Nothing ever prepared it for the task of memorizing dozens of intermingled multiplication facts, or of flawlessly executing the ten or fifteen steps of a two-digit subtraction. An innate sense of approximate numerical quantities may well be embedded in our genes; but when faced with exact symbolic calculation, we lack proper resources. Our brain has to tinker with alternate circuits in order to make up for the lack of a cerebral organ specifically designed for calculation. This tinkering takes a heavy toll. Loss of speed, increased concentration, and frequent errors illuminate the shakiness of the mechanisms that our brain contrives in order to "incorporate" arithmetic.

Counting: The ABC of Calculation

In the first six or seven years of life, a profusion of calculation algorithms sees the light. Young children reinvent arithmetic. Spontaneously or by imitating their peers, they imagine new strategies for calculation. They also learn to select the best strategy for each problem. The majority of their strategies are based on counting, with or without words, with or without fingers. Children often discover them by themselves, even before they are taught to calculate.

Does this imply that counting is an innate competence of the human brain? Rochel Gelman and Randy Gallistel, from the psychology department of UCLA, have championed this point of view. According to them, children are endowed with unlearned principles of counting. They do not have to be taught that each object must be counted once and only once, that the number words must be recited in fixed order, or that the last number represents the cardinal of the whole set. Gelman and Gallistel maintain that such counting knowledge is innate and even precedes and guides the acquisition of the number lexicon.

Few theories have been as harshly debated as that of Gelman and Callistel's. For many psychologists and educators, counting is a typical example of learning by imitation. Initially, it is just a rote behavior devoid of meaning. According to Karen Fuson, children initially recite "onetwothreefourfive . . ." as an uninterrupted chain. Only later do they learn to segment this sequence into words, to extend it to larger numerals, and to apply it to concrete situations. They progressively infer what counting is about by observing other people count. Initially, according to Fuson, counting is just parroting.

The truth, which is being progressively unveiled after years of controversy and tens of experiments, seems to stand somewhere between the "all innate" and the "all acquired" extremes. Some aspects of counting are mastered quite precociously, while others seem to be acquired by learning and imitation.

As an example of an amazingly precocious competence for counting, consider the following experiment by Karen Wynn. At two and a half, children have probably not had many occasions to see someone count sounds or actions. Yet if one asks them to watch a *Sesame Street* videotape and count how many times Big Bird jumps, they easily lend themselves to this task. Likewise, they can count sounds as diverse as trumpeting, a bell, a splash, and a computer beep that have been recorded on tape and whose source is not visible. So children seem to understand, quite early on and without explicit teaching, that counting is an abstract procedure that applies to all kinds of visual and auditory objects.

Here is another precocious competence: As early as three and half years of age, children know that the order in which one recites numerals is crucial, while the order in which one points toward objects is irrelevant as long as each object is counted once and only once. In an innovative series of experiments, Gelman and her colleagues presented children with situations that violate the usual conventions of counting. The results indicate that three-and-a-half-year-olds can identify and correct rather subtle counting errors. They never fail to notice when someone recites numerals out of order, forgets to count an item, or counts the same item twice. Most important, they maintain a clear distinction between such patent errors and other correct though unusual ways of counting. For instance, they find it perfectly acceptable to start counting at the middle of a row of objects, or to count every other object first, as long as one eventually counts all items once and only once. Better yet, they are willing to start counting at any point in a row, and they can even devise strategies to systematically reach a predesignated object in third position.

What these experiments show is that by their fourth year, children have mastered the basics of how to count. They are not content with slavishly imitating the behavior of others: They generalize counting to novel situations. The origins of this precocious competence remain poorly understood. From where does a child draw the idea of reciting words in a perfect one-to-one correspondence with the objects to be counted? Like Gelman and Gallistel, I believe that this aptitude belongs to the genetic endowment of the human species. Reciting words in a fixed order is probably a natural outcome of the human faculty for language. As to the principle of one-to-one correspondence, it is actually widespread in the animal kingdom. When a rat forages through a maze, it tries to visit each arm once and only once, a rational behavior that minimizes exploration time. When we look for a given object in a visual scene, our attention is oriented in turn toward each object. The counting algorithm stands at the intersection of these two elementary abilities of the human brain—word recitation and exhaustive search. That is why our children easily dominate it.

Though children rapidly grasp the how to of counting, however, they seem to initially ignore the *why*. As adults, we know what counting is for. To us, counting is a tool that serves a precise goal: enumerating a set of items. We also know that what really matters is the final numeral, which represents the cardinal of the entire set. Do young children have this knowledge? Or do they just view counting as an entertaining game in which one recites funny words while pointing to various objects in turn?

According to Karen Wynn, children do not appreciate the meaning of counting until the end of their fourth year. Let your three-year-old daughter count up her toys and then ask her, "How many toys do you have?" Chances are, she will give a random number, not necessarily the one she just reached. Like all children of this age, she does not seem to relate the "how many" question to her previous counting. She may even count everything up again, as if the act of counting itself was an adequate answer to a "how many" question. Likewise, ask a two-and-a-half-year-old boy to give you three toys. Most likely he will pick a handful at random, even if he can already count up to five or ten. At that age, although the mechanisms of counting have largely fallen into place, children do not seem to understand what counting is for, and they do not think of counting when the situation commands it.

Around four, the meaning of counting eventually settles in. But how? The preverbal representation of numerical quantities probably plays a crucial role in this process. Remember that right from birth, way before they start to count, children have an internal accumulator that informs them of the approximate number of things that surround them. This accumulator can help bring meaning to counting. Suppose that a child is playing with two dolls. His accumulator automatically activates a cerebral representation of the quantity 2. . . . The child has learned that the word "two" applies to this quantity, so that he can say "two dolls" without having to count. Now suppose that for no particular reason, he decides to "play the counting game" with the dolls, and recites the words "one, two." He will be surprised to discover that the last number of the count, "two," is the very word that can apply to the entire set. After ten or twenty such occasions, he may soundly infer that whenever one counts, the last word arrived at has a special status: It represents a numerical quantity that matches the one provided by the internal accumulator. Counting, which was only an entertaining word game, suddenly acquires a special meaning: Counting is the best way of saying how many!

Preschoolers as Algorithm Designers

Understanding what counting is for is the starting point of an outburst of numerical inventions. Counting is the Swiss Army knife of arithmetic, the tool that children spontaneously put to all sorts of uses. With the help of counting, most children find ways of adding and subtracting numbers without requiring any explicit teaching.

The first calculation algorithm that all children figure out for themselves consists in adding two sets by counting them both on the fingers. Ask a very young child to add 2 and 4. She will typically start by counting up to the first number, 2, while successively raising two fingers. Then she will count up to the second number, 4, while raising four other fingers. And finally she will recount them all and reach a total of 6. This first "digital" algorithm is conceptually simple but very slow. Executing it can be truly awkward: At the age of four, to compute 3 + 4, my son would put up three fingers on the left hand and four on the right hand. Then he would proceed to count them using the only pointing device that remained at his disposal—the tip of his nose!

Initially, young children find it difficult to calculate without using their fingers. Words vanish as soon as they have been uttered, but fingers can be kept constantly in sight, preventing one from losing count in case of a temporary distraction. After a few months though, children discover a more efficient addition algorithm than finger counting. When adding two and four, they can be heard muttering "one *two* . . . three . . . four . . . five . . . *six*." They first count up to the first operand, 2, then move forward by as many steps as specified by the second operand, 4. This is an attention-demanding strategy because it implies some sort of recursion: In the second phase, one has to count how many times one counts! Children often make this recursion explicit: "one *two* . . . three is one . . . four is two . . . five is three . . . six is four . . . *six*." The difficulty of this step is reflected by a drastic slowing and extreme concentration.

Refinements are quickly found. Most children realize that they need not recount both numbers, and that they can compute 2 + 4 by starting right from the word "two." They then simply say "two . . . three . . . four . . . five . . . *six*." To shorten calculation even further, they learn to systematically start with the larger of the two numbers. When asked to compute 2 + 4, they spontaneously transform this problem into the equivalent 4 + 2. As a result, all they now have to do is count a number of times equal to the smaller of the two addends. This is called the "minimum strategy." It is a standard algorithm that underlies most of children's calculations before the onset of formal schooling.

It is rather remarkable that children spontaneously think of counting from the larger of the two numbers to be added. This indicates that they have a very precocious understanding of the commutativity of addition (the rule that $a + b$ is always equal to $b + a$). Experiments show that this principle is already in place by five years of age. Never mind the legions of educators and theorists who have claimed that children couldn't possibly understand arithmetic unless they first received years of solid education in logic. The truth is just the opposite: As children count on their fingers, years before going to school, they develop an intuitive understanding of commutativity, whose logical foundations they will come to appreciate only much later (if ever).

Children select their calculation algorithms with an extraordinary flair. They quickly master many addition and subtraction strategies. Yet far from being lost in this abundance of possibilities, they learn to carefully select the strategy that seems most suited for each particular problem. For 4 + 2, they may decide to count on from the first operand. For 2 + 4, they will not forget to reverse the two operands. Confronted with the more difficult 8 + 4, they might remember that 8 + 2 is 10. If they manage to decompose 4 into 2 + 2, then they'll be able to simply count "ten, eleven, *twelve.*"

Calculation abilities do not emerge in an immutable order. Each child behaves like a cook's apprentice who tries a random recipe, evaluates the quality of the result, and decides whether or not to proceed in this direction. Children's internal evaluation of their algorithms takes into account both the time it takes them to complete the computation and the likelihood that they have reached the correct result. According to child psychologist Robert Siegler, children compile detailed statistics on their success rate with each algorithm. Little by little, they acquire a refined database of the strategies that are most appropriate for each numerical problem. There is no doubt that mathematical education plays an extremely important role in this process, both by inculcating new algorithms into children and by providing them with explicit rules for selecting the best strategy. Yet the best part of this process of invention followed by selection is established in most children before they even reach their preschool years.

Would you like a final example of children's shrewdness in designing their own calculation algorithms? Consider the case of subtraction. Ask a young boy to compute $8 - 2$, and you may hear him muttering: "eight . . . seven is one . . . six is two . . . *six*": He counts backward starting from the larger number 8. Now ask him to solve $8 - 6$. Does the child have to count backward "eight seven six five four three two"? No. Chances are, he will find a more expeditious solution: "six . . . seven is one . . . eight is two . . . *two!*" He counts the number of steps it takes to go from the smaller number to the larger. By cunningly planning his course of action, the child realizes a remarkable economy. It takes him the same number of steps—only two—to compute $8 - 2$ and $8 - 6$. But how does he select the appropriate strategy? The optimal choice is dictated by the size of the number to be subtracted. If it is greater than half the starting number, as in $8 - 5$, $8 - 6$, or $8 - 7$, the second strategy is the winner; otherwise, as in $8 - 1$, $8 - 2$, or $8 - 3$, backward counting is faster. Not only is the child a sufficiently clever mathematician to spontaneously discover this rule, but he manages to use his natural sense of numerical quantities to apply it. The selection of an exact calculation strategy is guided by an initial quick guess. Between the age of four and seven, children exhibit an intuitive understanding of what calculations mean and how they should best be selected.

Memory Appears on the Scene

Take a stopwatch and measure how long a seven-year-old child takes to add two numbers. You will discover that the calculation time increases in direct proportion to the smaller addend, a sure sign that the child is using the minimum algorithm. Even if the child betrays no evidence of counting either verbally or on his fingers, response times indicate that he is reciting the numbers in his head. Computing $5 + 1$, $5 + 2$, $5 + 3$, or $5 + 4$ takes him an additional four-tenths of a second for each additional unit: At that age, each counting step takes about 400 milliseconds.

What happens in older subjects? When they first conducted this experiment in 1972, Carnegie-Mellon University psychologist Guy Groen and his student John Parkman were puzzled to discover that even in college students, the duration of an addition is predicted by the size of the smaller addend. The only difference is that the size of the time increment is much smaller: 20 milliseconds per unit. How should this finding be interpreted? Surely even talented students cannot count at the incredible speed of 20 milliseconds per digit, or 50 digits per second. Groen and Parkman thus proposed a hybrid model. On 95 percent of trials, the students would directly retrieve the result from memory. On the remaining 5 percent of trials, their memory would collapse, and they would have to count at the speed of 400 milliseconds per digit. On average, therefore, addition times would increase by only 20 milliseconds for each unit.

Despite its ingenuity, this proposal was quickly challenged by new findings. It was soon realized that students' response time did not increase linearly with the size of the addends. Large addition problems such as 8 + 9 took a disproportionately long time. The time to add two digits was actually best predicted by their product or by the square of their sum—two variables that were hard to reconcile with the hypothesis that the subjects were counting. The final blow against the counting theory came when it was discovered that the time to multiply two digits was essentially identical to the time taken to add them. In fact, addition and multiplication times were predicted by the very same variables. If subjects counted, even on only 5 percent of trials, multiplication should have been much slower than addition.

There was only one way out of this conundrum. In 1978, Mark Ashcraft and his colleagues at Cleveland State University proposed that young adults hardly ever solve addition and multiplication problems by counting. Instead, they generally retrieve the result from a memorized table. Accessing this table, however, takes an increasingly longer time as the operands get larger. It takes less than a second to retrieve the result of 2 + 3 or 2 × 3, but about 1.3 seconds to solve 8 + 7 or 8 × 7.

This effect of number size on memory retrieval probably has multiple origins. . . . The accuracy of our mental representation drops quickly with number size. Order of acquisition may also be a factor, because simple arithmetic facts, which involve small operands, are often learned before more difficult ones with large operands. A third factor is the amount of drilling. Because the frequency of numerals decreases with size, we receive less training with larger multiplication problems. Mark Ashcraft and his colleagues have tallied up how often each addition or multiplication problem appears in children's textbooks. The outcome is surprisingly inane: Children are drilled far more extensively with multiplications by 2 and by 3 than by 7, 8, or 9, although the latter are more difficult.

The hypothesis that memory plays a central role in adult mental arithmetic is now universally accepted. This does not imply that adults do not also have many other calculation strategies at their disposal. Indeed, most adults confess to using indirect methods such as computing 9 × 7 as (10 × 7) − 7, a factor that also contributes to slowing down the resolution of large addition and multiplication problems. It does mean, however, that a major upheaval in the mental arithmetic system occurs during preschool years. Children suddenly shift from an intuitive understanding of numerical quantities, supported by simple counting strategies, to a rote learning of arithmetic. It is hardly surprising if this major turn coincides with the first serious difficulties that children encounter in mathematics. All of a sudden, progressing in mathematics means storing a wealth of numerical knowledge in memory. Most children get through as best as they can. But as we will see, they often lose their intuitions about arithmetic in the process.

The Multiplication Table: An Unnatural Practice?

Few lessons are drilled as extensively as the addition and multiplication tables. We have all spent a portion of our childhood learning them, and as adults we constantly appeal to them. Any student executes tens of elementary calculations daily. Over a lifetime, we must solve more than ten thousand multiplication problems. And yet our arithmetic memory is at best mediocre. It takes a well-trained young adult considerable time, often more than 1 second, to solve a multiplication such as 3×7. Error rates average 10 to 15 percent. On the most difficult problems such as 8×7 or 7×9, failure occurs at least once in every four attempts, often following more than 2 seconds of intense reflection.

Why is this? Multiplications by 0 or 1 obviously do not have to be learned by rote. Furthermore once 6×9 or $3 + 5$ are stored, the responses to 9×6 and $3 + 5$ easily follow by commutativity. This leaves us with only forty-five addition and thirty-six multiplication facts to be remembered. Why is it so difficult for us to store them? After all, hundreds of other arbitrary facts crowd our memory. The names of our friends, their ages, their addresses, and the many events of our lives occupy entire sections of our memory. At the very age when children labor over arithmetic, they effortlessly acquire a dozen new words daily. Before adulthood, they will have learned at least twenty thousand words and their pronunciation, spelling, and meaning. What makes the multiplication table so much harder to retain, even after years of training?

The answer lies in the particular structure of addition and multiplication tables. Arithmetic facts are not arbitrary and independent of each other. On the contrary, they are closely intertwined and teeming with false regularities, misleading rhymes, and confusing puns. What would happen if you had to memorize an address book that looked like this:

- ○ Charlie David lives on George Avenue.
- ○ Charlie George lives on Albert Zoe Avenue.
- ○ George Ernie lives on Albert Bruno avenue.

And a second one for professional addresses like this:

- ○ Charlie David works on Albert Bruno Avenue.
- ○ Charlie George works on Bruno Albert Avenue.
- ○ George Ernie works on Charlie Ernie Avenue.

Learning these twisted lists would certainly be a nightmare. Yet they are nothing but addition and multiplication tables in disguise. They were composed by replacing each of the digits 0, 1, 2, 3, 4 . . . by a surname (Zoe, Albert, Bruno, Charlie, David . . .). Home address was substituted for addition, and professional address for multiplication. The six above addresses are thus equivalent to the additions $3 + 4 = 7$, $3 + 7 = 10$, and $7 + 5 = 12$, and to the multiplications $3 \times 4 = 12$, $3 \times 7 = 21$, and $7 \times 5 = 35$. Seen from this unusual angle, arithmetic tables regain for our adult eyes the intrinsic difficulties that they pose for children who first discover them. No wonder we have trouble remembering them: The most amazing thing may well be that we do eventually manage to memorize most of them!

We haven't quite answered our question, though: Why is this type of list so difficult to learn? Any electronic agenda with a minuscule memory of less than a kilobyte has no trouble storing them all. In fact, this computer metaphor almost begs the answer. If our brain fails to retain arithmetic facts, that is because the organization of human memory, unlike that of a computer, is *associative:* It weaves multiple links among disparate data. Associative links permit the reconstruction of memories on the basis of fragmented information. We invoke this reconstruction process, consciously or not, whenever we try to retrieve a past fact. Step by step, the perfume of Proust's madeleine evokes a universe of memories rich in sounds, visions, words, and past feelings.

Associative memory is a strength as well as a weakness. It is a strength when it enables us, starting from a vague reminiscence, to unwind a whole ball of memories that once seemed lost. No computer program to date reproduces anything close to this "addressing by content." It is a strength again when it permits us to take advantage of analogies and allows us to apply knowledge acquired under other circumstances to a novel situation. Associative memory is a weakness, however, in domains such as the multiplication table where the various pieces of knowledge must be kept from interfering with each other at all costs. When faced with a tiger, we must quickly activate our related memories of lions. But when trying to retrieve the result of 7×6, we court disaster by activating our knowledge of $7 + 6$ or of 7×5. Unfortunately for mathematicians, our brain evolved for millions of years in an environment where the advantages of associative memory largely compensated for its drawbacks in domains like arithmetic. We are now condemned to live with inappropriate arithmetical associations that our memory recalls automatically, with little regard for our efforts to suppress them.

Proof of the pernicious influence of interference in associative memory is easy to come by. Throughout the world, scores of students have contributed hundreds of thousands of response times and tens of thousands of errors to the scientific study of calculation processes. Thanks to them, we now know precisely which calculation errors are the most frequent. Multiply 7 by 8. It is probable that instead of 56, you will answer 63, 48, or 54. Nobody ever replies 55, although this number is only one unit off the correct result. Practically all errors belong to the multiplication table, most often to the same line or column as the original multiplication problem. Why? Because the mere presentation of 7×8 is enough for us to not only recall the correct result 56, but also its tightly associated neighbors 7×9, 6×8, or 6×9. All of these facts compete in gaining access to speech production processes. All too often we try to retrieve 7×8 and the result of 6×8 pops up.

The automatization of arithmetic memory starts at a young age. As early as seven, whenever we see two digits, our brain automatically cranks up their sum. To prove this, psychologist JoAnne Lefevre and her colleagues at the University of Alberta in Canada concocted a clever experiment. They explained to subjects that they were going to see a pair of digits such as 2 and 4 that they had to memorize for a second. They would then see a third digit and were to decide whether it was identical to one of the first two numbers. The results revealed an unconscious addition process. When the target digit was equal to the sum of the pair (6), although the subjects generally responded correctly that it was not equal to any of the initial digits, there was a noticeable slowing of responses, which was not seen for neutral targets such as 5 or 7. In a recent study by Patrick Lemaire and collaborators, this effect was replicated with children as young as seven. Apparently, the mere flashing of the digits 2 and 4, even without a plus sign, suffices for our memory to automatically retrieve their sum. Subsequently, because this number is active in our memory, we are not quite sure whether we have seen it or not.

Here is another striking demonstration of the automaticity of arithmetic memory that you can try for yourself. Answer the following questions as *fast as you can:*

$$-2 + 2?$$
$$-4 + 4?$$
$$-8 + 8?$$
$$-16 + 16?$$

Now quick! Pick a number between 12 and 5. Got it?

The number you picked is 7, isn't it?

How did I read your mind? The mere presentation of the numbers 12 and 5 seems enough to trigger an unconscious subtraction $12 - 5 = 7$. This effect is probably amplified by the initial addition drill, the reversed order of the numbers 12 and 5, and the ambiguous phrase "between 12 and 5" that may incite you to compute the distance between the two numbers. All these factors conspire to enhance the automatic activation of $12 - 5$ up to a point where its result enters consciousness. And you believed that you were exercising your "free will" when selecting a digit!

Our memory also has a hard time keeping addition and multiplication facts in distinct compartments. Not infrequently do we automatically answer an addition problem with the corresponding multiplication fact $(2 + 3 = 6)$; more rarely, the contrary occurs $(3 \times 3 = 6)$. It also takes us longer to realize that $2 \times 3 = 5$ is false than to reject $2 \times 3 = 7$ because the former result would be correct under addition.

Kevin Miller, at the University of Texas, has studied how such interference evolves during the acquisition of new arithmetic facts. In third grade, most pupils already know many additions by heart. As they start to learn multiplication, the time they take to solve an addition temporarily *increases,* while the first memory slips of the $2 + 3 = 6$ kind begin to appear. Thus, the integration of multiple arithmetic facts in long-term memory seems to be a major hurdle for most children.

Verbal Memory to the Rescue

If storing arithmetic tables in memory is so difficult, how does our brain eventually catch up? A classic strategy consists in recording arithmetic facts in verbal memory. "Three times seven, twenty-one" can be stored word for word alongside "Twinkle twinkle little star" or "Our Father who art in Heaven." This solution is not unreasonable because verbal memory is vast and durable. Indeed, who does not still have a head full of slogans and songs heard years earlier? Educators have long realized the huge potential of verbal memory. In many countries, recitation remains the prime method for teaching arithmetic. I still remember the ungracious chorus at elementary school as my fellow budding mathematicians and I loudly recited multiplication tables in perfect synchrony.

The Japanese seem to have pushed this method even further. Their multiplication table is made up of little verses called "ku-ku." This word, which literally means "nine-nine," is directly drawn from the last verse of the table, $9 \times 9 = 81$. In the Japanese table, times and equal symbols are silent, leaving only the two operands and the result. Thus $2 \times 3 = 6$ is learned as "ni san na-roku"—literally, "two three zero six." Several conventions have been consecrated by history. In kuku, numbers are pronounced in their Chinese form, and their pronunciation varies with context. For instance, eight is normally "hashi," but can be abbreviated as "hap" or even as "pa," as in "hap-pa roku-ju shi," $8 \times 8 = 64$. The resulting system is complex and often arbitrary, but its singularities probably ease the load on memory.

The fact that arithmetic tables are learned verbatim seems to have an intriguing consequence: calculation becomes tied to the language in which it is learned at school. An Italian colleague of mine, after spending more than twenty years in the United States, is now an accomplished bilingual. He speaks and writes in fluent English, with a rigorous syntax and an extensive vocabulary. Yet when he has to calculate mentally, he can still be heard mumbling numbers in his native Italian. Does this mean that after a certain age, the brain loses its plasticity for learning arithmetic? This is a possibility, but the real explanation may be more trivial. Learning arithmetic tables is so laborious that it may be more economical for a bilingual to switch back to the mother tongue for calculation rather than relearn arithmetic from scratch in a new language.

Non-bilinguals can experience the same phenomenon. We all find it hard to refrain from naming numbers aloud when we have to perform complex calculations. The crucial role played by the verbal code in arithmetic becomes fully apparent when one is asked to calculate while simultaneously reciting the alphabet aloud. Try it, and you will easily convince yourself that this is quite hard, because speaking saturates the cerebral language production systems necessary for mental calculation.

Yet a better proof of the verbatim coding of the multiplication table comes from the study of calculation errors. When confronted with 5×6, we often mistakenly respond "36" or even "56," as if the 5 and the 6 of the problem contaminated our response. Our cerebral circuits tend to automatically read the problem as a two-digit number: 5×6 irrepressibly evokes the words "fifty-six." Most strangely, this reading bias interacts in a complex way with the plausibility of the result. One never observes gross blunders such as $6 \times 2 = 62$ or $3 \times 7 = 37$. Most of the time, we mistakenly read the operands only when the resulting two-digit number is a plausible result that belongs to the multiplication table (for instance, $3 \times 6 = 36$ or $2 \times 8 = 28$). This suggests that reading errors do not occur *after* multiplication retrieval, but during it—at a time when the reading bias can still influence access to arithmetic memory without completely overriding it. Hence, reading and arithmetic memory are highly interconnected procedures that make use of the same verbal encoding of numbers. For the adult brain, multiplying merely means reading out 3×6 as "eighteen."

In spite of its importance, verbal memory is not the only source of knowledge to be exploited during mental calculation. When confronted with the difficult task of memorizing arithmetic tables, our brain uses every available artifice. When memory fails, it falls back on other strategies like counting, serial addition, or subtraction from some reference (for instance, $8 \times 9 = (8 \times 10) - 8 = 72$). Above all, it never misses any opportunity to take a shortcut. Please verify whether the following calculations are true or false: $5 \times 3 = 15$, $6 \times 5 = 25$, $7 \times 9 = 20$. Do you have to calculate to reject the third multiplication? Probably not, for at least two good reasons. First, the proposed result, 20, is grossly false. Experiments have shown that response time drops as the degree of falsehood increases. Results whose magnitude departs considerably from the truth are rejected in less time than it would take to actually complete the operation, suggesting that in parallel to calculating the exact result, our brain also computes a coarse estimate of its size. Second, in $7 \times 9 = 20$, parity is violated. Since both operands are odd, the result should be odd. An analysis of response times shows that our brain implicitly checks the parity rules that govern addition and multiplication and quickly reacts whenever a violation is found.

Mental Bugs

Let us now briefly tackle the issue of multidigit calculations. Suppose that you have to compute $24 + 59$. No computer would need more than a few microseconds, yet it will take you more than two seconds, or at least a hundred thousand times longer. This problem will mobilize all your power of concentration (as we will see later on, the prefrontal sectors of the brain, which are involved in the control of nonautomated activities, are highly active during complex calculations). You will have to go carefully through a series of steps: Isolate the right-most digits (4 and 9), add them up (4 + 9 = 13), write down the 3, carry the 1, isolate the left-most digits (2 and 5), add them up (2 + 5 = 7), add the carry over (7 + 1 = 8), and finally write down the 8. These stages are so reproducible that given the magnitude of the digits, one can estimate the duration of each operation and predict, to within a few tens of a second, at which point you will finally lift your pen.

At no time during such a calculation does the meaning of the unfolding operations seem to be taken into account. Why did you carry the 1 over to the left-most column? Perhaps you now realize that this 1 stands for 10 units and that it must therefore land in the tens column. Yet this thought never crossed your mind while you were computing. In order to calculate fast, the brain is forced to ignore the meaning of the computations it performs.

As another example of the divorce between the mechanical aspects of calculation and their meaning, consider the following subtraction problems, which are quite typical of a young child:

54	54	612	317
−23	−28	−39	−81
31	34	627	376
(correct)	(false)	(false)	(false)

Do you see the problem? This child is not responding at random. Every single answer obeys the strictest logic. The classical subtraction algorithm is rigorously applied, digit after digit, from right to left. The child, however, reaches an impasse whenever the top digit is smaller than the bottom. This situation calls for carrying over, but for some reason the child prefers to invert the operation and subtract the top digit from the bottom one. Little does it matter that this operation is meaningless. Indeed, the result often exceeds the starting number, without disturbing the pupil in the least. Calculation appears to him as a pure manipulation of symbols, a surrealist game largely devoid of meaning.

John Brown, Richard Burton, and Kurt Van Lehn, from Carnegie-Mellon University, studied mental subtraction with such meticulous scrutiny that they wound up collecting the responses of more than a thousand children to tens of problems. In this way, they discovered and classified dozens of systematic errors similar to the ones we've just examined. Some children have difficulties only with zeroes, while others fail only with the digit 1. A classical error consists in a leftward shift of all carry-overs that apply to the digit 0. In $307 - 9$, some children correctly compute $17 - 9 = 8$, but then fail to subtract the carryover from 0. Instead, they wrongly simplify the task by carrying over the 1 into the hundreds column; therefore, $307 - 9 = 208$. Errors of this kind are so reproducible that Brown and his colleagues have described them in computer science terms: children's subtraction algorithms are riddled with "bugs."

Where do these bugs come from? Strange as it might seem, no textbook ever describes the correct subtraction recipe in its full generality. A computer scientist can vainly search his kid's arithmetic manual for instructions precise enough to program a general subtraction routine. All school manuals are content with providing rudimentary instructions and a panoply of examples. Pupils are supposed to study the examples, analyze the behavior of their teacher, and derive their own conclusions. It is hardly surprising, then, that the algorithm they arrive at is not correct. Textbook examples generally do not cover all possible cases of subtraction. Hence they leave the door open to all sorts of ambiguities. In due course, any child is confronted with a novel situation where he or she will have to improvise, and gaps in his or her understanding of subtraction will show up.

Consider this example studied by Kurt Van Lehn: A child subtracts correctly except that each time he has to subtract two identical digits, he wrongly carries 1 over to the next column (e.g., $54 - 4 = 40$; $428 - 26 = 302$). This child has correctly figured out that one must carry over whenever the top digit is smaller than the bottom. However, he wrongly generalizes this rule to the case where the two digits are equal. Most likely, this particular case was never dealt with in his textbook.

Another edifying example: Many arithmetic textbooks illustrate only the subtraction procedure with two-digit numerals ($17 - 8$, $54 - 6$, $64 - 38$, etc.). Initially then, pupils only learn to carry over to the tens column, which is always the first column from the left. Hence the first time they are confronted with a three-digit subtraction, many children wrongly decide to carry over to the left-most column as they have in the past (e.g., $621 - 2 = 529$). How could they guess, without further instruction, that one should always carry over from the column *immediately left of the present one,* rather than from the left-most column? Only a refined understanding of the algorithm's design and purpose can help. Yet the very occurrence of such absurd errors suggests that the child's brain registers and executes most calculation algorithms without caring much about their meaning.

Pros and Cons of the Electronic Calculator

What coherent picture emerges from this panorama of human arithmetic abilities? Clearly, the human brain behaves unlike any computer that we currently know of. It has not evolved for the purpose of formal calculation. This is why sophisticated arithmetic algorithms are so difficult for us to faithfully acquire and execute. Counting is easy because it exploits our fundamental biological skills for verbal recitation and one-to-one correspondence. But memorizing the multiplication table, executing the subtraction algorithm, and dealing with carryovers are purely formal operations without any counterpart in a primate's life. Evolution can hardly have prepared us for them. The *Homo sapiens* brain is to formal calculation what the wing of the prehistoric bird *Archaeopteryx* was to flying: a clumsy organ, functional but far from optimal. To comply with the requirements of mental arithmetic, our brain has to tinker with whatever circuits it has, even if that implies memorizing a sequence of operations that one does not understand.

We cannot hope to alter the architecture of our brain, but we can perhaps adapt our teaching methods to the constraints of our biology. Since arithmetic tables and calculation algorithms are, in a way, counternatural, I believe that we should seriously ponder the necessity of inculcating them in our children. Luckily, we now have an alternative—the electronic calculator, which is cheap, omnipresent, and infallible. Computers are transforming our universe to such an extent that we cannot confine ourselves thoughtlessly to the educational recipes of yesteryear. We have to face this question: Should our pupils still have to spend hundreds of hours reciting multiplication tables, as their grandparents did, in the hope that arithmetic facts will eventually be engraved in their memories? Would it not be wiser to give them early training in electronic calculators and computers?

Reducing the part played by rote arithmetic at school may be judged a heresy. Yet there is nothing sacred in the way arithmetic is currently taught. Until recently, in many countries, the abacus and finger counting were the privileged vectors of arithmetic. Even today, millions of Asians pull out their "soro-ban," the Japanese abacus, whenever they have to calculate. The most experienced of them practice the "mental abacus": By visualizing abacus moves in their heads, they can add two numbers mentally in less time than it takes us to type them into a calculator! These examples show that there are alternatives to the rote learning of arithmetic.

One might object that electronic calculators atrophy children's mathematical intuitions. This opinion has been vehemently defended, for instance, by the famous French mathematician and Fields Medal winner René Thom, who wrote, "In primary school we learned the addition and multiplication tables. It was a good thing! I am convinced that when children as young as six or seven are allowed to use a calculator, they eventually attain a less intimate knowledge of number than the one we reached through the practice of mental calculation."

Yet what may have been true for schoolboy Thom need not hold for the average child today. Anyone can judge for himself the purported ability of our schools to teach an "intimate knowledge of number." When a pupil readily concludes, without batting an eyelid, that $317 - 81$ is 376, perhaps there is something rotten in the educational kingdom.

I am convinced that by releasing children from the tedious and mechanical constraints of calculation, the calculator can help them to concentrate on meaning. It allows them to sharpen their natural sense of approximation by offering them thousands of arithmetic examples. By studying a calculator's results, children can discover that subtraction always yields a result smaller than the starting number, that multiplying by a three-digit number always increases the size of the starting number by two or three digits, and thousands of similar facts. The mere observation of a calculator's behavior is an excellent way of developing number sense.

The calculator is like a road map for the number line. Give a calculator to a five-year-old, and you will teach him how to make friends with numbers instead of despising them. There are so many fascinating regularities to be discovered about arithmetic. Even the most elementary of them looks like pure magic to children. Multiplying by 10 adds a zero on the right. Multiplying by 11 duplicates a digit ($2 \times 11 = 22$, $3 \times 11 = 33$, etc.). Multiplying by 3, then by 37, makes three copies of it ($9 \times 3 \times 37 = 999$). Can you figure out why? Because these childish examples might leave mathematically advanced readers unsatisfied, here are some more sophisticated ones:

- $11 \times 11 = 121$; $111 \times 111 = 12321$; $1111 \times 1111 = 1234321$; and so on. Do you see why?
- $12345679 \times 9 = 111111111$. Why? Note that the 8 is lacking!
- $11 - 3 \times 3 = 2$; $1111 - 33 \times 33 = 22$; $111111 - 333 \times 333 = 222$; and so on. Prove it!
- $1 + 2 = 3$; $4 + 5 + 6 = 7 + 8$; $9 + 10 + 11 + 12 = 13 + 14 + 15$; and so on. Can you find a simple proof?

Do you find these arithmetic games barren and dull? Do not forget that before the age of six or seven, children do not yet despise mathematics.

Everything that looks mysterious and excites their imagination feels like a game to them. They are open and ready to develop a passion for numbers if only one were willing to show them how magical arithmetic can be. Electronic calculators, as well as mathematical software for children, hold the promise of initiating them to the beauty of mathematics, a role that teachers, all too occupied in teaching the mechanics of calculation, often do not accomplish.

This being said, can and should the calculator serve as substitute to rote mental arithmetic? It would be foolish to pretend that I have the definitive answer. Reaching for a pocket calculator in order to compute $2 - 3$ is obviously absurd, but no one is pushing toward such extremes. Yet it should be acknowledged that today the vast majority of adults never perform a multidigit calculation without resorting to electronics. Whether we like it or not, division and subtraction algorithms are endangered species quickly disappearing from our everyday lives—except in schools, where we still tolerate their quiet oppression.

At the very least, using calculators in school should lose its taboo status. Mathematics curricula are not immutable, much less perfect. Their sole objective should be to improve children's fluency in arithmetic, not perpetuate a ritual. Calculators and computers are only a few of the promising paths that educators have begun to explore. Perhaps we should study the teaching methods used in China or Japan in a less condescending manner. Recent studies by psychologists Harold Stevenson, from the University of Michigan, and Jim Stigler, from UCLA, suggest that these methods are often superior in many ways to those used in most Western countries. Just consider this simple example: In the West, we generally learn multiplication tables line after line, starting with the "times two" facts and ending with the "times nine" facts, for a total of 72 facts to be remembered. In China, children are explicitly taught to reorder multiplications by placing the smallest digit first. This elementary trick, which avoids relearning $9 - 6$ when one already knows 6×9, cuts the amount of information to be learned by almost one-half. It has a notable impact on calculation speed and error rates of Chinese pupils. Obviously, we do not have the monopoly on a well-conceived curriculum. Let us keep our eyes open to all potential improvements, whether they come from computer science or psychology.

Innumeracy: Clear and Present Danger?

In the Western educational system, children spend much time learning the mechanics of arithmetic. Yet there is a growing suspicion that many of them reach adulthood without having really understood when to apply this knowledge appropriately. Lacking any deep understanding of arithmetic principles, they are at risk of becoming little calculating machines that compute but do not think. John Paulos has given their plight a name: *innumeracy*, the analogue of illiteracy in the arithmetical domain. Innumerates are prompt in drawing hazardous conclusions based on a reasoning that is mathematical only in appearance. Here are a few examples:

○ $\frac{1}{5} + \frac{2}{5} = \frac{3}{10}$ because $1 + 2 = 3$ and $5 + 5 = 10$.

○ $0.2 + 4 = 0.6$ because $4 + 2 = 6$.

○ 0.25 is greater than 0.5 because 25 is greater than 5.

○ A basin of water at 35°C, plus another basin of water at 35°C, makes for a tub of very hot water at 70°C (stated by my six-year-old son).

○ The temperature is in the 80s today, twice as warm as last night, when the temperature was 40°F.

○ There is a 50 percent chance of rain for Saturday, and also a 50 percent chance of rain for Sunday, so there is a 100 percent certainty that it will rain over the weekend (heard on the local news by John Paulos).

○ One meter equals 100 centimeters. Since the square root of 1 is 1, and the square root of 100 is 10, shouldn't one conclude that 1 meter equals 10 centimeters?

○ Mrs. X is alarmed: the new cancer test that she took was positive. Her doctor certifies that the test is highly reliable and reads positive in 98 percent of cancer cases. So Mrs. X is 98 percent certain of having cancer. Right? (Wrong. The available information supports absolutely no conclusion. Suppose that only one person in 10,000 ever develops this type of cancer, and that the test yields a 5 percent rate of false positives. Of 10,000 people taking the test, about 500 will test positive, but only one of them will really suffer from cancer. In that case, despite her results, Mrs. X still only has one chance in 500 of developing cancer.)

In the United States, innumeracy has been promoted as a cause for national concern. Alarming reports suggest that, as early as preschool, American children lag way behind their Chinese and Japanese peers. Some educators view this "learning gap" as a potential threat to American supremacy in science and technology. The designated culprit is the educational system, its mediocre organization, and the poor training of its teachers. On the French side of the Atlantic, about every other year a similar controversy announces a new drop in children's mathematical achievement.

A French mathematics educator, Stella Baruk, has shrewdly analyzed the share of responsibility that is borne by the educational system in children's mathematical difficulties. Her favorite example is the following Monty Pythonesque problem: "Twelve sheep and thirteen goats are on a boat. How old is the captain?" Believe it or not, this problem was officially presented to French first- and second-graders in an official survey, and a large proportion of them earnestly responded "Twenty-five years, because $12 + 13 = 25$"—an amazing example of innumeracy!

Though there are serious reasons for being concerned by the widespread incompetence in mathematics, my own belief is that our school system is not the only one to blame. Innumeracy has much deeper roots: Ultimately, it reflects the human brain's struggle for storing arithmetical knowledge. There are obviously many degrees of innumeracy, from the young child who thinks that temperatures can be added to the medical student who fails to compute a conditional probability. Yet all such errors share one feature: Their victims directly jump to conclusions without considering the relevance of the computations they perform. This is an unfortunate counterpart to the automatization of mental calculation. We become so skillful at the mechanics of calculation that arithmetic operations sometimes start automatically in our heads. Check your reflexes on the following problems:

- A farmer has eight cows. All but five die. How many cows remain?
- Judy owns five dolls, which is two fewer than Cathy. How many dolls does Cathy have?

Did you feel an impulse to answer "three" to both problems? The mere presentation of the words "fewer than" or "all but" suffices to trigger an automatic subtraction scheme in our minds. We have to fight against this automatism. A conscious effort is needed to analyze the meaning of each problem and form a mental model of the situation. Only then do we realize that we should *repeat* the number 5 in the first problem, and *add* 5 and 2 in the second problem. The inhibition of the subtraction scheme mobilizes the anterior portion of the brain, a region called the prefrontal cortex, which is involved in implementing and controlling nonroutine strategies. Because the prefrontal cortex matures very slowly—at least up to puberty and probably beyond—children and adolescents are most vulnerable to arithmetical impulsiveness. Their prefrontal cortical areas have not yet had much opportunity to acquire the large repertoire of refined control strategies required to avoid falling into arithmetic traps.

My hypothesis, then, is that innumeracy results from the difficulty of controlling the activation of arithmetic schemas distributed in multiple cerebral areas. . . . Number knowledge does not rest on a single specialized brain area, but on vast distributed networks of neurons, each performing its own simple, automated, and independent computation. We are born with an "accumulator circuit" that endows us with intuitions about numerical quantities.

With language acquisition, several other circuits that specialize in the manipulation of number symbols and in verbal counting come into play. The learning of multiplication tables recruits yet another circuit specialized for rote verbal memory; and the list could probably go on for a long while. Innumeracy occurs because these multiple circuits often respond autonomously and in a disconcerted fashion. Their arbitration, under the command of the prefrontal cortex, is often slow to emerge. Children are left at the mercy of their arithmetical reflexes. Regardless of whether they are learning to count or to subtract, they focus on calculation routines and fail to draw appropriate links with their quantitative number sense. And so innumeracy sets in.

Teaching Number Sense

If my hypothesis is correct, innumeracy is with us for a long time, because it reflects one of the fundamental properties of our brain: its modularity, the compartmentalization of mathematical knowledge within multiple partially autonomous circuits. In order to become proficient in mathematics, one must go beyond these compartmentalized modules and establish a series of flexible links among them. The numerical illiterate performs calculations by reflex, haphazardly and without any deep understanding. The expert calculator, on the contrary, juggles mentally with number notations, moves fluently from digits to words to quantities, and thoughtfully selects the most appropriate algorithm for the problem at hand.

From this perspective, schooling plays a crucial role not so much because it teaches children new arithmetic techniques, but also because it helps them draw links between the mechanics of calculation and its meaning. A good teacher is an alchemist who gives a fundamentally modular human brain the semblance of an interactive network. Unfortunately, our schools often do not quite meet this challenge. All too often, far from smoothing out the difficulties raised by mental calculation, our educational system increases them. The flame of mathematical intuition is only flickering in the child's mind; it needs to be fortified and sustained before it can illuminate all arithmetic activities. But our schools are often content with inculcating meaningless and mechanical arithmetical recipes into children.

This state of affairs is all the more regrettable because, as we have seen, most children enter preschool with a well-developed understanding of approximation and counting. In most math courses, this informal baggage is treated as a handicap rather than as an asset. Finger counting is considered a childish activity that a good education will quickly do away with. How many children try to hide when they count on their fingers because "the teacher said not to"? Yet the history of numeration systems repeatedly proves that finger counting is an important precursor to learning base 10. Likewise, failing to retrieve 6 + 7 = 13 from rote memory is considered an error, even if the child later proves his or her excellent command of arithmetic by recovering the result indirectly—for instance, by remembering that 6 + 6 is 12 and that 7 is one unit after 6. Blaming a child for calling on indirect strategies blatantly ignores that adults use similar strategies when their memory fails.

Despising children's precocious abilities can have a disastrous effect on their subsequent opinion of mathematics. It accredits the idea that mathematics is an arid domain, detached from intuition and ruled by arbitrariness. Pupils feel that they are supposed to do as the teacher does, whether or not they can make any sense of it. A random example: Developmental psychologist Jeffrey Bisanz asked six- and nine-year-old pupils to calculate 5 + 3 − 3. The six-year-olds often responded 5 without calculating, rightly noting that + 3 and −3 cancel each other. However the nine-years-olds, although they were more experienced, stubbornly performed the calculation in full (5 + 3 = 8, then 8 − 3 = 5). "It would be cheating to take short-cuts," explained one of them.

The insistence on mechanical computation at the expense of meaning is reminiscent of the heated debate that divides the formalist and intuitionist schools of mathematical research. The formalist trend, which was founded by Hilbert and was pursued by major French mathematicians grouped under the pseudonym of Bourbaki, set as its goal the anchoring of mathematics on a firm axiomatic base. Their objective was to reduce demonstration to a purely formal manipulation of abstract symbols. From this arid vision stemmed the all-too-famous reform of "modern mathematics," which ruined the mathematical sense of a generation of French pupils by presenting, according to an actor of this period, "an extremely formal education, cut from any intuitive support, presented on the basis of artificial situations, and highly selective." For instance, the reformers thought that children should be familiar with the general theoretical principles of numeration before being taught the specifics of our base-10 system. Hence, believe it or not, some arithmetic textbooks started off by explaining that 3 + 4 is 12—in base 5! It is hard to think of a better way to befuddle children's thinking.

This erroneous conception of the brain and of mathematics, in which intuition is discouraged, leads to failure. Studies conducted in the United States by David Geary and his colleagues at the University of Missouri-Columbia indicate that about 6 percent of pupils are "mathematically disabled." I cannot believe that a genuine neurological handicap affects that many children. Although cerebral lesions can selectively impair mental calculation, . . . they are relatively infrequent. It seems more likely that many of these "mathematically disabled" children are normally abled pupils who got off to a false start in mathematics. Their initial experience unfortunately convinces them that arithmetic is a purely scholastic affair, with no practical goal and no obvious meaning. They rapidly decide that they will never be able to understand a word about it. The already considerable difficulties posed by arithmetic to any normally constituted brain are thus compounded by an emotional component, a growing anxiety or phobia about mathematics.

We can fight these difficulties if we ground mathematical knowledge on concrete situations rather than on abstract concepts. We need to help children realize that mathematical operations have an intuitive meaning, which they can represent using their innate sense of numerical quantities. In brief, we must help them build a rich repertoire of "mental models" of arithmetic. Consider the example of an elementary subtraction, $9 - 3 = 6$. As adults, we know of many concrete situations to which this operation applies: a set scheme (a basket containing nine apples, from which one takes away three apples, now only has six), a distance scheme (in any board game, in order to move from cell 3 to cell 9, six moves are required), a temperature scheme (if it is 9 degrees and the temperature drops 3 degrees, then it will be only 6 degrees), and many others. All such mental models seem equivalent to our adult eyes, but they are not so to the child who must discover that subtraction is the operation suited to all of them. The day the teacher introduces negative numbers and asks pupils to compute $3 - 9$, a child who only masters the set scheme judges this operation impossible. Taking 9 apples from 3 apples? That's absurd! Another child who relies exclusively on the distance scheme concludes that $3 - 9 = 6$, because indeed the distance from 3 to 9 is 6. If the teacher merely maintains that $3 - 9$ equals "minus six," the two children run the risk of failing to understand the statement. The temperature scheme, however, can provide them with an intuitive picture of negative numbers. Minus six degrees is a concept that even first-graders can grasp.

Consider a second example: the addition of two fractions $\frac{1}{2}$ and $\frac{1}{3}$. A child who has in mind an intuitive picture of fractions as portions of a pie—half a pie, and then another third of a pie—will have little difficulty figuring out that their sum falls just below 1. He or she may even understand that the portions must be cut into smaller identical pieces (i.e., reduced to the same denominator) before they can be regrouped in order to compute the exact total. $\frac{1}{2} + \frac{1}{3} = \frac{5}{6}$. In contrast, a child for whom fractions have no intuitive meaning and are merely two digits separated by a diagonal bar is likely to fall into the classic trap of adding the numerator and denominator: $\frac{1}{2} + \frac{1}{3} = (1 + 1)/(2 + 3) = \frac{2}{5}$! This error may even be justified by a concrete model. Suppose that in the first period Michael Jordan scores once in two shots, for an average of $\frac{1}{2}$, and that in second period he scores once in three shots, for an average of $\frac{1}{3}$. Over the entire game he would have scored twice in five shots. Here is a situation in which $\frac{1}{2}$ "plus" $\frac{1}{3}$ equals $\frac{2}{5}$! When one teaches fractions, it is vital to let the child know that one has a "portion of pie" scheme in mind rather than a "scoring average" scheme. The brain is not content with abstract symbols: Concrete intuitions and mental models play a crucial role in mathematics. This is probably why the abacus works so well for Asian children; it provides them with a very concrete and intuitive representation of numbers.

But let us leave this chapter with a note of optimism. The craze for "modern mathematics," based on a formalist vision of mathematics, is losing momentum in many countries. In the United States, the National Council of Teachers of Mathematics is now deemphasizing the rote learning of facts and procedures and is focusing instead on teaching an intuitive familiarity with numbers. In France—the country that was most directly struck by "Bourbakism"—many teachers no longer wait for psychologists' advice to tell them to head back to a more concrete approach to mathematics. Schools have slowly readopted concrete educational material such as Maria Montessori's bicolored bars, Sequin's tables, unit cubes, ten bars, hundreds plaques, dice, and board games. The French Ministry of Education, after several reforms, seems to have dropped the idea of turning each schoolchild into a symbol-crunching machine. Number sense—indeed, common sense—is making a comeback.

In parallel to this welcome change, education psychologists in the United States have demonstrated empirically the merits of an arithmetic curriculum that stresses concrete, practical, and intuitive mental models of arithmetic. Sharon Griffin, Robbie Case, and Robert Siegler, three North American developmental psychologists, have joined efforts to study the impact of different educational strategies on children's understanding of arithmetic. Their theoretical analysis, like mine, emphasizes the central role played by an intuitive representation of quantities on the mental number line. On this basis, Griffin and Case designed the "Right-Start" program, an arithmetic curriculum for kindergartners that comprises entertaining numerical games with varied concrete pedagogical materials (thermometers, board games, number lines, rows of objects, etc.). Their goal was to teach children from low-income inner-city neighborhoods the rudiments of arithmetic: "The central objective of the program is to enable children to relate the world of numbers to the world of quantity and consequently, to understand that numbers have meaning and can be used to predict, to explain, and to make sense of the real world."

Most children spontaneously understand the correspondence between numbers and quantities. Underprivileged children, however, may not have grasped it before entering preschool. Lacking the conceptual prerequisites for learning arithmetic, they run the risk of losing ground in mathematics courses. The RightStart program attempts to set them back on the right path using simple interactive arithmetic games. For example, in one section of the program, children are invited to play a simple board game that teaches them to count their moves, to subtract in order to find out how far they are from the goal, and to compare numbers in order to discover who is closest to winning the game.

The results are remarkable. Griffin, Case, and Siegler have tried their program in several inner-city schools in Canada and the United States, mostly with immigrant children from low-income families. Children who were lagging behind their peers participated in forty 20-minute sessions of the RightStart program and were propelled to the top of their class as of the next semester. They even outranked pupils with a better initial command of arithmetic but who had followed a more traditional curriculum. Their advance was consolidated in the next school year. This extraordinary success story should bring some consolation to the teachers and parents who feel that their children are allergic to mathematics. In fact, most children are only too pleased to learn mathematics if only one shows them the playful aspects before the abstract symbolism. Playing

Snakes and Ladders may be all children need to get a head start in arithmetic.

REFERENCES

Gelman and Gallistel's famous book *The Child's Understanding of Number* (1978) remains a central reference on numerical development in children. See also Bideaud, Meljac, and Fischer (1992), Case (1985, 1992), Fuson (1988), and Hiebert (1986) for more recent references. The research on calculation in adults has been recently summarized by two of its major contributors, Mark Ashcraft (1992, 1995) and Jamie Campbell (1992, 1994). Excellent discussions of issues in mathematical teaching can be found in Baruk (1973, 1985), Paulos (1988), and Stevenson and Stigler (1992).

Ashcraft, M. H. (1992). Cognitive arithmetic: A review of data and theory. *Cognition, 44,* 75–106.

Ashcraft, M. H. (1995). Cognitive psychology and simple arithmetic: A review and summary of new directions. *Mathematical Cognition, 1,* 3–34.

Baroody, A. J., & Ginsburg, H. P. (1986). The relationship between initial meaningful and mechanical knowledge of arithmetic. In J. Hiebert (Ed.), *Conceptual and Procedural Knowledge: The Case of Mathematics,* pp. 75–112. Hillsdale, NJ: Erlbaum.

Baruk, S. (1973). *Echec et maths.* Paris: Editions du Seuil.

Baruk, S. (1985). *L'dge du capitaine.* Paris: Editions du Seuil.

Bideaud, J., Meljac, C., & Fischer, J.-P. (1992). *Pathways to Number.* Hillsdale, NJ: Erlbaum.

Bkouche, R., Chariot, B., & Rouche, N. (1991). *Faire des mathematiques: Le plaisir du sens.* Paris: Armand Colin.

Brown, J. S., & Burton, R. B. (1978). Diagnostic models for procedural bugs in basic mathematical skills. *Cognitive Science, 2,* 155–192.

Campbell, J. I. D. (Ed.). (1992). *The Nature and Origins of Mathematical Skills.* Amsterdam: North-Holland.

Campbell, J. I. D. (1994). Architectures for numerical cognition. *Cognition, 53,* 1–44.

Case, R. (1985). *Intellectual Development: Birth to Adulthood.* San Diego: Academic Press.

Case, R. (1992). *The Mind's Staircase: Exploring the Conceptual Underpinnings of Children's Thought and Knowledge.* Hillsdale, NJ: Erlbaum.

Fuson, K. C. (1988). *Children's Counting and Concepts of Number.* New York: Springer-Verlag.

Gelman, R., & Gallistel, C. R. (1978). *The Child's Understanding of Number.* Cambridge, MA: Harvard University Press.

Gelman, R., & Meck, E. (1983). Preschooler's counting: Principles before skill. *Cognition, 13,* 343–359.

Gelman, R., Meck, E., & Merkin, S. (1986). Young children's numerical competence. *Cognitive Development, 1,* 1–29.

Griffin, S., Case, R., & Siegler, R. S. (1994). RightStart: Providing the central conceptual prerequisites for first formal learning of arithmetic to students at risk for school failure. In K. McGilly (Ed.), *Classroom Lessons: Integrating Cognitive Theory and Classroom Practice,* pp. 25–49. Cambridge, MA: MIT Press.

Groen, G. J., & Parkman, J. M. (1972). A chronometric analysis of simple addition. *Psychological Review, 79,* 329–343.

Hiebert, J. (Ed.). (1986). *Conceptual and Procedural Knowledge: The Case of Mathematics.* Hillsdale, NJ: Erlbaum.

LeFevre, J., Bisanz, J., & Mrkonjic, L. (1988). Cognitive arithmetic: Evidence for obligatory activation of arithmetic facts. *Memory and Cognition, 16,* 45–53.

Lemaire, P., Barrett, S. E., Fayol, M., & Abdi, H. (1994). Automatic activation of addition and multiplication facts in elementary school children. *Journal of Experimental Child Psychology, 57,* 224–258.

Miller, K. F., & Paredes, D. R. (1990). Starting to add worse: Effects of learning to multiply on children's addition. *Cognition, 37,* 213–242.

Paulos, J. A. (1988). *Innumeracy: Mathematical Illiteracy and Its Consequences.* New York: Vintage Books.

Resnick, L. B. (1983). A developmental theory of number understanding. In H. P. Ginsburg (Ed.), *The Development of Mathematical Thinking,* pp. 109–151. New York: Academic Press.

Siegler, R. S., & Jenkins, E. A. (1989). *How Children Discover New Strategies.* Hillsdale, NJ: Erlbaum.

Stevenson, H. W., & Stigler, J. W. (1992). *The Learning Gap.* New York: Simon & Schuster.

VanLehn, K. (1986). Arithmetic procedures are induced from examples. In *Conceptual and Procedural Knowledge: The Case of Mathematics,* J. Hiebert (Ed.), pp. 133–179. Hillsdale, NJ: Erlbaum.

Wynn, K. (1990). Children's understanding of counting. *Cognition, 36,* 155–193.

19

MATH SKILLS

James P. Byrnes

THROUGHOUT THE SCHOOL YEAR, children are asked to take a variety of aptitude tests, achievement tests, and teacher-made tests. For the most part, teachers and administrators use these tests in order to gauge their students' learning, place students into various ability groups, or determine the effectiveness of particular instructional techniques. For hundreds of years, it has been observed that test scores often array themselves into a characteristic bell-shaped distribution; that is, about one-sixth of students score below average, two-thirds score near the average, and one-sixth score above the average (Bernstein, 1996). This low-to-high performance continuum is thought to occur because (1) most tests are intentionally designed to identify the "actual" level of talent or mastery in each student and (2) students tend to differ in the amount of ability they seem to possess, or the amount of content they seem to master in a given time period (due to differences in effort, differing levels of access to adequate instruction, differing levels of talent, or various combinations of these factors). If all students received the same scores each time a test was given, the issue of ability would probably fall into the background of everyday existence and scientific enterprises. In other words, we all would probably not even think about abilities. The fact that scores always seem to vary, however, pushes the constructs of ability (and individual differences in these abilities) to the forefront of most people's consciousness. In recent years, it has been claimed that children and adults notice these differences (and other variations in the environment) because the human mind is "built" to see them and naturally motivated to want to explain them (Pinker, 1997). Whereas scientists construct formal theories to explain variations in ability and other kinds of variations, nonscientists are thought to create so-called naive or folk theories.

In this chapter, I shall examine several scientific theories regarding the nature of mathematical abilities. In the first section, my focus is on psychological accounts that were constructed to explain the variations in performance that occur on classroom tests, standardized tests, or experimenter-made tests. This psychological view is supplemented by a related view that has recently emerged from the field of mathematics education. Scholars in the latter field have often gained their inspiration from psychological accounts, but they also have elaborated on these accounts using classroom experiences, expert models, and logical argumentation as guides. In the second section, my focus is on neuroscientific accounts that were constructed to explain the variations in performance that occur when the following groups have been compared: (1) neurologically intact individuals versus individuals who have known brain injuries or mathematical disabilities, (2) students with high mathematical talent versus students with lower amounts of math talent, and (3) males versus females. In the final section, I assess the compatibility of the psychological and neuroscientific perspectives, and describe the instructional implications of an integrated account.

Psychological and Educational Perspectives on Mathematical Abilities

To a large extent, psychologists have tried to answer the following question: What is the nature of mathematical ability? Their answers to this question have tended to be theoretical (i.e., componential) descriptions of what it means to have math skills. In contrast, educators have usually sought answers to slightly different questions. For example, they have often asked, What *should* students know and be able to do in math when they graduate from high school? Thus, the math education perspective tends to be both descriptive and prescriptive.

When these two perspectives are synthesized, they suggest that mathematical ability involves the following components.

Declarative Knowledge

. . . A person's declarative knowledge is his or her knowledge of the facts in some field. In the present case, declarative knowledge would refer to a person's knowledge of math facts (Byrnes, 2001). In most people, these facts amount to the answers to various computations (e.g., knowing that 9 is the right answer to 3 × 3, or that 25 is the square root of 625). Individuals who have considerable math talent usually know a number of math facts that are highly accessible (i.e., it does not take a long time for them to retrieve these facts). However, in recent years, this aspect of mathematical expertise has been downplayed in its importance (especially in the math education community) because people can have considerable knowledge of facts but still lack the ability to solve problems in the classroom or in the real world. In effect, declarative knowledge is thought to be a necessary but not sufficient condition for math talent (Byrnes, 1992).

Procedural Knowledge

A *procedure* is a set of operations or actions that is implemented to achieve some goal (Anderson, 1993; Byrnes, 2001). Thus, a person who has procedural knowledge in math knows how to achieve certain ends using a series of actions, operations, or steps. Examples include knowing how to (1) count an array of objects; (2) add, subtract, multiply, or divide whole numbers, fractions, integers, or algebraic symbols; (3) determine the area under a curve; (4) set up and carry out a geometric proof; and (5) use statistics to determine whether a correlation is significantly larger than zero. As I implied earlier, regular use of certain procedures on a finite set of mathematical objects (e.g., whole numbers between 1 and 20) yields answers that will ultimately comprise one portion of a person's declarative knowledge base. Moreover, certain forms of procedures have a "syntax" (Hiebert & LeFevre, 1987) in the sense that the steps must be performed in a certain way in order for correct answers to emerge (e.g., lining up the decimal points when manually adding numbers with decimals).

Psychologists and educators further assume that procedures can exist in the mind at different levels of abstraction (Byrnes, 1999). At the lowest level of abstraction, for example, are specific actions or algorithms (e.g., the actions involved in frying an egg or adding two fractions). These actions are "specific" in the sense that they apply to a limited range of objects and situations. For example, a person would presumably not attempt to crack open a hamburger before frying it or add negative integers with the least common denominator method.

At a somewhat higher level of abstraction are strategies and heuristics. A *strategy* is a plan that (1) describes, in outline, how a problem will be approached and (2) includes some specification of the overall goal (e.g., find out what angle X is) and the subgoals that need to be achieved in order to attain the overall goal (e.g., First I need to find out . . . Then I have to . . .). Strategies are more abstract than action-based procedures because the former may be formulated well before particular methods for attaining each subgoal are even envisioned. Moreover, the same general strategy may be applied in a variety of situations. A related kind of procedural knowledge is a *heuristic,* or a rule of thumb (e.g., "When in doubt, ask the teacher").

An interesting aspect of the research on math strategies is the finding that children and adults seem to rely on a repertoire of five to seven strategies to solve even structurally similar problems (Siegler, 1991). For example, for the problem "3 + 7," a child may count out three using one hand, count out seven using the other hand, then add up all the extended fingers (the *count-all* strategy). For the problem "18 + 2," however, the same child may start counting at the largest number, then add two numbers onto that (the *min* strategy). The general approach is to use strategies that are not only efficient but likely to yield the correct answer.

In sum, then, psychologists and educators assume that mathematical ability requires a rich procedural knowledge base. However, again it is not enough to simply have facts, procedures, strategies, and heuristics stored in long-term memory. Mathematical competence involves the ability to call on the *right* facts, procedures, and strategies at the *right* time. The component to be described next has been alleged to support this kind of context-sensitive use.

Conceptual Knowledge

. . . People would be expected to develop conceptual knowledge in math as they (1) struggle to understand the *meaning* of mathematical facts and procedures, (2) learn to relate mathematical symbols to their referents and construct categories of mathematical entities, and (3) construct cardinal and ordinal representations of mathematical entities (Byrnes, 2001; Case & Okamoto, 1996). Clearly, there is a critical difference between knowing certain facts and knowing *why* these facts are true. Similarly, there is a difference between knowing how to execute a procedure and knowing why it should be performed in a particular instance (and why it should be executed in a particular way). Individuals with conceptual knowledge understand the meaning and appropriate use of mathematical facts and procedures. Moreover, they relate various mathematical symbols to their referents in appropriate ways (in the same way that literate individuals relate words to their referents). The latter skill requires the construction of mathematical categories and definitions (e.g., *odd number, integer, rational number, integral,* etc.). One particularly important type of categorical representation for math is called a *schema* (plural, *schemata*).

Schemata are abstract representations of what all instances of something (e.g., word problems that require addition) have in common. Schemata form through repeated encounters with the same kind of problem or situation, especially when analogous or identical solutions are required (Byrnes, 2001; Mayer, 1982). When problems are recognized as being of a particular type, their solutions can be immediately retrieved instead of having to be reinvented on the spot. Hence, schemata probably provide the basis of *conditional knowledge,* knowing when and where to apply a procedure. However, certain theoretical models of procedural knowledge build conditions of use into the procedure itself.

The final kind of conceptual knowledge refers to the fused, linear representation of the cardinal and ordinal representations of mathematical quantities. Cardinal representations describe the amount or extent of a set of objects (i.e., how many objects might be present in a particular situation). When the cardinal representations for various quantities are arranged in increasing magnitude, a student can be said to have an ordinal representation of these numbers as well. An example would be a mental number line of integer amounts. To assess cardinal and ordinal knowledge, a researcher could present two arrays of objects and ask a person to identify the larger amount.

Thus, conceptual knowledge involves mappings of mental representations to things in the external world (so-called *extension relations*), as well as mappings between multiple representations in the mind (so-called *intension relations*). Together, these representations help a student understand and make sense of math facts and procedures. By "make sense," it is meant that a child truly understands "the big picture" when it comes to concepts as well as the likely effects of some procedures. For example, a student with math sense would appreciate what might happen if the 3 in $3 \times 4 = 12$ were to be replaced by a 4 and how such a change would be different from substituting a 4 for the 3 in $3 + 4 = 7$ (Byrnes, 2001; Markovits & Sowder, 1994). Hence, the child essentially knows what is going on in math class.

Moreover, the construction of mathematical categories helps a child to avoid inappropriate applications of procedures. For example, a child with conceptual knowledge of fractions would not simply add the numerators and denominators of two fractions together because the two categories of fractions and whole numbers are representationally distinct in their minds (Byrnes, 1992). Each of these categories, in turn, is linked to its own set of procedures. Whereas individuals with high math ability have large amounts of declarative, procedural, and conceptual knowledge of math, their less competent peers often only have declarative and procedural knowledge (if that). In other words, the latter may often do the right things but have no idea what they are doing or why.

Estimation Skills

Sometimes a problem requires only an approximate solution. For example, an employer may only wish to know the probable month (or even time of year) when a job will be completed, not the exact date. Or a homeowner may wish to get only a rough idea of how much a monthly payment would go down with refinancing, or how much money to bring to the supermarket. In such cases, a skilled individual needs to know how to use math facts, procedures, concepts, and strategies to generate an approximate but still useful solution. For example, consider the case of a third grader who wanted to know the approximate answer to the problem, $25 \times 25 = ?$ She may already know that 20×20 is 400 and that 30×30 is 900. From these two math facts and her ordinal representations of whole numbers (i.e., 25 is midway between 20 and 30), she may deduce that 25×25 is probably somewhere in between 400 and 900, and perhaps close to the halfway mark of 650 (again using ordinal representations or quick computations to determine the halfway mark). The estimate of 650 is, of course, reasonably close to the correct answer of 625. On important tests like the National Assessment of Educational Progress (NAEP) or the Scholastic Achievement Test (SAT), estimation skills are required for scoring in the highest ranges because most problems have to be solved in 60 seconds or less. Whereas approximate answers can be generated in a few seconds and be compared to possible answers, complete computations often take more than the allotted 60 seconds. Given earlier arguments, one could say that estimation skills are simply a form of math sense. It should also be clear that one could not be proficient at estimating without having large amounts of declarative, procedural, and conceptual knowledge in math. But again, there are students who have the latter kinds of knowledge but lack the ability or tendency to engage in estimation when it is appropriate to do so.

Graphing and Modeling Skills

Mathematics has often been said to be a discipline that can be used to identify patterns and functional relationships in the world. When data points are presented in a serial fashion or one by one, it is often difficult to get an overall sense of what is going on. For example, if a person wanted to get a rough sense of the housing prices in a given neighborhood, he or she could read an unorganized list of prices for the last 100 houses that sold in that neighborhood (one by one), but such an activity would not be very helpful. A better approach would be to make a bar graph or tally sheet to see where most of the prices fall (using prices arranged in increasing order along the bottom of the graph). Similarly, researchers in multiple fields use an approach called *regression* to see which of a set of predictor variables is statistically related to some outcome for a large sample of cases. For example, a scientist can use regression to predict someone's yearly income using variables such as age, occupation, and mortgage payment. Here, statistical programs in computers link up such variables in a mathematical function. This function indicates which variables are useful for prediction and which are not. The equations generated by the computer also indicate which variables (e.g., mortgage payments) are better predictors than others (e.g., age). Graphs, charts, and mathematical equations, then, help a person develop a good conceptual understanding of patterns in the data. These aides also reduce the amount of information processing that has to be performed to see the patterns and also greatly facilitate inference making (Bruner, 1966). People with high levels of math ability use graphic aides in a strategic fashion. Moreover, they rely on their extensive knowledge to create these models. Note that these tendencies reflect something other than spatial ability.

Problem Solving

To sum up, then, mathematical ability requires (1) high levels of declarative, procedural, and conceptual knowledge *and* (2) a tendency to use this knowledge in a strategic, efficient, and context-sensitive way. This analysis suggests that in a national sample of students, there would probably be four kinds of individuals. The first would be students who do not use math knowledge in a strategic, efficient, or context-sensitive way because they have low levels of declarative, procedural, and conceptual knowledge. The second would be students who have adequate levels of declarative and procedural knowledge but are unable to use this knowledge to solve problems due to the fact that they have insufficient levels of conceptual knowledge, were given inadequate guidance, or had too few opportunities to practice. The third would be students who have all three kinds of knowledge but do not use this knowledge to solve problems because of inadequate instruction or insufficient opportunities to practice.

The final would be students who can solve a wide range of problems because they have the requisite knowledge, and have received multiple, guided opportunities to apply this knowledge.

Neuroscientific Perspectives on Math Ability

By and large, neuroscientists have attempted to explain mathematical abilities and disabilities by appealing to individual differences in the operation of specific brain mechanisms. In what follows, the neuroscientific literature on math skills is summarized in five sections. In the first, the focus is on several models of math skills that were constructed to explain the calculation deficits that sometimes occur following brain injury. In the second, the literature on math disabilities in children is summarized. In the third, neuroimaging studies of math skills are reviewed. In the fourth, the focus shifts from math disabilities to mathematical talent. In the fifth and final section, a summary of the neuroscientific literature is provided.

Neuroscientific Models of Calculation

Two models have recently been proposed to account for the patterns of calculation deficits that have sometimes occurred following brain injuries. For expository purposes, these theoretical frameworks are called the *McCloskey model* and the *Dehaene model,* respectively, though the focal individuals have had several collaborators.

THE MCCLOSKEY MODEL. After conducting a detailed analysis of 14 case studies of brain-injured adults, Michael McCloskey and colleagues (e.g., McCloskey, Caramazza, & Basili, 1985; McCloskey, Aliminosa, & Sokol, 1991) proposed that calculation abilities can be decomposed into two clusters of functionally autonomous components. The first cluster, which comprise *a number processing system,* includes one set of components for comprehending numbers and another set for producing them. Within each of the comprehension and production subsystems, moreover, there are distinct components for processing arabic numbers (e.g., 53) and verbal numbers (e.g., *fifty-three).* All of these components were originally proposed to account for various forms of double dissociations that appeared in the focal cases. For example, some of the patients could recognize arabic numbers but could not write them down when asked. Similarly, some could write down arabic numbers but not verbal numbers.

The components in the second cluster comprise the *calculation system.* McCloskey et al. (1985, 1991) argue that these components perform three kinds of processes: (1) comprehension of the signs or words for operations (e.g., ÷ *divided by*), (2) retrieval of arithmetic facts (e.g., that 39 is the answer to 13 × 3), and (3) execution of calculation procedures (e.g., the algorithm for long division). Again, these components were inferred on the basis of certain double dissociations. Some patients, for example, could recognize the signs for operations but could not perform the operations indicated by these signs. Others, however, could perform the operations, but could not retrieve math facts associated with these operations. Moreover, there were individuals who could do some of the operations from the calculation system but could not do others from the number processing system (McCloskey et al., 1991). When the two systems are intact, however, they are thought to be linked via the ability to create abstract representations of the numbers and operations in a problem. This abstract representation is also linked to action systems that are alleged to regulate the implementation of goal-directed procedures.

Beyond such double dissociations, five other interesting aspects of the 14 cases emerged. The first is that, in most of the patients (64 percent), problems developed after these patients experienced a cerebrovascular accident in the left hemisphere. In two other patients (14 percent), the cerebrovascular accident occurred in the right hemisphere. The remaining patients experienced a closed head injury (14 percent) or anoxia (7 percent). Thus, calculation skills in arithmetic seem to be localized in the left hemisphere, but the data are not completely consistent in this regard. These findings are, however, analogous to those that have been observed in postmortem studies of dyslexic children. In these studies, 66 percent of the children showed either symmetry or reversed asymmetry of the plana temporale. . . . The rest showed the normal pattern of asymmetry. It is curious that in both cases, two-thirds of subjects showed problems in the same region of the brain, but one-third did not.

The second interesting finding was that in all 14 cases the calculation deficits were limited to multiplication (i.e., arithmetic skills for addition and subtraction were left largely intact). Thus, these findings suggest that there are brain regions associated with multiplication, and other regions associated with arithmetic and subtraction. The third finding was that all patients showed uneven patterns of performance across particular kinds of multiplication problems. For example, some patients could solve all problems except those involving zero (e.g., 3 × 0 or 0 × 4). Others could solve problems with zero when it was the first but not the second multiplicand. Still others had no problem with items involving zeros and ones (e.g., 3 × 0 and 1 × 4), but had problems with all other combinations that had multiplicands between 2 and 9. The fourth finding was that each person seemed to have problems with their own types of items. Such findings combined with related evidence from other case studies (e.g., Hittmair-Delazer, Semenza, & Denes, 1994) suggest that each fact seems to be stored in its own format. Further analysis showed that many patients forgot the facts associated with all types of problems but could quickly reconstruct the facts for the problems with zero or one because the more abstract rules for these items were spared (e.g., "any number multiplied by 1 is itself"). Thus, there seem to be brain regions that store such abstract rules and others that store other kinds of multiplication algorithms (e.g., how to line things up in columns for problems such as 317×32). This finding regarding the abstract rules has been replicated in other case studies (e.g., Pesenti, Seron, & Van Der Linden, 1994).

THE DEHAENE MODEL. Dehaene and Cohen (1997) reviewed the neuropsychological literature related to mathematical deficits and proposed a "triple-code" model to account for the myriad of findings. As the name implies, the triple-code model suggests that there are three main representations of numbers: (1) a *visual arabic code* that is localized in the left and right inferior occipital-temporal areas, (2) an *analogical quantity* or *magnitude code* that is localized in the left and right inferior parietal areas, and (3) a *verbal code* that is localized in the left perisylvian areas. The visual arabic code, which subserves multidigit operations, is utilized during the identification of strings of digits and during judgments of parity (e.g., knowing that numbers that end in 2 are even). The magnitude code, in contrast, is assumed to correspond to distributions of activation on an oriented number line. This code subserves the ability to evaluate proximity (e.g., that 18 is close to 20) and ordinal relations (e.g., that 20 is larger than 18). The verbal code, finally, represents numbers via a parsed sequence of words. It is involved when an individual accesses rote verbal memories of arithmetic facts.

Dehaene and Cohen further suggest that there are two basic routes through which arithmetic problems can be solved. In the direct route, the problem (e.g., 2×9) is first encoded into a verbal representation (e.g., "two times nine is . . ."). The verbal representation, in turn, triggers the rote-learned verbal answer that is stored in memory (e.g., "eighteen"). The latter process is thought to involve a left cortico–subcortical loop through the basal ganglia and thalamus. Hence, the direct route does not require conceptual analysis of any type and is largely devoid of meaning. In contrast, the second route is more indirect and calls on stored semantic knowledge of numbers. When problems are solved by the indirect route, a person recodes the arabic symbols into quantity representations. These quantity representations (thought to be localized in the left and right parietal areas) subserve semantically meaningful operations, such as when one alters a representation of the quantity 5 to make it into a representation of 7 or 3. The results of such manipulations are thought to be transmitted from the left inferior parietal cortex to the left perisylvian language network for naming.

Dehaene and Cohen's model, then, proposes that there are two major sets of brain areas that are critical for calculation: (1) the bilateral inferior parietal areas that are responsible for semantic knowledge about numerical quantities and (2) the left cortico–pallidum–thalamic loop that is involved in the storage of the verbal sequences that correspond to arithmetic facts. The model further assumes that brain lesions would have different effects depending on which of these two areas were damaged. The calculation deficits (or *acalculias*) that arise from damage to the inferior parietal areas should be domain-specific (i.e., damage should only affect number knowledge and not other kinds of knowledge) and be limited to problems that rely heavily on semantic math knowledge such as estimation, comparison, and ordinality (i.e., automatized facts should be uneffected). In contrast, acalculias that arise from damage to the cortico–subcortical loop should be domain-general (i.e., other kinds of rote-learned material besides math facts may be affected as well), and should involve loss of math facts combined with spared semantic skills (e.g., estimation, comparison, and ordinal relations).

Dehaene and Cohen (1997) demonstrated the utility of this model by applying it to two case studies. Whereas one of these patients had a localized inferior parietal lesion in the right hemisphere, the other had a left subcortical infarct. As predicted, the patient with the parietal lesion demonstrated the following double dissociation: he had difficulty considering semantic relations (e.g., comparing two numbers) but could recall automatized math facts. The other patient, in contrast, demonstrated the opposite kind of double dissociation.

Developmental Disabilities in Math

The aforementioned models were constructed to explain the calculation deficits that sometimes arise in brain-injured adults. Such acquired disabilities can be contrasted with so-called developmental disabilities in math (or MD). The latter term applies to problems that present themselves in children who have no known history of brain injury.

Children with MD have been found to have both procedural and fact-retrieval deficits. Moreover, these deficits appear to follow different developmental trajectories (Geary, 1993). In the case of procedural problems, for example, it has been found that children with MD usually lag behind their nondisabled peers in the sense that they often (1) use less mature strategies (e.g., "count all" vs. "min"), (2) perform the same strategies more slowly, and (3) make calculation errors more often. By the end of second grade, however, the computational skills of children with MD approach those of their non-MD peers. In contrast, fact-retrieval deficits tend to persist indefinitely and are resistant to remediation through extensive training. When children with MD attempt to recall facts, they tend to recall fewer facts, the retrieval times associated with these facts are very unsystematic, and they make a large number of retrieval errors (Geary, 1993).

It is notable that the two primary deficits of children with MD correspond to two of the three component operations of the calculation system proposed by McCloskey and colleagues (see above). The fact-retrieval problem is also consistent with aspects of Dehaene and Cohen's model. The research on which these models are based further suggests that procedural and fact-retrieval problems are particularly likely to arise following lesions to the left hemisphere or the left corticosubcortical systems. This left hemisphere bias is interesting given the fact that 40 percent of the children who have MD have been found to have a reading disability as well (Geary, 1993). . . . Many important reading skills seem to be localized in the left hemisphere.

Studies Using Neuroimaging and Gross Electrical Recording Techniques

So far, the discussion has been limited to the math deficits that arise in disabled children and adults. In the present and next sections, the focus shifts somewhat to the math abilities of nonimpaired individuals. The two studies to be described next employed neuroimagining or gross electrical recording techniques while subjects performed math tasks. Studies of this sort are surprisingly rare (in contrast to the large number of neuroimagining studies of reading, attention, or memory).

Dehaene et al. (1996) presented number pairs to eight healthy adults. On one-third of the trials, subjects were asked to mentally identify the larger of the two numbers. On another third of trials, they were asked to multiply the two numbers together. On the remaining third of trials, they simply rested with their eyes open. Using PET [positron emission tomography] scans, Dehaene et al. considered the differences in blood flow patterns that were evident when any of the two conditions were compared to each other (e.g., multiplying numbers vs. identifying the larger one). Results showed selective increases or decreases in blood flow in a number of brain areas. Notably, the number comparison task "did not yield any significant activations over and above those that . . . are related to stimulus identification and response selection (lateral occipital cortex, precentral gyrus, and supplementary motor areal). . . . Hence, no critical brain areas for number comparison emerged" (Dehaene et al., 1996, p. 1103). Small activations, however, did emerge in the left and right inferior parietal region, but these activations were not significant (contrary to predictions based on Dehaene and Cohen's model; see above). It is not clear whether the use of PET scans, inadequate control trials, or a small sample size were responsible for these inconclusive results.

Using a 64-channel EEG [electroencephalogram] technology . . . , Dehaene (1996) limited his focus to just number identification and comparison. He attempted to verify a three-stage processing model that suggested that number comparison involved an initial stage of number comprehension (with distinct components for comprehending arabic and verbal symbols) that was followed by comparative processes that operate on the mental representations that emerge after the symbols are interpreted. Results suggested that arabic digits are initially comprehended bilaterally in posterior occipito–temporal regions. Verbal digits, however, seem to be processed mainly in the left posterior region. As for the second stage of number comparison, activation seemed to occur mainly in the right parieto–occipito–temporal junction. This finding is consistent with the results of a case study reported by Dehaene and Cohen (1997) in which a right parietal lesion caused problems in quantity estimation. Dehaene (1996) concluded his paper by noting that "the right hemisphere appears to possess both the ability to identify a digit and to represent its magnitude relative to other numbers" (p. 64).

The Neural Basis of Mathematical Ability

Perhaps the most controversial portion of the neuroscientific literature on math is the segment concerned with the neural basis of mathematical talent. To understand the origins of this controversy, we need to return to the bell-shaped (i.e., normal) distribution that was described earlier. Recall that in a normal distribution any given score falls into one of three categories: below average, average, or above average. Many years of research have shown that students always seem to fall into the same category (e.g., below average) each time they take a math test. Hence, there is a fair amount of stability over time in a student's performance as well as in his or her relative ranking in the distribution.

Although this pattern of results can be explained in a variety of ways (see Byrnes, 2001), advocates of the neural explanation of math talent (or NEMT, for short) suggest that there may be inborn differences in math ability that are reflected in distinct neural architectures. In the extreme, the NEMT perspective is reflected in the numerous attempts to reveal differences between Albert Einstein's brain and the brains of nongeniuses. Researchers who have done so have asked questions such as the following: Was his brain bigger? If so, in what areas of the brain were the differences in size most pronounced? Did he have more neurons of a particular type in particular layers of the cortex? Did he have more synaptic connections?

. . . This atheoretical, bottom-up approach is not very efficient nor likely to be terribly informative. If math ability is like other kinds of abilities, it is likely to be comprised of a set of component skills that are carried out in specific regions of the brain. As such, two things have to occur before it even makes sense to look at structural or functional differences in brains: (1) psychologists have to create theories that carve math ability into component skills and (2) neuroscientists have to locate the brain regions responsible for carrying out these component skills. In the absence of such information, an individual could spend a great deal of time examining slices from brain regions that have nothing to do with math ability. In addition, most higher order skills are widely distributed throughout the brain. . . . Examination of slices of cortical tissue from one or two areas of the brain would not reveal the overall, brain-wide *organization* or neural architecture of a skill like math ability.

Third, there are two basic kinds of psychological theories: (1) those that merely subdivide a process into its component operations and (2) those that describe how the components should operate to produce *high levels* of performance. To see the difference between these types of theories, it is useful to consider the following analogy involving automobiles. The first kind of theory is like the answer that would be given to the question "How does a car engine work?" Here, one merely says what the component parts and processes are (e.g., "A *battery* sends a charge to a set of *spark plugs* that make sparks inside a set of *cylinders*. At the same time, *fuel injectors* spray atomized gas into the cylinders . . . "). The second kind of theory, in contrast, would be more like the answer given to the question "Why is a race car faster than a family car?" Here, one elaborates on the basic description of components by referring to the *optimal* operation of the components and the system as a whole (e.g., faster cars have more cylinders, each of which permit a larger quantity of fuel to be ignited, etc.). Thus, a prerequisite for discovering possible differences in the brains of high-ability and low-ability students is a psychological theory that specifies the nature of mathematical *expertise* or talent. It is not enough to simply list the component operations of math skills. Once the optimal operation of the components has been defined, one can then consider how particular kinds of neural assemblies could support this optimal performance. For example, if one element of a theory of math ability suggests that math experts *quickly* retrieve facts, procedures, and strategies that are *relevant* to a given problem (e.g., Byrnes & Takahira, 1994), a neuroscientific approach would then attempt to consider possible brain architectures that would permit rapid, but selective, retrieval of problem-relevant information. A less informative approach would be to look for brain regions that seem to be active when math knowledge is retrieved. Such an approach is uninformative because it may not help a scientist discriminate among three kinds of people: (1) those who tend to retrieve relevant information, but do so fairly slowly; (2) those who tend to retrieve relevant information quickly; and (3) those who tend to retrieve irrelevant information quickly. It is conceivable that the same region of the brain could be active in all three types of individuals.

A fourth complicating issue pertains to the difference between *natural* ability (aptitude) and *acquired* expertise. Most advocates of the NEMT tend to focus on architectural differences that are alleged to be present *before* children have experiences that promote math knowledge. In other words, these advocates assume that the initial state of brain organization (or neural functioning) determines the manner in which mathematical knowledge and skill is acquired and utilized. One might argue, for example, that some students have more neurons in their frontal and parietal lobes that are available for being configured into performance-enhancing neural assemblies. Or one could argue that the process of myelination occurs more quickly in some people than in others. If so, then exposure to the same content in math class would not necessarily lead to the creation of similar kinds of neural assemblies in two individuals who are exposed to this content.

In contrast, the acquired expertise explanation would not focus on the initial differences in brain assemblies in people as much as differences that arise much later in development after formative experiences have transpired. Here, advocates of the latter position would agree that math experts probably have different brains than their less competent peers, but they would argue that experts have different brains because they have had experiences that nonexperts did not have. These experiences, in turn, helped to create appropriate neural assemblies. . . . Returning to the car analogy, then, the natural ability view would suggest that some people are born with "race cars" for brains while others are born with "family cars." The acquired expertise view, in contrast, would suggest that we all start off with "family cars" but some of us transform these cars into "race cars" through experience.

With all of these introductory comments in mind, we can now turn to several recent proposals regarding the origins of extreme mathematical talent (and gender differences in this regard). In an effort to understand the nature of giftedness, researchers at several universities in the United States have created summer programs to enhance the math skills of gifted seventh graders. In such programs, children are initially identified and selected on the basis of their very high standardized test scores in math or other subject areas. Once enrolled in a particular program, children are given a variety of tests, including the SATs. Remarkably, some of these children (less than 1 percent) have been found to score over 700 on the SAT (Benbow, 1988). This is quite a feat considering the fact that only 6 percent of much older students (i.e., twelfth graders) normally score that high. Moreover, further analyses showed that nearly all of the seventh graders who scored above 700 were male (the ratio is actually 12 males to every 1 female).

Confronted with such findings, it seems reasonable to ask two questions: (1) How is it possible for 13-year-olds to perform so well on a math test that is difficult for even twelfth graders (i.e., the SAT)? and (2) Why are gifted males more likely than gifted females to score above 700 on the SAT? Several different proposals have been advanced to explain these outcomes (Byrnes, 2001), but the explanation that has generated the most interest suggests that mathematical talent has a neural basis (see, e.g., Benbow, 1988, and commentaries). This NEMT begins by showing how gifted males and gifted females do not differ in their attitudes toward math. Moreover, their parents do not appear to hold sexist attitudes regarding math. Finally, these students have not attended high school, so a researcher could not argue that gender differences in extreme talent are due to the fact that males tend to take more high school math courses than females.

Inasmuch as various alternative explanations seemed to be inadequate, advocates of the NEMT began searching for evidence of possible anatomical or physiological indicators of math skill. They eventually found what they needed in the work of the late Norman Geschwind and colleagues on the anatomical basis of dyslexia. . . . Geschwind et al. sought to account for three sets of findings: (1) a higher incidence of language problems in boys than in girls, (2) symmetry or reversed asymmetry in the size of certain brain areas in dyslexic children, and (3) unexpected empirical links between left-handedness, language disorders, and immune disorders (Geschwind & Behan, 1982; Geschwind & Galaburda, 1985). To explain all these findings, Geschwind and colleagues proposed the following. During prenatal development, testosterone levels affect the growth of the left cerebral hemisphere in such a way that an anomalous form of dominance develops. Instead of being right-handed and having language lateralized in the left hemisphere, affected individuals become left-handed with language lateralized in the right or both hemispheres. This altered physiology, in turn, leads to problems such as developmental dyslexia, impaired language development, and autism. Testosterone levels also affect the thymus, resulting in disorders of the immune system (e.g., allergies, colitis, AIDS). To explain asymmetries in the size of the left and right hemispheres, Geschwind and colleagues suggested the testosterone may either retard the growth of the left hemisphere or interfere with normal reductions in the right.

This proposal seemed promising to advocates of the NEMT because of the claim that some individuals might be born with atypical dominance and a larger-than-normal right hemisphere (Benbow, 1988). The reasoning was that "the right hemisphere is traditionally considered specialized for non-verbal tasks and the left for verbal, although these differences may not be qualitative but quantitative. Mathematical reasoning ability, especially in contrast to computational ability, may be more strongly under the influence of the right hemisphere" (Benbow, 1988, p. 180).

To test these speculations, Benbow and colleagues considered whether gifted children were more likely than nongifted children to be left-handed and to have immune disorders (e.g., allergies). To assess handedness, Benbow and colleagues gave the Edinburgh Handedness Inventory (Oldfield, 1971) to two kinds of children who were drawn from their sample of over 100,000 gifted students: (1) an extremely precocious group of children $(N = 303)$ who scored above 700 on the SAT–Math or above 630 on the SAT–Verbal, and (2) a less precocious group who scored closer to 500 on the SAT–Math $(N = 127)$. Whereas the norms for Edinburgh Handedness Inventory suggest that 8 percent of Scottish adults use their left hands occasionally or often to perform everyday tasks, 13 percent of children who were extremely precocious for math and 10 percent of the less precocious group were left-handed in this way (Benbow, 1986). Whereas the incidence of left-handedness was found to be significantly higher in the extremely precocious children than in the Scottish adults ($p < .04$), two other comparisons revealed no significant differences: (1) less precocious children versus the Scottish adults and (2) extremely precocious children versus less precocious children. Note that the significant difference between the extremely precocious students and Scottish adults is largely a function of sample size. The adult sample contained over 1,000 adults. Had it contained as few as 600 individuals, the difference between 13 percent and 8 percent would no longer be significant.

As for gender differences in the extent of left-handedness in extremely precocious students, Benbow (1988) reports that more males (16 percent) than females (11 percent) were left-handed in the study ($p < .05$, using an unspecified test). However, the present author applied the standard test for comparing frequencies (i.e., the chi-square test) to Benbow's (1986) data and found that the difference between 16 percent and 11 percent is not significant ($p = .17$). In addition, the key difference between mathematically precocious males (14 percent) and mathematically precocious females (6 percent) was also not significant ($p = .33$).

With respect to immune disorders, Benbow (1988) reports that students with extremely high mathematical ability are twice as likely to have allergies as children in the general population (53 percent vs. 25 percent), but no statistical tests were employed in this instance presumably because the population figure was an estimate provided to Benbow by the author of the test for immune disorders. Such a difference would, however, be significant if the population rate of 25 percent were based on 10 or more children. A chi-square test applied to the percentages of extremely precocious students in math (53 percent) and less precocious students in the gifted sample (35 percent) revealed a highly significant difference ($p < .001$). As for extremely precocious males (53 percent) and females (54 percent), the difference in the incidence of allergies was not significant.

Thus, the preliminary findings based on handedness and allergies were not terribly supportive of the idea of greater right hemisphere involvement in gifted children, in general, and in gifted males, in particular. It could be argued, however, that these studies really do not test the right-hemisphere (RH) proposal directly because indices such as handedness and allergies are fairly imprecise. A more direct approach would be to look at patterns of activation in the right and left hemisphere using either neuroimaging or gross electrical recording techniques. In their review of the literature using the latter, O'Boyle and Gill (1998) report that gifted adolescents appear to engage their right hemispheres more than nongifted adolescents when they listen to auditory stimuli or process facial expressions. In addition, gifted adolescents show a pattern of resting activation that is similar to that of college students and significantly different from nongifted adolescents (i.e., greater activation in the frontal and occipital lobes).

Finally, comparisons of gifted males and females have revealed gender differences with respect to the involvement of the right hemisphere for the processing of faces and mental rotation (more involvement for males), but not for verbal stimuli. In addition, charts presented in Alexander, O'Boyle, and Benbow (1996) also suggest greater resting activations in the parietal and possibly frontal lobes in gifted males than in gifted females, but these specific comparisons were not reported in the text. The one study that had the potential to consider whether greater right hemisphere involvement was associated with higher SAT–Math scores (i.e., O'Boyle & Benbow, 1990) failed to report this correlation because the authors expressed concerns over a restricted range problem with the SAT–Math scores (i.e., most students scored over 500). The authors did report a correlation of $r = -.29$ between laterality scores and SAT scores, but it was not clear from the text whether total SAT scores or just SAT–Verbal scores were used to compute this correlation.

Thus, there is very little evidence in support of the idea that gifted children, in general, and gifted males, in particular, are better in math because they tend to engage their right hemispheres more than other individuals. In addition, there are other reasons to have serious doubts about this RH proposal. First, most neuroscientists assume that the frontal lobes are the most likely sites of higher order reasoning (Luria, 1973). More posterior regions of the right hemisphere could be associated with certain aspects of conceptual knowledge in math or certain types of spatial reasoning (but not all), but these regions are also active when working memory and attention are engaged. . . . Thus, even if evidence suddenly did accumulate that suggested that extremely talented mathematicians engage their right hemispheres more than less talented individuals, this difference could reflect the former's greater reliance on math concepts, spatial skills, or working memory. These capacities may relate to the kind of reasoning required to do well on the SAT, but the core processes of problem comprehension and strategic planning are likely to be associated with the frontal lobes.

Second, it is not at all clear why a theory designed to account for reading disabilities (i.e., the model of Geschwind and colleagues) would even be appropriate for explaining high levels of *math* talent. If the Geschwind model really did apply, one would expect to find reading disabilities in many of the extremely precocious children. In fact, however, most of these children have a great deal of verbal ability in addition to having considerable math ability (Benbow, 1986, 1988). Third, . . . there is a very little evidence in support of the proposals of Geschwind and colleagues.

Fourth, advocates of the neural account have never really shown how knowledge-based or experience-based explanations are not viable. For example, whereas it is true that 13-year-olds tend not to take high school math courses, these children must get their knowledge and reasoning skills somewhere. Note that tests like the SAT–Math require knowledge of arithmetic, algebra, and geometry. Many nongifted children receive direct instruction on these topics by the seventh or eighth grade, and most gifted children receive instruction on these topics 2 or more years before that. In addition, gifted children's enrichment in school involves exercises in problem-solving games and the like and they undoubtedly pursue math-related activities outside of school as well. The only alternative to such an experience-based view is some form of radical nativism (i.e., these children did not need to be exposed to arithmetic, algebra, or geometry because they were born with knowledge of these topics). Thus, the question is not whether they have more knowledge than their nongifted peers, but how they learned it before their peers did.

Finally, it is worth noting that researchers may eventually find subtle, but important, architectural differences between the brains of gifted and nongifted children. What can be made of such differences if they are found? The arguments presented so far suggest the answer to this question is "very little." The key issue is not whether such differences exist but *how* and *when* they arose. Regarding the "how" aspect, the research [I present] suggests that there are a number of factors that affect brain structure (e.g., genetics, hormones, and experience). With respect to the "when" aspect, note that some accounts claim that differences in brain structure exist prior to exposure to math content (the natural ability view), while others assume that differences arise in response to differential exposure to content (the acquired expertise view).

Summary of the Neuroscientific Literature

As can be surmised from the present chapter, there seem to be very few neuroscientific studies of math skills. As such, it is difficult to draw firm conclusions from this literature. What we can tentatively say is that (1) calculation skills seem to be largely confined to the left hemisphere (though not always); (2) individual math facts and procedures seemed to be stored in their own, separate areas of the cortex (e.g., one area for multiplication facts, another for subtraction procedures, etc.); (3) comparison and ordinality skills seem to be localized in the posterior regions of the right hemisphere (though not always); and (4) gifted children tend to have more allergies and engage their right hemisphere more often than non-gifted children (though not always). There is, then, much to learn about the neuroscientific basis of math skills.

Conclusions, Caveats, and Instructional Implications

. . . I will address the implications of the research on math ability through a consideration of four questions:

1. How much overlap is there between the psychological and neuroscientific accounts of math skills?
2. Is it possible to fuse these accounts into a single integrated perspective?
3. How confident can we be in the portrait of math ability that has emerged from these two traditions?
4. When and how should children be taught math skills, given what we have learned from these two traditions?

The Overlap Question

Comparison of the psychological and neuroscientific perspectives on math ability suggests that these perspectives overlap very little. Whereas psychologists (and educators) have tended to emphasize multiple kinds of knowledge, strategies, and problem-solving skills, neuroscientists have tended to emphasize fairly low-level skills such as arithmetic calculation or ordinal judgments. Moreover, there is little indication that neuroscientists have used psychological accounts as "road maps" to help them locate regions of the brain that are responsible for performing the core operations of mathematical reasoning. Relatedly, it would appear that neuroscientific studies of math have had very little impact on contemporary psychological theories.

The reasons for this lack of overlap are not entirely clear, but two explanations seem plausible. The first is that relatively few neuroscientific studies of math have been conducted. Moreover, these studies are hard to find and easily missed. The second explanation is that math-specific deficits may be less common than language-specific, attention-specific, or memory-specific deficits (Dehaene, 1996). In other words, many of the people who experience math deficits also experience deficits in other domains. Individuals with such comorbidities seem to have been overlooked in the literature in favor of much rarer cases of "pure" acalculias. The greater preponderance of mixed disorders suggests that higher level performance in math may require the recruitment of important domain-general capacities such as working memory and a tendency to plan. The latter processes have been alleged to be centered in the frontal lobes (Luria, 1973 . . .).

There is, however, a sense in which the psychological and neuroscientific perspectives can be said to overlap. In particular, the intriguing cases of double dissociations in math (see above) strongly support the assertions of psychologists and educators regarding the distinctions among declarative, conceptual, and procedural knowledge in math (Byrnes & Fox, 1998). Unfortunately, however, the same findings have little bearing on proposals regarding the possible links among these kinds of knowledge. Logically, at least three possibilities exist. The first is that math experts have all of the requisite knowledge (i.e., declarative, conceptual, and procedural) but this knowledge is not intrinsically interconnected. Instead, goal-related thinking and metacognitive processes search out the needed information (and strategies) and put these unconnected elements together. The second possible link is that high levels of conceptual knowledge help a student avoid procedural errors (Hiebert & LeFevre, 1987). The third is that conceptual knowledge serves as a foundation for learning procedures and also enhances motivation. Motivation is enhanced because students seem to be more attracted to content when it makes sense than when it does not make sense. The available brain research cannot be used to decide among these perspectives, and it is not clear whether brain research ever could.

The Integration Question

The constructs of "overlap" and "integration" are based on paradigms analogous to Venn diagrams or Hegel's discussion of thesis, antithesis, and synthesis. In the typical case (e.g., two competing theories), there are portions of the integrated quantities that overlap and portions that do not. In the case of the psychological and neuroscientific perspectives on math, however, the neuroscientific perspective is essentially subsumed by the psychological perspective with the exception of some specification of the brain areas that may be related to calculation and ordinal judgments. Hence, the psychological account has nearly everything the neuroscientific account has, and elaborates on this basic proposal considerably. As such, the simple answer to the question "Is it possible to fuse the psychological and neuroscientific perspectives into a single integrated perspective" is "Yes."

The Confidence Question

... The confidence question hinges on two primary aspects of psychological and neuroscientific research: (1) the validity of the measures used and (2) the consistency of the results across studies. Applied to math research, the first issue is whether the measurement techniques used (e.g., paper-and-pencil tasks, EEG recordings, etc.) are valid indicators of math skills. A measure is valid to the extent that it assesses what you think it assesses (i.e., you think it measures X and it really does). Nonvalid measures, in contrast, are either misleading (i.e., we think it measures X but it really measures Y) or equivocal (i.e., a response could mean either X or mean Y). The consistency issue pertains to whether researchers in the psychological and neuroscientific camps have repeatedly found the same thing.

A comprehensive discussion of the validity and consistency of psychological research on math is beyond the scope of this chapter. It suffices to say that the research has been fairly consistent across studies, though controversies remain about such things as age trends (e.g., When do children first understand addition?) and the need to posit multiple forms of knowledge (e.g., conceptual, procedural, and declarative knowledge). For example, when we ask children to compute the answer to "$0.35 + 2.19$," is this task a measure of procedural knowledge or of other kinds of knowledge as well (e.g., conceptual knowledge)? Similarly, when we ask children to explain why $\frac{5}{6}$ is the answer to "$\frac{1}{2} + \frac{1}{3}$," is it accurate to say that they only rely on their conceptual knowledge when they provide an explanation? Even so, there is a growing consensus regarding the merits of the psychological description that was presented at the beginning of this chapter. In effect, psychologists and educators are reasonably confident that this description is accurate.

In contrast, it is far too early to be confident in the results of the neuroscientific studies described in this chapter. ... All neuroscientific methods have their problems. As a result, we cannot feel confident about neuroscientific claims about math skills until multiple researchers find the same thing using different methods (e.g., case studies, PET, fMRI, EEG, and computer simulations). Thus, there is a real need for additional neuroscientific studies of math skills. Ideally, these new studies should be grounded in the description of mathematical talent that has emerged from the field of psychology. It would also be useful to begin to explore the architectures that would support superior levels of performance. Clues to the macrostructure of such an architecture could come from fMRI studies of gifted and nongifted children as they solve SAT-like problems. Once the active brain regions are revealed, researchers can then consider within-region and across-region microstructures that could support fast, accurate, and creative mathematical reasoning.

Instructional Implications

The preceding section can be summarized as follows: whereas we can be reasonably confident about the portrait of math skills that has emerged from the field of psychology, we cannot yet be confident about the math-related claims made by neuroscientists. As such, it would be most prudent to base all instructional implications on the psychological perspective (at least until more neuroscientific studies are conducted). Byrnes (2001) reviewed the extensive literature on the development of math skills and suggested the following implications:

1. Preschool experiences should be structured in such a way to enhance children's existing mathematical conceptual and procedural knowledge (however informal or implicit this knowledge may be). In other words, there is no need to wait until the first grade to have children begin to interact with mathematical ideas.

2. Instruction should form bridges between children's informal math ideas and the formal mathematics presented in school.

3. Instruction at all levels should be consistent with the "Math 2000" recommendations of the National Council of Teachers of Mathematics (1998). The consensus view of math skills that was presented earlier serves as a foundation for many of these recommendations.

4. Instructional activities should promote the acquisition of number concepts as well as schemata for various kinds of word problems. One of the best ways to instill such knowledge in students is to have them solve structurally similar problems and consider how these problems are similar (Gick & Holyoak, 1983; Sweller & Cooper, 1985).

5. Exercises should be designed to promote an accurate meta-cognitive understanding of when an answer is sensible and correct, and when it is not.

6. Finally, there is no substitute for extensive practice. Even when teachers tie procedures to concrete referents or rely on meaningful problem solving, students still make a variety of procedural errors (Byrnes,

1992; Peterson, Carpenter, Fennema, & Loef, 1989; Resnick & Omanson, 1987). Although there is no dichotomy between "meaning," on the one hand, and "repetition," on the other, many people often assume there is. The best approach involves embedding practice within meaningful, goal-directed activities.

REFERENCES

Alexander, J. E., O'Boyle, M. W., & Benbow, C. P. (1996). Developmentally advanced EEG power in gifted male and female adolescents. *International Journal of Psychophysicology, 23,* 25–31.

Anderson, J. R. (1993). Problem solving and learning. *American Psychologist, 48,* 35–44.

Benbow, C. P. (1986). Physiological correlates of extreme intellectual precocity. *Neuropsychologia, 24,* 719–725.

Benbow, C. P. (1988). Sex differences in mathematical reasoning ability in intellectually talented preadolescents: Their nature, effects, and possible causes. *Behavioral and Brain Sciences, 11,* 169–232.

Bernstein, P. L. (1996). *Against the gods: The remarkable story of risk.* New York: Wiley.

Bruner, J. S. (1966). *Toward a theory of instruction.* Cambridge, MA: Belknap Press of Harvard University Press.

Byrnes, J. P. (1992). The conceptual basis of procedural learning. *Cognitive Development, 7,* 235–257.

Byrnes, J. P. (1999). The nature and development of representation: Forging a synthesis of competing approaches. In I. Siegel (Ed.), *Development of representation* (pp. 273–294). Mahwah, NJ: Erlbaum.

Byrnes, J. P. (2001). *Cognitive development and learning in instructional contexts.* Needham Heights, MA: Allyn & Bacon.

Byrnes, J. P., & Fox, N. A. (1998). The educational relevance of research in cognitive neuroscience. *Educational Psychology Review, 10,* 297–342.

Byrnes, J. P., & Takahira, S. (1994). Why some students perform well and others perform poorly on SAT-math items. *Contemporary Educational Psychology, 19,* 63–78.

Case, R., & Okamoto, Y. (1996). The role of central conceptual structures in the development of children's thought. *Monographs of the Society for Research in Child Development, 61,* v-265.

Dehaene, S. (1996). The organization of brain activations in number comparison: Event-related potentials and the additive factors method. *Journal of Cognitive Neuroscience, 8,* 47–68.

Dehaene, S., & Cohen, L. (1997). Cerebral pathways for calculation: Double dissociation between rote verbal and quantitative knowledge of arithmetic. *Cortex, 33,* 219–250.

Dehaene, S., Tzourio, N., Frak, V., Raynaud, L., Cohen, L., Mehler, J., & Mazoyer, B. (1996). Cerebral activations during number multiplication and comparison: A PET study. *Neuropsychologia, 34,* 1097–1106.

Geary, D. C. (1993). Mathematical disabilities: Cognitive, neuropsychological, and genetic components. *Psychological Bulletin, 114,* 345–362.

Geschwind, N., & Behan, P. (1982). Left-handedness: Association with immune disease, migraine, and developmental learning disorder. *Proceedings of the National Academy of Sciences, 79,* 5097–5100.

Geschwind, N., & Galaburda, A. M. (1985). Cerebral lateralization: Biological mechanisms, associations, and pathology, 1: A hypothesis and a program for research. *Archives of Neurology, 42,* 428–459.

Gick, M. L., & Holyoak, K. J. (1983). Schema induction and analogical transfer. *Cognitive Psychology, 15,* 1–38.

Hiebert, J., & LeFevre, P. (1987). Conceptual and procedural knowledge in mathematics: An introductory analysis. In J. Hiebert (Ed.), *Conceptual and procedural knowledge in mathematics* (pp.1–27). Hillsdale, NJ: Erlbaum.

Hittmair-Delazer, M., Semenza, C., & Denes, G. (1994). Concepts and facts in calculation. *Brain, 117,* 715–728.

Luria, A. R. (1973). *The working brain.* New York: Basic Books.

Markovits, Z., & Sowder, J. (1994). Developing number sense: An intervention study in grade 7. *Journal for Research in Mathematics Education, 25,* 4–29.

Mayer, R. E. (1982). Memory for algebra story problems. *Journal of Educational Psychology, 74,* 199–216.

McCloskey, M., Aliminosa, D., & Sokol, S. M. (1991). Facts, rules, and procedures in normal calculation: Evidence from multiple single-patient studies of impaired arithmetic fact retrieval. *Brain and Cognition, 17,* 154–203.

McCloskey, M., Caramazza, A., & Basili, A. (1985). Cognitive mechanisms in number processing and calculations: Evidence from dyscalculia. *Brain and Cognition, 4,* 171–196.

National Council of Teachers of Mathematics. (1998). *Principles and standards for school mathematics: Discussion draft.* Reston, VA: Author.

O'Boyle, M. W., & Benbow, C. P. (1990). Enhanced right hemisphere involvement during cognitive processing may relate to intellectual precocity. *Neuropsychologia, 28,* 211–216.

O'Boyle, M. W., & Gill, H. S. (1998). On the relevance of research findings in cognitive neuroscience to educational practice. *Educational Psychology Review, 10,* 397–410.

Oldfield, R. C. (1971). The assessment and analysis of handedness: Edinburgh inventory. *Neuropsychologia, 9,* 97–113.

Pesenti, M., Seron, X., & Van Der Linden, M. (1994). Selective impairment as evidence for mental organization of arithmetical facts: BB, a case of preserved subtraction? *Cortex, 30,* 661–671.

Peterson, P. L., Carpenter, T. P., Fennema, E., & Loef, M. (1989). Teacher's pedagogical content beliefs in mathematics. *Cognition and Instruction, 6,* 1–40.

Pinker, S. (1997). *How the mind works.* New York: Norton.

Resnick, L. B., & Omanson, S. F. (1987). Learning to understand arithmetic. In R. Glaser (Ed.), *Advances in instructional psychology* (Vol. 3, pp. 41–95). Hillsdale, NJ: Erlbaum.

Siegler, R. S. (1991). Strategy choice and strategy discovery. *Learning and Instruction, 1,* 89–102.

Sweller, J., & Cooper, G. A. (1985). The use of examples as a substitute for problem solving in learning algebra. *Cognition and Instruction, 2,* 59–89.

PART SIX

THE LEARNING BRAIN

THE ARTS

20

THE BRAIN AND THE ARTS

David A. Sousa

The quality of civilization can be measured through its music, dance, drama, architecture, visual art, and literature. We must give our children knowledge and understanding of civilization's most profound works.

—Ernest L. Boyer

WE HAVE NEVER DISCOVERED a culture on this planet, past or present, that doesn't have art. Yet there have been a number of cultures—even today—that don't have reading and writing. Why is that? One likely explanation is that the activities represented by the arts—dance, music, drama, and visual arts—are basic to the human experience and necessary for survival. If they weren't, why would they have been part of every civilization from the Cro-Magnon cave dwellers to the urban citizens of the 21st century?

The Arts Are Basic to the Human Experience

As we learn more about the brain, we continue to find clues as to why the activities required for the arts are so fundamental to brain function. Music: It seems that certain structures in the auditory cortex respond only to musical tones. Dance: A portion of the cerebrum and most of the cerebellum are devoted to initiating and coordinating all kinds of movement, from intense running to the delicate sway of the arms. Drama: Specialized areas of the cerebrum focus on spoken language acquisition and call on the limbic system to provide the emotional component. Visual arts: The internal visual processing system can recall reality or create fantasy with the same ease.

These cerebral talents did not develop by accident. They are the result of many centuries of interaction between humans and their environment, and the continued existence of these talents indicates they contribute in some way to our survival. In those cultures that do not have reading and writing, the arts are the media through which that culture's history, mores, and values are transmitted to the younger generations and perpetuated. They also transmit more basic information necessary for the culture's survival, such as how and what to hunt for food and how to defend the village from predators.

Consequently, art is an important force behind group survival. For example, about 1,000 of the 6,500 languages on this planet are spoken in just one place—New Guinea! Each language is totally unrelated to any other known language in New Guinea (or elsewhere) and is spoken by a tribe of just a few thousand people living within a ten-mile radius. Even more astonishing is that each tribe has its own music, visual arts, and dance (Diamond, 1992).

In modern cultures, the arts are rarely thought of as survival skills, but rather as frills—the esthetic product of a wealthy society with lots of time to spare. In fact, people pay high ticket prices to see the arts performed professionally, leading to the belief that the arts are highly valued. This cultural support is often seen in high schools, which have their choruses, bands, drama classes, and an occasional dance troupe.

Yet seldom do public elementary schools enjoy this continuous support, precisely when the young brain is most adept at refining the skills needed to develop artistic talent (several private school initiatives have been the exception, most notably the Montessori schools and the Waldorf schools). Furthermore, when school budgets get tight, elementary grade art and music programs are among the first to be reduced or eliminated. Now, pressure from the No Child Left Behind Act to improve reading and mathematics achievement is prompting elementary schools to trade off instruction in the arts for more classroom preparation for the Act's high-stakes testing.

Why Teach the Arts?

The basic arguments I make here are these:

  ○ The arts play an important role in human development, enhancing
    the growth of cognitive, emotional, and psychomotor pathways.

○ Schools have an obligation to expose children to the arts at the earliest possible time and to consider the arts as fundamental—not optional—curriculum areas.

○ Learning the arts provides a higher quality of human experience throughout a person's lifetime.

The Arts and the Young Brain

. . . Much of what young children do as play—singing, drawing, dancing—are natural forms of art. These activities engage all the senses and help wire the brain for successful learning. When children enter school, these art activities need to be continued and enhanced. The cognitive areas are developed as the child learns songs and rhymes, and creates drawings and finger paintings. The dancing and movements during play develop gross motor skills, and the sum of these activities enhances emotional well-being.

The arts also contribute to the education of young children by helping them realize the breadth of human experience, see the different ways humans express sentiments and convey meaning, and develop subtle and complex forms of thinking (Eisner, 2002a).

The Arts Develop Cognitive Growth

Although the arts are often thought of as separate subjects, like chemistry or algebra, they really are a collection of skills and thought processes that transcend all areas of human engagement. When taught well, the arts develop cognitive competencies that benefit learners in every aspect of their education and prepare them for the demands of the 21st century. Elliot Eisner (2002b) of Stanford University identifies these eight competencies:

○ *The perception of relationships.* Creating a work in music, words, or any other art discipline helps students recognize how parts of a work influence each other and interact. For example, this is the kind of skill that enables an executive to appreciate the way a particular system affects every other subsystem in an organization.

○ *An attention to nuance.* The arts teach students that small differences can have large effects. Great amounts of visual reasoning go into decisions about nuance, form, and color to make an art work satisfying. In writing, similarly, great attention to detail in use of language is needed to employ allusion, innuendo, and metaphor.

○ *The perspective that problems can have multiple solutions, and questions can have multiple answers.* Good things can be done in different ways. Schools often emphasize learning focused on a single correct answer. In business and in life, most difficult problems require looking at multiple options with differing priorities.

○ *The ability to shift goals in process.* Work in the arts helps students recognize and pursue goals that were not thought of at the beginning. Too often in schools, the relationship of means to ends is oversimplified. Arts help us see that ends can shift in process.

○ *The permission to make decisions in the absence of a rule.* Arithmetic has rules and measurable results, but many other things lack that kind of rule-governed specificity. In the absence of rules, it is personal judgment that allows one to assess what feels right and to decide when a task is well done.

○ *The use of imagination as the source of content.* Arts enhance the ability to visualize situations and use the mind's eye to determine the rightness of a planned action.

○ *The acceptance of operating within constraints.* No system, whether linguistic, numerical, visual, or auditory covers every purpose. Arts give students a chance to use the constraints of a medium to invent ways to exploit those constraints productively.

○ *The ability to see the world from an aesthetic perspective.* Arts help students frame the world in fresh ways—like seeing the Golden Gate Bridge from a design or poetic angle.

It is encouraging that more states have recently promoted the arts in their curriculum through policies, such as including the arts as part of high school graduation requirements, standards, and assessments. Although the extent of commitment varies, some states have developed more extensive programs in the arts for schools and created partnerships with state arts councils and local arts organizations. The Education Commission of the States is sponsoring a two-year initiative (2004 to 2006) to ensure that every child has the opportunity to learn about, enjoy, and participate in the arts.

My point is that the arts should be taught for the arts' sake, and one should not have to suggest that we teach the arts only because they enhance the learning of other academic subjects. Nonetheless, I am a realist, and I recognize that it is important, nonetheless, to document any spillover effects that learning the arts can have on learning other subjects. That is because of the risk that the arts will fall by the wayside as schools are held more accountable for improving achievement in language arts and mathematics, despite strong public support for arts programs.

The Sciences Need the Arts

Few people will argue against studying the natural sciences in the elementary and middle schools, and support remains strong for the sciences—including Advanced Placement courses—in high schools. When budgets get tight, some people even view music and other arts courses as a drain on the funds needed to preserve science and mathematics courses. Others often see science and the arts as polar opposites. The sciences are thought of as objective, logical, analytical, reproducible, and useful; the arts are supposed to be subjective, intuitive, sensual, unique, and frivolous. In the competition between the arts and sciences in U.S. society, the arts have frequently lost. Typically, more public and private funds are given to any single technical or scientific discipline than all the arts combined.

But scientists and mathematicians know that the arts are vital to their success and use skills borrowed from the arts as scientific tools. These include the ability to observe accurately, to think spatially (how does an object appear when I rotate it in my head?), and perceive kinesthetically (how does it move?). These skills are not usually taught as part of the science curriculum but are at home in writing, drama, painting, and music.

Indeed, the arts often inform the sciences (Root-Bernstein, 1997). For example:

○ Buckminster Fuller's geodesic domes can describe soccer balls and architectural buildings, as well as the structure of viruses and some recently discovered complex and enormous molecules.

○ NASA employs artists to design displays that present satellite data so that it is accurate, yet understandable.

○ A biochemist looks at the fiber folds in her weaving cloth as another way of explaining protein folding.

○ Computer engineers code messages to the frequencies of a specific song to prevent interception or blocking of the message, unless the decoder knows the song.

○ Genetic researchers convert complex data into musical notation to facilitate analysis of the data, as for example, decoding the sequence of genes in a chromosome.

Thus, playing the piano, writing a poem, or creating a painting sharpen observations, hone details, and put things into context. These are the same tools needed by a good scientist. The study of the arts not only allows students to develop skills that will improve the quality of their lives but also sustains the same creative base from which scientists and engineers seek to develop their innovations and breakthroughs of the future.

Impact of the Arts on Student Learning and Behavior

Arts Education and Arts Integration

Numerous research studies show that well-designed arts experiences produce positive academic and social effects as well as assist in the development of critical academic skills, basic and advanced literacy, and numeracy. The studies look at both stand-alone arts programs as well as programs that integrate concepts and skills from the arts into the many areas of study. One intriguing and important revelation of these studies is that the most powerful effects are found in programs that *integrate* the arts with subjects in the core curriculum.

Researchers speculate that arts integration causes both students and teachers to rethink how they view the arts and generates conditions that educational researchers and cognitive scientists say are ideal for learning. The arts are not just expressive and affective, they are deeply cognitive. They develop essential thinking tools: pattern recognition and development; mental representations of what is observed or imagined; symbolic, allegorical, and metaphorical representations; careful observation of the world; and abstraction from complexity. Studies repeatedly show that in schools where arts are integrated into the core curriculum (Rabkin & Redmond, 2004):

- Students have a greater emotional investment in their classes.
- Students work more diligently and learn from each other.
- Cooperative learning groups turn classrooms into learning communities.
- Parents become more involved.
- Teachers collaborate more.
- Art and music teachers become the center of multi-class projects.
- Learning in all subjects becomes attainable through the arts.
- Curriculum becomes more authentic, hands-on, and project-based.
- Assessment is more thoughtful and varied.
- Teachers' expectations for their students rise.

The following research studies are but a few of the many that have accumulated in recent years about the effects of art instruction on student learning. They include results from both stand-alone and arts integration programs.

SAT SCORES. The association between students taking arts courses and their SAT scores is one of the largest studies of its kind. It included over several years more than 10 million American high schoolers who responded to a questionnaire indicating the number of years of arts classes they took. The results were amazingly consistent (Vaughn & Winner, 2000).

- Students who took arts classes had higher math, verbal, and composite SAT scores than students who did not take arts classes.
- SAT scores increased linearly with the addition of more years of arts classes, that is, the more years of arts classes, the higher the SAT scores.
- The strongest relationship with SAT scores was found with students who took four or more years of arts classes.
- The correlations with mathematics scores were consistently smaller than those for verbal scores.
- Acting classes had the strongest correlation with verbal SAT scores. Acting classes and music history, theory, or appreciation had the strongest relationship with math SAT scores. However, all classifications of arts classes were found to have significant relationships with both verbal and math SAT scores.

It is important to note that although enrollment in arts courses is positively correlated with higher SAT verbal and mathematics scores, it does not prove that one caused the other. Perhaps there are other variables involved. Nonetheless, it is difficult to challenge the strength of this relationship, given the magnitude of the study.

DISAFFECTED STUDENTS. The arts reach students who are not otherwise being reached. Arts sometimes provide the only reason that certain students stay in touch with school. Without the arts, these young people would be left with no access to a community of learners. A ten-year ongoing study in the Chicago public schools shows test scores rising faster on the Iowa Test of Basic Skills reading section than a matched population (for neighborhood, family income, and academic performance) of sixth graders in the regular schools. A study of the Minneapolis schools showed that arts integration had positive effects on all students, but much more so with disadvantaged students (Rabkin & Redmond, 2004). In Florida, 41 percent of potential dropout students said something about the arts kept them in school. Further, these students were more engaged in their art classes than in academic classes (Barry, Taylor, & Walls, 2002).

DIFFERENT LEARNING STYLES. Ample research evidence indicates that students learn in many different ways. This research also notes that some students can become behavior problems if conventional classroom practices are not engaging them. Success in the arts is often a bridge to successful learning in other areas, thereby raising a student's self-concept. Table 20.1 shows how students involved in arts-based youth organizations have a better self-concept than a standard student population. These numbers are particularly significant considering that students in the arts organizations are twice as likely to have stressful home situations involving parents getting a divorce, going on and off welfare, or losing a job. The students in this sample noted how the arts allowed them to express pent-up feelings and to gain some distance from these problems by talking about them, thinking, and listening (Fiske, 1999).

PERSONAL AND INTERPERSONAL CONNECTIONS. The arts connect students to themselves and each other. Creating art is a personal experience, as students draw upon their own resources to produce the result.

Table 20.1. Percentage of Students in Standard School Population and in Arts-Based Youth Organizations Reporting a Positive Perception of Self.

	Standard School Population	Arts-Based Youth
Organizations		
Student feels good about him/herself.	76.2	92.3
Student feels s/he is a person of worth.	75.9	90.9
Student is able to do things as well as others.	76.2	88.8
Student, on the whole, is satisfied with self.	70.7	84.6

Source: Fiske (1999).

This is a much deeper involvement than just reading text to get an answer. Studies indicate that the attitudes of young people toward one another improve through their arts learning experiences. For instance, more than 2,400 elementary and middle school students from 18 public schools participated in a study that showed students in arts-rich schools scoring higher in creativity and several measures of academic self-concept than students in schools without that level of arts instruction (Burton, Horowitz, & Abeles, 2000).

SCHOOL AND CLASSROOM CLIMATE. The arts transform the environment for learning. Schools become places of discovery when the arts are the focus of the learning environment. Arts change the school culture, break down barriers between curriculum areas, and can even improve the school's physical appearance. Because administrators and teachers determine a school's climate, a study of 29 arts-rich New York City schools compared some indicators of school climate to the remaining, non-arts schools. In the arts-rich schools, administrators encouraged teachers to take risks, broaden the curriculum, and learn new skills. The teachers had a significantly higher degree of innovation in their instruction, were more supportive of students, and had greater interest in their own professional development. Once again, the arts-rich program had a much greater impact on these results than did the students' socioeconomic status (Fiske, 1999).

GIFTED AND TALENTED STUDENTS. The arts provide new challenges for students already considered successful. Students who outgrow their learning environment usually get bored and complacent. The arts offer a chance for unlimited challenge. For instance, older students may teach and mentor younger ones who are learning to play musical instruments, and some advanced students may work with professional artists.

THE WORLD OF WORK. The arts connect learning experiences to the world of everyday work. The adult workplace has changed. The abilities to generate ideas, bring ideas to life, and communicate them to others are keys to workplace success. Whether in a classroom or in a studio as an artist, the student is learning and practicing future workplace behaviors.

Let's take a look at the three major forms of artistic expression—music, visual arts, and dance and drama—and observe what brain research is telling us. What impact will these studies have on student learning and success?

Music

Music exerts a powerful effect on the brain through intellectual and emotional stimulation. It can also affect our body by altering our heart rate, breathing, blood pressure, pain threshold, and muscle movements. These responses result from the activation of neural networks that include the frontal cortex, the amygdala, and other limbic areas involved in motivation and reward.

Is Music Inborn?

Many researchers now believe that the ability to perceive and enjoy music is an inborn human trait. But is there any credible evidence to support this biological basis of music? First of all, any behavior thought to have a biological foundation must be universal. Even though the uses of music may vary across past and current cultures, all cultures do sing and associate certain meanings and emotions with music.

Second, biologically based behaviors should reveal themselves early in life. Researchers have shown that infants of just three months old can learn and remember to move an overhead crib mobile when a certain song is played. Thus, infants can use music as a retrieval cue. In addition, the memory of the specific song lasted more than seven days (Fagan et al., 1997). Babies can also differentiate between two adjacent musical tones and can recognize a melody when it is played in a different key (Weinberger, 2004). At the age of seven months, infants can categorize rhythmic and melodic patterns on the basis of underlying meter (Hannon & Johnson, 2005). Moreover, preschool children spontaneously use music in their communication and play.

Third, if music has a strong biological component, then it should exist in other animals. Monkeys, for example, can form musical abstractions, such as determining harmonic patterns. Although many animals use musical sounds to attract mates and signal danger, only humans have developed a sophisticated and unlimited musical repertoire.

Fourth, if music has biological roots, we might expect the brain to have specialized areas for music—and it does. For example, areas in the auditory cortex are organized to process pitch. Furthermore, the brain's ability to respond emotionally to music is connected to biology and culture. The biological aspect is supported by the fact that the brain has specialized areas that respond only to music, and these areas are able to stimulate the limbic system, provoking an emotional response. PET [positron emission tomography] scans show that the neural areas stimulated depend on the type of music—melodic tunes stimulate areas that evoke pleasant feelings, whereas dissonant sounds activate other limbic areas that produce unpleasant emotions (Blood, Zatorre, Bermudez, & Evans, 1999; Menon & Levitin, 2005).

Effects of Listening to Music Versus Creating Instrumental Music

No one arts area has gained more notoriety in recent years than the impact of music on the brain. Numerous books are on the market touting the so-called Mozart Effect and promising that music can do all sorts of things from relieving pain, to increasing a child's IQ, to improving mathematics skills. To what degree are these claims backed by credible scientific evidence? As with most claims of this nature, there is a growing body of scientific data, followed by media attention and a lot of hype. Let's try to sort out what the research in music is saying so that we can reap its benefits while making informed decisions about the validity of the assertions.

Research on the effects of music on the brain and body can be divided into the effects of *listening* to music, and the effects of *creating* or *producing* music on an instrument, especially an acoustic rather than an electronic one. The brain and body respond differently in these two situations. Unfortunately, not enough attention has been paid to this crucial distinction. Consequently, people have mistakenly assumed that the results of studies that involved creating music would be repeated when listening to music. If educators want to use the research on the effects of music to benefit students, then it is important that they differentiate the studies on listening from those on creating music.

HOW THE BRAIN LISTENS TO MUSIC. The sounds of music are transmitted to the inner ear and are broken down according to the specific frequencies that make up the sounds (Figure 20.1). Different cells in the *cochlea* respond to different frequencies, and their signals are mapped out in the auditory cortex, especially in the right hemisphere in which perceptions of pitch, melody, timbre, and harmony emerge. This information is then transmitted to the frontal lobe where the music can be linked to emotion, thoughts, and past experiences. Over time, the auditory cortex is "retuned" by experience so that more cells become sensitive to important sounds and musical tones. This sets the stage for the processing of the more complex music patterns of melody, harmony, and rhythm.

Each hemisphere of the brain contains areas that respond to both music and language. But . . . the left hemisphere also contains regions of

Figure 20.1.

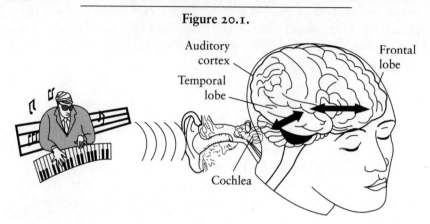

Sound entering the ear is converted into nerve impulses in the cochlea. These impulses are transmitted to the auditory cortex in the temporal lobe in which specialized regions, especially in the right hemisphere, analyze pitch and timbre. Information from the auditory cortex is transmitted to the frontal lobe, which associates the sound of music with thought and stimulates emotions and past experiences.

specialization that respond only to language, and the right hemisphere has areas devoted exclusively to music perception. This explains why some people can be extraordinarily talented in language skills but have difficulty humming a melody. The reverse situation occurs in the brains of individuals with savant syndrome, who are talented musicians despite severe language retardation.

The discovery that the auditory cortex (located in the temporal lobes) in the right hemisphere has regions that respond only to music came from studies comparing patients who have damage to their left or right temporal lobes. Patients with right temporal lobe damage have lost the ability to recognize familiar songs, a condition known as *amusia*. However, only the response to music is affected. The patients can still recognize human voices, traffic sounds, and other auditory information.

Music can also be imagined because people have stored representations of songs and the sounds of musical instruments in their long-term memory. When a song is imagined, the brain cells that are activated are identical to those used when a person actually hears music from the outside world. But when a song is imagined, brain scans show that the visual cortex is also stimulated so that visual patterns are imaged as well. The mechanism that triggers musical imagery is not yet understood, but it is not uncommon for people to have songs running through their heads when they get up in the morning.

THE BENEFITS OF LISTENING TO MUSIC

Therapeutic Benefits. For many years, medical researchers and practitioners have reported on the therapeutic effects of music to relieve stress, diminish pain, and treat other more severe disabilities, such as mental retardation, Parkinson's disease, Alzheimer's disease, and visual and hearing impairments. Other studies have shown that listening to music can boost immune function in children and that premature babies exposed to lullabies in the hospital went home earlier. The sheer volume of studies and positive results attest to music's therapeutic benefits.

How does music work this magic? That is still a mystery, but there are some important hints. Researchers have known for a long time that music can directly influence blood pressure, pulse, and the electric activity of muscles. Newer evidence shows that music may even help build and strengthen connections between brain cells in the cortex. This effect is important, and some doctors are already using music to help rehabilitate stroke patients. Some stroke patients who have lost their ability to speak retain their ability to sing. By getting patients to sing what they want to say their fluency improves, and therapists can use existing pathways to retrain the speech centers of the brain.

EDUCATIONAL BENEFITS. The notion that music could affect cognitive performance catapulted from the research laboratory to the television talk shows in 1993 when Frances Rauscher and Gordon Shaw conducted a study using 84 college students. They reported that the students' spatial-temporal reasoning—the ability to form mental images from physical objects, or to see patterns in time and space—improved after listening to Mozart's Sonata for Two Pianos in D Major (K.448) for 10 minutes. But the students' improved abilities faded within an hour (Rauscher, Shaw, & Ky, 1993).

The results of this study, promptly dubbed "The Mozart Effect," were widely publicized and soon reinterpreted to incorrectly imply that listening to a Mozart sonata would enhance intelligence by raising IQ. In fact, the study reported that the music improved only spatial-temporal reasoning (one of many components of total IQ) and that the effect quickly faded. But the results did encourage the researchers to go further and test whether *creating* music would have a longer-lasting effect.

Shaw was convinced that listening to the complex melodic variations in Mozart's sonata (K.448) stimulated the frontal cortex more than simpler music. He and several colleagues tested this idea by having subjects take turns listening to Mozart's sonata (K.448), Beethoven's *Für Elise*, and popular piano music. The fMRIs showed that both the popular and the Beethoven piano music activated only the auditory cortex in all subjects.

The Mozart sonata, however, activated the auditory as well as the frontal cortex in all of the subjects, leading Shaw to suggest that there *is* a neurological basis for the "Mozart Effect" (Muftuler, Bodner, Shaw, & Nalcioglu, 1999).

Subsequent studies confirm that listening to Mozart enhances various types of spatial and temporal reasoning tasks, especially problems requiring a sequence of mental images to correctly reassemble objects. The data suggest that the effect is real, yet it can occur with other kinds of music besides Mozart. However, researchers do not yet know conclusively why the effect occurs. Nonetheless, the effect is important to educators because it shows that passive listening to music appears to stimulate spatial thinking, and that neural networks normally associated with one kind of mental activity can readily share the cognitive processes involved in a different activity. So learning or thinking in one discipline may not be completely independent of another (Hetland, 2000a).

Several studies have shown that listening to certain music can stimulate the parts of the brain that are responsible for memory recall and visual imagery (Nakamura et al., 1999). Researchers have also found that listening to background music enhances the efficiency of those working with their hands. In a study of surgeons, for example, background music enhanced their alertness and concentration (Restak, 2003). This explains why background music in the classroom helps many students stay focused while completing certain learning tasks. However, one must exercise caution in selecting the *type* of background music. Several studies show that overly stimulating music serves more as a distraction and interferes with cognitive performance (Hallam, 2002).

Creating Music

Although passive listening to music does have some therapeutic and short-term educational benefits, the making of music seems to provide many more cerebral advantages. Learning to play a musical instrument challenges the brain in new ways. In addition to being able to discern different tone patterns and groupings, new motor skills must be learned and coordinated in order to play the instrument. These new learnings cause profound and seemingly permanent changes in brain structure. For example, the auditory cortex, the motor cortex, the cerebellum, and the corpus callosum are larger in musicians than in non-musicians.

This raises an interesting question: Are the brains of musicians different because of their training and practice in music, or did these differences exist before they learned music? The answer came when researchers trained non-musicians to listen for small changes in pitch and similar musical components. In just three weeks, their brains showed increased activation in the auditory cortex. This suggests that the brain differences in highly skilled musicians are more likely the result of training and not inherited (Restak, 2003). In support of this notion, another study compared 5- to 7-year-olds who were beginning piano or string lessons with a similar group not beginning instrument training. The researchers found no pre-existing neural, cognitive, motor, or musical differences between the two groups and no correlations between music perceptual skills or visual-spatial measures. As in previous studies, correlations were found between music perceptual skills and phonemic awareness (Norton et al., 2005). No doubt some genetic traits enhance music learning, but it seems that most musicians are made, not born.

Benefits of Creating Music

The effects of learning to play an instrument can begin at an early age. One major study involved 78 preschoolers from three California preschools, including one serving mostly poor, inner-city families. The children were divided into four groups. One group (Keyboard) took individual, 12- to 15-minute piano lessons twice a week along with singing instruction. Another group (Singing) took 30-minute singing lessons five days a week, and a third group (Computer) trained on computers. The fourth group received no special instruction. All students took tests before the lessons began to measure different types of spatial-reasoning skills.

SPATIAL-TEMPORAL TASK. After six months, the children who received six months of piano keyboard training had improved their scores by 34 percent on tests measuring spatial-temporal reasoning (Figure 20.2). On other tasks, there was no difference in scores. Furthermore, the enhancement lasted for days, indicating a substantial change in spatial-temporal function. The other three groups, in comparison, had only slight improvement on all tasks (Rauscher et al., 1997). Subsequent studies continue to show a strong relationship between creating music with keyboards and the enhancement of spatial reasoning in young children (Hetland, 2000b; Rauscher & Zupan, 2000).

Why did piano keyboard training improve test performance by 34 percent while the computer keyboard training didn't? Remember that the study measured spatial-temporal improvements only. As this and other studies show, music training seems to specifically influence neural

Figure 20.2. Spatial-Temporal Task.

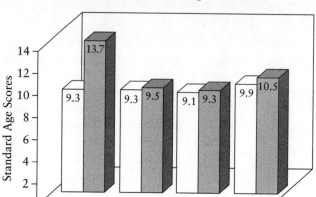

The graph shows the results of a spatial-temporal task performed by the preschool students before and after piano keyboard training, group singing, training on the computer, and no lessons. National standard age scores for all ages are 10, showing that these were average children before training.

pathways responsible for spatial-temporal reasoning, and that effect is more noticeable in the young brain. This may be due to the combination of tactile input from striking the piano keys, auditory input from the sounds of the notes, and the visual information of where one's hand is on the keyboard. This is a much more complex interaction than from the computer keyboard. Computers, of course, are very valuable teaching tools, but when it comes to developing the neural pathways responsible for spatial abilities, the piano keyboard is much more effective.

CREATING MUSIC BENEFITS VERBAL MEMORY. Numerous studies have shown that musical training improves verbal memory. Researchers in one study administered memory tests to 90 boys between the ages of 6 and 15. Half belonged to their school's strings program for one to five years, while the other half had no musical training. The musically trained students had better verbal memory, but showed no differences in visual memory. Apparently, musical training's impact on the left temporal lobe seems to improve the ability of that region (where Broca's and Wernicke's areas are located) to handle verbal learning. Furthermore, the memory benefits of musical training are long-lasting. Students who dropped out of the music training group were tested a year later and found to retain the verbal memory advantage they had gained earlier (Ho, Cheung, & Chan, 2003).

Does Creating Music Affect Ability in Other Subjects?

Research studies continue to look for the impact that music instruction can have on learning in other subject areas. Two subject areas of particular interest are mathematics and reading.

MUSIC AND MATHEMATICS. Of all the academic subjects, mathematics seems to be most closely connected to music. Music relies on fractions for tempo and on time divisions for pacing, octaves, and chord intervals. Here are some mathematical concepts that are basic to music.

- ○ *Patterns.* Music is full of patterns of chords, notes, and key changes. Musicians learn to recognize these patterns and use them to vary melodies. Inverting patterns, called counterpoint, helps form different kinds of harmonies.
- ○ *Counting.* Counting is fundamental to music because one must count beats, count rests, and count how long to hold notes.
- ○ *Geometry.* Music students use geometry to remember the correct finger positions for notes or chords. Guitar players' fingers, for example, form triangular shapes on the neck of the guitar.
- ○ *Ratios and Proportions, and Equivalent Fractions.* Reading music requires an understanding of ratios and proportions, that is, a whole note needs to be played twice as long as a half note, and four times as long as a quarter note. Because the amount of time allotted to one beat is a mathematical constant, the duration of all the notes in a musical piece is relative to one another on the basis of that constant. It is also important to understand the rhythmic difference between ¼ and ⁴⁄₄ time signatures.
- ○ *Sequences.* Music and mathematics are related through sequences called intervals. A mathematical interval is the difference between two numbers; a musical interval is the ratio of their frequencies. Here's another sequence: Arithmetic progressions in music correspond to geometric progressions in mathematics.

Because of the many common mathematical concepts that underlie music, scientists have long wondered how these two abilities are processed in the brain. Several recent fMRI studies have shown that musical training activated the same areas of the brain (mainly the left frontal cortex) that are also activated during mathematical processing. It may be, then, that early musical training begins to build the very same neural networks that will later be used to complete numerical and mathematical tasks (Schmithhorst & Holland, 2004).

Keyboard Training. Motivated by the studies showing that music improved spatial-temporal reasoning, Gordon Shaw set out to determine whether this enhancement would help young students learn specific mathematics skills. He focused on proportional mathematics, which is particularly difficult for many elementary students, and which is usually taught with ratios, fractions, and comparative ratios. Shaw and his colleagues worked with 136 second-grade students from a low socioeconomic neighborhood in Los Angeles. One group (Piano-ST) was given four months of piano keyboard training, as well as computer training and time to play with a newly designed computer software to teach proportional mathematics. The second group (English-ST) was given computer training in English and time to play with the software; the third group (No Lessons) had neither music nor specific computer lessons, but did play with the computer software.

The Piano-ST group scored 27 percent higher on proportional math and fractions subtests than the English-ST students, and 166 percent higher than the No Lessons group (Figure 20.3). These findings are significant because proportional mathematics is not usually introduced until fifth or sixth grade, and because a grasp of proportional mathematics is essential to understanding science and mathematics at higher levels (Graziano, Peterson, & Shaw, 1999).

Strings Training. Begun in 2000, the Newark (NJ) Early Strings Program created a partnership with the New Jersey Symphony Orchestra to provide Suzuki-based string instruction to students in Newark's elementary schools, starting in second grade. A recent assessment showed that students in the program in grades two through four performed significantly better on standardized tests in language arts and mathematics than their peers. The program also had a positive effect on the students' self-esteem and self-discipline, and increased parent involvement in the schools (Abeles & Sanders, 2005).

A 1998 study showed how creating music can make a difference for students from low socioeconomic status. The low socioeconomic students who took music lessons from eighth through twelfth grade increased their

Figure 20.3. Piano and Computer Study Groups.

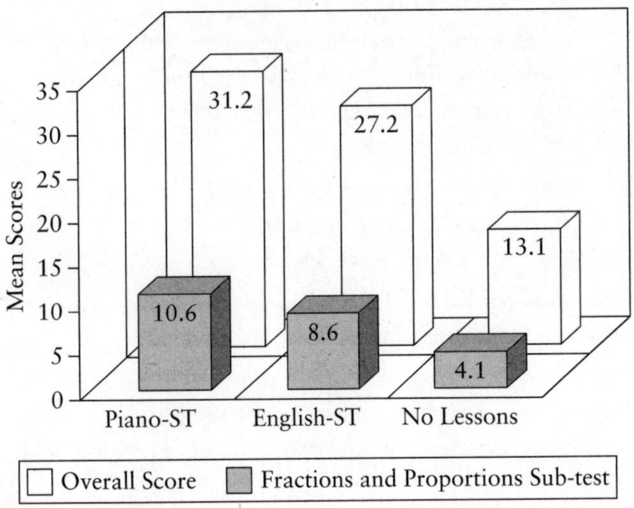

The mean overall, and fraction and proportions sub-test scores of the group that had piano and computer training with special software (Piano-ST), the group with computer and software (English-ST), and the group with no lessons.

test scores in mathematics and scored significantly higher than those low socioeconomic students who were not involved in music. Mathematics scores more than doubled, and history and geography scores increased by 40 percent (Catterall, Chapleau, & Iwanga, 1999). A subsequent review of studies involving more that 300,000 secondary school students confirmed the strong association between music instruction and achievement in mathematics. Of particular interest is an analysis of six experimental studies that revealed a causal relationship between music and mathematics performance, and that the relationship had grown stronger in recent years (Vaughn, 2000). Isn't this something that educators should consider in planning the core curriculum? If numeracy is so important, perhaps every student should learn to play a musical instrument.

MUSIC AND READING. Several studies confirm a strong association between music instruction and standardized tests of reading ability. Although we cannot say that this is a causal association (that taking music instruction *caused* improvement in reading ability), this consistent finding in a large group of studies builds confidence that there is a strong relationship (Butzlaff, 2000). Researchers suggest that this strong relationship may result because of positive transfer occurring between language and reading. Their rationale is as follows:

- Although music and written language use highly differentiated symbol systems, both involve similar decoding and comprehension reading processes, such as reading from left to right, sequential ordering of content, etc.
- There are interesting parallels in the underlying concepts shared between music and language reading skills, such as sensitivity to phonological or tonal distinctions.
- Reading music involves the simultaneous incorporation and reading of written text with music.
- Learning in the context of a highly motivated social context, such as music ensembles, may lead to a greater desire for academic responsibility and performance that enhances reading achievement.

Studies done with 4- and 5-year-old children revealed that the more music skills children had, the greater their degree of phonological awareness and reading development. Apparently, music perception taps and enhances auditory areas that are related to reading (Anvari, Trainor, Woodside, & Levy, 2002).

The Visual Arts

The human brain has the incredible ability to form images and representations of the real world or sheer fantasy within its mind's eye. Solving the mystery of DNA's structure, for example, required Watson and Crick in the early 1950s to imagine numerous three-dimensional models until they hit on the only image that explained the molecule's peculiar behavior—the spiral helix. This was an incredible marriage of visual art and biology that changed the scientific world forever. Exactly how the brain performs the functions of imagination and meditation may be uncertain, but no one doubts the importance of these valuable talents, which have allowed human beings to develop advanced and sophisticated cultures.

Imagery

For most people, the left hemisphere specializes in coding information verbally whereas the right hemisphere codes information visually. Although teachers spend much time talking (and sometimes have their students talk) about the learning objective, little time is given to developing visual cues. This process, called *imagery,* is the mental visualization of objects, events, and arrays related to the new learning and represents a major way of storing information in the brain. Imagery can take place in two ways: *imaging* is the visualization in the mind's eye of something that the person has actually experienced; *imagining* depicts something the person has not yet experienced and, therefore, has no limits.

A mental image is a pictorial representation of something physical or of an experience. The more information an image contains, the richer it is. Some people are more capable of forming rich images than others, but the research evidence is clear: Individuals can be taught to search their minds for images and be guided through the process to select appropriate images that, through hemispheric integration, enhance learning and increase retention. When the brain creates images, the same parts of the visual cortex are activated as when the eyes process real world input. Thus, the powerful visual processing system is available even when the brain is creating internal pictures in the mind's eye (Kosslyn et al., 1999; Mazard, Laou, Joliot, & Mellet, 2005).

The human brain's ability to do imagery with such efficiency is likely due to the importance of imagery in survival. When confronted with a potentially life-threatening event—say, a car speeding toward you in the wrong traffic lane—the brain's visual processing system and the frontal lobes process several potential scenarios in a fraction of a second and initiate a reflex reaction that is most likely to keep you alive. As students today engage with electronic media that produce images, they are not getting adequate practice in generating their own imaging and imagining, skills that not only affect survival but also increase retention and, through creativity, improve the quality of life.

Training students in imagery encourages them to search long-term memory for appropriate images and to use them more like a movie than a photograph. For example, one recalls the house one lived in for many years. From the center hall with its gleaming chandelier, one mentally turns left and "walks" through the living room to the sun room beyond. To the right of the hall is the paneled dining room and then the kitchen with the avocado green appliances and oak cabinets. In the back, one sees the flagstone patio, the manicured lawn, and the garden with its variety of flowers. The richness of the image allows one to focus on just a portion of it and generate additional amounts of detail. In this image, one could mentally stop in any room and visualize the furniture and other decor. Imagery should become a regular part of classroom strategies as early as kindergarten. In the primary grades, the teacher should supply the images to ensure accuracy.

Imagery can be used in many classroom activities, including notetaking, cooperative learning groups, and alternative assessment options. Mindmapping is a specialized form of imagery that originated when the left-brain/right-brain research emerged in the 1970s. The process combines language with images to help show relationships between and among concepts, and how they connect to a key idea. Buzan (1989) and Hyerle (2004) illustrate different ways in which mind maps can be drawn.

Research on Visual Arts and Learning

A review of the research literature shows a serious lack of studies that examine the impact of the visual arts and imagery on learning. One reason is the difficulty in determining which aspects of visual arts training (apart from imagery) are at work in programs that integrate visual art into core curriculum subjects.

Most studies in this area relate to imagery in sports. Coaches have known for a long time that athletes who use imagery to mentally rehearse what they intend to do perform better than if they do not use imagery. Studies reveal that the more time and intensity devoted to imagery, the better the athletic performance (Cumming & Hall, 2002; Harwood, Cumming, & Hall, 2003).

Apart from sports, one meta-analysis did look at imagery and creativity. Data from nine studies involving nearly 1,500 students were analyzed and showed a statistically significant association between imagery and creativity. Not surprisingly, students who used more imagery during learning displayed more creativity in their discussions, modeling, and assessments (LeBoutillier & Marks, 2003).

Movement

The mainstream educational community has often regarded thinking and movement as separate functions, assigning them different priorities. Activities involving movement, such as dance, theater, and occasionally sports, are often reduced or eliminated when school budgets get tight. But as brain studies probe deeper into the relationship between body and mind, the importance of movement to cognitive learning becomes very apparent.

Movement and the Brain

A NEW ROLE FOR THE CEREBELLUM. . . . The cerebellum [has a long-known role] in coordinating the performance of motor skills. For several decades, neuroscientists assumed that the cerebellum carried out its coordinating role by communicating exclusively with the cerebrum's motor cortex. But this view did not explain why some patients with damage to the cerebellum also showed impaired cognitive function. Recent research using scans centered on the cerebellum shows that its nerve fibers communicate with other areas of the cerebrum as well.

Studies have found that the cerebellum plays an important role in attention, long-term memory, spatial perception, impulse control, and the frontal lobe's cognitive functions—the same areas that are stimulated during learning (Bower & Parsons, 2003). It seems that the more we study the cerebellum, the more we realize that movement is inescapably linked to learning and memory (Figure 20.4).

Autism and ADHD. Further evidence of the link between the cerebellum and cognitive function has come from some studies of autism.

Figure 20.4.

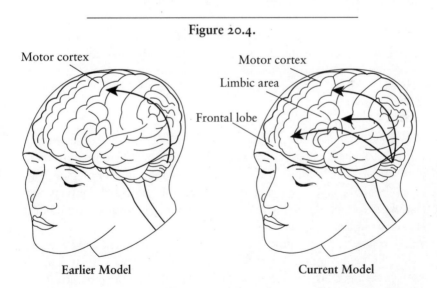

Earlier Model   Current Model

Researchers earlier thought that the cerebellum's role was limited to coordinating movement with the motor cortex. Recent studies indicate that the cerebellum also acts to support limbic functions (such as attention and impulse control) and cognitive processes in the frontal lobe.

Brain images show that many autistic children have smaller brain stems and cerebellums and fewer cerebellar neurons. This cerebellar deficit may explain the impaired cognitive and motor functions seen in autism (Courchesne, 1999; Rodier, 2000). Using movement and other intense sensory experiences, therapy centers working with autistic children and those with attention-deficit hyperactivity disorder (ADHD) are reporting remarkable improvement in their ability to focus their attention to complete a task, as well as an increased ability to listen quietly when others share ideas.

PHYSICAL EXERCISE IMPROVES BRAIN PERFORMANCE. Even short, moderate physical exercise can improve brain performance. Studies indicate that physical activity increases the number of capillaries in the brain, thus facilitating blood transport. It also increases the amount of oxygen in the blood, which the brain needs for fuel. The concentration of oxygen affects the brain's ability to carry out its tasks. Studies confirm that higher concentrations of oxygen in the blood significantly enhanced cognitive performance in healthy young adults. They were able to recall more words from a list and perform visual and spatial tasks faster. Moreover, their cognitive abilities varied directly with the amount of oxygen in the brain (Chung et al., 2004; Scholey et al., 1999).

Despite the realization that physical activity enhances brain function and learning, secondary students spend most of their classroom time sitting. Although enrollment in high school daily physical education classes has risen slightly in recent years, it is only about 25 percent.

Implications for Schools

Armed with the knowledge that movement is connected to cognitive learning, teachers and administrators need to encourage more movement in all classrooms at all grade levels. At some point in every lesson, students should be up and moving about, preferably talking about their new learning. Not only does the movement increase cognitive function, but it also helps students use up some kinesthetic energy—the "wiggles," if you will—so they can settle down and concentrate better later. Mild exercise before a test also makes sense. So does teaching dance to all students in K–8 classrooms. Dance techniques help students become more aware of their physical presence, spatial relationships, breathing, and of timing and rhythm in movement.

Summarizing the research on the interplay of motion and the cognitive functions of the brain, we should consider using movement activities (Patterson, 1997) because they

○ Involve more sensory input, which is likely to hold the students' attention for a longer period of time.

○ More closely resemble what students would be doing outside of school. Many students are involved with interesting kinesthetic activities after school. Doing these types of activities in school awakens and maintains that interest.

○ Engage other cerebral aptitudes, such as music or visual-spatial skills, thus enhancing integration of sensory perception. This process will help students make connections between new and past learnings.

○ Are more likely to lead to long-term recall. You can easily recall that time you participated in the school play or other public performance. Your memory is clear because this experience activated your kinesthetic sensory system.

○ Stimulate the right hemisphere and help the student perceive concepts in their totality, rather than in the traditional language patterns (left hemisphere) that are so common.

REFERENCES

Abeles, H. F., & Sanders, E. M. (2005). *Final assessment report: New Jersey Symphony Orchestra's Early Strings Program.* New York: Center for Arts Education Research, Columbia University.

Anvari, S. H., Trainor, L. J., Woodside, J., & Levy, B. A. (2002, October). Relations among musical skills, phonological processing, and early reading ability in preschool children. *Journal of Experimental Child Psychology, 83,* 111–130.

Barry, N., Taylor, J. & Walls, K. (2002). The role of the fine and performing arts in high school dropout prevention. In R. J. Deasy (Ed.), *Critical links: Learning in the arts and student academic and social development* (pp. 74–75). Washington, DC: Arts Education Partnership.

Blood, A. J., Zatorre, R. J., Bermudez, P. & Evans, A. C. (1999, April). Emotional responses to pleasant and unpleasant music correlate with activity in paralimbic brain regions. *Nature Neuroscience, 2,* 382–387.

Bower, J. M., & Parsons, L. M. (2003, August). Rethinking the lesser brain. *Scientific American, 289,* 51–57.

Burton, J. M., Horowitz, R., & Abeles, H. (2000). Learning in and through the arts: The question of transfer. *Studies in Art Education, 41,* 228–257.

Butzlaff, R. (2000, Fall). Can music be used to teach reading? *Journal of Aesthetic Education, 34,* 167–178.

Buzan, T. (1989). *Use both sides of your brain* (3rd ed.). New York: Penguin.

Catterall, J., Chapleau, R., & Iwanga, J. (1999, Fall). *Involvement in the arts and human development: Extending an analysis of general associations and introducing the special cases of intense involvement in music and in theater arts.* Monograph Series No. 11. Washington, DC: Americans for the Arts.

Chung, S-C., Tack, G-R., Lee, B., Eom, G-M., Lee, S-Y., & Sohn, J-H. (2004, December). The effect of 30% oxygen on visuospatial performance and brain activation: An fMRI study. *Brain and Cognition, 56,* 279–285.

Courchesne, E. (1999, March 23). An MRI study of autism: The cerebellum revisited. *Letter in Neurology, 52,* 1106–1107.

Cumming, J., & Hall, C. (2002, February). Deliberate imagery practice: The development of imagery skills in competitive athletes. *Journal of Sports Sciences, 20,* 137–145.

Diamond, J. (1992). *The third chimpanzee: The evolution and future of the human animal.* New York: Harper Perennial.

Eisner, E. (2002a, September). What the arts do for the young. *School Arts, 102,* 16–17.

Eisner, E. (2002b). *The arts and the creation of mind.* New Haven, CT: Yale University Press.

Fagan, J., Prigot, J., Carroll, M., Pioli, L., Stein, A., & Franco, A. (1997, December). Auditory context and memory retrieval in young infants. *Child Development, 68,* 1057–1066.

Fiske, E. B. (Ed.). (1999). *Champions of change: The impact of the arts on learning.* Washington, DC: President's Committee on the Arts and the Humanities.

Graziano, A. B., Peterson, M., & Shaw, G. L. (1999, March 15). Enhanced learning of proportional math through music training and spatial-temporal training. *Neurological Research, 21,* 139–152.

Hallam, S. (2002). The effects of background music on studying. In R. J. Deasy (Ed.), *Critical links: Learning in the arts and student academic and social development* (pp. 74–75). Washington, DC: Arts Education Partnership.

Hannon, E. E., & Johnson, S. P. (2005, June). Infants use meter to categorize rhythms and melodies: Implications for musical structure learning. *Cognitive Psychology, 50,* 354–377.

Harwood, C., Cumming, J., & Hall, C. (2003, September). Imagery use in elite youth sport participants: Reinforcing the applied significance of achievement goal theory. *Research Quarterly for Exercise and Sport, 74,* 292–300.

Hetland, L. (2000a, Fall). Listening to music enhances spatial-temporal reasoning: Evidence for the "Mozart Effect." *Journal of Aesthetic Education, 34,* 105–148.

Hetland, L. (2000b, Fall). Learning to make music enhance spatial reasoning. *Journal of Aesthetic Education, 34,* 179–238.

Ho, Y-C., Cheung, M-C., & Chan, A. S. (2003, July). Music training improves verbal but not visual memory: Cross-sectional and longitudinal explorations in children. *Neuropsychology, 17,* 439–450.

Hyerle, D. (2004). *Student successes with thinking maps: School-based research, results, and models for achievement using visual tools.* Thousand Oaks, CA: Corwin Press.

Kosslyn, S. M., Pascual-Leone, A., Felician, O., Camposano, S., Keenan, J. P., Thompson, W. L., Ganis, G., Sukel, K. E., & Alpert, N. M. (1999, April 2). The role of Area 17 in visual imagery: Convergent evidence from PET and rTMS. *Science, 284,* 167–170.

LeBoutillier, N., & Marks, D. F. (2003, February). Mental imagery and creativity: A meta-analytic review study. *British Journal of Psychology, 94,* 29–44.

Mazard, A., Laou, L., Joliot, M., & Mellet, E. (2005, August). Neural impact of the semantic content of visual mental images and visual percepts. *Cognitive Brain Research, 24,* 423–435.

Menon, V., & Levitin, D. J. (2005, October). The rewards of music listening: Response and physiological connectivity of the mesolimbic system. *Neuroimage, 28,* 175–184.

Muftuler, L. T., Bodner, M., Shaw, G. L., & Nalcioglu, O. (1999). *fMRI of Mozart effect using auditory stimuli.* Abstract presented at the 7th meeting of the International Society for Magnetic Resonance in Medicine, Philadelphia.

Nakamura, S., Sadato, N., Oohashi, T., Nishina, E., Fuwamoto, Y., & Yonekura, Y. (1999, November 19). Analysis of music-brain interaction with simultaneous measurement of regional cerebral blood flow and elec-troencephalogram beta rhythm in human subjects. *Neuroscience Letters, 275,* 222–226.

Norton, A., Winner, E., Cronin, K., Overy, K., Lee, D. J., & Schlaug, G. (2005). Are there pre-existing neural, cognitive, or motoric markers for musical ability? *Brain and Cognition.*

Patterson, M. N. (1997). *Every body can learn.* Tucson, AZ: Zephyr.

Rabkin, N., & Redmond, R. (2004). *Putting the arts in the picture: Reforming education in the 21st century.* Chicago: Columbia College.

Rauscher, F. H., Shaw, G. L., & Ky, K. N. (1993). Music and spatial task performance. *Nature, 365,* 311.

Rauscher, F. H., Shaw, G. L., Levine, L. J., Wright, E. L., Dennis, W. R., & Newcomb, R. L. (1997). Music training causes long-term enhancement of preschool children's spatial-temporal reasoning. *Neurological Research, 19,* 2–8.

Rauscher, F. H., & Zupan, M. A. (2000). Classroom keyboard instruction improves kindergarten children's spatial-temporal performance: A field experiment. *Early Childhood Research Quarterly, 15,* 215–228.

Restak, R. M. (2003). *The new brain: How the modern age is rewiring your mind.* New York: Rodale.

Rodier, P. (2000, February). The early origins of autism. *Scientific American, 282,* 56–63.

Root-Bernstein, R. S. (1997, July 11). Art for science's sake. *Chronicle of Higher Education,* B6.

Schmithhorst, V. J., & Holland, S. K. (2004, January). The effect of musical training on the neural correlates of math processing: A functional magnetic resonance imaging study in humans. *Neuroscience Letters, 354,* 193–196.

Scholey, A. B., Moss, M. C., Neave, N., & Wesnes, K. (1999, November). Cognitive performance, hyperoxia, and heart rate following oxygen administration in healthy young adults. *Physiological Behavior, 67,* 783–789.

Vaughn, K. (2000, Fall). Music and mathematics: Modest support for the oft-claimed relationship. *Journal of Aesthetic Education, 34,* 149–166.

Vaughn, K., & Winner, E. (2000, Fall). SAT scores of students who study the arts: What we can and cannot conclude about the association. *Journal of Aesthetic Education, 34,* 77–89.

Weinberger, N. M. (2004, November). Music and the brain. *Scientific American, 291,* 89–95.

21

THE ROLE OF THE ARTS IN TRANSFORMING CONSCIOUSNESS

EDUCATION IS THE PROCESS OF LEARNING HOW TO INVENT YOURSELF

Elliot W. Eisner

To understand the role of the arts in transforming consciousness we must start with the biological features of the human organism, for it is these features that make it possible for us humans to establish contact with the environment in and through which we live. That environment is, in its most fundamental state, a qualitative one made up of sights and sounds, tastes and smells that can be experienced through our sensory system. Although the world of the newborn may indeed be the blooming, buzzing confusion that William James once described, it is, even in its apparently chaotic condition, an empirical environment, an environment that all humans, even newborns, can experience.[1]

Experiencing the environment is, of course, a process that continues throughout life; it's the very stuff of life. It is a process that is shaped by culture, influenced by language, impacted by beliefs, affected by values, and moderated by the distinctive features of that part of ourselves we sometimes describe as our individuality. We humans give simultaneously

---

[1]William James, *The Principles of Psychology* (New York: Holt, 1896), 488.

both a personal and a cultural imprint to what we experience; the relation between the two is inextricable. But despite these mediating factors, factors that personalize and filter experience, our initial contact with the empirical world is dependent upon our biologically evolved sensory system. That system, an extension of our nervous system, is, as Susanne Langer says, "the organ of the mind." Listen as Susanne Langer, in her classic *Philosophy in a New Key,* describes the connection between the sensory system and the mind:

> The nervous system is the organ of the mind; its center is the brain, its extremities the sense-organs; and any characteristic function it may possess must govern the work of all of its parts. In other words, the activity of our senses is "mental" not only when it reaches the brain, but in its very inception, whenever the alien world outside impinges on the furthest and smallest receptor. All sensitivity bears the stamp of mentality. "Seeing," for instance, is not a passive process, by which meaningless impressions are stored up for the use of an organizing mind, which constructs forms out of these amorphous data to suit its own purposes. "Seeing" is itself a process of formulation; our understanding of the visible world begins in the eyes.[2]

The senses are our first avenues to consciousness. Without an intact sensory system we would be unaware of the qualities in the environment to which we now respond. That absence of consciousness would render us incapable of distinguishing friend from foe, of nourishing ourselves, or of communicating with others.

The ability to experience the qualitative world we inhabit is initially reflexive in character; we are biologically designed to suckle, to respond to temperature, to be sated with milk. Our biological system is designed to enable us to survive—with the help of others.[3] But we also learn. We learn to see, to hear, to discern the qualitative complexities of what we taste and touch. We learn to differentiate and discriminate, to recognize and to recall. What first was a reflex response, a function of instinct, becomes a gradual search for stimulation, differentiation, exploration, and eventually for meaning. Our sensory system becomes a means through which we pursue our own development. But the sensory system

---

[2]Susanne Langer, *Philosophy in a New Key* (Cambridge: Harvard University Press, 1979), 84.

[3]The human infant is one of the most dependent of living organisms over the longest period of time. Without adult assistance, it would perish.

does not work alone; it requires for its development the tools of culture: language, the arts, science, values, and the like. With the aid of culture we learn how to create ourselves.

The term *culture* is said to have hundreds of meanings. Two are particularly relevant to education, one anthropological, the other biological. A culture in the anthropological sense is a shared way of life. But the term *culture* in the biological sense refers to a medium for growing things. Schools, I believe, like the larger society of which they are a part, function as cultures in both senses of the term. They make possible a shared way of life, a sense of belonging and community, and they are a medium for growing things, in this case children's minds. How schools are organized, what is taught in them, the kind of norms they embrace, and the relationships they foster among adults and children all matter, for they all shape the experiences that students are likely to have and in the process influence who children will become. Experience is central to growth because experience is the medium of education.[4] Education, in turn, is the process of learning to create ourselves, and it is what the arts, both as a process and as the fruits of that process, promote. Work in the arts is not only a way of creating performances and products; it is a way of creating our lives by expanding our consciousness, shaping our dispositions, satisfying our quest for meaning, establishing contact with others, and sharing a culture.

Humans, of all living species, have the distinctive, if perhaps not the unique, ability to create a culture through which those in their community can grow. Humans can leave a legacy. Even chimpanzees, our closest genetic relatives, have, as far as we know, no cultural development that is transmitted in a progressive way from generation to generation.[5] Three hundred years ago chimps lived as they do today. We are not only able to experience the qualitative world, as can chimps; we can also form concepts. Concepts are distilled images in any sensory form or combination of forms that are used to represent the particulars of experience. With concepts we can do two things that may very well be unique to our species: we can imagine possibilities we have not encountered, and we can try to create, in the public sphere, the new possibilities we have imagined in the private precincts of our consciousness. We can make the private public by sharing it with others.

---

[4]John Dewey, *Experience and Education* (New York: Macmillan, 1938).
[5]For a view sympathetic to the idea that chimpanzees possess a culture see Frans B. M. DeWaal, "Cultural Primatology Comes of Age," *Nature* 399 (1999): 635–636.

Transforming the private into the public is a primary process of work in both art and science. Helping the young learn how to make that transformation is another of education's most important aims. It is a process that depends initially upon the ability to experience the qualities of the environment, qualities that feed our conceptual life and that we then use to fuel our imaginative life.

I do not want to draw too sharp a distinction between the formation of concepts and the imaginative generation of the forms needed to create, for example, twentieth-century architecture or the improvisational riffs of an Ella Fitzgerald solo; concept formation is itself an imaginative act. Yet there is a difference between recalled images and their imaginative transformation. Were we limited to the recall of the images we had once experienced, cultural development would be in trouble. Imagination gives us images of the possible that provide a platform for seeing the actual, and by seeing the actual freshly, we can do something about creating what lies beyond it. Imagination, fed by the sensory features of experience, is expressed in the arts through the image. The image, the central term of imagination, is qualitative in character. We do indeed see in our mind's eye.

The Role of the Arts in Refining the Senses and Enlarging the Imagination

The arts have an important role to play in refining our sensory system and cultivating our imaginative abilities. Indeed, the arts provide a kind of permission to pursue qualitative experience in a particularly focused way and to engage in the constructive exploration of what the imaginative process may engender. In this sense, the arts, in all their manifestations, are close in attitude to play.[6] Constraints on the imagination are loosened. In the arts, in the West at least, permission is provided to explore, indeed to surrender, to the impulsions the work sends to the maker, as well as those sent from the maker to the work. We see this perhaps most vividly when we watch preschoolers engaged in play. It is during this period that children take special pleasure in the sheer exploration of the sensory potential of the materials they use. It is at this time that their imaginative abilities, uninhibited by the constraints of culture, make it possible for them to convert a stick of wood into a plane they can fly, a sock into a doll they can cuddle, or an array of lines drawn so they

---

[6]Johan Huizinga, *Homo Ludens: A Study of the Play-Element in Culture* (Boston: Beacon Press, 1955).

stand for daddy. For young children the sensory world is a source of satisfaction, and imagination a source of exploratory delight. And it is these inclinations toward satisfaction and exploration that enlightened educators and parents wish to sustain rather than to have dry up under the relentless impact of "serious" academic schooling. A culture populated by a people whose imagination is impoverished has a static future. In such a culture there will be little change because there will be little sense of possibility.

Imagination, that form of thinking that engenders images of the possible, also has a critically important cognitive function to perform aside from the creation of possible worlds. Imagination also enables us to try things out—again in the mind's eye—without the consequences we might encounter if we had to act upon them empirically. It provides a safety net for experiment and rehearsal.[7]

As for sensibility, the arts invite us to attend to the qualities of sound, sight, taste, and touch so that we experience them; what we are after in the arts is the ability to perceive things, not merely to recognize them.[8] We are given permission to slow down perception, to look hard, to savor the qualities that we try, under normal conditions, to treat so efficiently that we hardly notice they are there.

Sensibility and imagination can, of course, remain entirely private affairs: we can enjoy the rosy radiance of dusk in private, the colored brilliance of a Cézanne still life in silence, the symmetrical strength of a Baule mask in quiet awe. The contents of our imaginative life can be kept to ourselves. Appreciation, though active, can be mute. Something else is needed if the products of our imagination are to make a social contribution to our culture. That something else is representation.

The Meaning of Representation

Representation, like sensibility and imagination, also performs critically important cognitive functions. Consider the process through which it occurs.

Representation can be thought of, first, as aimed at transforming the contents of consciousness within the constraints and affordances of

---

[7]John Dewey, How We Think (Boston: D. C. Heath, 1910).
[8]Dewey distinguishes between perception and recognition. Perception requires exploration. It seeks to further experience. Recognition takes place when a percept is given a label and then discussed. See his Art as Experience (New York: Minton, Balch, 1934).

a material.[9] Representation can and often does begin with an elusive and sometimes evanescent idea or image. I say evanescent because there is nothing quite so slippery as an idea; here now, gone a moment later. Images emerge and, like the subtle changes of the setting sun, may be altered irrevocably with a blink of the eye. Representation stabilizes the idea or image in a material and makes possible a dialogue with it. It is through "inscription" (I use the term metaphorically) that the image or idea is preserved—never, to be sure, in the exact form in which it was originally experienced, but in a durable form: a painting is made, a poem is written, a line is spoken, a musical score is composed.

It is through this very concreteness that representation makes possible a second, critically important process of editing. Although editing is usually associated with writing, it occurs in all art forms—painting and sculpture, music performance and music composition, theater, film and video, dance, and the rest. Editing is the process of working on inscriptions so they achieve the quality, the precision, and the power their creator desires. It is through the editing process that attention to the "wee bit" that Tolstoy believed defined art is conferred upon a work.[10] It is in the process of editing that transitions are made graceful, colors harmonized, intensities modulated, and, indeed, seasoning to suit the palette adjusted. In the domain of writing, editing allows us carefully to inspect the precision of language, the aptness of metaphor, the logic of argument. In painting it consists in brightening a passage of color. In music it involves shifting to the minor mode. In dance it is changing the pace of a movement. Editing is paying attention to relationships and attending to details; it is a process of making the work, work. Unless one is a genius, editing is a crucial aspect of the creative process, a way of removing the rough edges from one's work.

Inscription and editing are directly related to a third cognitive function of representation, one we usually take for granted: communication. The transformation of consciousness into a public form, which is what representation is designed to do, is a necessary condition for communication; few of us read minds. How this transformation occurs, I believe, is taken much too much for granted. It is so natural a process that we hardly notice it. Yet we can ask, "How does speech, or an imagined image, or a melody we hear in our head get communicated? What must

[9]J. J. Gibson, *The Senses Considered as Perceptual Systems* (Boston: Houghton Mifflin, 1966).

[10]Leo Tolstoy, *What Is Art?* trans. Aylmer Maud (1896; reprint, Indianapolis, Ind.: Bobbs-Merrill, 1960).

the maker do? And then what must the 'reader' do for it to make sense, that is, to be meaningful?"

What is clear is that culture depends upon these communications because communication patterns provide opportunities for members of a culture to grow. We develop, in part, by responding to the contributions of others, and in turn we provide others with material to which they respond. The relationship, at its best, is symbiotic. Thus the social contribution of the educational process is to make it possible for individuals to create symbiotic relationships with others through the development of their distinctive and complementary abilities and in so doing to enrich one another's lives.

Inscribing, editing, and communicating are three cognitive processes used in the act of representation. As I have described them, each appears as if the process of representation occurred from the top down, that is, from idea or image, through the hand, into the material, and then into the head of an eager reader of text or image, sound, or movement. However, the process is not so linear. The process of representation is more of a conversation than it is like speaking into a tape recorder. The ideas and images are not so much blueprints for action detailing specific directions and destinations; they are more like embarkation points. Once into the sea, the ship rides the currents of the ocean, which also help set the course. In the process of working with the material, the work itself secures its own voice and helps set the direction. The maker is guided and, in fact, at times surrenders to the demands of the emerging forms. Opportunities in the process of working are encountered that were not envisioned when the work began, but that speak so eloquently about the promise of emerging possibilities that new options are pursued. Put succinctly, surprise, a fundamental reward of all creative work, is bestowed by the work on its maker.

Thus we can add to inscription, editing, and communication a fourth cognitive function of representation, the discovery of ends in process, which in turn generates surprise. Surprise is itself a source of satisfaction. Familiarity and routine may provide security, but not much in the way of delight. Surprise is one of the rewards of work in the arts. In addition, it is from surprise that we are most likely to learn something. What is learned can then become a part of the individual's repertoire, and once it is a part of that repertoire, new and more complex problems can be generated and successfully addressed. At the same time it must be acknowledged that it is quite possible to do something very well in a particular work and not know how to repeat it.

The process of representation is always mediated through some form. Some of these forms are carried by the meanings that language makes possible, including prosody, the cadences and melodies of the language itself. The way language is crafted, especially through its form and its connotative qualities, expresses emotions and adumbrates meanings that cannot be conveyed through literal denotation. But language, while a central and primary form of representation, is by no means the only form of representation. Forms that appeal to our sense of sight are also fundamental modes of communication and have been since humans inscribed images on the walls of the caves in Lascaux some seventeen thousand years ago. Sound in the form of music is also a means through which meanings are conveyed. Indeed, there is no sensory modality that humans have not used to express what imagination has generated. Forms of representation are means through which the contents of consciousness are made public. The process of making the contents of consciousness public is, as I indicated earlier, a way of discovering it, stabilizing it, editing it, and sharing it.

The selection of a form of representation is a choice having profound consequences for our mental life, because choices about which forms of representation will be used are also choices about which aspects of the world will be experienced. Why? Because people tend to seek what they are able to represent. If your camera is loaded with black-and-white film, you look for shadows, for light and dark, but if the same camera is loaded with color film, you seek color. What the film in your camera can do influences what you will do. If the only tool you have is a yardstick, you look for what you can measure. Put another way, the tools you work with influence what you are likely to think about. Measuring tools lead to quantification; the tools used in the arts lead to qualification.

Consider the implications of the relationship between forms of representation for the selection of content in the school curriculum. Learning to use particular forms of representation is also learning to think and represent meaning in particular ways. How broad is the current distribution? What forms of representation are emphasized? In what forms are students expected to become "literate"? What modes of cognition are stimulated, practiced, and refined by the forms that are made available? Questions such as these direct our attention to the relationship of the content of school programs to the kinds of mental skills and modes of thinking that students have an opportunity to develop. In this sense, the school's curriculum can be considered a mind-altering device.[11] And it should be.

---

[11]Elliot Eisner, *The Educational Imagination: On the Design and Evaluation of School Programs,* 3d ed. (New York: Prentice-Hall, 1994).

Although we seldom think about the curriculum this way, parents send their children to school to have their minds made. In school, children learn how to think about the world in new ways. The culture provides the options in the various fields of study included, and various communities make the selections through choices reflected in graduation requirements, state education codes, college admission requirements, and the like. These selections are among the most significant policy decisions a community can make. Such decisions help influence how we think.

The Cognitive Functions of the Arts

What are the cognitive functions performed by the arts? By the term *cognition* I mean to include all those processes through which the organism becomes aware of the environment or its own consciousness. It includes the most sophisticated forms of problem-solving imaginable through the loftiest flights of the imagination. Thinking, in any of its manifestations, is a cognitive event. The noncognitive pertains to forms of life of which we have no awareness. Blood flows through our veins, but typically we are not aware of the course it takes. Events occur about which we are unaware. This is not to say that factors about which we are unaware cannot influence our behavior or attitudes; they can. But to the extent that we are unaware of them, those events are outside the realm of cognition.

With respect to art and its meaning, I share Dewey's view that art is a mode of human experience that in principle can be secured whenever an individual interacts with any aspect of the world. The arts are typically crafted to make aesthetic forms of experience possible. Works of art do not ensure that such experience will emerge, but they increase the probability that it will as long as those in their presence are inclined to experience such work with respect to their aesthetic features. The Parthenon and the Sistine ceiling can be ignored by someone in their presence; yet even a stone can be attended to so that its aesthetic character can serve as a source of that special form of life we call art.

One cognitive function the arts perform is to help us learn to notice the world. A Monet landscape or a Paul Strand photograph makes possible a new way of seeing: Monet's shimmering color gives us a new way to see light. Paul Strand's photographs provide a new way to experience the geometry of industrial cities. Art provides the conditions for awakening to the world around us. In this sense, the arts provide a way of knowing.

Aside from promoting our awareness of aspects of the world we had not experienced consciously before, the arts provide permission to engage the imagination as a means for exploring new possibilities. The arts liberate us from the literal; they enable us to step into the shoes of others and to experience vicariously what we have not experienced directly. Cultural development depends upon such capacities, and the arts play an extraordinarily important role in their contribution to such an aim.

Work in the arts also invites the development of a disposition to tolerate ambiguity, to explore what is uncertain, to exercise judgment free from prescriptive rules and procedures. In the arts, the locus of evaluation is internal, and the so-called subjective side of ourselves has an opportunity to be utilized. In a sense, work in the arts enables us to stop looking over our shoulder and to direct our attention inward to what we believe or feel. Such a disposition is at the root of the development of individual autonomy.

Another cognitive function of the arts is that in the process of creation they stabilize what would otherwise be evanescent. Ideas and images are very difficult to hold on to unless they are inscribed in a material that gives them at least a kind of semipermanence. The arts, as vehicles through which such inscriptions occur, enable us to inspect more carefully our own ideas, whether those ideas emerge in the form of language, music, or vision. The works we create speak back to us, and we become in their presence a part of a conversation that enables us to "see what we have said."

Finally, the arts are means of exploring our own interior landscape. When the arts genuinely move us, we discover what it is that we are capable of experiencing. In this sense, the arts help us discover the contours of our emotional selves. They provide resources for experiencing the range and varieties of our responsive capacities.

To discover the cognitive functions of other visual forms of representation, consider the use of maps. Why do we draw them? Why do we use them? Maps are drawn and used because they help us grasp relationships that would be harder to grasp, for example, in narrative or number. We use maps because they display, by a structural analogue, relationships in space that provide a useful image of the world we wish to navigate. Maps lay it out for us. So do histograms, charts, diagrams, and sketches. The inscription of visual images makes vivid certain relationships. They help us to notice and understand a particular environment and our place in it.

They also obscure. Thus the paradox: a way of seeing is also, and at the same time, a way of not seeing. Relationships that are made visible through maps also obscure what any particular map does not illuminate— the feel of a place, its look and color, what is idiosyncratic about it, its aroma, the lifestyles of the people who live there. Maps effectively simplify. We want them to, but we should not forget that the map is not the territory. The view they provide is always partial—as is any view. And precisely because any single view is partial, it is important, depending upon our purpose, to secure other views that provide other pictures.

I have been speaking of the cognitive functions of the arts largely in terms of the way they illuminate, that is, what they help us see. But the arts go well beyond making visible the visible; they also tell us something about how places and relationships feel. They speak to us, as Susanne Langer said, through the emotions: "A work of art presents feeling (in the broad sense I mentioned before, as everything that can be felt) for our contemplation, making it visible or audible or in some way perceivable through a symbol, not inferable from a symptom. Artistic form is congruent with the dynamic forms of our direct sensuous, mental, and emotional life; works of art are projections of 'felt life,' as Henry James called it, into spatial, temporal, and poetic structures. They are images of feeling, that formulate it for our cognition."[12]

Through the arts we learn to see what we had not noticed, to feel what we had not felt, and to employ forms of thinking that are indigenous to the arts. These experiences are consequential, for through them we engage in a process through which the self is re-made. What are the features of this transformational process? How does it proceed? What does it mean in the context of education?

---

[12]Susanne Langer, *Problems of Art* (New York: Scribner, 1957), 25.

22

MY FAVORITE THING

WHY DO WE LIKE THE MUSIC WE LIKE?

Daniel J. Levitin

A STUDY MADE THE newspapers and morning talk shows several years ago, claiming that listening to Mozart for ten minutes a day made you smarter ("the Mozart Effect"). Specifically, music listening, it was claimed, can improve your performance on spatial-reasoning tasks given immediately after the listening session (which some journalists thought implied mathematical ability as well). U.S. congressmen were passing resolutions, the governor of Georgia appropriated funds to buy a Mozart CD for every newborn baby Georgian. Most scientists found ourselves in an uncomfortable position. Although we do believe intuitively that music can enhance other cognitive skills, and although we would all like to see more governmental funding for school music programs, the actual study that claimed this contained many scientific flaws. The study was claiming some of the right things but for the wrong reasons. Personally, I found all the hubbub a bit offensive because the implication was that music should not be studied in and of itself, or for its own right, but only if it could help people to do better on other, "more important" things. Think how absurd this would sound if we turned it inside out. If I claimed that study-ing mathematics helped musical ability, would policy makers start pump-ing money into math for that reason? Music has often been the poor stepchild of public schools, the first program to get cut when there are funding problems, and people frequently try to justify it in terms of its collateral benefits, rather than letting music exist for its own rewards.

The problem with the "music makes you smarter" study turned out to be straightforward: The experimental controls were inadequate, and the tiny difference in spatial ability between the two groups, according to research by Bill Thompson, Glenn Schellenberg, and others, all turned on the choice of a control task. Compared to sitting in a room and doing nothing, music listening looked pretty good. But if subjects in the control task were given the slightest mental stimulation—hearing a book on tape, reading, etc.—there was no advantage for music listening. Another problem with the study was that there was no plausible mechanism proposed by which this might work—how could music listening increase spatial performance?

Glenn Schellenberg has pointed out the importance of distinguishing short-term from long-term effects of music. The Mozart Effect referred to immediate benefits, but other research *has* revealed long-term effects of musical activity. Music listening enhances or changes certain neural circuits, including the density of dendritic connections in the primary auditory cortex. The Harvard neuroscientist Gottfried Schlaug has shown that the front portion of the corpus callosum—the mass of fibers connecting the two cerebral hemispheres—is significantly larger in musicians than nonmusicians, and particularly for musicians who began their training early. This reinforces the notion that musical operations become bilateral with increased training, as musicians coordinate and recruit neural structures in both the left and right hemispheres.

Several studies have found microstructural changes in the cerebellum after the acquisition of motor skills, such as are acquired by musicians, including an increased number and density of synapses. Schlaug found that musicians tended to have larger cerebellums than nonmusicians, and an increased concentration of gray matter; gray matter is that part of the brain that contains the cell bodies, axons, and dendrites, and is understood to be responsible for information processing, as opposed to white matter, which is responsible for information transmission.

Whether these structural changes in the brain translate to enhanced abilities in nonmusical domains has not been proven, but music listening and music therapy have been shown to help people overcome a broad range of psychological and physical problems. But, to return to a more fruitful line of inquiry regarding musical taste . . . Lamont's results are important because they show that the prenatal and newborn brain are able to store memories and retrieve them over long periods of time. More practically, the results indicate that the environment—even when mediated by amniotic fluid and by the womb—can affect a child's development and preferences. So the seeds of musical preference are sown in the womb, but there must be more to the story than that, or children would simply gravitate toward the music their mothers like, or that plays in Lamaze classes. What we can say is that musical preferences are influenced, but not determined, by what we hear in the womb. There also is an extended period of acculturation, during which the infant takes in the music of the culture she is born into. There were reports a few years ago that prior to becoming used to the music of a foreign (to us) culture, all infants prefer Western music to other music, regardless of their culture or race. These findings were not corroborated, but rather, it was found that infants do show a preference for consonance over dissonance. Appreciating dissonance comes later in life, and people differ in how much dissonance they can tolerate.

There is probably a neural basis for this. Consonant intervals and dissonant intervals are processed via separate mechanisms in the auditory cortex. Recent results from studying the electrophysiological responses of humans and monkeys to sensory dissonance (that is, chords that sound dissonant by virtue of their frequency ratios, not due to any harmonic or musical context) show that neurons in the primary auditory cortex—the first level of cortical processing for sound—synchronize their firing rates during dissonant chords, but not during consonant chords. Why that would create a preference for consonance is not yet clear.

We do know a bit about the infant's auditory world. Although infant ears are fully functioning four months before birth, the developing brain requires months or years to reach full auditory processing capacity. Infants recognize transpositions of pitch and of time (tempo changes), indicating they are capable of relational processing, something that even the most advanced computers still can't do very well. Jenny Saffran of the University of Wisconsin and Laurel Trainor of McMaster University have gathered evidence that infants can also attend to absolute-pitch cues if the task requires it, suggesting a cognitive flexibility previously unknown: Infants can employ different modes of processing—presumably mediated by different neural circuits—depending on what will best help them to solve the problem at hand.

Trehub, Dowling, and others have shown that contour is the most salient musical feature for infants, who can detect contour similarities and differences even across thirty seconds of retention. Recall that *contour* refers to the pattern of musical pitch in a melody—the sequence of ups and downs that the melody takes—regardless of the size of the interval. Someone attending to contour exclusively would encode only that the melody goes up, for example, but not by how much. Infants' sensitivity to musical contour parallels their sensitivity to linguistic contours—which separate questions from exclamations, for example, and which are part of what linguists call prosody. Fernald and Trehub have documented the ways in which parents speak differently to infants than to older children and adults, and this holds across cultures. The resulting manner of speaking uses a slower tempo, an extended pitch range, and a higher overall pitch level.

Mothers (and to a lesser extent, fathers) do this quite naturally without any explicit instruction to do so, using an exaggerated intonation that the researchers call infant-directed speech or motherese. We believe that motherese helps to call the babies' attention to the mother's voice, and helps to distinguish words within the sentence. Instead of saying, as we would to an adult, "This is a ball," motherese would entail something like, "Seeeeee?" (with the pitch of the eee's going up to the end of the sentence). "See the BAAAAAALLLLLL?" (with the pitch covering an extended range and going up again at the end of the word *ball*). In such utterances, the contour is a signal that the mother is asking a question or making a statement, and by exaggerating the differences between up and down contours, the mother calls attention to them. In effect, the mother is creating a prototype for a question and a prototype for a declaration, and ensuring that the prototypes are easily distinguishable. When a mother gives an exclamatory scold, quite naturally—and again without explicit training—she is likely to create a third type of prototypical utterance, one that is short and clipped, without much pitch variation: "No!" (pause) "No! Bad!" (pause) "I said no!" Babies seem to come hardwired with an ability to detect and track contour, preferentially, over specific pitch intervals.

Trehub also showed that infants are more able to encode consonant intervals such as perfect fourth and perfect fifth than dissonant ones, like the tritone. Trehub found that the unequal steps of our scale make it easier to process intervals even early in infancy. She and her colleagues played nine-month-olds the regular seven-note major scale and two scales she invented. For one of these invented scales, she divided the octave into eleven equal-space steps and then selected seven tones that made one- and two-step patterns, and for the other she divided the octave into seven equal steps. The infants' task was to detect a mistuned tone. Adults performed well with the major scale, but poorly with both of the artificial, never-before-heard scales. In contrast, the infants did equally well on both unequally tuned scales and on the equally tuned ones. From prior work, it is believed that nine-month-olds have not yet incorporated a mental schema for the major scale, so this suggests a general processing advantage for unequal steps, something our major scale has.

In other words, our brains and the musical scales we use seem to have coevolved. It is no accident that we have the funny, asymmetric arrangement of notes in the major scale: It is easier to learn melodies with this arrangement, which is a result of the physics of sound production . . . ; the set of tones we use in our major scale are very close in pitch to the tones that constitute the overtone series. Very early in childhood, most children start to spontaneously vocalize, and these early vocalizations can sound a lot like singing. Babies explore the range of their voices, and begin to explore phonetic production, in response to the sounds they are bringing in from the world around them. The more music they hear, the more likely they are to include pitch and rhythmic variations in their spontaneous vocalizations.

Young children start to show a preference for the music of their culture by age two, around the same time they begin to develop specialized speech processing. At first, children tend to like simple songs, where *simple* means music that has clearly defined themes (as opposed to, say, four-part counterpoint) and chord progressions that resolve in direct and easily predictable ways. As they mature, children start to tire of easily predictable music and search for music that holds more challenge. According to Mike Posner, the frontal lobes and the anterior cingulate—a structure just behind the frontal lobes that directs attention—are not fully formed in children, leading to an inability to pay attention to several things at once; children show difficulty attending to one stimulus when distracters are present. This accounts for why children under the age of eight or so have so much difficulty singing "rounds" like "Row, Row, Row Your Boat." Their attentional system—specifically the network that connects the cingulate gyrus (the larger structure within which the anterior cingulate sits) and the orbitofrontal regions of the brain—cannot adequately filter out unwanted or distracting stimuli. Children who have not yet reached the developmental stage of being able to exclude irrelevant auditory information face a world of great sonic complexity with all sounds coming in as a sensory barrage. They may try to follow the part of the song that their group is supposed to be singing, only to be distracted and tripped up by the competing parts in the round. Posner has shown that certain exercises adapted from attention and concentration games used by NASA can help accelerate the development of the child's attentional ability.

The developmental trajectory, in children, of first preferring simple and then more complex songs is a generalization, of course; not all children like music in the first place, and some children develop a taste for music that is off the beaten path, oftentimes through pure serendipity. I became fascinated with big band and swing music when I was eight, around the time my grandfather gave me his collection of 78 rpm records from the World War II era. I was initially attracted by novelty songs, such as "The Syncopated Clock," "Would You Like to Swing on a Star," "The Teddy Bear's Picnic," and "Bibbidy Bobbidy Boo"—songs that were made for children. But sufficient exposure to the relatively exotic chord patterns and voicings of Frank de Vol's and Leroy Anderson's orchestras became part of my mental wiring, and I soon found myself listening to all kinds of jazz; the children's jazz opened the neural doors to make jazz in general palatable and understandable.

Researchers point to the teen years as the turning point for musical preferences. It is around the age of ten or eleven that most children take on music as a real interest, even those children who didn't express such an interest in music earlier. As adults, the music we tend to be nostalgic for, the music that feels like it is "our" music, corresponds to the music we heard during these years. One of the first signs of Alzheimer's disease (a disease characterized by changes in nerve cells and neurotransmitter levels, as well as destruction of synapses) in older adults is memory loss. As the disease progresses, memory loss becomes more profound. Yet many of these old-timers can still remember how to sing the songs they heard when they were fourteen. Why fourteen? Part of the reason we remember songs from our teenage years is because those years were times of self-discovery, and as a consequence, they were emotionally charged; in general, we tend to remember things that have an emotional component because our amygdala and neurotransmitters act in concert to "tag" the memories as something important. Part of the reason also has to do with neural maturation and pruning; it is around fourteen that the wiring of our musical brains is approaching adultlike levels of completion.

There doesn't seem to be a cutoff point for acquiring new tastes in music, but most people have formed their tastes by the age of eighteen or twenty. Why this is so is not clear, but several studies have found it to be the case. Part of the reason may be that in general, people tend to become less open to new experiences as they age. During our teenage years, we begin to discover that there exists a world of different ideas, different cultures, different people. We experiment with the idea that we don't have to limit our life's course, our personalities, or our decisions to what we were taught by our parents, or to the way we were brought up. We also seek out different kinds of music. In Western culture in particular, the choice of music has important social consequences. We listen to the music that our friends listen to. Particularly when we are young, and in search of our identity, we form bonds or social groups with people whom we want to be like, or whom we believe we have something in common with.

As a way of externalizing the bond, we dress alike, share activities, and listen to the same music. Our group listens to this kind of music, those people listen to that kind of music. This ties into the evolutionary idea of music as a vehicle for social bonding and societal cohesion. Music and musical preferences become a mark of personal and group identity and of distinction.

To some degree, we might say that personality characteristics are associated with, or predictive of, the kind of music that people like. But to a large degree, it is determined by more or less chance factors: where you went to school, who you hung out with, what music they happened to be listening to. When I lived in northern California as a kid, Creedence Clearwater Revival was huge—they were from just down the road. When I moved to southern California, CCR's brand of quasi-cowboy, country-hick music didn't fit in well with the surfer/Hollywood culture that embraced the Beach Boys and more theatrical performance artists like David Bowie.

Also, our brains are developing and forming new connections at an explosive rate throughout adolescence, but this slows down substantially after our teenage years, the formative phase when our neural circuits become structured out of our experiences. This process applies to the music we hear; new music becomes assimilated within the framework of the music we were listening to during this critical period. We know that there are critical periods for acquiring new skills, such as language. If a child doesn't learn language by the age of six or so (whether a first or a second language), the child will never learn to speak with the effortlessness that characterizes most native speakers of a language. Music and mathematics have an extended window, but not an unlimited one: If a student hasn't had music lessons or mathematical training prior to about age twenty, he can still learn these subjects, but only with great difficulty, and it's likely that he will never "speak" math or music like someone who learned them early. This is because of the biological course for synaptic growth. The brain's synapses are programmed to grow for a number of years, making new connections. After that time, there is a shift toward pruning, to get rid of unneeded connections.

Neuroplasticity is the ability of the brain to reorganize itself. Although in the last five years there have been some impressive demonstrations of brain reorganization that used to be thought impossible, the amount of reorganization that can occur in most adults is vastly less than can occur in children and adolescents.

Of course, there are individual differences. Just as some people can heal broken bones or skin cuts faster than others, so, too, can some people forge new connections more easily than others. Generally, between the ages of eight and fourteen, pruning starts to occur in the frontal lobes, the seat of higher thought and reasoning, planning, and impulse control. Myelination starts to ramp up during this time. Myelin is a fatty substance that coats the axons, speeding up synaptic transmission. (This is why as children get older, generally, problem solving becomes more rapid and they are able to solve more complex problems.) Myelination of the whole brain is generally completed by age twenty. Multiple sclerosis is one of several degenerative diseases that can affect the myelin sheath surrounding the neurons.

The balance between simplicity and complexity in music also informs our preferences. Scientific studies of like and dislike across a variety of aesthetic domains—painting, poetry, dance, and music—have shown that an orderly relationship exists between the complexity of an artistic work and how much we like it. Of course, complexity is an entirely subjective concept. In order for the notion to make any sense, we have to allow for the idea that what seems impenetrably complex to Stanley might fall right in the "sweet spot" of preference for Oliver. Similarly, what one person finds insipid and hideously simple, another person might find difficult to understand, based on differences in background, experience, understanding, and cognitive schemas.

In a sense, schemas are everything. They frame our understanding; they're the system into which we place the elements and interpretations of an aesthetic object. Schemas inform our cognitive models and expectations. With one schema, Mahler's Fifth is perfectly interpretable, even upon hearing it for the first time: It is a symphony, it follows symphonic form with four movements; it contains a main theme and subthemes, and repetitions of the theme; the themes are manifested through orchestral instruments, as opposed to African talking drums or fuzz bass. Those familiar with Mahler's Fourth will recognize that the Fifth opens with a variation on that same theme, and even at the same pitch. Those well acquainted with Mahler's work will recognize that the composer includes quotations from three of his own songs. Musically educated listeners will be aware that most symphonies from Haydn to Brahms and Bruckner typically begin and end in the same key. Mahler flouts this convention with his Fifth, moving from C-sharp minor to A minor and finally ending in D major. If you had not learned to hold in your mind a sense of key as the symphony develops, or if you did not have a sense of the normal trajectory of a symphony, this would be meaningless; but for the seasoned listener, this flouting of convention brings a rewarding surprise, a violation of expectations, especially when such key changes are done skillfully so as not to be jarring. Lacking a proper symphonic schema, or if the listener holds another schema, perhaps that of an aficionado of Indian ragas, Mahler's Fifth is nonsensical or perhaps rambling, one musical idea melding amorphously into the next, with no boundaries, no beginnings or endings that appear as part of a coherent whole. The schema frames our perception, our cognitive processing, and ultimately our experience.

When a musical piece is too simple we tend not to like it, finding it trivial. When it is too complex, we tend not to like it, finding it unpredictable—we don't perceive it to be grounded in anything familiar. Music, or any art form for that matter, has to strike the right balance between simplicity and complexity in order for us to like it. Simplicity and complexity relate to familiarity, and *familiarity* is just another word for a schema.

It is important in science, of course, to define our terms. What is "too simple" or "too complex"? An operational definition is that we find a piece too simple when we find it trivially predictable, similar to something we have experienced before, and without the slightest challenge. By analogy, consider the game tic-tac-toe. Young children find it endlessly fascinating, because it has many features that contribute to interest at their level of cognitive ability: It has clearly defined rules that any child can easily articulate; it has an element of surprise in that the player never knows for sure exactly what her opponent will do next; the game is dynamic, in that one's own next move is influenced by what one's opponent did; when the game will end, who will win, or whether it will be a draw is undetermined, yet there is an outer limit of nine moves. That indeterminacy leads to tension and expectations, and the tension is finally released when the game is over.

As the child develops increasing cognitive sophistication, she eventually learns strategies—the person who moves second cannot win against a competent player; the best the second player can hope for is a draw. When the sequence of moves and the end point of the game become predictable, tic-tac-toe loses its appeal. Of course, adults can still enjoy playing the game with children, but we enjoy seeing the pleasure on the child's face and we enjoy the process—spread out over several years—of the child learning to unlock the mysteries of the game as her brain develops.

To many adults, Raffi and Barney the Dinosaur are the musical equivalents of tic-tac-toe. When music is too predictable, the outcome too certain, and the "move" from one note or chord to the next contains no element of surprise, we find the music unchallenging and simplistic. As the music is playing (particularly if you're engaged with focused attention), your brain is thinking ahead to what the different possibilities for the next note are, where the music is going, its trajectory, its intended direction, and its ultimate end point. The composer has to lull us into a state of trust and security; we have to allow him to take us on a harmonic journey; he has to give us enough little rewards—completions of expectations—that we feel a sense of order and a sense of place.

Say you're hitchhiking from Davis, California, to San Francisco. You want the person who picks you up to take the normal route, Highway 80. You might be willing to tolerate a few shortcuts, especially if the driver is friendly, believable, and is up-front about what he's doing. ("I'm just going to cut over here on Zamora Road to avoid some construction on the freeway.") But if the driver takes you out on back roads with no explanation, and you reach a point where you no longer see any landmarks, your sense of safety is sure to be violated. Of course, different people, with different personality types, react differently to such unanticipated journeys, musical or vehicular. Some react with sheer panic ("That Stravinsky is going to kill me!") and some react with a sense of adventure

Figure 22.1.

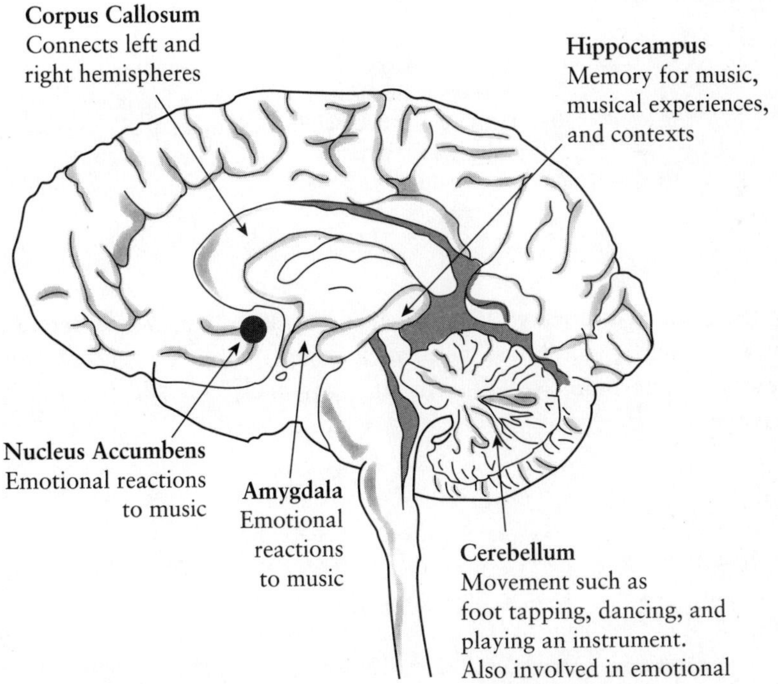

Corpus Callosum
Connects left and right hemispheres

Hippocampus
Memory for music, musical experiences, and contexts

Nucleus Accumbens
Emotional reactions to music

Amygdala
Emotional reactions to music

Cerebellum
Movement such as foot tapping, dancing, and playing an instrument. Also involved in emotional reactions to music

Figure 22.2.

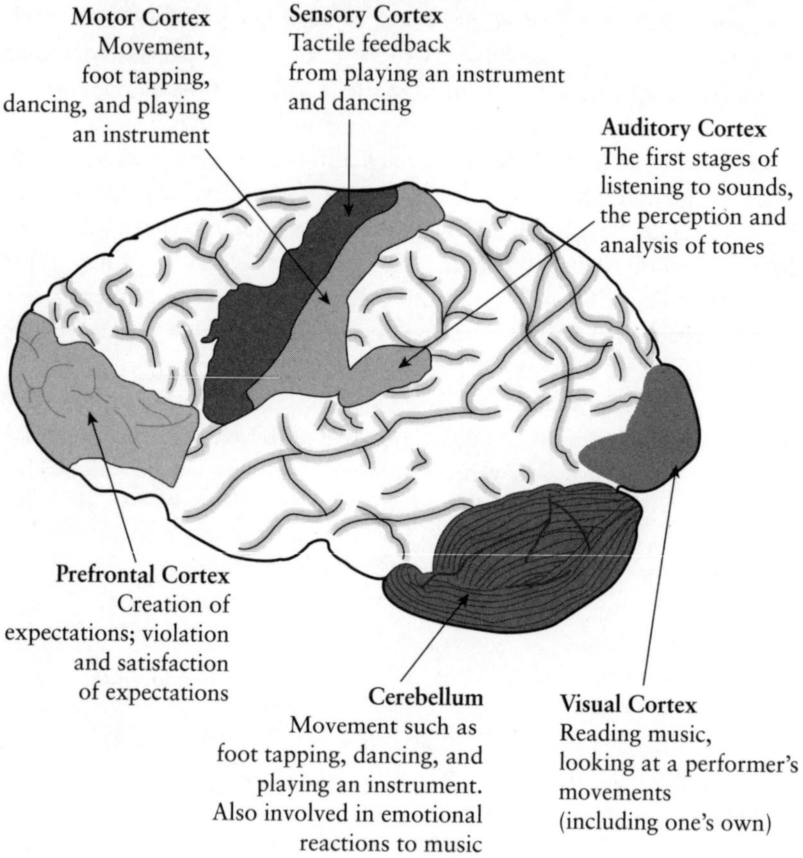

Motor Cortex
Movement,
foot tapping,
dancing, and playing
an instrument

Sensory Cortex
Tactile feedback
from playing an instrument
and dancing

Auditory Cortex
The first stages of
listening to sounds,
the perception and
analysis of tones

Prefrontal Cortex
Creation of
expectations; violation
and satisfaction
of expectations

Cerebellum
Movement such as
foot tapping, dancing, and
playing an instrument.
Also involved in emotional
reactions to music

Visual Cortex
Reading music,
looking at a performer's
movements
(including one's own)

at the thrill of discovery ("Coltrane is doing something weird here, but what the hell, it won't hurt me to stick around awhile longer, I can take care of my harmonic self and find my way back to musical reality if I have to").

REFERENCES

Berlyne, D. E. 1971. *Aesthetics and Psychobiology*. New York: Appleton-Century-Crofts. On the "inverted-U" hypothesis of musical liking.
Grier, C., and G. Schlaug. 2003. Gray matter differences between musicians and nonmusicians. *Annals of the New York Academy of Sciences* 999:514–517. Differences between the brains of musicians and nonmusicians.

Husain, G., W. F. Thompson, and E. G. Schellenberg. 2002. Effects of musical tempo and mode on arousal, mood, and spatial abilities. *Music Perception* 20(2):151–171. The "Mozart Effect" explained.

Hutchinson, S., L. H. Lee, N. Gaab, and G. Schlaug. 2003. Cerebellar volume of musicians. *Cerebral Cortex* 13:943–949. Differences between the brains of musicians and nonmusicians.

Lamont, A. M. 2001. Infants' preferences for familiar and unfamiliar music: A socio-cultural study. Paper read at Society for Music Perception and Cognition, August 9, 2001, at Kingston, Ont. On infants' prenatal musical experience.

Lee, D. J., Y. Chen, and G. Schlaug. 2003. Corpus callosum: Musician and gender effects. *NeuroReport* 14:205–209. Differences between the brains of musicians and nonmusicians.

Rauscher, F. H., G. L. Shaw, and K. N. Ky. 1993. Music and spatial task performance. *Nature* 365:611. The original report of the "Mozart Effect."

Saffran, J. R. 2003. Absolute pitch in infancy and adulthood: The role of tonal structure. *Developmental Science* 6(1):35–47. On the use of absolute pitch cues by infants.

Schellenberg, E. G. 2003. Does exposure to music have beneficial side effects? In *The Cognitive Neuroscience of Music,* edited by I. Peretz and R. J. Zatorre. New York: Oxford University Press.

Thompson, W. F., E. G. Schellenberg, and G. Husain. 2001. Arousal, mood, and the Mozart Effect. *Psychological Science* 12(3):248–251. The "Mozart Effect" explained.

Trainor, L. J., L. Wu, and C. D. Tsang. 2004. Long-term memory for music: Infants remember tempo and timbre. *Developmental Science* 7(3):289–296. On the use of absolute-pitch cues by infants.

Trehub, S. E. 2003. The developmental origins of musicality. *Nature Neuroscience* 6(7):669–673.

Trehub, S. E. 2003. Musical predispositions in infancy. In *The Cognitive Neuroscience of Music,* edited by I. Peretz and R. J. Zatorre. Oxford: Oxford University Press. On early infant musical experience.

PART SEVEN

THE EXCEPTIONAL BRAIN

WHEN IT WORKS DIFFERENTLY

23

EXPLORING EXCEPTIONAL BRAINS

Eric Jensen

What Makes a Brain Gifted?

You cannot have functional or behavioral differences (such as being smarter) without some kind of corresponding difference in the brain from a more typical brain. As understanding of the causes of those differences improves, researchers will know better how to identify and develop them. On the whole, brain differences fall into four distinct categories. They are morphology, operations, real estate, and electro-chemical cellular functions, or M-O-R-E as a way to remember them easily.

○ *Morphology:* Size, quantity, and shape of brain structures

○ *Operations:* Neural efficiency and speed of internal connectivity in the brain

○ *Real estate:* Strategic differences in which or how brain areas are used

○ *Electro-chemical cellular function:* Differences in electrical and chemical activity

The difference most associated with gifted children is the effectiveness with which they learn; as a generalization, they pay closer attention, absorb information, stay focused, learn the interrelationships more quickly, and remember longer. Those are the observable consequences of the four differences I just described. The following sections describe how each of them plays out.

Morphology

The first category—brain morphology—refers to the shape, size, and boundaries of structures within the brain. Some correlations suggest that more brain volume equals more computing power.[1] Total brain volume accounts for about 16 percent of the variance in general intelligence scores. If this study was true, you'd also expect overall head size to correlate with intelligence, and it does.[2] Interestingly, students with AD/HD [attention deficit/hyperactivity disorder] have both lower overall IQ scores *and* smaller brain volume, by 3 to 4 percent.[3] Data like these suggest at least some kind of a correlation between overall computing capacity and the brain's morphology. Bigger head size does increase the chances for greater IQ. This obviously does not mean that all melon-headed kids are geniuses, but the correlations are well above chance levels.

Another set of animal studies measured (postmortem) the total number of both neurons and glial cells (the highly important support tissue) in rats. In the gifted, there were far more glial cells (more than double!) as compared with the nongifted learners. But what about humans?[4] As a vivid example, when Marian Diamond studied a sample of Einstein's brain tissue in the mid-1980s, she found that his brain had more glia per neuron than did the average brain (73 percent, compared with eleven others) in one area: the left inferior parietal lobe (Figure 23.1).[5] This difference exceeded the expected ranges for both age and individual variability and may be typical for the frontal area of exceptionally gifted people—or it may have been the specific area Einstein used for complex mathematical theories.

---

[1]R. J. Haier, R. E. Jung, R. A. Yeo, K. Head, and M. T. Alkire, "Structural Brain Variation and General Intelligence," *Neuroimage,* 2004, 23(1), 425–433.

[2]D. M. Ivanovic, B. P. Leiva, H. T. Perez, M. G. Olivares, N. S. Diaz, M. S. Urrutia, A. F. Almagia, T. D. Toro, P. T. Miller, E. O. Bosch, and C. G. Larrain, "Head Size and Intelligence, Learning, Nutritional Status and Brain Development," *Neuropsychologia,* 2004, 42(8), 1118–1131.

[3]F. Castellanos and M. Acosta, "The Neuroanatomy of Attention Deficit/Hyperactivity Disorder," *Revista de neurologia,* 2002, 38(1), S131–S136.

[4]N. S. Orzhekhovskaia, "The Cytoarchitectonic Characteristics of the Frontal Fields of the Brain in Gifted People," *Morfologiia,* 1996, 109(3), 7–9; M. Soffie, K. Hahn, E. Terao, and F. Eclancher, "Behavioural and Glial Changes in Old Rats Following Environmental Enrichment," *Behavioral Brain Research,* 1999, 101, 37–49.

[5]M. Diamond, A. Schiebel, G. Murphy, and T. Harvey, "On the Brain of a Scientist: Albert Einstein," *Experimental Neurology,* 1985, 88(1), 198–204.

Figure 23.1. Einstein's Brain Had Higher Counts of Glial Cells in the Left Parietal Lobe.

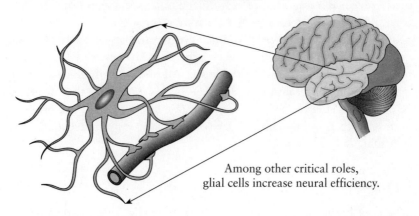

Among other critical roles, glial cells increase neural efficiency.

As a historical note—and evidence of the difficulty many have in accepting the idea that exceptional brains can differ physically from the norm—it's interesting to observe that Diamond's paper ran into a firestorm of publicity. Her fellow scientists concocted headlines based on her findings ("Einstein's Extra Brain Cells: The Secret to His Genius!") as icebreakers in their presentations, setting crowds of skeptical researchers roaring with laughter.[6] Diamond herself never generalized her results to all geniuses, merely saying that they were potentially meaningful, and her work has since been vindicated. Today, we do know that larger numbers of glial cells are correlated with improved learning and memory.[7] In another study with highly gifted individuals, there was a significantly greater level of individual variability, especially in the right hemisphere.[8] This may reflect space, time, and sensory processing skills.

Surprisingly, gifted brains also include larger proportions of "extreme neurons"—those very small and very large neurons. These are ones that seem to either start off that way, enabling a greater number of connections, or develop in ways that may have some additional processing capacity.

[6]C. Abraham, *Possessing Genius: The Bizarre Odyssey of Einstein's Brain* (New York: St. Martin's Press, 2001).

[7]Orzhekhovskaia, "The Cytoarchitectonic Characteristics"; Soffie and others, "Behavioural and Glial Changes in Old Rats."

[8]I. Bogolepova and L. Malofeeva, "Variability in the Structure of Field 39 of the Lower Parietal Area of the Cortex in the Left and Right Hemispheres of Adult Human Brains," *Neuroscience and Behavioral Physiology*, 2004, 34(4), 363–367.

In another study that compared people with strongly creative, highly gifted talents to a control group of average performers, postmortem evidence revealed a much more customized and specialized brain.[9] More cortical fields were streamlined, there were greater numbers of pyramidal neuron glial cells, and there was much greater distinctiveness of how the neurons were grouped. This suggests the extensiveness to which gifted people use particular areas of the brain. All told, the giftedness may be more likely a combination of differences or a threshold that needs to be reached. There are correlations for it in a larger-than-typical brain or in those with unusual neuronal development, and it may have more glial cells than a typical brain.

Operations

When our brains do things that we ask them to (tie our shoe, turn on the lights, figure out the change from a ten-dollar bill, type a sentence in our computer, or calculate the tip in a restaurant), we call that "brain work" an operation. Some operations are merely functional (brushing our teeth or driving our car, and so on), and others are strategic (solving a problem, calculating the odds on a decision, or figuring out how to approach a problem from another's point of view). Gifted people are usually better at working memory and attention span.

Even though the functional operations seem like they are more physical, they still involve our brains. But those can be and are typically learned by people at most levels of intelligence. The more strategic operations are different. Strategic operations are done faster and more efficiently and often more creatively by those who deserve a gifted label. The mental computations are not just "fun work" for their brains; they often do them enough so that they become automatic and fast.

CONNECTIVITY. There are between seventy-five and one hundred billion neurons in the brain and nearly a trillion glial cells. Each neuron has between several hundred and tens of thousands of synaptic connections, depending on where in the brain it is. Overall, this means the human brain has several trillion connections that enable everyday life. Neurons are linked to one another both locally and at a distance.

---

[9]I. Bogolepova, "The Cytoarchitectonic Characteristics of the Speech Center of the Brain in Gifted People in the Plan to Study Individual Variability of Human Brain Structure," *Morfologiia*, 1994, 106(4–6), 31–38.

For comparison, think about all the technology that surrounds you right now. You needn't be deeply into the high-tech life to have a computer or two in the house, along with several phones of various types, a few TV sets (probably with DVD player and VCR), TIVO, Internet access, videogames, an iPod, and any number of other devices, from a PDA to a talking oven. Each device has different needs and varying capacity. In most homes, these separate systems don't talk to each other. Could you imagine the work in networking together all those devices in just one house, your own? This would mean a complete wireless network within your house. Let's say you did have the savvy to interface all your different types of systems into one streaming, trouble-free, seamless network. That would be tricky, but it could be done. Now add this: next you're making every bit of technology in your home talk to every bit of technology in someone's home down the street. Now add this: you're making every bit of technology in your home talk to one in three homes around the world. You've just bumped your home-networking problem into a global challenge of near-biblical proportions. If that sounds complex, that's the equivalent of what every human brain does! The gifted brain simply does it all quicker.

Does the gifted brain have a much greater number of connections as compared with a more typical brain? The answer is not known for sure, but there is speculation that the gifted brain does work faster and has up to 10 percent more connections. One wouldn't want too many connections. The human brain uses probably 30 to 40 percent of the total possible connections already.[10] But a brain with too many connections would not be any smarter. In fact, at an extreme case, a child with the Fragile X Syndrome has way too many connections and is severely mentally retarded.[11] Computer modeling simulations show that having some unused capacity in the brain is actually a smart concept. It gives a computational advantage for a brain that needs a high degree of flexibility in responses at the more global level.[12]

[10]D. J. Felleman and D. C. Van Essen, "Distributed Hierarchical Processing in the Primate Cerebral Cortex," *Cerebral Cortex,* 1991, 1(1), 1–47.

[11]J. D. Churchill, A. W. Grossman, S. A. Irwin, R. Galvez, A. Y. Klintsova, I. J. Weiler, and W. T. Greenough, "A Converging-Methods Approach to Fragile X Syndrome," *Developmental Psychobiology,* 2002, 40(3), 323–338.

[12]K. J. Friston, "Testing for Anatomically Specified Regional Effects," *Human Brain Mapping,* 1997, 5(2), 133–136; G. Tononi, O. Sporns, and G. M. Edelman, "Reentry and the Problem of Integrating Multiple Cortical Areas: Simulation of Dynamic Integration in the Visual System," *Cerebral Cortex,* 1992, 2(4), 310–335.

Therefore, it's likely that a gifted brain has the right combination of sufficient connections in the right places and high processing speed. Any brain system that has both reciprocal and sparse connections can learn faster and integrate a great deal more information than a brain that is 100 percent interconnected.

CONNECTION AND PROCESSING SPEED. Why is speed so essential? Greater complexity creates greater possibility of confusion without another key feature: connectivity. Once all the connections are in place, the next ingredient needed to make it functional is speed.

The gifted learn things more quickly, they develop and use more connections, and they have faster connections. It's as if they are using high-speed Internet access while the rest of the population is still struggling with dial-up lines. In fact, there's a decrease in cortical usage with increasing intelligence: electrical-chemical activity from pretest to post-test correlates negatively with intelligence. This suggests that the higher the subjects' general competence, the larger the decrease in the amount of cortical activation.[13] These findings suggest intelligence-related individual differences in becoming neurally efficient. The brains of the gifted are just flat out faster at processing. That means they can move larger quantities of signals around more easily.

Other researchers have been more concerned with speed of processing. Two studies found different results. One found an inherited (genetic) correlation between intelligence and speed of information processing.[14] But in a practical manner, higher processing speed did not always mean faster decision making. Another group studied peripheral nerve conduction velocity and found no relation to IQ.[15] In fact, in a very practical study testing for memory and speed, the higher-ability participants devoted

---

[13]R. J. Haier, B. V. Siegel Jr., A. MacLachlan, E. Soderling, S. Lottenberg, and M. S. Buchsbaum, "Regional Glucose Metabolic Changes After Learning a Complex Visuospatial/Motor Task: A Positron Emission Tomographic Study," *Brain Research*, 1992, 570(1–2), 134–143.

[14]L. A. Baker, P. A. Vernon, and H. Z. Ho, "The Genetic Correlation Between Intelligence and Speed of Information Processing," *Behavior Genetics*, 1991, 21(4), 351–367.

[15]F. V. Rijsdijk, D. I. Boomsma, and P. A. Vernon, "Genetic Analysis of Peripheral Nerve Conduction Velocity in Twins," *Behavior Genetics*, 1995, 25(4), 341–348.

more time to stimulus analysis and planning than did lower-ability participants, suggesting more processing time on an activity.[16]

Generally, the gifted have the ability to acquire new and complex information more rapidly than their average-ability peers in situations involving simple acquisition. Multiple studies have shown a stronger focus ability in those with higher IQ, suggesting an ability to filter out distractions. Higher-ability people's effectiveness in controlling attention and gating sensory information seems to be a critical factor.[17] It differentiates and identifies those individuals with complex cognitive abilities.

Some correlations also show up between mental speed of processing and specific abilities. For example, musical ability, as one might guess, is correlated with higher mental speed.[18] But I would also expect competencies in martial arts, race car driving, and videogames to correlate with mental speed, too. This suggests that many people who have faster mental processing may have chosen to use the advantage in nonacademic arenas. So far, human intelligence seems much like a mental juggling act in which the smartest performers use specific brain regions to resist distraction and keep attention focused on pieces of information that *they regard* as critical, which may or may not be anything involved with their schooling.

GLOBAL CONNECTIONS. One of the keys to understanding cognition is understanding the networking operations of the brain. For the various brain areas to be most efficient, they need rapid and thorough communications. Most research has found clear links between intelligence and brain activation patterns in the frontal lobe. These make for higher-order cognitive functions. The brain has to be able to activate, process the learning, and then wait for the next activation. Sluggish learning won't work in the gifted brain. This "transient response plasticity" occurs over a very

---

[16]M. Houlihan, R. Stelmack, and K. Campbell, "Intelligence and the Effects of Perceptual Processing Demands, Task Difficulty and Processing Speed on P300, Reaction Time and Movement Time," *Intelligence,* 1998, 26(1), 9–25.

[17]C. R. Brumback, K. A. Low, G. Gratton, and M. Fabiani, "Sensory ERPs Predict Differences in Working Memory Span and Fluid Intelligence," *Neuroreport,* 2004, 15(2), 373–376.

[18]W. Gruhn, N. Galley, and C. Kluth, "Do Mental Speed and Musical Abilities Interact?" *Annals of the New York Academy of Sciences,* 2003, 999, 485–496.

Figure 23.2. Exceptional or "Gifted" Brains.

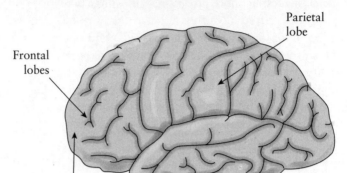

short time scale and is typically considered to be a property of higher-order, more cognitive brain regions such as the prefrontal cortex.[19]

It's a bit like a city; the more roads, highways, and alternative routes available, the faster anyone can get to any other place. The fewer the connections, the weaker they are, the more sluggish they are, the slower the traffic. In the brain, if you want general intelligence, connecting to the right place at a high speed is a must. As an example of connectivity, consider the brain of the severely retarded savant; the savant has great connectivity in one neighborhood of the brain, but a gifted brain is far more globally connected.

In general, the brain typically called smarter or gifted has different neural wiring (Figure 23.2). One study measured interaction between the left and right hemispheres in mathematically gifted adolescents, average-ability youths, and college students. The task showed hierarchical letter pairs in three viewing conditions: (a) only to the right hemisphere—to the subject's left side, (b) only to the left hemisphere—to their right side, or (c) bilaterally—to both hemispheres at once. Participants had to make quick letter-match or no-match judgments, and some did much better than

---

[19]M. M. Mesulam, "From Sensation to Cognition," *Brain,* 1998, 121(6), 1013–1052.

the others.[20] These data suggest to us that greater interhemispheric traffic may be a functional characteristic of the mathematically gifted brain.

Real Estate

In general, it's difficult to say that gifted people consistently use their brains differently from more typical learners. But what the research tells us is that a slew of efficiencies in the gifted brain help it use the right areas, use areas that it is very good at, and use the smallest amount of brain real estate necessary to do the task. This is important in looking at imaging studies, because the area of the brain may not light up in the same way it would for a more typical or disadvantaged learner. In fact, it may give a contradictory story that has a temporal component. Many gifted learners seem to be switching gears constantly, like an old-time car transmission, trying to get the right task into the right part of the brain. This means that the areas activated will change more dramatically during a task than would be likely among other more typical learners.

The brains of gifted people often show these differences:

○ Greater focus skills (frontal lobe function)

○ Greater global connectivity (more overall brain usage)

○ Greater alpha brainwave pattern (supports concentration and input)

○ Better brain chemistry balance (supports attention, mood, and memory)

FOCUS THAT BRAIN! The amount of brain activation in each network depends on how skilled individuals are in verbal or visual learning. In other words, the more skilled we are in the strategy used, the less brain activation or effort is required to perform higher-level thinking tasks. When given a choice as to which thinking strategy to use, the brain often uses the method that requires the least effort, namely the strategy in which the individual is most efficient. This means that it takes greater skills to manage your own resources, even if it means damping down the emotions. Those who test higher are typically less influenced by affect (that is, by emotional state). Feeling ecstatic, very sad, or anxious all

[20]H. Singh and M. O'Boyle, "Interhemispheric Interaction During Global-Local Processing in Mathematically Gifted Adolescents, Average-Ability Youth, and College Students," *Neuropsychology*, 2004, 18(2), 371–377.

create competing stimuli for the brain to deal with. Problem solving and other processes require focus, and too much affect slows us down. In fact, neutral affect is associated with faster learning because the emotional processing is dampened.[21] Having some positive affect enhances thinking, but too much affect will negatively influence cognition.

Those who are gifted tend to use their frontal lobes very effectively and to manage incoming sensory information better than those who have a lower IQ (Figure 23.3). This area is used to filter the incoming data and then figure out the task, then things literally slow down. Generally, the higher the subject's overall mental ability, the more quickly the task is mastered, and the larger the decrease in the amount of cortical activation as the subject shifts gears. These findings suggest intelligence-related individual differences in becoming neurally efficient.[22]

Effectiveness in controlling attention and gating sensory information is a critical determinant of individual differences in complex cognitive abilities.[23] To be effective at a consistently high level takes the constant engagement of higher-order brain functions to sort tasks, focus, move tasks, switch brain areas used, and process tasks quickly. Generally, those with higher and more flexible, fluid intelligence keep distracting information at bay by activating regions in both the pre-frontal and parietal cortexes, as well as a number of other regions. Naturally, how well subjects perform in any given situation depends on the complex interaction of many abilities, but frontal lobe execution is paramount.

To confirm this theory, we could ask if those who have difficulty with focus and impulsivity regulation (both frontal lobe functions) do worse on IQ tests; they do! Studies of students with attention deficit tell us that for overall intellectual ability (Full Scale IQ), scores were lower for those with AD/HD than for healthy participants.[24] Of course, many highly successful adults have AD/HD, but these results may tell you that they

---

[21]F. G. Ashby, A. M. Isen, and A. U. Turken, "A Neuropsychological Theory of Positive Affect and Its Influence on Cognition," *Psychological Review*, 1999, 106(3), 529–550.

[22]A. C. Neubauer, R. H. Grabner, H. H. Freudenthaler, J. F. Beckmann, and J. Guthke, "Intelligence and Individual Differences in Becoming Neurally Efficient," *Acta Psychologica*, 2004, 116(1), 55–74.

[23]Brumback and others, "Sensory ERPs Predict Differences in Working Memory Span."

[24]T. W. Frazier, H. A. Demaree, and E. A. Youngstrom, "Meta-Analysis of Intellectual and Neuropsychological Test Performance in Attention-Deficit/ Hyperactivity Disorder," *Neuropsychology*, 2004, 18(3), 543–555.

Figure 23.3. Areas of the Brain Dedicated to Attention and Focus Skills.

Dorsolateral
prefrontal
cortex

Parietal

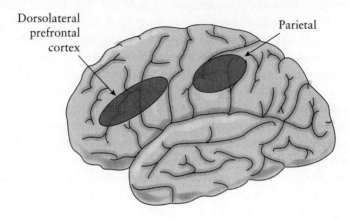

were able to compensate and beat the odds. This is just one of the many differences that crop up between paper IQ scores and real-world success.

TRY LESS, ACCOMPLISH MORE. The relationship of the more gifted with brain usage is complex and often delicate. Gifted adolescents often have a developmentally enhanced (closer to a college age) state of brain activity.[25] This typically gives them unusually strong focus, motivation, and concentration on tasks for their age. In general, they have a greater "force of will" as characterized by greater left hemisphere alpha brainwave activity levels (8–12 Hz per second). As a generalization, those with lower IQ use certain areas more, to try harder, even though their efficiency in using that area is not strong. In one study, the higher-IQ subjects were found to be using an entirely different part of the brain to do a given task as compared with the lower-IQ subjects.[26]

Again we see the same pattern. It's not just using the frontal lobes, it's being able to use them successfully that counts. One high school boy had moderate mental retardation, with an IQ in the 70 to 80 range. But he also had exceptional calculation abilities and was referred to as a savant.

[25]J. Alexander, M. O'Boyle, and C. Benbow, "Developmentally Advanced EEG Alpha Power in Gifted Male and Female Adolescents," *International Journal of Psychophysiology,* 1966, 23(1–2), 25–31.
[26]N. Jausovec and K. Jausovec, "Differences in Induced Brain Activity During the Performance of Learning and Working-Memory Tasks Related to Intelligence," *Brain and Cognition,* 2004, 54(1), 65–74.

When asked to perform, he actually used the frontal lobes excessively, suggesting that it was his previously diagnosed obsessive-compulsive nature combined with a probable failure in his brain's central executive functioning.[27] This shows the dual nature of skill and deficit; his sheer will (obsessive, in fact) forces his frontal lobes to work overtime at tasks. As you may have guessed, one could be both gifted and have a learning disability.

Overall, there appears to be support for the idea that gifted people have more balanced thinking ("whole brain" was the buzzword years ago). Some researchers contend that enhanced right hemisphere involvement during cognitive processing is a correlate of mathematical precocity.[28] In addition, the general pattern of activation observed tells us that those of higher ability more effectively coordinate left and right hemisphere processing. Later studies have supported this lingering notion that gifted males have a greater reliance on their right hemisphere as a physiological correlate of mathematical giftedness.[29] One older but very interesting study using EEG showed that, as compared with lower-IQ subjects, greater symmetry between hemispheres is associated with superior performance among those more gifted.[30] Again we see that those with greater intellectual prowess are literally using "more" of their brain at times, while at other times they are simply integrating its areas much better.

It is also believed that the gifted use the spatial-temporal areas of the temporal lobes to support higher-level functions. Under the supervision of physicist Gordon Shaw, a group of researchers in Irvine, California, used a very challenging videogame to understand spatial-temporal reasoning. The game is based on the mathematics of knot theory and was used for understanding DNA structure prior to this application.

---

[27]A. A. Gonzalez-Garrido, J. L. Ruiz-Sandoval, F. R. Gomez-Velazquez, J. L. de Alba, and T. Villasenor-Cabrera, "Hypercalculia in Savant Syndrome: Central Executive Failure?" *Archives of Medical Research,* 2002, 33(6), 586–589.

[28]M. W. O'Boyle, J. E. Alexander, and C. P. Benbow, "Enhanced Right Hemisphere Activation in the Mathematically Precocious: A Preliminary EEG Investigation," *Brain Cognition,* 1991, 17(2), 138–153.

[29]W. W. O'Boyle, H. S. Gill, C. P. Benbow, and J. E. Alexander, "Concurrent Finger-Tapping in Mathematically Gifted Males: Evidence for Enhanced Right Hemisphere Involvement During Linguistic Processing," *Cortex,* 1994, 30(3), 519–526.

[30]D. G. Fischer, D. Hunt, and B. S. Randhawa, "Spontaneous EEG Correlates of Intellectual Functioning in Talented and Handicapped Adolescents," *Perceptual and Motor Skills,* 1982, 54(3), 751–762.

Some elementary and middle school students showed game mastery so quickly that researchers conjectured that the spatial temporal reasoning capacity is innate.[31] Is there a way you could test this theory? Could someone influence intelligence by changing where in the brain they are processing a task? Yes—in one experiment, researchers in Sydney, Australia, used electromagnetic pulses to suppress the left frontal temporal lobe for a task, forcing the brain to use the right side. In a statistically significant number of subjects, there was an increase in drawing skills (typically thought of as more right-brained) and even proofreading (very sequential task).[32] These studies suggest that some strengths would be available to all of us, if we could get our brains to use the right areas for the right jobs.

Electro-Chemical Cellular Function

It turns out that brains do differ right down to the electrical and chemical levels. Researchers at the University of Tennessee did an interesting experiment using cortical event-related potential (ERP). That's the one where the subject wears that fashionable little cloth polka-dot skullcap (usually with thirty-two or more electrodes connected to the scalp) to measure electrical current. Then a stimulus is presented, and the speed, amplitude, and location of the brain's response are measured. Sensory ERPs can successfully predict differences in working memory span and fluid intelligence.[33] This suggests that electrical activity is one of the indicators for efficient or effective cognitive processing.

One study used learning disabled, gifted, and typical control children of ages eight to twelve. The common "distracter" stimulus consisted of random nouns generated 80 percent of the time. The target stimulus was animal names presented the other 20 percent of the time. The research was designed to find out what differences, if any, would appear among the subject groups. There were differences, and—as you might guess—the

---

[31]M. R. Peterson, D. Balzarini, M. Bodner, E. G. Jones, T. Phillips, D. Richardson, and G. L. Shaw, "Innate Spatial-Temporal Reasoning and the Identification of Genius," *Neurological Research*, 2004, 26(1), 2–8.

[32]A. W. Snyder, E. Mulcahy, J. L. Taylor, D. J. Mitchell, P. Sachdev, and S. C. Gandevia, "Savant-Like Skills Exposed in Normal People by Suppressing the Left Fronto-Temporal Lobe," *Journal of Integrated Neuroscience*, 2003, 2(2), 149–158.

[33]Brumback and others, "Sensory ERPs Predict Differences in Working Memory Span."

gifted performed much better than those with learning disabilities and the typical subjects.[34] But the study differences suggested the possibility of delays or gaps in the attention and information processing for those with learning disabilities. Again, it was the speed and ability to filter out and focus that made the gifted subjects do better. The electrical-chemical capacity of their brains helped create a more efficient response.

What about hormone levels—are they correlated with intelligence? The best-researched hormones are the stress and sex hormones. It is believed that those who are more intellectually curious have a lower baseline of cortisol—that's a hormone related to stress. Higher levels of cortisol are associated with a more contracted response. When we feel too stressed, we are less likely to show exploratory, curious, novelty-seeking behaviors. Those who do show this early habit of curiosity, even as three-year-olds, turn out to be much more competent intellectually in later years.[35]

Using saliva samples, researchers measured the testosterone levels of 247 children, 100 of them gifted and the others randomly chosen. Lower salivary testosterone levels were found in intellectually gifted children of both sexes (all females have some testosterone). There was an overall negative relationship between testosterone levels and cognitive abilities in preadolescent children.[36] Greater levels of salivary testosterone are correlated with lower student achievement. This is not to say that athletes are dullards; it suggests that testosterone comes with a price. Remember that with any population sample, you'll see a bell-shaped curve. Some with higher levels of testosterone may have a dozen other, far stronger factors that support a gifted brain, including high motivation and better concentration.

And finally, certain neurotransmitter levels are associated with greater intellectual performance. Having just the right levels of dopamine is associated with better frontal lobe function. Too much dopamine (the "pleasure" or "reward" neurotransmitter) is associated with schizophrenia.[37]

---

[34]J. F. Lubar, C. A. Mann, D. M. Gross, and M. S. Shively, "Differences in Semantic Event-Related Potentials in Learning-Disabled, Normal, and Gifted Children," *Biofeedback and Self-Regulation*, 1992, 17(1), 41–57.

[35]A. Raine, C. Reynolds, P. Venables, and S. Mednick, "Stimulation Seeking and Intelligence: A Prospective Longitudinal Study," *Journal of Personality & Social Psychology*, 2002, 82(4), 663–674.

[36]D. Ostatnikova, M. Dohnanyiova, A. Mataseje, Z. Putz, J. Laznibatova, and J. Hajek, "Salivary Testosterone and Cognitive Ability in Children," *Bratislayske Lekarske Lis*, 2000, 101(8), 470–473.

[37]T. C. Neylan, "Pathophysiology of Schizophrenia: Dopamine Hypothesis," *The Journal of Neuropsychiatry and Clinical Neurosciences*, 1996, 8(2), 222.

The brain's frontal lobes need just the right amount of dopamine to fuel working memory. Excess dopamine is counterproductive for cognitive processing.[38] However, too little is bad, too.[39] Dopamine is known as an upper for the brain; in the same way that amphetamines, cocaine, and caffeine ramp up the activity of the prefrontal cortex, dopamine does also. It just does it in a more sane way.

There's no doubt that highly intelligent, gifted thinkers display a greater degree of cognitive flexibility. Gifted thinking requires just the right amount of serotonin. That's the neurotransmitter associated with mood, memory, and attention. Those with little flexibility typically are lower in serotonin. Studies show that cognitive inflexibility is typical after prefrontal serotonin depletion.[40] Serotonin depletion can be influenced by dietary changes. Foods with a higher amount of the amino acid tryptophan (used to make serotonin in the brain) include bananas, turkey, milk, and avocados. Creative problem solving is improved when serotonin is at the middle healthy level. Together with increased dopamine release for better processing speed and attention, serotonin improves the flexibility needed for maximum cognitive achievement.

Overview of the Exceptional Brain

No one single difference makes someone gifted. In some cases, being very strong in one area allows the gifted learner to compensate for being less gifted in another. As a generalization, the gifted brain is better designed to pay attention, filter out trivial information, learn quicker, and remember longer. It is stronger in the frontal lobes, and tends to work on tasks there quickly, then farms them out to other areas. The gifted brain is more likely to use both hemispheres to solve a problem, not just one, and is more neurally efficient. It may have more connections, but not an

---

[38]S. Castner, G. Williams, and P. Goldman-Rakic, "Reversal of Antipsychotic-Induced Working Memory Deficits by Short-Term Dopamine DI Receptor Stimulation," *Science*, 2000, 287(5460), 2020.

[39]S. Bandyopadhyay, C. Gonzalez-Islas, and J. J. Hablitz, "Dopamine Enhances Spatiotemporal Spread of Activity in Rat Prefrontal Cortex," *Journal of Neurophysiology*, February 2004, 93(2), 864–872; P. R. Montague, S. E. Hyman, and J. D. Cohen, "Computational Roles for Dopamine in Behavioural Control," *Nature*, 2004, 431(7010), 760–767.

[40]H. F. Clarke, J. W. Dalley, H. S. Crofts, T. W. Robbins, and A. C. Roberts, "Cognitive Inflexibility After Prefrontal Serotonin Depletion," *Science*, 2004, 304(5672), 878–880.

extraordinary amount more. It is faster and more cognitively flexible. It's better regulated by hormones and the right balance of neurotransmitters. On the whole, an aggregate of factors makes the gifted brain both unusually effective and unusually efficient at neural processing.

What's going on inside gifted children? No single profile can be drawn that describes all the gifted. But they do share some strong common tendencies. Conversations with teachers and parents of gifted children as well as with authors and consultants in this area revealed four personality traits or qualities that are most consistent with giftedness:

- o *Perfectionism:* They want to get it right and dislike sloppy work. This also means they can be very critical of themselves.

- o *Creativity:* They are constantly attracted to novel and creative ways to see, hear, and do things.

- o *Sensitivity:* They can be emotionally intense and often have a greater moral, ethical, and social awareness of the world and its dangers. As an example of this awareness, gifted girls often hide their abilities and learn to blend in with other children. In elementary school they may typically focus on developing social relationships at the cost of notoriety for "smarts."

- o *Intensity:* They have a dogged ability to focus relentlessly. They can be high achievers because they're willing to put in the effort. This often works against them in the social world, since there is a social likeability price to pay for isolation and focus.

Many parents and educators of gifted children note an advanced vocabulary, a tendency to ask complex questions, a preference for older companions, perceptive observations, high creativity, a strong problem-solving ability, and excellent memory. Many gifted people also display an aptitude or talent in a specific area such as mathematics, language arts, or music. We've all heard about other qualities associated with giftedness such as a natural concern with moral, ethical, and social issues. But those concerns will develop only in a supportive environment.[41]

As I've noted, those who are truly gifted are not just faster or more accurate at a task, they really do think differently. Surprisingly, most of the gifted who were high in math giftedness got no outside tutoring or training. We all know that nearly anyone can become good at mathematics. And if they're willing to put in the hours, anyone who works hard at

---

[41]L. K. Silverman and L. P. Leviton, "Advice to Parents in Search of the Perfect Program," *The Gifted Child Today,* 1991, 14(6), 31–34.

it can become a mathematician. Now, for a moment, think of the kind of mathematical genius seen in the movie *A Beautiful Mind*, which portrayed 1994 Nobel Laureate Dr. John Nash. That kind of genius is different, and only a few are "born with the gift" and can become truly great. Here are some examples to clarify the differences:

Mathematically Gifted	Typical Student
Prefers elegant solutions	Takes any solution
Views world mathematically	Disconnected from world of math
Switches strategies easily	Tends toward inflexible thinking
Studies hard problems first	Jumps into hard problems quickly
Recalls problem structures	Recalls contextual details
Generalizes quickly	Slow to generalize
Long chains of reasoning	Simple reasoning
Reverses methods easily	Has trouble working backwards

Many excellent books have been written about the gifted learner. One of my favorites is Susan Winebrenner's *Teaching Gifted Kids in the Regular Classrooms*.[42] In this book she notes the following characteristics:

- *Coping mechanisms.* The gifted have varied ways of coping. Gifted girls often hide their abilities and learn to blend in with other children. In elementary school they may typically focus on developing social relationships. In middle school peers value appearance and sociability more than intelligence. Gifted boys are often considered "immature" and often get held back when they don't socialize with peers with whom they have no common interests.

- *Discipline.* Many gifted students act out in class from frustration. Although they can appear to be troublemakers or unmotivated, they often feel that class time is wasted for them. You may see symptoms such as disruptiveness, restlessness, and inattentiveness, often confused with AD/HD. The gifted are more likely to challenge authority figures by questioning classroom rules that they feel are unfair.

- *Disabilities.* One-sixth of the gifted children may have some type of learning disability. Both the disability and the giftedness often go undetected because giftedness can hide disabilities and disabilities depress IQ scores. For some with disabilities, strong abstract reasoning helps children make adjustments and compensations for weaknesses, making them very much harder for others to uncover.

---

[42]S. Winebrenner, *Teaching Gifted Kids in the Regular Classroom* (Minneapolis: Free Spirit Press, 2001).

○ *Sociability*. Gifted children are introverted at twice the rate of typical children (60 percent versus 30 percent). Of those who are highly gifted, the introvert numbers go up further, to 75 percent. Introversion correlates with introspection, reflection, the ability to inhibit aggression, deep sensitivity, moral development, high academic achievement, scholarly contributions, leadership in academic and aesthetic fields in adult life, and smoother passage through midlife; however, it is very likely to be misunderstood and "corrected" in children by well-meaning adults. Social self-concept improves when children come in contact with true peers.

Making the Case for Gifted Education

As I've said, any attempt to profile the gifted can get a bit controversial. Some people view all such discussion as a thinly veiled attempt to justify an elitist position for those who hit the genetic lottery. Nothing could be further from the truth. In total, far more gifted students come from middle- and lower-income families than from upper-income families; that's where the largest populations are! The discussion deserves to be held, the research has to be done, and policy has to be implemented that supports this population.

There are many public precedents for specific national policy changes for an underserved minority. Head Start, the 1997 IDEA (Individuals with Disabilities Education Act), and the congressionally mandated and funded Title I, Title II, and Title IX acts have all been targeted educational legislation. The question is, Why?

Most important, these acts were not implemented to level the playing field. You can't level the playing field unless you make equal the impossible: socioeconomic status, parental knowledge, love, parental education, environment, family history, safety, genes. These legislative actions are all attempts at ensuring that no one segment of the population is unfairly treated, discriminated against, or disadvantaged by educational policy.

That distinction is important. In today's schools, being gifted is commonly a disadvantage. For a child who already knows the material being presented to the class but has no choice but to sit through the lesson, the day stretches out unbearably—and no education whatsoever takes place. Quality education, after all, works by a simple principle: contrast. If there is no difference between what you already know and what is offered, there is no contrast and there is no new learning. Netscape guru Jim Clark and comedian Chris Rock were two high school dropouts who thought school made no sense for them. Jan and Bob Davidson, authors of *Genius Denied,* say that up to 20 percent of dropouts are "gifted" but quit school because they feel ignored and unchallenged, bored, and frustrated.[43] As the Davidsons point out, if you taught the alphabet every day to senior high school students, they'd not only learn nothing and be insulted, over time they would lose ground. That's what gifted students are up against.

If we take the attitude that those on the margin (or even the extremes) are to be ignored, then one could argue that we shouldn't have special needs classes, either. This is dead wrong. And although everyone is important, an argument could be made that the gifted make unique contributions to society. The numbers show that they are overrepresented in the arts, in higher education, in research, economics, science, and other highly valued fields in society. In addition, they stay married longer, pay more taxes, and use fewer social and medical services than their more typical counterparts.[44] This supports a position that says, just as others who are disadvantaged in school should be supported, so should the gifted.

The key here is that without contrast, there is no learning, no enrichment, and no point in being in school. If there's no contrast in the schooling from the home life, no enrichment can take place. The children who are truly most disadvantaged by current schooling are those in the top 3 percent of the population. If you broaden the concept of gifted to include the top 5, 10, or 15 percent, the resulting group is less different from the more typical student, so there's less reason to differentiate or provide enrichment.

In the current climate of identifying students who have special needs, it is critical that gifted populations get their share of understanding, attention, and policy support. The gifted advocates are simply asking that the same rules be applied to everybody.

Summary

Can anyone become gifted? One view holds that giftedness is all about training the brain. The thinking goes that, "If anyone provides enough resources and training, the child receiving it will be gifted." This turns

---

[43]J. Davidson and B. Davidson, *Genius Denied: How to Stop Wasting Our Brightest Young Minds* (New York: Simon & Schuster, 2004).
[44]C. Jencks, *Who Gets Ahead? The Determinants of Economic Success in America* (New York: Basic Books, 1979).

out to be somewhat true, somewhat false. A strong positive environment has been shown to be able to raise a child's IQ by 10 to 20 points, but it may take months or years to do this. It's probably only likely if the child starts with an IQ in the below-average range. For the moment, there's no evidence that you can turn a moderately retarded child into a Mensa (IQ of 165+) student by enhancing his or her world (although futurist Ray Kurzweil may disagree). By the way, you still want to enhance his or her world in a dozen other ways; improvement comes in many forms and formal IQ is just one indicator. The improvement may not be in the IQ area, but might be more lateral (social, emotional, and practical skills are powerful, too). Everyone can get the enrichment response; it just shows up in different ways.

If you combine some of the innate brain differences typical of gifted learners in a positive resource-laden environment, with good encouragement, you'll get a strong achiever. Will the child be on the dean's list, a Mensa regular, or a MacArthur Foundation "Genius Grant" winner? That's possible, but not at all guaranteed. However, you are likely to have a productive student who grows into a happy, resourceful adult: someone who is more likely to attain a higher education, be married longer, earn more money, and have greater life satisfaction than others in the class. Any fewer of the positive variables for being gifted and you'll get (maybe) less of a star—but you'll nonetheless have the satisfaction of building toward and not diminishing whatever potential was there. Remember that everyone can and should become enriched. That should be the whole point of school: to turn one into what one is capable of. There is no middle ground; you are either making headway toward an enrichment response or losing ground toward a neural wasteland.

24

SELECTIONS FROM
THE MINDS OF BOYS

Michael Gurian
Kathy Stevens

The Male Brain

PET SCANS AND MRIS allow all of us to observe the structural and functional differences between the brains of boys and girls. When you look at a scan of male and female brains doing any kind of task, you see different parts of the brain light up, with differing levels of brain activity in these cortical sections. This is a primary way we've been able to discern the nature of boys and the nature of how boys learn.

Nancy Forger, of the University of Massachusetts at Amherst, reported recently that "at least 100 differences in male and female brains have been described so far."[1] She is joined by other researchers . . . such as

---

[1] Quoted in Amanda Onion, "Sex in the Brain: Research Showing Men and Women Differ in More Than One Area." *ABC News,* Sept. 21, 2004. A fascinating new development has emerged in the study of brain differences, one that will lead to deeper research. British scientists believe they have discovered a third area of the brain involved in language. They base this belief on innovative use of a process called "diffusion tensor magnetic resonance imaging," a very powerful type of MRI. They have called this third area Geschwind's territory. You can learn more in the *Annals of Neurology* online, under January 2005, at www3.interscience.wiley.com/cgi-bin/fulltext/109857315/HTMLSTART.

Jill Goldstein, a professor of psychiatry at Harvard Medical School, who studies male and female brain differences in order to help cure diseases in males and females. Kathy and I specifically apply such gender science research in order to help develop educational and parenting strategies that work for boys and for girls.

[Here are] some biological tendencies that we have observed from studying what is hardwired into male nature:

- Boys tend to have more dopamine in their bloodstream—which can increase impulsive risk behavior—and they process more blood flow in the cerebellum (the part of the brain that controls "doing" and "physical action").[2] (Although dopamine can't cross the "blood-brain barrier," L-dopa, an amino acid in the brain, is converted to dopamine.)[3] These factors are believed to contribute to boys' tendency to learn less well than girls (on average) when sitting still or being sedentary. Boys are more likely than girls to attach their learning to physical movement.[4] This movement is in fact often crucial to male brain learning (and to the learning style of females with higher dopamine-cerebellum functioning as well).

- A boy's corpus callosum (the connecting bundle of tissues between hemispheres) is a different size than a girl's (some studies show up to a 25 percent difference in size).[5] Researchers have shown that the female corpus callosum (as well as other related nerve fibers) allows more crosstalk between hemispheres than does that of the male. One of the obvious behavioral differences that grow from higher levels of cross-talk between hemispheres is the greater ability to do more than one task at once with equal success (multitasking). On average, girls test out better at multitasking.

- Girls have, in general, stronger neural connectors in their temporal lobes than boys do; these stronger connectors appear to facilitate more sensorially detailed memory storage and better listening, especially for tones of voice. Boys in general pick up less of what is aurally going on around them, *especially when it is said in words,*

---

[2]Daniel Amen. Personal interview with Michael Gurian, July 2004.

[3]Robert P. Iacono. "The Nervous System: The Blood-Brain Barrier." Available at www.pallidotomy.com/index.html.

[4]Michael W. Smith and Jeffrey D. Wilhelm. *Reading Don't Fix No Chevy's.* Portsmouth, N.H.: Heinemann, 2002.

[5]Rita Carter. *Mapping the Mind.* Berkeley: University of California Press, 1998.

and need more sensory-tactile experience than girls in order for their brains to light up with learning.[6]

○ The hippocampus (another memory storage area in the brain) works differently in boys than in girls.[7] Boys will tend to need even more time to memorize classroom items—especially written items—than girls. However, because the male hippocampus favors list making, boys tend to succeed well in memorization when greater amounts of information come in list organization and in listed substrata of categorization (point, subpoint, subsubpoint).

○ Girls' frontal lobes are generally more active than boys, and grow at earlier ages.[8] For this reason, girls tend to make less impulsive executive decisions than boys. Impulsivity used to be much more useful and desirable in learning, especially when children did more of their learning outdoors and independently.

○ Girls tend to get earlier and more advanced development of the Broca's and Wernicke's areas in the frontal and temporal lobes— these are the main language centers of the brain.[9] In general, the female brain utilizes more neural pathways and brain centers for word production and expression of experience, emotion, and cognition through words.

○ Girls have more estrogen and oxytocin than boys. (These chemicals have a direct impact on the use of words.) Boys have higher levels of testosterone (a hormone closely associated with aggression and sex) and vasopressin (which relates to territoriality and hierarchy). Oxytocin rises when girls communicate verbally with a friend or family member. Boys, with less oxytocin in the bloodstream and less verbal emphasis in the brain, don't learn as much through sitting and talking, nor gravitate toward it as naturally. Their formation of learning bonds often develops through action-response, hierarchical competition,[10] and aggression nurturance. . . .

---

[6]Deborah Blum. *Sex on the Brain*. New York: Penguin Books, 1998.

[7]Simon Baron-Cohen. *The Essential Difference*. New York: Basic Books, 2003.

[8]Marian Diamond. *Male and Female Brains*. Lecture at the annual meeting of the Women's Forum West, San Francisco, 2003. Available at http://newhorizons.org/neuro/diamond_male_female.htm.

[9]Anna Moir and David Jessel. *Brain Sex*. New York: Dell, 1989.

[10]Steven E. Rhoads. *Taking Sex Differences Seriously*. San Francisco: Encounter Books, 2004.

○ Boys compartmentalize brain activity (that is, they use less of the brain), their brains overall operate with 15 percent less blood flow than do girls',[11] and they are structured to learn with less multi-tasking. Boys therefore tend to do better when focusing for long periods on one task in which depth of learning takes place; they do less well when required to move from task to task very quickly. One primary brain response to the overstimulation of doing many things at once is frustration (a swelling of the amygdala, which is an anger and aggression center in the brain and has a significantly higher volume of tissue in males).[12] Gradually, increasing frustration levels lead to heightened levels of stress hormone (cortisol), which also link to heightened adrenalin—thus, it ought not surprise us that males create more discipline problems in classrooms.

○ Research continues to explore the implications of gender on the functioning of many brain areas, including the occipital lobe (involved primarily in visual processing), the parietal lobe (involved mainly in movement, orientation, calculation, and some types of recognition), and the brain stem (often referred to as the reptilian brain because of its similarity to the entire brain of a reptile—responsible for much involuntary movement and vital bodily functioning, such as heartbeat, breathing, and temperature).

○ The male brain is set to renew, recharge, and reorient itself between tasks by moving to what neurologist Ruben Gur has called a "rest state."[13] The boy in the back of the classroom whose eyes are drooping, his mind ready to doze off, may have entered a neural rest state. The man zoning out in front of the television after a long day at work is recharging his brain by entering a neural rest state; so too the grandfather sitting in his fishing boat for hours, content but unstimulated. The rest state, which MRIs

---

[11]Hara Estroff Marano, "The Opposite Sex: The New Sex Scorecard." *Psychology Today*. July/Aug. 2003, pp. 38–44.

[12]Holly VanScoy. "Hot Headed Guys? It's All in the Brain." *HealthScoutNews*, Oct. 1, 2002. Available at http://kprc-tvhealth.ip2m.com/index.cfm.

[13]Ruben Gur. *Weekend House Call* (CNN Saturday Morning News), Dec. 6, 2003. Transcripts available at www.fdch.com. Dr. Gur has pioneered research into male-female difference in white and gray matter (with males having more white matter and females more gray). His work has been corroborated by researcher Richard Haier of the University of California–Irvine and Rex Jung at the University of New Mexico. These new results are available through the online journal *NeuroImage* (February 2005).

have now discovered to be essential to male brain activity, can create big problems in a classroom. Boys make up the vast majority of students who drift off without completing assignments, who stop taking notes or fall asleep during a lecture, and even who begin to tap pencils or fidget in order to self-stimulate (and thus keep themselves awake and learning). With greater blood flow in the brain, girls and women tend to recharge and reorient neural focus without pronounced rest states; thus a girl can be bored with a lesson but nonetheless keep her eyes open and take notes. As Ruben Gur has observed, "In the resting female brain, we find just as much neural activity as in the male brain that is solving problems." The female brain, in other words, doesn't really go to a rest state in the way the male does. Female blood flow even during brain rest is very active. Male blood flow during a rest state is not.

The issue of brain difference becomes increasingly important the more words a teacher uses to teach a lesson (that is, the less diagrammatic a teacher is). The male brain, on average, relies more heavily than does the female on spatial-mechanical stimulation and thus is inherently more stimulated by diagrams, pictures, and objects moving through space than by the monotony of words. If a teacher uses a lot of words, the male brain is more likely than the female to get bored, drift, sleep, fidget. This is just one difference.

The Inherent Fragility of the Male Brain

"Boys are naturally fragile as learners," wrote Helene Crouper, a high school math teacher. "I can see the fragility in their eyes when they don't understand something, or think they've failed. In fact, when I stop seeing it, I really start to worry. When their eyes go blank or 'too cool to learn,' I know they've crushed their own vulnerability or they've had it crushed. That's when I know we've lost them as learners. In our special education classes and learning disability teams, I see a lot of those lost boys. I don't see tough guys, I see fragile minds."

Over the last decade, many of us have learned about men's vulnerability in areas of physical health—how much more likely males are to get various diseases (especially when ethnicity is also a factor) and how much earlier than women our men are dying (seven years for white males, twelve years for black).

We've also heard a great deal in the last decade about how emotionally fragile boys and men can be; we've seen that fragility expressed in suicide, homicide, and other violence. We've learned that boys do, quite often, have tough exteriors, but have profound and powerful feelings in their hearts. As Jamal, sixteen, wrote in a paper on gender roles in his social studies class in a Michigan high school, "Boys are tough, but we get hurt like anyone else. I cry a lot—just not with tears."

Now that our culture has opened the door of understanding to men's and boys' bodies and feelings, we are ready to understand a crucial element of human brain biology: *the male learning brain is inherently fragile.* Neurally speaking, it just isn't as tough as our cultural myths and stereotypes tell us males are or should be.

Neural Vulnerability in the Male Mind

Metaphors about porcelain dolls generally describe girls, not boys, yet a good gender-bender metaphor would be this one: "The male learning brain is more porcelain than the female; the female learning brain is more steel."

Although girls experience their own unique kind of painful vulnerability, consider this research on the male brain, summarized in the bullets below:

- ○ Males are diagnosed with the majority of brain disorders in our schools, predominantly ADD/ADHD (seven boys for every one girl).

- ○ Over two-thirds of children labeled learning-disabled and 90 percent of children labeled behaviorally disabled are boys. As the learning or behavioral disability becomes more severe, boys constitute an increasingly higher statistical number.

- ○ Neurobiologist Jay Belsky, who has studied the whole life span, has summed up the gender-bender conclusion we face as a society: "Actually, males have a more vulnerable biology than females."[14]

When Belsky, Rappaport, and other researchers share these results, some people are skeptical. Our culture is so accustomed to the stereotypes of tough males and fragile females that it's often difficult to believe the new brain research. Fortunately, however, MRIs and PET scans allay skepticism, especially when we localize our discussion to *learning fragility*. A picture, as the saying goes, speaks a thousand words.

When the brains of boys and girls are scanned, researchers see not only less attention activity for a greater number of boys than girls but also less

---

[14]Jay Belsky. "Quantity Counts." *Developmental and Behavioral Pediatrics,* June 2002, pp. 167–170. Also see Dianne Connell and Betsy Gunzelmann. "The New Gender Gap." *Scholastic Instructor,* 2003. . . .

blood flow in the learning male brain between the parts of the brain that control impulse. The frontal lobe, a part of the brain crucial to general learning and to impulse control, grows later in the majority of males and is more vulnerable to disruptions in infant and toddler development in the male brain than in the female.

The Cerebral Cortex

. . . The fragility of the "thinking brain" [the cerebral cortex] . . . led to Nancy Bayley's findings in the late 1990s.[15] At UC Berkeley, she studied the effect of attachment (nurture) on boys' and girls' learning brains, discovering that daughters of mothers who had problems forming secure attachments to their children as infants did not test out significantly lower in intellectual functioning during adolescence than daughters of securely attached mothers (though these girls did have other emotional and relational problems). In contrast, sons of insecurely attached mothers tested out *significantly lower in high school intellectual markers*. Bayley's studies indicate that in the area of educational learning in the cerebral cortex, the female brain seems, in some ways, stronger than the male.

New Genetic Research

Male neural fragility goes beyond the cognitive and intellectual brain centers in the cerebral cortex, as geneticists have discovered. New genetics research shows us neural fragility of the male brain at a *cellular* level. In the last five years, DNA research has revealed a cellular fragility in male development that affects the educational ability of the male brain. As the geneticist Bryan Sykes has researched and reported in his book *Adam's Curse,* the Y chromosome itself (the single chromosome out of our forty-six human chromosomes that creates the male gender and brain) is more fragile than the X chromosome of the female. He points out, "Ironically, although the Y chromosome has become synonymous with male aggression, it is intrinsically unstable." Sykes reports that damaging changes "are ten to fifteen times more likely to happen in male chromosomal cells than in their female counterparts" and that DNA is better protected in the cells of the female body and brain than in the male.[16]

---

[15]Cited in Blum. *Sex on the Brain.*
[16]Brian Sykes. *Adam's Curse: A Future Without Men.* London: Norton, 2004, pp. 286–287.

The impact of genetics and brain research on male vulnerability is important for the whole culture. One parent, one teacher, one person at a time, we are each called to help our civilization absorb this impact and use it to break down the "tough male" stereotype. In few places is this more important than in our diagnostic and treatment procedures for male brain and learning disorders in schools.

Boys constitute the vast majority of our school's learning disorder, brain disorder, and behavioral disorder referrals in our school system, but the school system is diagnosing and treating boys for these disorders without understanding the male mind.

Many boys diagnosed with learning disabilities are "learning-fragile," not "learning-disabled." The starting point for addressing these disabilities lies here, in convincing our educational culture to pay attention from the outset to this inherent male vulnerability—to understand, be sensitive to, and accommodate the needs of learning fragility, without labeling boys as learning-disabled. Boys do not need any more pathologizing—they need understanding.

25

THE GREAT CONTINUUM

DIAGNOSING AUTISM

Temple Grandin

THE FIRST SIGN that a baby may be autistic is that it stiffens up and resists being held and cuddled. It may be extremely sensitive to touch and respond by pulling away or screaming. More obvious symptoms of autism usually occur between twelve and twenty-four months of age. I was my mother's first child, and I was like a little wild animal. I struggled to get away when held, but if I was left alone in the big baby carriage I seldom fussed. Mother first realized that something was dreadfully wrong when I failed to start talking like the little girl next door, and it seemed that I might be deaf. Between nonstop tantrums and a penchant for smearing feces, I was a terrible two-year-old.

At that time, I showed the symptoms of classic autism: no speech, poor eye contact, tantrums, appearance of deafness, no interest in people, and constant staring off into space. I was taken to a neurologist, and when a hearing test revealed that I was not deaf, I was given the label "brain-damaged." Most doctors over forty years ago had never heard of autism. A few years later, when more doctors learned about it, that label was applied.

I can remember the frustration of not being able to talk at age three. This caused me to throw many a tantrum. I could understand what people said to me, but I could not get my words out. It was like a big stutter, and starting words was difficult. My first few words were very difficult to produce and generally had only one syllable, such as "bah" for ball. I can remember logically thinking to myself that I would have to scream because I had no other way to communicate. Tantrums also occurred when I became tired or stressed by too much noise, such as horns going off at a birthday party. My behavior was like a tripping circuit breaker. One minute I was fine, and the next minute I was on the floor kicking and screaming like a crazed wildcat.

I can remember the day I bit my teacher's leg. It was late in the afternoon and I was getting tired. I just lost it. But it was only after I came out of it, when I saw her bleeding leg, that I realized I had bitten her. Tantrums occurred suddenly, like epileptic seizures. Mother figured out that like seizures, they had to run their course. Getting angry once a tantrum started just made it worse. She explained to my elementary school teachers that the best way to handle me if I had a tantrum was not to get angry or excited. She learned that tantrums could be prevented by getting me out of noisy places when I got tired. Privileges such as watching *Howdy Doody* on TV were withdrawn when I had a bad day at school. She even figured out that I'd sometimes throw a tantrum to avoid going to class.

When left alone, I would often space out and become hypnotized. I could sit for hours on the beach watching sand dribbling through my fingers. I'd study each individual grain of sand as it flowed between my fingers. Each grain was different, and I was like a scientist studying the grains under a microscope. As I scrutinized their shapes and contours, I went into a trance which cut me off from the sights and sounds around me.

Rocking and spinning were other ways to shut out the world when I became overloaded with too much noise. Rocking made me feel calm. It was like taking an addictive drug. The more I did it, the more I wanted to do it. My mother and my teachers would stop me so I would get back in touch with the rest of the world. I also loved to spin, and I seldom got dizzy. When I stopped spinning, I enjoyed the sensation of watching the room spin.

Today, autism is regarded as an early childhood disorder by definition, and it is three times more common in boys than girls. For the diagnosis to be made, autistic symptoms must appear before the age of three. The most common symptoms in young children are no speech or abnormal speech, lack of eye contact, frequent temper tantrums, oversensitivity to touch, the appearance of deafness, a preference for being alone, rocking or other rhythmic stereotypic behavior, aloofness, and lack of social contact with parents and siblings. Another sign is inappropriate play with toys. The child may spend long periods of time spinning the wheel of a toy car instead of driving it around on the floor.

Diagnosing autism is complicated by the fact that the behavioral criteria are constantly being changed. These criteria are listed in the *Diagnostic and Statistical Manual* published by the American Psychiatric Association. Using those in the third edition of the book, 91 percent of young children displaying autistic symptoms would be labeled autistic. However, using the newest edition of the book, the label would apply to only 59 percent of the cases, because the criteria have been narrowed.

Many parents with an autistic child will go to many different specialists looking for a precise diagnosis. Unfortunately, diagnosing autism is not like diagnosing measles or a specific chromosomal defect such as Down syndrome. Even though autism is a neurological disorder, it is still diagnosed by observing a child's behavior. There is no blood test or brain scan that can give an absolute diagnosis, though brain scans may partially replace observation in the future.

The new diagnostic categories are autism, pervasive developmental disorder (PDD), Asperger's syndrome, and disintegrative disorder, and there is much controversy among professionals about them. Some consider these categories to be true separate entities, and others believe that they lie on an autistic continuum and there is no definite distinction between them.

A three-year-old child would be labeled autistic if he or she lacked both social relatedness and speech or had abnormal speech. This diagnosis is also called classic Kanner's syndrome, after Leo Kanner, the physician who first described this form of autism, in 1943. These individuals usually learn to talk, but they remain very severely handicapped because of extremely rigid thinking, poor ability to generalize, and no common sense. Some of the Kanner people have savant skills, such as calendar calculation. The savant group comprises about 10 percent of the children and adults who are diagnosed.

A child with classic Kanner's syndrome has little or no flexibility of thinking or behavior. Charles Hart describes this rigidity in his autistic brother, Sumner, who had to be constantly coached by his mother. He had to be told each step of getting undressed and going to bed. Hart goes on to describe the behavior of his autistic son, Ted, during a birthday party when ice cream cones were served. The other children immediately began to lick them, but Ted just stared at his and appeared to be afraid of it. He didn't know what to do, because in the past he had eaten ice cream with a spoon.

Another serious problem for people with Kanner's syndrome is lack of common sense. They can easily learn how to get on a bus to go to school, but have no idea what to do if something interrupts the routine.

Any disruption of routine causes a panic attack, anxiety, or a flight response, unless the person is taught what to do when something goes wrong. Rigid thinking makes it difficult to teach people with Kanner-type autism the subtleties of socially appropriate behavior. For example, at an autism meeting, a young man with Kanner's syndrome walked up to every person and asked, "Where are your earrings?" Kanner autistics need to be told in a clear simple way what is appropriate and inappropriate social behavior.

Uta Frith, a researcher at the MRC Cognitive Development Unit in London, has found that some people with Kanner's syndrome are unable to imagine what another person is thinking. She developed a "theory of mind" test to determine the extent of the problem. For example, Joe, Dick, and a person with autism are sitting at a table. Joe places a candy bar in a box and shuts the lid. The telephone rings, and Dick leaves the room to answer the phone. While Dick is gone, Joe eats the candy bar and puts a pen in the box. The autistic person who is watching is asked, "What does Dick think is in the box?" Many people with autism will give the wrong answer and say "a pen." They are not able to figure out that Dick, who is now outside the room, thinks that the box still contains a candy bar.

People with Asperger's syndrome, who tend to be far less handicapped than people with Kanner-type autism, can usually pass this test and generally perform better on tests of flexible problem-solving than Kanner's syndrome autistics. In fact, many Asperger individuals never get formally diagnosed, and they often hold jobs and live independently. Children with Asperger's syndrome have more normal speech development and much better cognitive skills than those with classic Kanner's. Another label for Asperger's syndrome is "high-functioning autism." One noticeable difference between Kanner's and Asperger's syndromes is that Asperger children are often clumsy. The diagnosis of Asperger's is often confused with PDD, a label that is applied to children with mild symptoms which are not quite serious enough to call for one of the other labels.

Children diagnosed as having disintegrative disorder start to develop normal speech and social behavior and then regress and lose their speech after age two. Many of them never regain their speech, and they have difficulty learning simple household chores. These individuals are also referred to as having low-functioning autism, and they require supervised living arrangements for their entire lives. Some children with disintegrative disorder improve and become high-functioning, but overall, children in this category are likely to remain low-functioning. There is a large group of children labeled autistic who start to develop normally and then regress and lose their speech before age two. These early regressives sometimes have a better prognosis than late regressives. Those who never learn to talk usually have severe neurological impairments that show up on routine tests. They are also more likely to have epilepsy than Kanner or Asperger children. Individuals who are low-functioning often have very poor ability to understand spoken words. Kanner, Asperger, and PDD children and adults usually have a much better ability to understand speech.

Children in all of the diagnostic categories benefit from placement in a good educational program. Prognosis is improved if intensive education is started before age three. I finally learned to speak at three and a half, after a year of intensive speech therapy. Children who regress at eighteen to twenty-four months of age respond to intensive educational programs when speech loss first occurs, but as they become older they may require calmer, quieter teaching methods to prevent sensory overload. If an educational program is successful, many autistic symptoms become less severe.

The only accurate way to diagnose autism in an adult is to interview the person about his or her early childhood and obtain descriptions of his or her behavior from parents or teachers. Other disorders with autistic symptoms, such as acquired aphasia (loss of speech), disintegrative disorder, and Landau-Kleffner syndrome, occur at an older age. A child may have normal or near-normal speech and then lose it between the ages of two and seven. In some cases disintegrative disorder and Landau-Kleffner syndrome may have similar underlying brain abnormalities. Landau-Kleffner syndrome is a type of epilepsy that often causes a child to lose speech. Small seizures scramble hearing and make it difficult or impossible for the child to understand spoken words. A proper diagnosis requires very sophisticated tests, because the seizures are difficult to detect. They will not show up on a simple brain-wave (EEG) test. These disorders can often be successfully treated with anticonvulsants (epilepsy drugs) or corticosteroids such as prednisone. Anticonvulsant medications may also be helpful to autistic children who have abnormal EEGs or sensory scrambling. Other neurological disorders that have symptoms of autism are Fragile X syndrome, Rhea's syndrome, and tuberous sclerosis. Educational and treatment programs that help autistic children are usually helpful for children with these disorders also.

There is still confusion in diagnosing between autism and schizophrenia. Some professionals claim that children with autism develop schizophrenic characteristics in adulthood. Like autism's, schizophrenia's current diagnostic criteria are purely behavioral, though both are neurological disorders. In the future, brain scans will be sophisticated enough to provide an accurate diagnosis. Thus far, brain research has shown that these conditions have different patterns of abnormalities. By definition, autism starts in early childhood, while the first symptoms of schizophrenia usually occur in adolescence or early adulthood. Schizophrenia has two major components, the positive symptoms, which include full-blown hallucinations and delusions accompanied by incoherent thinking, and the negative symptoms, such as flat, dull affect and monotone speech. These negative symptoms often resemble the lack of affect seen in adults with autism.

In the *British Journal of Psychiatry,* Dr. P. Liddle and Dr. T. Barnes wrote that schizophrenia may really be two or three separate conditions. The positive symptoms are entirely different from symptoms of autism, but the negative ones may partially overlap with autistic symptoms. Confusion of the two conditions is the reason that some doctors attempt to treat autism with neuroleptic drugs such as Haldol and Mellaril. But neuroleptics should not be the first-choice medications for autism, because other, safer drugs are often more effective. Neuroleptic drugs have very severe side effects and can damage the nervous system.

Over ten years ago, Dr. Peter Tanguay and Rose Mary Edwards, at UCLA, hypothesized that distortion of auditory input during a critical phase in early childhood development may be one cause of handicaps in language and thinking. The exact timing of the sensory processing problems may determine whether a child has Kanner's syndrome or is a nonverbal, low-functioning autistic. I hypothesize that oversensitivity to touch and auditory scrambling prior to age two may cause the rigidity of thinking and lack of emotional development found in Kanner-type autism. These children partially recover the ability to understand speech between the ages of two and a half and three. Disintegrative disorder children, who develop normally up to two years of age, may be more emotionally normal because emotional centers in the brain have had an opportunity to develop before the onset of sensory processing problems. It may be that a simple difference in timing determines which type of autism develops. Early sensory processing problems may prevent development of the emotional centers of the brain in Kanner-type autistics, while the acquisition of language is more disturbed when sensory processing difficulties occur slightly later.

Research has very clearly shown that autism is a neurological disorder that reveals distinct abnormalities in the brain. Brain autopsy research by Dr. Margaret Bauman has shown that those with both autism and disintegrative disorder have immature development of the cerebellum and the limbic system. Indications of a delay in brain maturation can also be seen in autistic children's brain waves. Dr. David Canter and his associates at the University of Maryland found that low-functioning children between the ages of four and twelve have EEG readings that resemble the brain-wave pattern of a two-year-old. The question is what causes these abnormalities. Studies by many researchers are showing that there may be a cluster of genes that can put a person at risk for many disorders, including autism, depression, anxiety, dyslexia, attention deficit disorder, and other problems.

There is no single autism gene, though most cases of autism have a strong genetic basis. If a person is autistic, his or her chances of having an autistic child are greatly increased. There is also a tendency for the siblings of autistic children to have a higher incidence of learning problems than other children. Studies by Susan Folstein and Mark Rutter in London showed that in 42 percent of the families surveyed, either a sibling or a parent of an autistic child had delayed speech or learning problems.

Genetics, however, does not completely control brain development. Studies of identical twins by Folstein and Rutter show that sometimes one twin is severely autistic and the other has only a few autistic traits. MRI (magnetic resonance imaging) brain scans of identical twin schizophrenics have shown that the more severely afflicted twin has greater brain abnormalities. The brain is so complex that genetics cannot tell every little developing neuron exactly where it should be connected. There is a 10 percent variation in brain anatomical structure that is not controlled by genetics. Brain scans of normal identical twins by Michael Gazzaniga, at the Dartmouth Medical School, showed an easily observable variation in brain structure, but twins' brains are more similar than the brains of unrelated people. Likewise, the personalities of identical twins are similar. Studies at the University of Minnesota by Thomas Bouchard and his colleagues of twins reared in different families show that basic traits such as mathematical ability, athletic ability, and temperament are highly inheritable. A summary of these studies concluded that roughly half of what a person becomes is determined by genetics and the other half is determined by environment and upbringing.

Other theories suggest that if a fetus is exposed to certain toxins and viruses, these may interact with genes to cause the abnormal brain development typical of autism. If either parent is exposed to chemical toxins that slightly damage his or her genetic material, that could increase the likelihood of autism or some other developmental disorder. Some parents suspect that an allergic reaction to early childhood vaccinations triggers autistic regression. If this is true it is likely that the vaccine interacts with genetic factors. Another possibility is immune system abnormalities which interfere with brain development. However, there is still too much that is not known, and neither parent should be held responsible for an autistic child. Scientific studies and interviews with families indicate that both the father's and the mother's side contribute genetically to autism.

The Autistic Continuum

Countless researchers have attempted to figure out what factors determine the difference between high- and low-functioning autism. High-functioning children with Kanner's or Asperger's syndrome usually develop good speech and often do well academically. Low-functioning children are often unable to speak or can say only a few words. They also have trouble learning simple skills such as buttoning a shirt. At age three, both types have similar behaviors, but as they grow older the difference becomes more and more apparent.

When my speech therapist held my chin and directed me to look at her, it jerked me out of my private world, but for others forcing eye contact can cause the opposite reaction—brain overload and shutdown. For instance, Donna Williams, the author of *Nobody Nowhere,* explained that she could use only one sensory channel at a time. If a teacher had grabbed her chin and forced eye contact, she would have turned off her ears. Her descriptions of sensory jumbling provide an important bridge to understanding the difference between high-functioning and low-functioning autism, which I would describe as a sensory processing continuum. At one end of the continuum is a person with Asperger's or Kanner's autism who has mild sensory oversensitivity problems, and at the other end of the spectrum is the low-functioning person who receives jumbled, inaccurate information, both visually and aurally.

I was able to learn to speak because I could understand speech, but low-functioning autistics may never learn to speak because their brains cannot discriminate among speech sounds. Many of these people are mentally retarded, but a few individuals may have a near-normal brain trapped inside a sensory system that does not work. Those who escape the prison of low-functioning autism probably do so because just enough undistorted information gets through. They do not totally lose contact with the world around them.

Twenty years ago, Carl Delacato, a therapist who worked with autistic children, speculated that low-functioning individuals may have "white noise" in their sensory channels. In his book *The Ultimate Stranger,* he described three kinds of sensory processing problems: hyper, hypo, and white noise.

Hyper means oversensitive, hypo means undersensitive, and white noise means internal interference.

In questioning many people with autism, I soon found that there was a continuum of sensory abnormalities that would provide insight into the world of nonverbal people with autism. I imagine that the extent of sensory jumbling they experience would be equivalent to taking Donna's sensory problems and multiplying them tenfold. I am lucky in that I responded well when my mother, teachers, and governess kept encouraging social interaction and play. I was seldom allowed to retreat into the soothing world of rocking or spinning objects. When I daydreamed, my teachers yanked me back to reality.

Almost half of all very young children with autism respond well to gently intrusive programs in which they are constantly encouraged to look at the teacher and interact. Brightly colored wall decorations made learning fun for me, but they may be too distracting for a child with sensory jumbling. The popular Lovaas program, developed at UCLA, is being used successfully there to mainstream nearly half of young autistic children into a normal kindergarten or first grade. The Lovaas method pairs words with objects, and the children are rewarded with praise and food when they correctly match a word with an object. While this program is wonderful for some kids, it is certain to be confusing and possibly painful for children with severe sensory jumbling and mixing problems.

These children require a different approach. Touch is often their most reliable sense, and they learn best if teachers use a tactile system. One mother taught her nonverbal daughter to draw a circle by holding her hand and guiding it to make a circle. Plastic letters that can be felt are often useful for teaching words. The more protected these children are from distracting sights and sounds, the more likely it is that their dysfunctional nervous system will be able to perceive speech accurately. To help them hear better, teachers must protect them from visual stimuli that will cause sensory overload. They may hear best in a quiet, dimly illuminated room that is free of fluorescent lights and bright wall decorations. Sometimes hearing is enhanced if the teacher whispers or sings softly. Teachers need to speak slowly to accommodate a nervous system that processes information slowly. And sudden movements that will cause sensory confusion should also be avoided.

Children who are echolalic—who repeat what they hear—may be at a midpoint on the sensory processing continuum. Enough recognizable speech gets through for them to be able to repeat the words. Dr. Doris Allen, at the Albert Einstein Hospital in New York, emphasizes that echolalia should not be discouraged, so as not to inhibit speech. The child repeats what has been said to verify that he heard it correctly. Research by Laura Berk, at Illinois State University, has shown that normal children talk to themselves to help them control their behavior and learn new skills. Since autism is caused by immature brain development, it is likely that echolalia and self-talking, which occur in older autistic children, are the result of immature speech patterns.

Unlike normal children, who naturally connect language to the things in their lives at a remarkable rate, autistic children have to learn that objects have names. They have to learn that words communicate. All autistic children have problems with long strings of verbal information. Even very high-functioning people have difficulty following verbal instructions and find it easier to follow written instructions, since they are unable to remember the sequence of the information. My college math teacher once commented that I took excessive notes. He told me that I should pay attention and understand the concept. The problem was that it was impossible for me to remember the sequence of the problems without the notes. I learned to read with phonics and sounding out words, because I was able to understand speech by age three. Children with more severe auditory processing problems often learn to read before they can speak. They learn best if a written word is paired with an object, because many of them have very poor comprehension of spoken words.

As an adult my method for learning a foreign language may be similar to how a more severely impaired autistic child learns to understand language. I cannot pick words out of a conversation in a foreign language until I have seen them written first.

Two basic patterns of autistic symptoms can help identify which children will respond well to intensive, gently intrusive teaching methods, and which will not. The first kind of child may appear deaf at age two, but by age three he or she can understand speech. I was this kind. When adults spoke directly to me, I could understand them, but when they talked among themselves, it sounded like gibberish. The second kind of child appears to develop normally until one and a half or two and then loses speech. As the syndrome progresses, the ability to understand speech deteriorates and autistic symptoms worsen. A child that has been affectionate withdraws into autism as his sensory system becomes more and more scrambled. Eventually he may lose awareness of his surroundings, because his brain is not able to process and understand sights and sounds around him. There are also children who are mixtures of the two kinds of autism.

Children of the first kind will respond well to intensive, structured educational programs that pull them out of the autistic world, because their sensory systems provide a more or less accurate representation of things around them. There may be problems with sound or touch sensitivity, but they still have some realistic awareness of their surroundings. The second kind of child may not respond, because sensory jumbling makes the world incomprehensible. Gently intrusive teaching methods will work on some children who lose their speech before age two if teaching is started before their senses become totally scrambled. Catherine Maurice describes her successful use of the Lovaas program with her two children, who lost speech at fifteen and eighteen months of age, in her book, *Let Me Hear Your Voice*. Teaching was started within six months of the onset of symptoms. The regression into autism was not complete, and her children still had some awareness. If she had waited until they were four or five, it is very likely that the Lovaas method would have caused confusion and sensory overload. My experience and that of others has shown that an effective teaching method coupled with reasonable amounts of effort should work. Desperate parents often get hooked into looking for magic cures that require ten hours a day of intensive treatment. To be effective, educational programs do have to be done every day, but they usually do not require heroic amounts of effort. My mother spent thirty minutes five days a week for several months teaching me to read. Mrs. Maurice had a teacher spend twenty hours a week on the Lovaas method with her children. In addition to participating in formal educational programs, young autistic children need a structured day, both in the school and at home. Several studies have shown that twenty to twenty-five hours a week of intensive treatment which required the child to constantly interact with his teacher was most effective. A neurologist gave my mother some very good advice: to follow her own instincts. If a child is improving in an educational program, then it should be continued, but if there is no progress, something else should be tried. Mother had a knack for recognizing which people could help me and which ones could not. She sought out the best teachers and schools for me, in an era when most autistic children were placed in institutions. She was determined to keep me out of an institution.

A controversial technique called facilitated communication is now being used with nonverbal people with autism. Using the technique, the teacher supports the person's hand while he or she taps out messages on a typewriter keyboard. Some severely handicapped people have problems with stopping and starting hand movements, and they also have involuntary movements that make typing difficult. Supporting the person's wrist helps to initiate motion of the hand toward the keyboard and pulls his fingers off the keyboard after he pushes a key to prevent perseveration and multiple pushing of a single key. Merely touching the person's shoulder can help him initiate hand movements.

Several years ago, facilitated communication was hailed as a major breakthrough, and wild claims were made that the most severely handicapped autistic people had completely normal intelligence and emotions. Fifty scientific studies have now shown that in the vast majority of cases, the teacher was moving the person's hand, as if it were a planchet on a Ouija board. The teacher was communicating, instead of the person with autism. A summary of forty-three studies in the *Autism Research Review* showed that 5 percent of nonverbal, severely handicapped people can communicate with simple one-word responses. In the few cases where facilitated communication has been successful, someone has spent many hours teaching the person to read first.

It is likely that the truth about facilitated communication is somewhere between wishful hand-pushing and real communication. Carol Berger, of New Breakthroughs in Eugene, Oregon, found that low-functioning autistics could achieve 33 percent to 75 percent accuracy in typing one-word answers. Some of the poor results in controlled studies may have been due to sensory overload caused by the presence of strange people. Reports from parents indicate that a few adults and children initially need wrist support and then gradually learn to type independently. But the person must know how to read, and facilitator influence cannot be completely ruled out until wrist or arm support is removed.

Parents who are desperate to reach their autistic children often look for miracles. It's hard not to get caught up in new promises of hope, because there have been so few real breakthroughs in the understanding of autism.

The Autistic Continuum

It appears that at one end of the spectrum, autism is primarily a cognitive disorder, and at the other end, it is primarily a sensory processing disorder. At the severely impaired sensory processing end, many children may be diagnosed as having disintegrative disorder. At a midpoint along the spectrum, autistic symptoms appear to be caused by equal amounts of cognitive and sensory problems. There can be mild and severe cases at all points along the continuum. Both the severity and the ratio of these two components are variable, and each case of autism is different. When a person with autism improves because of either educational or medical intervention, the severity of a cognitive or sensory problem may diminish, but the ratio between the two seems to stay the same. What remains inexplicable, however, are rigid thinking patterns and lack of emotional affect in many high-functioning people. One of the perplexing things about autism is that it is almost impossible to predict which toddler will become high-functioning. The severity of the symptoms at age two or three is often not correlated with the prognosis.

The world of the nonverbal person with autism is chaotic and confusing. A low-functioning adult who is still not toilet-trained may be living in a completely disordered sensory world. It is likely that he has no idea of his body boundaries and that sights, sounds, and touches are all mixed together. It must be like seeing the world through a kaleidoscope and trying to listen to a radio station that is jammed with static at the same time. Add to that a broken volume control, which causes the volume to jump erratically from a loud boom to inaudible. Such a person's problems are further compounded by a nervous system that is often in a greater state of fear and panic than the nervous system of a Kanner-type autistic. Imagine a state of hyperarousal where you were being pursued by a dangerous attacker in a world of total chaos. Not surprisingly, new environments make low-functioning autistics fearful.

Puberty often makes the problem worse. Birger Sellin describes in his book *I Don't Want to Be Inside Me Anymore* how his well-behaved son developed unpredictable screaming fits and tantrums at puberty. The hormones of adolescence further sensitized and inflamed an overaroused nervous system. Dr. John Ratey, at Harvard University, uses the concept of noise in the nervous system to describe such hyperarousal and confusion. Medications such as beta-blockers and clonidine are often helpful because they can calm an overaroused sympathetic nervous system.

Autistics with severe sensory problems sometimes engage in self-injurious behavior such as biting themselves or hitting their heads. Their sensory sensations are so disordered that they may not realize they are hurting themselves. Though a recent study by Reed Elliot published in the *Journal of Autism and Developmental Disabilities* showed that very vigorous aerobic exercise reduced aggression and self-injury in half of mentally retarded autistic adults, educational and behavioral training will help almost all people with autism to function better. Early intervention in a good program can enable about 50 percent of autistic children to be enrolled in a normal first grade. Though most autistics will not function at my level, their ability to live a productive life will be improved. Medication can help reduce the hyperarousal of many low-functioning older children and help them control their behavior. Many nonverbal autistics are capable of doing simple jobs such as washing windows or routine manual work. Few nonverbal autistic adults are able to read and are capable of doing normal schoolwork.

Many parents and teachers have asked me where I fit on the autistic continuum. I still have problems with rapid responses to unexpected social situations. In my business dealings I can handle new situations, but every once in a while I panic when things go wrong. I've learned to deal with the fear of traveling, so that I have a backup plan if, for example, my plane is late. I have no problems if I mentally rehearse every scenario, but I still panic if I'm not prepared for a new situation, especially when I travel to a foreign country where I am unable to communicate. Since I can't rely on my library of social cues, I feel very helpless when I can't speak the language. Often I withdraw.

If I were two years old today, I would be diagnosed with classic Kanner's syndrome, because I had delayed abnormal speech development. However, as an adult I would probably be diagnosed as having Asperger's syndrome, because I can pass a simple theory-of-mind test and I have greater cognitive flexibility than a classic Kanner autistic. All of my thinking is still in visual images, though it appears that thinking may become less visual as one moves along the continuum away from classic Kanner's syndrome. My sensory oversensitivities are worse than the mild difficulties some Kanner autistics have, but I do not have sensory mixing and jumbling problems. Like most autistics, I don't experience the feelings attached to personal relationships. My visual world is a literal one, though I have made progress by finding visual symbols to carry me beyond the fixed and rigid worlds of other people with classic Kanner autism.

In an article written by Oliver Sacks in *The New Yorker,* I was quoted as saying, "If I could snap my fingers and be nonautistic, I would not. Autism is part of what I am." In contrast, Donna Williams says, "Autism is not me. Autism is just an information processing problem that controls who I am." Who is right? I think we both are, because we are on different parts of the autism spectrum. I would not want to lose my ability to think visually. I have found my place along the great continuum.

Update: Diagnosis and Education

Both parents and teachers make the mistake of thinking a diagnosis of autism, PDD (Pervasive Developmental Disorder), ADHD (Attention Deficit Hyperactivity Disorder), or Asperger's is precise. It is not precise the way a diagnosis for measles or meningitis is precise. It is a behavioral profile and different doctors and psychologists often come up with a different diagnosis because they interpret the child's behavior differently. At the time of writing this update, there is no definitive brain imaging or laboratory test for the diagnosis of autism.

. . . The mild Asperger diagnosis is being used more and more. At the many autism conferences that I attend, I am observing more and more very smart children with a diagnosis of Asperger's. Some of these children should be in a gifted and talented class instead of being sent to special education. There are other Asperger's individuals who may need special education in their area of weakness and be in an advanced class in their area of strength. I am worried that students who would be capable of a challenging career in science, engineering, or computers may be shunted into a special education rut. In fairness to special education teachers, it is difficult to work with a spectrum that can range from nonverbal to genius.

Diane Kennedy, author of *ADHD Autism Connection,* was one of the first people to write about the confusion of Asperger's with attention deficit problems. I talk to more and more parents of children with a diagnosis that switches back and forth between Asperger's and ADHD. Many parents have told me that stimulant ADHD medications such as Ritalin (metehylphenidate) and Adderall (a combination of four different types of amphetamines) have greatly helped their children. It is likely that some individuals on the high-functioning end of the autism spectrum share traits with ADHD. Children or adults who have more classical types of autism or are nonverbal often become agitated and worse on stimulants. A trial of only one or two pills is all that is needed to determine if stimulants will be helpful or terrible.

Brain Research and Early Diagnosis

During the last ten years, there has been an increased understanding of autistic brain abnormalities. A normal child's brain grows at a steady rate. Detailed brain scans of autistic children in Dr. Eric Courchesne's lab indicated that in the first year of life there is premature overgrowth of the brain followed by an arrest of growth. Children with greater amounts of abnormal overgrowth usually have more severe autism. Research has also shown that the serotonin systems in the autistic child's brain are highly abnormal. This may explain why doses for SSRI antidepressants often need to be kept very low to prevent agitation. The degree and pattern of abnormal overgrowth will be highly variable from child to child. David Amarel at the University of California found that the variability of overgrowth was greatest in low-functioning autism. He also discovered that the immune system is often abnormal and may affect the brain.

The excess of brain overgrowth causes the infant's head to become abnormally large between the ages of one and two. Later in childhood, the head size returns to normal due to later under growth of the brain. Measuring a young infant's head circumference (hat size) with a tape measure could be used as a simple screening tool for detecting babies who might be at risk for autism.

Other early screening tools that are being developed test for joint attention. Joint attention occurs when normal babies orient and follow an adult's gaze. When the adult is playing a little game, asking the baby to look at the pretty birdie, the baby will look where the adult is looking. The infant at risk for developmental problems will not follow an adult's gaze. Patricia Kohl at the University of Washington is working on another screening tool. This tool will detect children at risk for developmental problems who do not orient toward normal speech sounds. This is due to being unable to hear consonant sounds. Normal babies prefer to listen to "motherese"—expressive slowed-down speech where the mother enunciates the words. Autistic babies prefer computerized warbling nonspeech sounds. The test would be conducted by observing the infant to determine which sounds he orients toward.

Early Education

Both scientific studies and practical experience have fully confirmed that young children with autism need at least twenty hours a week of intensive one-to-one teaching by an adult. All experts agree that the *worst* thing to do with an autistic two- to five-year-old is to let him watch TV all day. There is much debate about the best early education programs. I have observed that the best teachers tend to use the same methods regardless of the theoretical basis of the program. A review of teaching methods by Sally Rogers at the University of California at Davis indicated that discrete trial or ABA (Applied Behavioral Analysis) teaching methods were the most effective to get language started. This structured highly repetitive method helps jump-start language in young two- to five-year-olds. The discrete trial programs used today are usually more natural and less rigid than the older Lovaas method. To teach socialization and play skills methods such as Greenspan's floor-time and Dr. Lynn Kern Koegel's program are more effective. Dr. Koegel's book *Overcoming Autism* is full of practical teaching methods. In the floor-time method, the teacher engages the child in many interactive games and encourages social play.

Autism and PDD are highly variable and the methods that work for each child should be used. Dr. Koegel found that some little children respond well to a highly structured Lovaas-style program and other types of autistic children, who are more socially engaged, may make more progress with a less structured program. Do not get too single-minded on one method. Use things that work and eliminate things that do not work. Sometimes a combination of methods is best. For older high-functioning children, highly repetitious programs are boring and they need lessons that will stimulate their minds. In elementary school children a child's fixation can be used to motivate learning. If a child loves trains, then read a book about a train or do a math problem involving trains.

If shooting-type video games had been available when I was little, I would have become a total addict and I may not have developed more career-related interests such as building things or flying kites and airplanes. The video games with lots of rapid movement are the most addictive. For me, rapid movement video games would have just been another way to "stim" and "zone out." I would rather encourage the older child to become really interested in doing science on a computer or learning programming. Free software is available that will turn a kid's computer into part of a super computer that crunches numbers on a real scientific project. The May 6, 2005, issue of *Science* is devoted to these fascinating projects. Looking at the NASA website and following a space probe during its journey is a wonderful way to use computers. The problem with video games is that both parents and teachers tell me that some students get so addicted that they have no other interests. I get hypnotized by screen savers with changing patterns that move rapidly. I cannot stop looking at them and for me to get any work done I have to shut them off. Video games or screen savers that move slowly do not have this effect.

Totally banning shooting-type games is probably a bad idea, but the time playing them should be severely limited. This is especially important for a child like me. They provide an activity that the autistic child can discuss with other kids at school and this may help the child socially. However, I want to direct the autistic child's interests into more constructive activities.

Genetics and Autism

Research during the last ten years confirms that autism, PDD, and Asperger's all have a strong genetic basis. Craig Newschaffer, Johns Hopkins School of Medicine, estimates that 60 to 90 percent of autism cases are genetic. Dr. Isabel Rapin and her colleagues at Albert Einstein College of Medicine reviewed papers published between 1961 and 2003. They concluded that interactions between multiple genes explain the highly variable nature of autism. Genome scans of families with many cases of autism indicate that at least ten genes are involved. They also found that the probability of having a second autistic child is 2 to 8 percent. Researchers have also confirmed previous studies that show that relatives of people with autism will often have many milder autistic-like symptoms. I have observed that the probability of having a child with low-functioning autism increases when *both* parents and their families have many autistic traits.

Many computer programmers exhibit autistic traits. Steve Silberman asked in an article entitled "The Geek Syndrome" in *Wired* magazine—are math and tech genes to blame? The computer and technical industries depend on people with attention to detail. The real social people are not interested in computers. Herbert Schreir of the Children's Hospital in Oakland, California, believes that intermarriage of "techies" explains why people have noticed high pockets of autism around Stanford and MIT Universities.

In 2004 and 2005, my webmaster for www.grandin.com (my livestock website) started giving me a list every month of the cities with the most hits on my webpage. Month after month, Redmond, Washington, where Microsoft is located and San Mateo, California, near Stanford University are in my top five cities. There is a total of one hundred cities on the list. The number one page downloaded is the first chapter of *Thinking in Pictures*. Even though my site is a livestock site, the autism book chapter gets the heaviest traffic. Is this because people in these areas are especially interested in the ways brains work, or does autism affect them more directly?

There are differences of opinion in the autism field about the relationship between autism and Asperger's. Are they really separate syndromes? Family and genetic studies done in the United Kingdom indicate that autism and Asperger's are part of the same spectrum. Research by Fred Volkmar at Yale showed that Asperger individuals with no speech delay are often poor at a visual thinking task such as the block design test on the WISC [Wechsler Intelligence Scale for Children] and high-functioning autistic individuals are more likely to be good at this test. In the block design test, the task is to assemble colored blocks to match patterns shown in a book. This difference could be explained by the differences in where the "computer cables" hook up. The underlying brain abnormality of underconnectivity problems would still be similar.

There is concern among people with Asperger's that genetic testing could eliminate them. This would be a terrible price to pay. Many gifted and talented people could be wiped out. A little bit of autism genetics may provide an advantage though too much creates a low-functioning, nonverbal individual. The development of genetic tests for autism will be extremely controversial.

Autism Epidemic

Many researchers agree that the increase in Asperger's syndrome is mostly increased detection. People who used to be labeled as science geeks or computer nerds are now diagnosed with Asperger's. Research in Sweden by Christopher Gillberg showed that some severe cases that used to be labeled mentally retarded are now labeled autistic. Another cause of the increase may be changes made to the DSMIV (Diagnostic and Statistical Manual) published by the American Psychiatric Association in 1994 to expand the diagnostic criteria to include Asperger's and Pervasive Developmental Disorders (PDD). The Centers for Disease Control (CDC) estimate that there are three to four autism cases per one thousand children. A CDC study in Atlanta, Georgia, indicated that 40 percent of all children on the spectrum are only diagnosed at school and 41 percent of special education students are on the autism spectrum. A fully verbal child with mild Asperger's will often not have any problems until he or she enrolls in school. Unfortunately there are severe cases of autism who do not receive services until they go to school. From my own observations there is one type of autism that I think has increased: the regressive type where the child loses language at age eighteen to twenty-four months. David Geier and Mark Geir, two autism consultants, state that exposure to mercury causes regression-type autism. Mercury has now been removed from many vaccines, but fish and power plant emissions are other sources of mercury. Other scientists question the effect of mercury in the incidence of autism.

There is increasing concern about environmental effects on the fetus during pregnancy. If these factors affect the incidence of autism, they probably could interact with susceptible genetics. An outside insult like toxic exposure could turn a brilliant Asperger baby into a nonverbal one. This is purely speculation. New research supports the idea that genetics susceptibility interacts with environmental insults. Scientists have developed a genetic line of mice that are highly susceptible to mercury toxicity. When the mice are given injections that mimic a vaccination schedule the normal mice have no ill effects and the susceptible mice develop autistic-like symptoms such as tail chewing and repetitive behaviors. Possibly there are some children who would have a similar susceptibility to mercury. Mady Horning at the Columbia University School of Public Health has a three-strikes model. The factors that all interact with each other to cause a developmental disability are:

1. Genetic susceptibility

2. Exposure to a toxic agent

3. The timing during development that exposure to a toxic agent occurs. A toxic agent may have no effect at one stage of development and bad effects at another stage.

Twin studies show further evidence of an interaction between environment and genetics. Mady Horning states that the concordance rate for autism in genetically identical twins is 90 percent. This means that 90 percent of the time both twins are autistic. In genetically different nonidentical twins the concordance rate is 35 percent and the autism rate in siblings is 4 percent. Further information on the mercury controversy can be found at the Autism Research Institute in San Diego, California, or in a new book by David Kirby entitled *Evidence of Harm*.

REFERENCES

Allen, D. 1994. Conference. The Virginia Foundation for the Exceptional Child and Adolescent, October 8, 1994. Richmond, Virginia.

American Psychiatric Association. 1994. *Diagnostic and statistical manual IV.* Washington, D.C.

Asperger, H. 1944. Autistic psychopathy in childhood. Translated by Uta Frith. In U. Frith (ed.), *Autism and Asperger's syndrome.* Cambridge University Press, Cambridge, England, pp. 37–92.

Bauman, M. L., and Kemper, T. L. 1994. Neuroanatomic observations of the brain in autism. In M. L. Bauman and T. L. Kemper (eds.), *The neurobiology of autism.* Johns Hopkins University Press, Baltimore, Maryland, pp. 119–145.

Berger, C. L. 1992. *Facilitated communication guide.* New Breakthroughs, Eugene, Oregon.

Berk, L. 1994. Why children talk to themselves. *Scientific American,* November 1994, pp. 78–83.

Bouchard, T. J. 1994. Genes, environment and personality. *Science,* 264: 1700–1701.

Canter, D. S., Thatcher, R. W., Hrybyk, M., and Kaye, H. 1986. Computerized EEG analysis of autistic children. *Journal of Autism and Development Disorders,* 16: 169–187.

Cunningham, A. 2005. Finding autism earlier. *Scientific American Mind,* 16(1): 7.

Delacato, C. H. 1974. *The ultimate stranger.* Arena, Novato, California.

Eastham, M. 1990. *Silent words.* Oliver Pate, Ottawa.

Elliot, R. O., Dobbin, A. R., Rose, G. D., and Soper, H. V. 1994. Vigorous aerobic exercise versus general motor training effects on maladaptive and stereotypic behavior of adults with both autism and mental retardation. *Journal of Autism and Developmental Disorders,* 24: 565–576.

Folstein, S., and Rutter, M. 1977. Infantile autism: A genetic study of 21 twin pairs. *Journal of Child Psychiatry,* 18: 297–321.

Frith, U. 1989. *Autism: explaining the enigma.* Basil Blackwell, Oxford, England.

Gazzaniga, M. S. 1989. Organization of the human brain. *Science,* 243: 947–952.

Geir, M. R., and Geier, D. A. 2003. Neurodevelopmental disorders following thimerosal containing vaccines. *Experimental Biology and Medicine,* 228: 660–664.

Gilchrist, A., Green, J., Cox, A., Burton, D., Rutter, M., and LeCooteur, A. 2001. Development and cortical functioning in adolescents with Asperger's syndrome: A comparative study. *Journal of Child Psychiatry,* 42: 227–240.

Holden, C. 2005. Mating for autism. *Science,* 308: 948.

Homey, M., Chian, D., and Lipkin, W. I. 2004. Neurotoxic effects of postnatal thimerosal mouse strain dependent. *Molecular Psychiatry,* 9: 833–845.

Kanner, L. 1943. Autistic disturbances of affective contact. *Nervous Child,* 2: 217–250.

Kennedy, D. 2002. *The ADHD autism connection.* Water Brook Press, Colorado Springs, Colorado.

Kirby, D. 2005. *Evidence of harm.* St. Martin's Press, New York.

Koegel, L., and Lazebnik, C. 2004. *Overcoming autism.* Viking (Penguin Group), New York.

Liddle, P., and Barnes, T. 1990. Symptoms of chronic schizophrenia. *British Journal of Psychiatry,* 157: 558–561.

Lovaas, I. 1987. Behavioral treatment and normal educational and intellectual functioning in young autistic children. *Journal of Consulting and Clinical Psychology,* 55: 3–9. (Long-term outcome of this treatment is discussed in a series of articles in the *American Journal of Mental Retardation,* 97: 359–391.)

Maurice, C. 1993. *Let me hear your voice.* Knopf, New York.

Muhle, R., Trentacoste, S. V., and Rapin, I. 2004. The genetics of autism. *Pediatrics,* 113: 472–486.

Plomin, R., Owen, M. J., and McGuffin, G. 1994. The genetic basis of complex human behaviors. *Science,* 264: 1733–1739.

Rimland, B., and Green, G. 1993. Controlled evaluations of facilitated communication. *Autism Research Review,* 7: 7.

Sacks, O. 1994. An anthropologist on Mars. *New Yorker,* December 27, pp. 106–125.

Sellin, B. 1995. *I don't want to be inside me anymore.* Basic Books, New York.

Silberman, S. 2001. The geek syndrome. *Wired,* December pp. 175–187.

Spence, S. J. 2004. The genetics of autism. *Seminar Pediatric Neurology,* 11: 196–204.

Tanguay, P. E., and Edwards, R. M. 1982. Electrophysiological studies of autism: The whisper of the bang. *Journal of Autism and Developmental Disabilities,* 12: 177–184.

Treasure Chest of Behavioral Strategies, Future Horizons, Arlington, Texas.

Volkmar, R. R., and Cohen, D. J. 1989. Disintegrative disorder or "late onset": Autism. *Journal of Child Psychiatry,* 30: 717–724.

Wainwright-Sharp, J. A. 1993. Visual orienting deficits in high-functioning people with autism. *Journal of Autism and Developmental Disorders,* 23: 1–13.

Williams, D. 1992. *Nobody nowhere.* Time Books, New York.

OTHER READINGS

Coleman, R. S., Frankel, E., Ritvoe, E., and Freeman, B. J. 1976. The effects of fluorescent and incandescent illumination upon repetitive behaviors in autistic children. *Journal of Autism and Developmental Disorders,* 6: 157–162.

Lovaas, I. O. 1992. *The me book.* Pro-Ed, Austin, Texas.

Martin, R. 1994. *Out of silence: a journey into language.* Henry Holt, New York.

Osterling, J., and Dawson, G. 1994. Early recognition of children with autism. *Journal of Autism and Developmental Disorders,* 24: 247–257.

Paquier, P. E, VanDongen, H. R., and Loonen, C. B. 1992. Landau-Kleffner syndrome or "acquired aphasia with convulsive disorder." *Archives of Neurology,* 49: 354–359.

Sands, S., and Ratey, J. J. 1986. The concept of noise. *Psychiatry,* 49: 290–297.

Simmons, J., and Sabine, O. 1987. *The hidden child.* Woodbine House, Kensington, Maryland.

Walters, R. G., and Walters, W. E. 1980. Decreasing self-stimulatory behavior with physical exercise in a group of autistic boys. *Journal of Autism and Developmental Disorders,* 10: 379–387.

26

BROKEN MIRRORS

A THEORY OF AUTISM

Vilayanur S. Ramachandran
Lindsay M. Oberman

AT FIRST GLANCE you might not notice anything odd on meeting a young boy with autism. But if you try to talk to him, it will quickly become obvious that something is seriously wrong. He may not make eye contact with you; instead he may avoid your gaze and fidget, rock his body to and fro, or bang his head against the wall. More disconcerting, he may not be able to conduct anything remotely resembling a normal conversation. Even though he can experience emotions such as fear, rage, and pleasure, he may lack genuine empathy for other people and be oblivious to subtle social cues that most children would pick up effortlessly.

In the 1940s two physicians—American psychiatrist Leo Kanner and Austrian pediatrician Hans Asperger—independently discovered this developmental disorder, which afflicts about 0.5 percent of American children. Neither researcher had any knowledge of the other's work, and yet by an uncanny coincidence each gave the syndrome the same name: autism, which derives from the Greek word *autos,* meaning "self." The name is apt, because the most conspicuous feature of the disorder is a withdrawal from social interaction. More recently, doctors have adopted the term "autism spectrum disorder" to make it clear that the illness has many related variants that range widely in severity but share some characteristic symptoms.

Ever since autism was identified, researchers have struggled to determine what causes it. Scientists know that susceptibility to autism is inherited, although environmental risk factors also seem to play a role. . . . Starting in the late 1990s, investigators in our laboratory at the University of California, San Diego [U.C.S.D.] set out to explore whether there was a connection between autism and a newly discovered class of nerve cells in the brain called mirror neurons. Because these neurons appeared to be involved in abilities such as empathy and the perception of another individual's intentions, it seemed logical to hypothesize that a dysfunction of the mirror neuron system could result in some of the symptoms of autism. Over the past decade, several studies have provided evidence for this theory. Further investigations of mirror neurons may explain how autism arises, and in the process physicians may develop better ways to diagnose and successfully treat the disorder.

Explaining the Symptoms

Although the chief diagnostic signs of autism are social isolation, lack of eye contact, poor language capacity, and absence of empathy, other less well known symptoms are commonly evident. Many people with autism have problems understanding metaphors, sometimes interpreting them literally. They also have difficulty miming other people's actions. Often they display an eccentric preoccupation with trifles yet ignore important aspects of their environment, especially their social surroundings. Equally puzzling is the fact that they frequently show an extreme aversion to certain sounds that, for no obvious reason, set off alarm bells in their minds.

The theories that have been proposed to explain autism can be divided into two groups: anatomical and psychological. (Researchers have rejected a third group of theories—such as the "refrigerator mother" hypothesis—that blame the disorder on poor upbringing.) Eric Courchesne of U.C.S.D. and other anatomists have shown elegantly that children with autism have characteristic abnormalities in the cerebellum, the brain structure responsible for coordinating complex voluntary muscle movements. Although these observations must be taken into account in any final explanation of autism, it would be premature to conclude that damage to the cerebellum is the sole cause of the disorder. Cerebellar damage inflicted by a stroke in a child usually produces tremors, swaying gait, and abnormal eye movements—symptoms rarely seen in autism. Conversely, one does not see any of the symptoms typical of autism in patients with cerebellar disease. It is possible that the cerebellar changes observed in children with autism may be unrelated side effects of abnormal genes whose *other* effects are the true causes of the disorder.

Perhaps the most ingenious of the psychological theories is that of Uta Frith of University College London and Simon Baron-Cohen of the University of Cambridge, who posit that the main abnormality in autism is a deficit in the ability to construct a "theory of other minds." Frith and Baron-Cohen argue that specialized neural circuitry in the brain allows us to create sophisticated hypotheses about the inner workings of other people's minds. These hypotheses, in turn, enable us to make useful predictions about others' behavior. Frith and Baron-Cohen are obviously on the right track, but their theory does not provide a complete explanation for the constellation of seemingly unrelated symptoms of autism. Indeed, saying that people with autism cannot interact socially because they lack a "theory of other minds" does not go very far beyond restating the symptoms. What researchers need to identify are the brain mechanisms whose known functions match those that are disrupted in autism.

One clue comes from the work of Giacomo Rizzolatti and his colleagues at the University of Parma in Italy, who in the 1990s studied neural activity in the brains of macaque monkeys while the animals were performing goal-directed actions. Researchers have known for decades that certain neurons in the premotor cortex—part of the brain's frontal lobe—are involved in controlling voluntary movements. For instance, one neuron will fire when the monkey reaches for a peanut, another will fire when the animal pulls a lever, and so on. These brain cells are often referred to as motor command neurons. (Bear in mind that the neuron whose activity is recorded does not control the arm by itself; it is part of a circuit that can be monitored by observing the signals in the constituent neurons.)

What surprised Rizzolatti and his coworkers was that a subset of the motor command neurons also fired when the monkey watched another monkey or a researcher perform the same action. For example, a neuron involved in controlling the reach-for-the-peanut action fired when the monkey saw one of his fellows making that movement. Brain-imaging techniques subsequently showed that these so-called mirror neurons also exist in the corresponding regions of the human cortex. These observations implied that mirror neurons—or, more accurately, the networks they are part of—not only send motor commands but also enable both monkeys and humans to determine the intentions of other individuals by mentally simulating their actions. In monkeys, the role of the neurons may be limited to predicting simple goal-directed actions, but in humans the mirror neuron system may have evolved the ability to interpret more complex intentions.

Later research showed that mirror neurons are located in other parts of the human brain, such as the cingulate and insular cortices, and that they may play a role in empathetic emotional responses. While studying the anterior cingulated cortex of awake human subjects, investigators found that certain neurons that typically fire in response to pain also fired when the person saw someone else in pain. Mirror neurons may also be involved in imitation, an ability that appears to exist in rudimentary form in the great apes but is most pronounced in humans. The propensity to imitate must be at least partly innate: Andrew Meltzoff of the University of Washington has shown that if you stick your tongue out at a newborn baby, the infant will do the same. Because the baby cannot see its own tongue, it cannot use visual feedback and error correction to learn the skill. Instead there must be a hardwired mechanism in the child's brain for mapping the mother's visual appearance—whether it be a tongue sticking out or a smile—onto the motor command neurons.

Language development in childhood also requires a remapping of sorts between brain areas. To imitate the mother's or father's words, the child's brain must transform auditory signals in the hearing centers of the brain's temporal lobes into verbal output from the motor cortex. Whether mirror neurons are directly involved in this skill is not known, but clearly some analogous process must be going on. Last, mirror neurons may enable humans to see themselves as others see them, which may be an essential ability for self-awareness and introspection.

Suppressing Mu Waves

What has all this to do with autism? In the late 1990s our group at U.C.S.D. noted that mirror neurons appear to be performing precisely the same functions that seem to be disrupted in autism. If the mirror neuron system is indeed involved in the interpretation of complex intentions, then a breakdown of this neural circuitry could explain the most striking deficit in people with autism, their lack of social skills. The other cardinal signs of the disorder—absence of empathy, language deficits, poor imitation, and so on—are also the kinds of things you would expect to see if mirror neurons were dysfunctional. Andrew Whitten's group at the University of St. Andrews in Scotland made this proposal at about the same time we did, but the first experimental evidence for the hypothesis came from our lab, working in collaboration with Eric L. Altschuler and Jaime A. Pineda of U.C.S.D.

To demonstrate mirror neuron dysfunction in children with autism, we needed to find a way to monitor the activity of their nerve cells without putting electrodes in their brains (as Rizzolatti and his colleagues did with their monkeys). We realized that we could do so using an electroencephalogram (EEG) measurement of the children's brain waves. For more than half a century, scientists have known that an EEG component called the mu wave is blocked anytime a person makes a voluntary muscle movement, such as opening and closing one's hands. Interestingly, this component is also blocked when a person watches someone else perform the same action. One of us (Ramachandran) and Altschuler suggested that mu-wave suppression might provide a simple, noninvasive probe for monitoring mirror neuron activity.

We decided to focus our first experiments on a high-functioning child with autism—that is, a child without severe cognitive impairments. (Very young, low-functioning children did not participate in this study because we wanted to confirm that any differences we found were not a result of problems in attention, understanding instructions, or the general effects of mental retardation.) The EEG showed that the child had an observable mu wave that was suppressed when he made a simple, voluntary movement, just as in normal children. But when the child watched someone else perform the action, the suppression did not occur. We concluded that the child's motor command system was intact but that his mirror neuron system was deficient. This observation, which we presented at the annual meeting of the Society for Neuroscience in 2000, provided a striking vindication of our hypothesis.

One has to be careful, however, of generalizing from a single case, so our lab group later conducted a more systematic series of experiments in 10 high-functioning individuals with autism spectrum disorder and 10 age- and gender-matched control subjects. We saw the expected suppression of mu waves when the control subjects moved their hands and watched videos of a moving hand, but the EEGs of the subjects with autism showed mu suppression only when they moved their own hands.

Other researchers have confirmed our results using different techniques for monitoring neural activity. A group led by Riitta Hari of the Helsinki University of Technology found mirror neuron deficits in children with autism by employing magnetoencephalography, which measures the magnetic fields produced by electric currents in the brain. More recently, Mirella Dapretto of the University of California, Los Angeles, and her colleagues used functional magnetic resonance imaging to show a reduction in mirror neuron activity in the prefrontal cortices of individuals with autism. And Hugo Théoret of the University of Montreal and his co-workers used transcranial magnetic stimulation, a technique that induces electric currents in the motor cortex to generate muscle movements, to study mirror neuron activity in subjects with autism. In the control subjects, induced hand movements became more pronounced when the subjects watched videos of the same movements; this effect was much weaker in the subjects with autism.

Taken together, these findings provide compelling evidence that people with autism have dysfunctional mirror neuron systems. Scientists do not yet know which genetic and environmental risk factors can prevent the development of mirror neurons or alter their function, but many research groups are now actively pursuing the hypothesis because it predicts symptoms that are unique to autism. In addition to explaining the primary signs of autism, deficiencies in the mirror neuron system can also account for some of the less well known symptoms. For instance, researchers have long known that children with autism often have problems interpreting proverbs and metaphors. When we told one of our subjects to "get a grip on yourself," he took the message literally and started grabbing his own body. Though seen in only a subset of children with autism, this difficulty with metaphors cries out for an explanation.

Understanding metaphors requires the ability to extract a common denominator from superficially dissimilar entities. Consider the bouba/kiki effect, which was discovered by German-American psychologist Wolfgang Köhler more than 60 years ago. In this test, a researcher displays two crudely drawn shapes, one jagged and one curvy, to an audience and asks, "Which of these shapes is bouba and which is kiki?" No matter what languages the respondents speak, 98 percent will pick the curvy shape as bouba and the jagged one as kiki. This result suggests that the human brain is somehow able to extract abstract properties from the shapes and sounds—for example, the property of jaggedness embodied in both the pointy drawing and the harsh sound of kiki. We conjectured that this type of cross-domain mapping is analogous to metaphors and must surely involve neural circuits similar to those in the mirror neuron system. Consistent with this speculation, we discovered that children with autism perform poorly at the bouba/kiki test, pairing the shapes and sounds incorrectly.

But which part of the human brain is involved in this skill? The angular gyrus, which sits at the crossroads of the brain's vision, hearing, and touch centers, seemed to be a likely candidate—not only because of its strategic location but because nerve cells with mirror neuron–like properties have been identified there. When we studied nonautistic subjects with damage to this area of the brain, we found that many of them fail the bouba/kiki test and have a disproportionate difficulty understanding metaphors, just like people with autism. These results suggest that cross-domain mapping may have originally developed to aid primates in complex motor tasks such as grasping tree branches (which requires the rapid assimilation of visual, auditory, and touch information) but eventually evolved into an ability to create metaphors. Mirror neurons allowed humans to reach for the stars, instead of mere peanuts.

Can the Mirrors Be Repaired?

The discovery of mirror neuron deficiencies in people with autism opens up new approaches to diagnosing and treating the disorder. For example, physicians could use the lack of mu-wave suppression (or perhaps the failure to mimic a mother sticking out her tongue) as a diagnostic tool to identify children with autism in early infancy, so that the currently available behavioral therapies can be started as quickly as possible. Timely intervention is critical; the behavioral therapies are much less effective if begun after autism's main symptoms appear (typically between ages two and four).

An even more intriguing possibility would be to use biofeedback to treat autism or at least alleviate its symptoms. Doctors could monitor the mu waves of a child with autism and display them on a screen in front of the patient. If the child's mirror neuron functions are dormant rather than completely lost, it may be possible for him or her to revive this ability by learning—through trial and error and visual feedback—how to suppress the mu waves on the screen. Our colleague Pineda is pursuing this approach, and his preliminary results look promising. Such therapies, though, should supplement rather than replace the traditional behavioral-training techniques.

Another novel therapeutic approach might rely on correcting chemical imbalances that disable the mirror neurons in individuals with autism. Our group (including students Mikhi Horvath and Mary Vertinsky) has suggested that specialized neuromodulators may enhance the activity of mirror neurons involved in emotional responses. According to this hypothesis, the partial depletion of such chemicals could explain the lack of emotional empathy seen in autism, and therefore researchers should look for compounds that stimulate the release of the neuromodulators or mimic their effects on mirror neurons. One candidate for investigation is MDMA, better known as ecstasy, which has been shown to foster emotional closeness and communication. It is possible that researchers may be able to modify the compound to develop a safe, effective treatment that could alleviate at least some of autism's symptoms.

Such treatments, however, may offer only partial relief, because other symptoms of autism cannot be explained by the mirror neuron hypothesis—for example, repetitive motions such as rocking to and fro, avoidance of eye contact, hypersensitivity, and aversion to certain sounds. In an attempt to determine how these secondary symptoms might arise, our lab group (in collaboration with William Hirstein of Elmhurst College and Portia Iversen of Cure Autism Now, a nonprofit foundation based in Los Angeles) has developed what we call the salience landscape theory.

When a person looks at the world, he or she is confronted with an overwhelming amount of sensory information—sights, sounds, smells, and so on. After being processed in the brain's sensory areas, the information is relayed to the amygdala, which acts as a portal to the emotion-regulating limbic system. Using input from the individual's stored knowledge, the amygdala determines how the person should respond emotionally—for example, with fear (at the sight of a burglar), lust (on seeing a lover), or indifference (when facing something trivial). Messages cascade from the amygdala to the rest of the limbic system and eventually reach the autonomic nervous system, which prepares the body for action. If the person is confronting a burglar, for example, his heart rate will rise and his body will sweat to dissipate the heat from muscular exertion. The autonomic arousal, in turn, feeds back into the brain, amplifying the emotional response. Over time, the amygdala creates a salience land-scape, a map that details the emotional significance of everything in the individual's environment.

Our group decided to explore the possibility that children with autism have a distorted salience landscape, perhaps because of altered connections between the cortical areas that process sensory input and the amygdala or between the limbic structures and the frontal lobes that regulate the resulting behavior. As a result of these abnormal connections, any trivial event or object could set off an extreme emotional response—an autonomic storm—in the child's mind. This hypothesis would explain why children with autism tend to avoid eye contact and any other novel sensation that might trigger an upheaval. The distorted perceptions of emotional significance might also explain why many children with autism become intensely preoccupied with trifles such as train schedules while expressing no interest at all in things that most children find fascinating.

We found some support for our hypothesis when we monitored auto-nomic responses in a group of 37 children with autism by measuring the increase in their skin conductance caused by sweating. In contrast with the control subjects, the children with autism had a higher overall level of autonomic arousal. Although they became agitated when exposed to trivial objects and events, they often ignored stimuli that triggered expected responses in the control group.

But how could a child's salience landscape become so distorted? Investigators have found that nearly one third of children with autism have had temporal lobe epilepsy in infancy, and the proportion may be much higher given that many epileptic seizures go undetected. Caused by repeated random volleys of nerve impulses traversing the limbic system, these seizures could eventually scramble the connections between the visual cortex and the amygdala, indiscriminately enhancing some links and diminishing others. In adults, temporal lobe epilepsy results in florid emotional disturbances but does not radically affect cognition; in infants, however, the seizures may lead to a more profound disability. And, like autism, the risk of temporal lobe epilepsy in infancy appears to be influenced by both genetic and environmental factors. Some genes, for example, could make a child more susceptible to viral infections, which could in turn predispose the child to seizures.

Our findings on autonomic responses may help explain the old clinical observation that high fever sometimes temporarily alleviates the symptoms of autism. The autonomic nervous system is involved in controlling body temperature; because fever and the emotional upheavals of autism appear to be regulated by the same neural pathways, perhaps the former can mitigate the latter.

The salience landscape theory could also provide an explanation for the repetitive motions and head banging seen in children with autism: this behavior, called self-stimulation, may somehow damp the child's autonomic storms. Our studies found that self-stimulation not only had a calming effect but also led to a measurable reduction in skin conductance. This result suggests a possible symptomatic therapy for autism. Hirstein is now developing a portable device that could monitor an autistic child's skin conductance; when the device detects autonomic arousal, it could turn on another device, called a squeeze vest, that provides a comforting pressure by gently tightening around the child's body.

Our two candidate theories for explaining the symptoms of autism— mirror neuron dysfunction and distorted salience landscape—are not necessarily contradictory. It is possible that the same event that distorts a child's salience landscape—the scrambled connections between the limbic system and the rest of the brain—also damages the mirror neurons. Alternatively, the altered limbic connections could be a side effect of the same genes that trigger the dysfunctions in the mirror neuron system. Further experiments are needed to rigorously test these conjectures. The ultimate cause of autism remains to be discovered. In the meantime, our speculations may provide a useful framework for future research.

GLOSSARY

Acetylcholine: A neurotransmitter in both the brain, where it may help regulate memory, and in the peripheral nervous system, where it controls the actions of skeletal and smooth muscle.

Action potential: This occurs when a neuron is activated and temporarily reverses the electrical state of its interior membrane from negative to positive. This electrical charge travels along the axon to the neuron's terminal where it triggers or inhibits the release of a neurotransmitter and then disappears.

Adrenal cortex: An endocrine organ that secretes corticosteroids for metabolic functions: aldosterone for sodium retention in the kidneys, androgens for male sexual development, and estrogens for female sexual development.

Adrenal medulla: An endocrine organ that secretes epinephrine and norepinephrine for the activation of the sympathetic nervous system.

Affective psychosis: A psychiatric disease relating to mood states. It is generally characterized by depression unrelated to events in the life of the patient, which alternates with periods of normal mood or with periods of excessive, inappropriate euphoria and mania.

Agonist: A neurotransmitter, a drug, or other molecule that stimulates receptors to produce a desired reaction.

Amino acid transmitters: The most prevalent neurotransmitters in the brain, these include glutamate and aspartate, which have excitatory actions, and glycine and gamma-amino butyric acid (GABA), which have inhibitory actions.

Amygdala: A structure in the forebrain that is an important component of the limbic system.

Androgens: Sex steroid hormones, including testosterone, found in higher levels in males than females. They are responsible for male sexual maturation.

Antagonist: A drug or other molecule that blocks receptors. Antagonists inhibit the effects of agonists.

Aphasia: Disturbance in language comprehension or production, often as a result of a stroke.

Auditory nerve: A bundle of nerve fibers extending from the cochlea of the ear to the brain, which contains two branches: the cochlear nerve that transmits sound information and the vestibular nerve that relays information related to balance.

Autonomic nervous system: A part of the peripheral nervous system responsible for regulating the activity of internal organs. It includes the sympathetic and parasympathetic nervous systems.

Axon: The fiberlike extension of a neuron by which the cell sends information to target cells.

Basal ganglia: Clusters of neurons, which include the caudate nucleus, putamen, globus pallidus, and substantia nigra, that are located deep in the brain and play an important role in movement. Cell death in the substantia nigra contributes to Parkinsonian signs.

Brainstem: The major route by which the forebrain sends information to and receives information from the spinal cord and peripheral nerves. It controls, among other things, respiration and regulation of heart rhythms.

Broca's area: The brain region located in the frontal lobe of the left hemisphere that is important for the production of speech.

Catecholamines: The neurotransmitters dopamine, epinephrine, and norepinephrine that are active both in the brain and the peripheral sympathetic nervous system. These three molecules have certain structural similarities and are part of a larger class of neurotransmitters known as monoamines.

Cerebral cortex: The outermost layer of the cerebral hemispheres of the brain. It is responsible for all forms of conscious experience, including perception, emotion, thought, and planning.

Cerebral hemispheres: The two specialized halves of the brain. The left hemisphere is specialized for speech, writing, language, and calculation; the right hemisphere is specialized for spatial abilities, face recognition in vision, and some aspects of music perception and production.

Cerebrospinal fluid: A liquid found within the ventricles of the brain and the central canal of the spinal cord.

Cholecystokinin: A hormone released from the lining of the stomach during the early stages of digestion which acts as a powerful suppressant of normal eating. It also is found in the brain.

Circadian rhythm: A cycle of behavior or physiological change lasting approximately 24 hours.

Classical conditioning: Learning in which a stimulus that naturally produces a specific response (unconditioned stimulus) is repeatedly paired with a neutral stimulus (conditioned stimulus). As a result, the conditioned stimulus can become able to evoke a response similar to that of the unconditioned stimulus.

Cochlea: A snail-shaped, fluid-filled organ of the inner ear responsible for transducing motion into neurotransmission to produce an auditory sensation.

Cognition: The process or processes by which an organism gains knowledge of or becomes aware of events or objects in its environment and uses that knowledge for comprehension and problem-solving.

Cone: A primary receptor cell for vision located in the retina. It is sensitive to color and used primarily for daytime vision.

Cornea: A thin, curved transparent membrane on the surface of the front of the eye. It begins the focusing process for vision.

Corpus callosum: The large bundle of nerve fibers linking the left and right cerebral hemispheres.

Cortisol: A hormone manufactured by the adrenal cortex. In humans, it is secreted in greatest quantities before dawn, readying the body for the activities of the coming day.

Dendrite: A tree-like extension of the neuron cell body. Along with the cell body, it receives information from other neurons.

Dopamine: A catecholamine neurotransmitter known to have multiple functions depending on where it acts. Dopamine-containing neurons in the substantia nigra of the brainstem project to the caudate nucleus and are destroyed in Parkinson's victims. Dopamine is thought to regulate emotional responses and plays a role in schizophrenia and cocaine abuse.

dorsal horn: An area of the spinal cord where many nerve fibers from peripheral pain receptors meet other ascending nerve fibers.

Endocrine organ: An organ that secretes a hormone directly into the bloodstream to regulate cellular activity of certain other organs.

Endorphins: Neurotransmitters produced in the brain that generate cellular and behavioral effects like those of morphine.

Epinephrine: A hormone, released by the adrenal medulla and the brain, that acts with norepinephrine to activate the sympathetic division of the autonomic nervous system. Sometimes called adrenaline.

Estrogens: A group of sex hormones found more abundantly in females than males. They are responsible for female sexual maturation and other functions.

Evoked potentials: A measure of the brain's electrical activity in response to sensory stimuli. This is obtained by placing electrodes on the surface of the scalp (or more rarely, inside the head), repeatedly administering a stimulus, and then using a computer to average the results.

Excitation: A change in the electrical state of a neuron that is associated with an enhanced probability of action potentials.

Follicle-stimulating hormone: A hormone released by the pituitary gland. It stimulates the production of sperm in the male and growth of the follicle (which produces the egg) in the female.

Forebrain: The largest division of the brain, which includes the cerebral cortex and basal ganglia. It is credited with the highest intellectual functions.

Frontal lobe: One of the four divisions (parietal, temporal, occipital) of each hemisphere of the cerebral cortex. It has a role in controlling movement and associating the functions of other cortical areas.

Gamma-amino butyric acid (GABA): An amino acid transmitter in the brain whose primary function is to inhibit the firing of neurons.

Glia: Specialized cells that nourish and support neurons.

Glutamate: An amino acid neurotransmitter that acts to excite neurons. Glutamate probably stimulates N-methyl-D-aspartate (NMDA) receptors that have been implicated in activities ranging from learning and memory to development and specification of nerve contacts in a developing animal. Stimulation of NMDA receptors may promote beneficial changes, while overstimulation may be the cause of nerve cell damage or death in neurological trauma and stroke.

Gonad: Primary sex gland: testis in the male and ovary in the female.

Growth cone: A distinctive structure at the growing end of most axons. It is the site where new material is added to the axon.

Hippocampus: A seahorse-shaped structure located within the brain and considered an important part of the limbic system. It functions in learning, memory, and emotion.

Hormones: Chemical messengers secreted by endocrine glands to regulate the activity of target cells. They play a role in sexual development, calcium and bone metabolism, growth, and many other activities.

Hypothalamus: A complex brain structure composed of many nuclei with various functions. These include regulating the activities of internal organs, monitoring information from the autonomic nervous system, and controlling the pituitary gland.

Immediate memory: A phase of memory that is extremely short-lived, with information stored only for a few seconds. It also is known as short-term and working memory.

Inhibition: In reference to neurons, it is a synaptic message that prevents the recipient cell from firing.

Ions: Electrically charged atoms or molecules.

Iris: A circular diaphragm that contains the muscles which alter the amount of light that enters the eye by dilating or constricting the pupil. It has an opening in its center.

Korsakoff's syndrome: A disease associated with chronic alcoholism, resulting from a deficiency of vitamin B-1. Patients sustain damage to part of the thalamus and cerebellum. Symptoms include inflammation of nerves, muttering delirium, insomnia, illusions and hallucinations, and a lasting amnesia.

Limbic system: A group of brain structures—including the amygdala, hippocampus, septum, and basal ganglia—that work to help regulate emotion, memory, and certain aspects of movement.

Long-term memory: The final phase of memory in which information storage may last from hours to a lifetime.

Mania: A mental disorder characterized by excessive excitement. A form of psychosis with exalted feelings, delusions of grandeur, elevated mood, psychomotor overactivity, and overproduction of ideas.

Melatonin: Produced from serotonin, melatonin is released by the pineal gland into the bloodstream. It affects physiological changes related to time and lighting cycles.

Memory consolidation: The physical and psychological changes that take place as the brain organizes and restructures information in order to make it a permanent part of memory.

Metabolism: The sum of all physical and chemical changes that take place within an organism and all energy transformations that occur within living cells.

Mitochondria: Small cylindrical particles inside cells that provide energy for the cell by converting sugar and oxygen into special energy molecules.

Monoamine oxidase (MAO): The brain and liver enzyme that normally breaks down the catecholamines norepinephrine, serotonin, and dopamine.

Motor neuron: A neuron that carries information from the central nervous system to the muscle.

Myasthenia gravis: A disease in which acetylcholine receptors on the muscle cells are destroyed, so that muscles can no longer respond to the acetylcholine signal in order to contract. Symptoms include muscular weakness and progressively more common bouts of fatigue. Its cause is unknown but is more common in females than in males and usually strikes between the ages of 20 and 50.

Myelin: Compact fatty material that surrounds and insulates axons of some neurons.

Nerve growth factor: A substance whose role is to guide neuronal growth during embryonic development, especially in the peripheral nervous system.

Neuron: Nerve cell. It is specialized for the transmission of information and characterized by long fibrous projections called axons and shorter, branch-like projections called dendrites.

Neurotransmitter: A chemical released by neurons at a synapse for the purpose of relaying information via receptors.

Nociceptors: In animals, nerve endings that signal the sensation of pain. In humans, they are called pain receptors.

Norepinephrine: A catecholamine neurotransmitter, produced both in the brain and in the peripheral nervous system. It seems to be involved in arousal, reward and regulation of sleep and mood, and the regulation of blood pressure.

Organelles: Small structures within a cell that maintain the cells and do the cells' work.

Parasympathetic nervous system: A branch of the autonomic nervous system concerned with the conservation of the body's energy and resources during relaxed states.

Parietal lobe: One of the four subdivisions of the cerebral cortex. It plays a role in sensory processes, attention, and language.

Peptides: Chains of amino acids that can function as neurotransmitters or hormones.

Periaqueductal gray area: A cluster of neurons lying in the thalamus and pons. It contains endorphin-producing neurons and opiate receptor sites and thus can affect the sensation of pain.

Peripheral nervous system: A division of the nervous system consisting of all nerves not part of the brain or spinal cord.

Phosphorylation: A process that modifies the properties of neurons by acting on an ion channel, neurotransmitter receptor, or other regulatory molecule. During phosphorylation, a phosphate molecule is placed on another molecule resulting in the activation or inactivation of the receiving molecule. It may lead to a change in the functional activity of the receiving molecule. Phosphorylation is believed to be a necessary step in allowing some neurotransmitters to act and is often the result of second messenger activity.

Pineal gland: An endocrine organ found in the brain. In some animals, it seems to serve as a light-influenced biological clock.

Pituitary gland: An endocrine organ closely linked with the hypothalamus. In humans, it is composed of two lobes and secretes a number of hormones that regulate the activity of other endocrine organs in the body.

Pons: A part of the hindbrain that, with other brain structures, controls respiration and regulates heart rhythms. The pons is a major route by which the forebrain sends information to and receives information from the spinal cord and peripheral nervous system.

Receptor cell: Specialized sensory cells designed to pick up and transmit sensory information.

Receptor molecule: A specific molecule on the surface or inside of a cell with a characteristic chemical and physical structure. Many neurotransmitters and hormones exert their effects by binding to receptors on cells.

Reuptake: A process by which released neurotransmitters are absorbed for subsequent reuse.

Rod: A sensory neuron located in the periphery of the retina. It is sensitive to light of low intensity and specialized for nighttime vision.

Second messengers: Recently recognized substances that trigger communications between different parts of a neuron. These chemicals are thought to play a role in the manufacture and release of neurotransmitters, intracellular movements, carbohydrate metabolism, and, possibly, even processes of growth and development. Their direct effects on the genetic material of cells may lead to long-term alterations of behavior, such as memory.

Sensitization: A change in behavior or biological response by an organism that is produced by delivering a strong, generally noxious, stimulus.

Serotonin: A monoamine neurotransmitter believed to play many roles including, but not limited to, temperature regulation, sensory perception, and the onset of sleep. Neurons using serotonin as a transmitter are found in the brain and in the gut. A number of antidepressant drugs are targeted to brain serotonin systems.

Short-term memory: A phase of memory in which a limited amount of information may be held for several seconds to minutes.

Stimulus: An environmental event capable of being detected by sensory receptors.

Stroke: The third largest cause of death in America, stroke is an impeded blood supply to the brain. It can be caused by a blood clot forming in a blood vessel, a rupture of the blood vessel wall, an obstruction of flow caused by a clot or other material, or by pressure on a blood vessel (as by a tumor). Deprived of oxygen, which is carried by blood, nerve cells in the affected area cannot function and die. Thus, the part of the body controlled by those cells cannot function either. Stroke can result in loss of consciousness and brain function, and death.

Sympathetic nervous system: A branch of the autonomic nervous system responsible for mobilizing the body's energy and resources during times of stress and arousal.

Synapse: A gap between two neurons that functions as the site of information transfer from one neuron to another.

Temporal lobe: One of the four major subdivisions of each hemisphere of the cerebral cortex. It functions in auditory perception, speech, and complex visual perceptions.

Thalamus: A structure consisting of two egg-shaped masses of nerve tissue, each about the size of a walnut, deep within the brain. It is the key relay station for sensory information flowing into the brain, filtering out only information of particular importance from the mass of signals entering the brain.

Ventricles: Of the four ventricles, comparatively large spaces filled with cerebrospinal fluid, three are located in the brain and one in the brainstem. The lateral ventricles, the two largest, are symmetrically placed above the brainstem, one in each hemisphere.

Wernicke's area: A brain region responsible for the comprehension of language and the production of meaningful speech.

CREDIT LINES